Psychological Themes in Classical Islamic Literature

بسم الله الرحمن الرحيم

Psychological Themes in Classical Islamic Literature

A Primary Source Reader

Edited by

Hooman Keshavarzi
Khalid Elzamzamy
Bilal Ali Ansari
Aamir Azhar Zaidi

BRILL

LEIDEN | BOSTON

Cover illustration: Sultan Han Kervansarayi, a 13th-Century Seljuk caravanserai in Sultanhani, Aksaray Province, Turkiye. Photograph by Amrin Malam, 2021.

The Library of Congress Cataloging-in-Publication Data is available online at https://catalog.loc.gov
LC record available at https://lccn.loc.gov/2025011415

Typeface for the Latin, Greek, and Cyrillic scripts: "Brill". See and download: brill.com/brill-typeface.

ISBN 978-90-04-72519-5 (hardback)
ISBN 978-90-04-72521-8 (paperback)
ISBN 978-90-04-72520-1 (e-book)
DOI 10.1163/9789004725201

Published by Koninklijke Brill BV, Plantijnstraat 2, 2321 JC Leiden, The Netherlands.
Koninklijke Brill BV incorporates the imprints Brill, Brill Nijhoff, Brill Schöningh, Brill Fink, Brill mentis, Brill Wageningen Academic, Vandenhoeck & Ruprecht, Böhlau and V&R unipress.

This book is printed on acid-free paper and produced in a sustainable manner.

Contents

Foreword XI
Preface XIII
Notes on Contributors XVI

Introduction 1
1 Central Objective 2
2 Content 3
3 Approach 4
4 Aims and Target Audience 4

1 **Epistemological Themes** 6
1 Sources of Knowledge. *Al-Kifāya fī al-Hidāya* by Imam Nūr al-Dīn al-Ṣābūnī (d. 580 AH/1184 AD) 6
1.1 *Author's Biography* 6
1.2 *Text Overview and Significance* 6
1.3 *Arabic Text* 7
1.4 *English Translation* 9
2 All That the Prophet (May Allah Bless Him and Grant Him Peace) Brought from Allah Is Self-Evident (Badīhī). *The Letters of Imam Rabānnī* (*Al-Maktūbāt al-Rabbāniyya*) by Mujaddid al-Alf al-Thānī al-Imam al-Rabbanī, Aḥmad al-Sirhindī (d. 1033 AH/1624 CE) 14
2.1 *Author's Biography* 14
2.2 *Text Overview and Significancc* 15
2.3 *Arabic Text* 16
2.4 *English Translation* 17

2 **Ontological Themes** 21
1 An Exposition on the Meanings of *Nafs, Rūh, ʿAql, Qalb* and What Is Intended by These Names. *The Revival of the Religious Sciences* (*Iḥyāʾ ʿUlūm al-Dīn*) by Imam Abū Ḥāmid Al-Ghazālī (d. 505 AH/1111 CE) 21
1.1 *Author's Biography* 21
1.2 *Text Overview and Significance* 22
1.3 *Arabic Text* 22
1.4 *English Translation* 25

2 The Nature of the ʿAql and Its Types. *Tuḥfat al-Murīd ʿalā Jawahart al-Tawḥid* by Ibrāhīm ibn Muḥammad al-Bājūrī (d. 1276/1860) 33
2.1 *Author's Biography* 33
2.2 *Text Overview and Significance* 33
2.3 *Arabic Text* 34
2.4 *English Translation* 35
3 On Man's Recognition of the Reality of His Soul and the Spiritual Disclosures of the Sufis regarding It. *Knowledge of the Spiritually Learned* (*ʿAwārif al-Maʿārif*) by Imam Shihab al-Din al-Suhrawardī (d. 632 AH/1191 CE) 40
3.1 *Author's Biography* 40
3.2 *Text Overview and Significance* 41
3.3 *Arabic Text* 41
3.4 *English Translation* 45
4 Inherent Faculties of Perception. *Al-Qānūn fī al-Ṭibb* (*The Canon of Medicine*) by Ibn Sīna (d. 428 AH/1037 CE) 53
4.1 *Author's Biography* 53
4.2 *Text Overview and Significance* 54
4.3 *Arabic Text* 54
4.4 *English Translation* 56
5 An Elucidation of the Malleability of Character Traits through Spiritual Exercises. *Iḥyāʾ ʿUlūm al-Dīn* by Imam Abu Hamid Al-Ghazali (d. 1111 AD) 60
5.1 *Author's Biography* 60
5.2 *Text Overview and Significance* 60
5.3 *Arabic Text* 61
5.4 *English Translation* 62
6 Types of Insanity (*Aqsām al-Junūn*). *Durar al-Ḥukkām Sharḥ Majallat al-Aḥkām* by Imam Ali Haydar Efendi (d. 1380 AH/1960 CE) 65
6.1 *Author's Biography* 65
6.2 *Text Overview and Significance* 66
6.3 *Arabic Text* 67
6.4 *English Translation* 70

3 **Cognitive Themes** 77
1 An Exposition of Shayṭān's Influence over the Heart through Subtle Whisperings (*Waswasa*), the Significance of *Waswasa*, and the Means through Which It Takes Hold [of a Person]. *Iḥyāʾ ʿUlūm al-Dīn* by Imam Abu Hamid Al-Ghazali (d. 1111 AD) 77

1.1 *Author's Biography* 77
1.2 *Text Overview and Significance* 77
1.3 *Arabic Text* 77
1.4 *English Translation* 80
2 An Introduction to Dream Interpretation (*Taʿbīr al-Manām*). *Taʿṭīr al-Anām fī Taʾbīr al-Manām* (*Dream Interpretation*) by Imam ʿAbd al-Ghanī al-Nābulsī (d. 1143 AH/1730 CE) 85
2.1 *Author's Biography* 85
2.2 *Text Overview and Significance* 86
2.3 *Arabic Text* 87
2.4 *English Translation* 92

4 **Emotional Themes** 102
1 Repelling Excess Sorrow. *Al-Ṭibb al-Ruhānī* (*Psycho-Spiritual Medicine*) by Imam ʿAbd al-Raḥmān Abū al-Faraj ibn al-Jawzī (d. 597 AH/1184 CE) 102
1.1 *Author's Biography* 102
1.2 *Text Overview and Significance* 102
1.3 *Arabic Text* 103
1.4 *English Translation* 105
2 The Station of Grief. *Madārij al-Sālikīn Bayn Manāzil Iyyāka Naʿbud wa-Iyyāka Nastaʿīn* (*Stations of the Seekers*) by Imam Ibn Qayyim al-Jawziyya (d. 751 AH/1351 CE) 110
2.1 *Author's Biography* 110
2.2 *Text Overview and Significance* 111
2.3 *Arabic Text* 112
2.4 *English Translation* 116
3 Worry and Sorrow. *Al-Hamm wa-l-Ḥazan* (*Worry and Sorrow*) by Imam Ibn Abī al-Dunyā (d. 281 AH/882 CE) 124
3.1 *Author's Biography* 124
3.2 *Text Overview and Significance* 125
3.3 *Arabic Text* 125
3.4 *English Translation* 128
4 Between Fear and Hope. *Mukhtaṣar Iḥyāʾ ʿUlūm al-Dīn* by Imam Abū Ḥāmid Muḥammad al-Ghazālī (d. 505 AH/1111 CE) 134
4.1 *Author's Biography* 134
4.2 *Text Overview and Significance* 134
4.3 *Arabic Text* 135
4.4 *English Translation* 141

5 An Exposition on the Essential Nature of Anger. *Iḥyāʾ ʿUlūm al-Dīn* (*The Revival of Religious Sciences*) by Imam Abū Ḥāmid Muḥammad al-Ghazālī (d. 505 AH/1111 CE) 152
5.1 *Author's Biography* 152
5.2 *Text Overview and Significance* 152
5.3 *Arabic Text* 153
5.4 *English Translation* 156
6 The Heart's Delight. *Mufarriḥ al-Nafs* (*The Heart's Delight*) by Ibn Qādi Baalbek (d. 650 AH/1256 CE) 163
6.1 *Author's Biography* 163
6.2 *Text Overview and Significance* 163
6.3 *Arabic Text* 164
6.4 *English Translation* 167

5 **Behavioral Themes** 173
1 Character Traits: Definitions, Origins, Types, and How to Change Them. *Al-Ṭarīqa al-Muḥammadiyya wa-l-Sīra al-Aḥmadiyya* (*The Muhammadan Path*) by Imam Taqī al-Dīn Muḥammad al-Birgivī (d. 981 AH/1573 CE) 173
1.1 *Author's Biography* 173
1.2 *Text Overview and Significance* 173
1.3 *Arabic Text* 174
1.4 *English Translation* 183
2 Chapter on *Waswasa*. *Mirqāt al-Mafātīḥ* by Mulla ʿAlī al-Qarī (d. 1014 AH/1620 CE) 200
2.1 *Author's Biography* 200
2.2 *Text Overview and Significance* 201
2.3 *Arabic Text* 202
2.4 *English Translation* 206

6 **Themes on General Well-Being** 220
1 Man's Discovery of His Own Vices. *Al-Ṭibb al-Ruhānī* (*Psycho-Spiritual Medicine*) by Abū Bakr Muḥammad ibn Zakariyā al-Rāzī (d. 251 AH/925 CE) 220
1.1 *Author's Biography* 220
1.2 *Text Overview and Significance* 220
1.3 *Arabic Text* 221
1.4 *English Translation* 222

2 The Means of Recognizing One's Own Flaws. *Iḥyā' ʿUlūm al-Dīn* (*The Revival of Religious Sciences*) by Imam Abū Ḥāmid Muḥammad al-Ghazālī (d. 505 AH/1111 CE) 224
2.1 *Author's Biography* 224
2.2 *Text Overview and Significance* 225
2.3 *Arabic Text* 225
2.4 *English Translation* 227
3 The Need for the Management of the Psyche. *Maṣālih al-Abdān wa-l-Anfus* (*Sustenance of the Body and the Psyche*) by Abū Zayd al-Balkhī (d. 322 AH/934 CE) 231
3.1 *Author's Biography* 231
3.2 *Text Overview and Significance* 232
3.3 *Arabic Text* 233
3.4 *English Translation* 235
4 Preservation of the Health of the Psyche. *Maṣālih al-Abdān wa al-Anfus* (*Sustenance of the Body and the Psyche*) by Abū Zayd al-Balkhī (d. 322 AH/934 CE) 238
4.1 *Author's Biography* 238
4.2 *Text Overview and Significance* 239
4.3 *Arabic Text* 239
4.4 *English Translation* 241
5 When One Loses It: Methods of Restoring Mental Health. *Maṣālih al-Abdān wa al-Anfus* (*Sustenance of the Body and the Psyche*) by Imam Abū Zayd al-Balkhī (d. 322 AH/934 CE) 246
5.1 *Author's Biography* 246
5.2 *Text Overview and Significance* 246
5.3 *Arabic Text* 247
5.4 *English Translation* 249
6 Explaining and Enumerating Psychological Symptoms. *Maṣālih al-Abdān wa-l-Anfus* (*Sustenance of the Body and the Psyche*) by Imam Abū Zayd al-Balkhī (d. 322 AH/934 CE) 252
6.1 *Author's Biography* 252
6.2 *Text Overview and Significance* 252
6.3 *Arabic Text* 253
6.4 *English Translation* 255

Bibliography 261
Index 269

Foreword

I am writing this foreword to draw attention to the importance of this particular book on *Psychological Themes in Classical Islamic Literature.* It has become exceedingly clear over the past decade that the Euro-American grip on the current literature on psychology needs to be softened and other diverse perspectives on psychology need to be introduced. While there are many recent publications discussing the diverse and rich intellectual heritage that Muslims have, there are not too many works that provide a direct exposure and reading of the classical Islamic scholarly works composed specifically related to psychology. This book provides a series of selected chapters from various classical texts across various Islamic specialties on topics related to Psychology. It provides readers with a flavor of the works and discussions regarding human psychology that great Muslim scholars have documented generations before the existence of a modern specialty in psychology. It also demonstrates that there is much to be unearthed and drawn out from the Islamic tradition that can provide valuable insights, advancements and perspective shifts in the field of psychology.

There are a few important distinguishing characteristics of this work that make it particularly valuable. First off, the team of editors and contributors consists of individuals who can bridge the gap between modern psychology and Islamic studies by possessing an understanding and familiarity with both fields. Additionally, the translation has been rendered in a manner that makes it comprehensible and highly relevant to those who are psychologically minded by encompassing and utilizing some important psychological terminologies to translate and capture the meanings of the classical texts. Finally, the commentary provides readers with a nice exploration and discussion of the relevance of these timeless traditions and works to the modern field of psychology.

Personally, I have had the pleasure of mentoring, teaching and working with Dr. Keshavarzi and many members of his team of contributors. This work makes me proud of their accomplishments and proud of the Islamic intellectual tradition. It provides me further reassurance that the road to advancement sometimes lies right beneath our noses, and we need not look too far to find it. Such translated works have been within the reach of Muslim academics, students and intellectuals for a long time. Such a compilation was long overdue and this work helps to demonstrate the immense need for further and more investigation of the rich Islamic legacy of psychology. While this book seems to be just a drop in the ocean, it serves as a great start and inspiration for others to potentially work on an encyclopedia of psychology drawn from the classical Islamic scholarly tradition that can be even more comprehensive than this short primer.

Lastly, I am very happy to see that our College of Islamic Studies at Hamad bin Khalifa University was able to support and facilitate open access for this book given its immense need and opportunity for broad exposure and utilization internationally. I have no doubt that this book will be an invaluable source for researchers and students of Islamic psychology first and foremost in our Counseling Psychology Program at the College of Islamic Studies. I hope to see this book utilized as a course textbook on psychology in the Islamic tradition across universities and academic institutions globally.

May Allah facilitate its acceptance and maximize its benefits and utility internationally and across time.

Recep Şentürk
Dean of College of Islamic Studies, Hamad bin Khalifa University

Preface

In the name of Allah, Most Beneficent, Most Merciful. Praise be to the one who has bestowed the light of prophethood and revelation upon humanity so that they may achieve true contentment and bliss in this life and in the hereafter.

May the choicest salutations and peace be upon our Master and Prophet Muhammad, who came to guide humanity out of the darkness and suffering of this temporal life and provided humanity with the glad tidings that the trials and tribulations of this life are a spiritual cleansing and elevation for the life hereafter, should they believe. And may salutations and peace be upon his noble family, companions and those who followed after them in excellence.

It is upon the request and insistence of my beloved friend, Dr. Hooman Keshavarzi, that I provide a preface to this book, entitled *Psychological Themes in Classical Islamic Literature*. It is important to note at the outset of reading this book the motivations and intentions by which Muslim scholars both in the past and present wrote their works and investigated intricate matters of knowledge. Muslim scholars have always chiefly been inspired and motivated by revelation and Islamic scripture in their academic works and construction of civilization. Thus, the rich Islamic intellectual heritage and civilization that has been transmitted to us, has its primary roots in revelation, i.e. the Qur'ān and the Sunnah. By reflecting and looking at scripture, Muslim scholars became keenly interested in a vast array of intellectual issues and matters. Within the context of healthcare, Muslims were inspired to investigate, construct and establish magnificent healthcare institutions and hospitals on account of thc tradition of the Prophet, may Allah bless him & grant him peace, when he instructed a female companion Rufaydah al-Aslamiyyah, may Allah be pleased with her, to establish a tent for the wounded members of the Battle of Khandaq (Tabaqāt 3:427). Such a tradition led Muslims to consider the possibilities of building upon the idea of establishing a place of healing and treatment for the sick in an institutional manner. This eventually led to the construction of the famous bimaristans and dar al-Shifas, that the world witnessed in Baghdad, Damascus, Cairo, Istanbul, Edirne, Bursa and various other cities throughout the Ottoman lands where both physical and mental illnesses were treated. Muslims were then motivated to find various treatments and uncover healthcare treatments on account of the famous prophetic tradition, wherein the Prophet Muḥammad, may Allah bless him & grant him peace, states, "For every sickness there is a treatment. And when the treatment is applied to the sickness, they shall be cured by the permission of Allah"

(Muslim, 2204). Such prophetic traditions led Muslims to uncover the treatment to various ailments that are well-documented.

More specifically, as it pertains to psychology and mental health, I would like to draw attention to the Prophetic cure and prayer that he, may Allah bless him & grant him peace, taught his companions, may Allah be pleased with them, and by extension the ummah for depression and anxiety. On one occasion, the Prophet, may Allah bless him & grant him peace, entered the Masjid and saw Hazrat Abū Umama, may Allah be pleased with him, a companion from among the Ansar sitting, wherein the Prophet, may Allah bless him & grant him peace, said to him, "Oh Abu Umamah, what is it that [has caused] you to sit in the Masjid outside of the prayer times?" He responded, "My anxieties and debts are overwhelming me oh Prophet of Allah". The Prophet, may Allah bless him & grant him peace, then responded, "shall I not teach you some words, that should you recite them, Allah, Most Exalted and Sublime, shall rid you of your anxieties and relieve you of your debt?" Hazrat Abu Umama, may Allah be pleased with him, replied, "Most certainly, Oh Prophet of Allah". The Prophet, may Allah bless him & grant him peace, stated, "then whenever you go to sleep in the evening and awake in the morning, say, 'Oh Allah, I seek refuge in you from [debilitating] anxiety and sadness, I seek refuge in you from incapacity and laziness, I seek refuge in you from cowardliness and miserliness, and I seek refuge in you from being overwhelmed [by] debt and being dominated by men'" (Abū Dawud, 1555). Furthermore, Hazrat Abū Bakr al-Siddīq, may Allah be pleased with him, once asked the Prophet, may Allah bless him & grant him peace, "Oh messenger of Allah, teach me some words that I can recite in the morning and in the evening. The Prophet, may Allah bless him & grant him peace, stated, "Say: Oh, Fashioner of the Heavens and the Earth, the Lord of all things and Possessor of everything, I testify that there is no god except You. I seek refuge in the evil of myself and the evil of the devil and his associates". He, may Allah bless him & grant him peace, then said, "Say this in the morning, evening and when you retire to bed" (Abu Dawud, 5067).

The following prayers of the Prophet, may Allah bless him & grant him peace, identify the importance of mental health. By virtue of asking to be relieved or protected from these conditions, it is an indication that such conditions may be commonplace among people and that it can have very debilitating and adverse effects on the human condition. As can be witnessed in this book, Muslim scholars therefore rose to the occasion to attempt to truly understand the nature of anxiety and depression (see section 4) and how to treat them. They were curious about, how these emotions manifest in people, their causes, triggers and psychological strategies that could be employed to rid themselves of these conditions in addition to seeking refuge in Allah. These burning concerns arose out of examining and being inspired by revelation that led them to these various rich discussions of mental health that are extremely relevant to this very day. Additionally, as seen by the second prophetic prescription above, Muslim scholars never divorced mental health conditions from metaphysical or spiritual issues. While it is important to employ prayers and strategies to ward off anxiety and depression, it is equally necessary to seek refuge in Allah from the evil influences of the self and from the unseen realm. Therefore, as you will notice in the book, many of the entries that deal with psychological techniques or topics are often intertwined with spiritual advice, litanies and practices.

Finally, I commend the editors and contributors of this work, who extracted various sections from the rich Islamic scholarly heritage as they relate to topics of human psychology to help answer and benefit modern psychological questions and issues. It is my firm belief that through the investigation of revelation, the prophetic prayers and the writings of the Islamic scholars in their commentaries, reflections, anecdotes and recommendations, the modern field of psychology and mental healthcare delivery can be transformed. It is time for modern psychologists to examine the rich Islamic heritage and revisit spirituality as a platform by which to understand and examine human psychology. I beseech Allah, Most High, that He accept this work as a service for His sake and a source of benefit, healing and transformation for all of humanity. Amīn.

Shaykh Moḥammed Zakariya ibn Ismāʿīl Patel al-Jogwarī
Imam of Masjid al-Taqwa, Toronto, Canada

Notes on Contributors

Sena Aycan
is a licensed clinical psychologist and serves as a Research & Content Development Fellow at the Khalil Center, where she integrates her expertise in psychology with a commitment to advancing Muslim mental health. She holds a master's degree in clinical psychology, a bachelor's degree in psychology, and is currently pursuing a bachelor's in Comparative Islamic Studies at Usul Academy. Sena's postgraduate research focused on developing an Islamically-integrated model of psychological well-being, and she continues to center her work on integrating Islamic perspectives into mental health paradigms. She has worked with disadvantaged and vulnerable populations as a clinical psychologist across various organizations. In addition to her role at the Khalil Center, Sena provides on-site and online psychotherapy for earthquake and trauma survivors in Türkiye.

Sena Akbay Safi
graduated with a degree in Psychology from Istanbul Sehir University in 2017 and earned a double major in Sociology in 2018 from the same institution. She completed her Master's in Trauma and Disaster Mental Health program at Istanbul Bilgi University in 2021 and is currently pursuing a PhD in Psychology at Uskudar University, where she also teaches in the Psychology department. As a trauma therapist, she works with clients from diverse cultural backgrounds, providing therapy in Turkish, Arabic, and English. She specializes in Cognitive Behavioral Therapy (CBT) and is a certified mental health trainer on several intervention programs from the World Health Organization. In addition, she serves as a supervisor for other therapists. With extensive experience in psychosocial support programs for vulnerable groups across multiple countries, she trains facilitators and implements individual and group therapy programs, which she continues to this day.

Munsif Mubarak
is a Hafidh of the Qur'an and a licensed psychotherapist registered with the College of Registered Psychotherapists of Ontario. He earned a Bachelor of Science degree from the University of Toronto and has a strong background in Islamic studies, having devoted seven years to the Islamic sciences in al-Madinah al-Munawwarah. While there, he studied under various scholars at Masjid-un-Nabawi and other educational institutions, obtaining an associate

degree in Arabic Language and a Bachelor of Arts in Classical Arabic Literature and Linguistics from the Islamic University of Medina. Munsif furthered his education by completing a Master of Psychospiritual Studies at the University of Toronto in 2021, which included certification in spiritual care and psychotherapy. Currently, Munsif holds several key positions at Khalil Center Toronto: Director of Community Relations, Clinical Supervisor, and Registered Psychotherapist. He is committed to connecting Islamic principles with modern psychological practice, offering essential support to those seeking mental wellness within the Muslim community. Munsif also actively delivers and facilitates psycho-spiritual education training across Canada and the USA.

Muhammed Furkan Cinisli
completed his undergraduate studies at Istanbul Şehir University, graduating from the Faculty of Islamic Studies in 2017 and obtaining a double major degree in Psychology from the same university in 2018. He went on to earn a master's degree in Qur'anic exegesis (tafsir al-Qur'an) at 29 Mayıs University in 2019, followed by a master's in Clinical Psychology at Ibn Haldun University in 2021. Currently, he is pursuing a doctorate in Clinical Psychology at Ibn Haldun University. His academic interests include exploring theoretical and practical sources of psychology within Islamic thought, and he conducts clinical research in the area of trauma. Muhammed Furkan is a member of the Association for Psychology and Psychotherapy Research and is proficient in Arabic and English. Additionally, he lectures on Islamic studies and psychology at various institutions.

Şuheda Ece Kaya
graduated from Kartal Anatolian Imam Hatip High School and later completed her bachelor's degree in Guidance and Psychological Counseling at Boğaziçi University. During her undergraduate studies, she participated in the honor program at the EDEP Center, where she received training in Arabic and Islamic studies. Her academic and professional interests include a focus on Islamic psychology, which continues to influence her scholarly work and engagements.

Abdullah Ansari
is a student of the Islamic sciences currently pursuing his education at Darul Qasim College in Hoffman Estates, Illinois. He began his education in Cairo, Egypt where he studied the Arabic language, Qur'ānic recitation, and tajwīd. He is currently enrolled in the Intermediate Islamic Studies program at Darul Qasim College, studying Islamic law, theology, and their subsidiary sciences.

Additionally, he holds a bachelor's degree in Information technology (IT) and human resource management (HRM) from Rutgers University in New Brunswick, New Jersey.

Huzaifa Ansari
is currently a student and assistant researcher at Darul Qasim College in Illinois. After completing the intermediate Islamic studies program, Huzaifa is continuing his studies and is pursuing an Advanced Diploma in Islamic law and theology. His interests include Islamic legal methodology, theology, and Arabic.

Sana Mohiuddin
LPC, attained her bachelor's from Texas A&M University majoring in History and Comparative Religious Studies. Sana went on to complete her graduate studies at Northeastern Illinois University in Counseling Education specializing in Marital and Family counseling. Along with her secular studies, Sana also has attained ijaazaat (permission to teach) in various Islamic studies including Jurisprudence (fiqh), Quranic exegesis (Tafseer), Arabic language, and Hadith studies. Sana is the founder and therapist at Sound Hearts Therapy.

Introduction

In the name of Allah, the Most Beneficent, Most Merciful. Praise be to the One who created human beings as the best of all creation and created the human mind in order to discern truth, come to know their true Lord and to worship Him. May the salutations and choicest blessings of Allah be upon our Master and Prophet Muḥammad and upon his family, progeny, companions, and those who follow him until the day of Reckoning.

The modern psychological literature, despite its richness, has generally overlooked the potential contributions of the Islamic intellectual heritage to the field. It is currently rooted in the historical and philosophical contributions of Euro-American intellectuals and figures that are overrepresented in the field. All the major schools of psychology from humanistic, cognitive, narrative, behavioral, psychodynamic, emotional psychologies stem from the ideas and theories of European and North American scholars that continue to shape the field and are taught and disseminated throughout the world. Despite the richness of the Islamic intellectual heritage and Islamic scholarly treatises that have discussed the subject matter of human psychology generations before their Euro-American counterparts, these figures are rarely given mention in the psychological literature. This is also the case within the Muslim world today, whereby Euro-American ideas are taught in Muslim Universities and such students come to know and memorize the names of these individuals of whom their parents could not even pronounce. Meanwhile in the same institutions of higher learning, the names of Islamic scholars that are so familiar to them are not readily accessible to them when the subject matter of psychology comes up.

Having said the above, there has been a growing interest in the contributions of the culturally and religiously diverse in modern psychology, particularly in a world that is increasingly globalized and shrinking. Thus, there is a clear recognition of the need for further investigation into diverse voices and traditions in psychology. However, there is a set of challenges that makes the endeavor of extracting contributions from the Islamic heritage exceedingly difficult. Firstly, most psychologists including Muslim psychologists are trained in Western institutions or in the Muslim world that has imported Euro-American psychology into its institutions. Even if such Muslim scholars wish to engage in this undertaking, there are yet another set of challenges that make it difficult for them to access the Islamic literature. This includes a language barrier, whereby they may not be able to read classical texts in the original languages such as Arabic, Persian, and Urdu. Though there may be translations of these works in their local languages, they are very limiting and often do not do justice to the original work. On the other hand, even if some of these scholars were to be able to read the original languages, they may not know how to engage with them since they are often replete with Islamic terminologies and organized in ways that may not be intuitive. For example, one may have a difficult time finding topics of human psychology in the voluminous work of Imam al-Ghazālī's *Iḥyāʾ*. And even if one were to find the sections where he addresses human psychology, oftentimes he utilizes terms that are specific to Islamic theology that may not be readily comprehensible to the non-expert. Therefore, it may in fact require an Islamic studies background for one to access such literature. One may consider Islamic studies experts to be the ones to take on this responsibility. However, there are also a few barriers that are in place for such experts. These include the lack of psychological mindedness that may be needed to consider which types of literature may be relevant for topics in modern psychology. Additionally, Islamic studies experts don't frequently focus on surveying the Islamic literature for psychological topics since this may be outside of their primary scope of topics that directly pertain to theology.

The ultimate result of the above is that Islamic scholarly contributions often feel out of reach for the field of modern psychology.

1 Central Objective

It is for this reason that this book project was conceived. This book provides a window into the Islamic scholarly tradition as it relates specifically to the subject of human psychology. The editors and contributors, all possessing some degree of dual training (i.e., behavioral and Islamic studies), came together to select segments from the Islamic scholarly literature in the Arabic language that spoke to major topics that tackle big questions in the field of psychology. These include the admissibility and validity of diverse sources of knowledge, the nature of the human psyche, nature of human drives, the mind and body problem, nature vs nurture, dreams, emotions, psychological resilience, and well-being among others. Oftentimes in the psychological literature these topics are discussed within the context of the Euro-American intellectual tradition. It is the belief of the editors that the field of modern psychology can be enriched through the inclusion of Islamic scholarly works that reflect such scholarly sophistication and comprehension of the topic at hand.

More specifically, this book attempted to bring together and provide a diverse representation of the Islamic intellectual heritage and its associated subfields. These included writings from discursive theology (*Kalām*), spirituality (Sufism), medical/health literature (*Tibb*), philosophical literature, and Islamic law (*fiqh*). Each one of these fields treats the subject matter of psychology in different ways. For example, the jurists' focus in human psychology is on the presence or absence of mens rea (*irāda/ikhtiyār*) and mental competence (*ahliyya*) for the determination of legal liability, responsibility (*taklīf*) and/or the affordance of disability accommodations (*rukhas*). Meanwhile, the epistemic focus that underlies *Tibb* or ancient Islamic medical practice centers on experiential trials and sensory information (*ḥiss*) that were the precursor to the empirical method. *Tassawuf* or Sufi scholars on the other hand, provide ontological models of the human psyche and spirit that inform experiential trials of behavioral interventions (*tahdhīb al-nafs*) guided by Islamic scripture (*waḥy*) rooted in metaphysical assumptions. While the predominant focus for the scholars of *kalām* is the very question of epistemology, and their conceptualization of admissible information that qualifies as objective truth (*qaṭʿī*) in contrast to subjective knowledge (*ẓannī*).

2 Content

Chapter 1 on Epistemological Themes explores the sources of knowledge in the Islamic tradition. Key texts include discussions on the nature of knowledge and its acquisition, featuring works by Imam Nūr al-Dīn al-Ṣābūnī and Mujaddid al-Alf al-Thānī al-Imam al-Rabbanī Aḥmad al-Sirhindī. These texts highlight the epistemological frameworks that integrate rational, sacred, and empirical knowledge, which are foundational for understanding human psychology from an Islamic perspective.

Chapter 2 on Ontological Themes delves into the nature of the human psyche. It includes works by Imams Abū Ḥāmid al-Ghazālī, al-Bājūrī, al-Suhrawardī, Ibn Sīna, and Ali Haydar Efendi. Topics covered include the definitions and interrelations of the qalb (heart), rūḥ (soul), nafs (self), and ʿaql (intellect), as well as discussions on the different traits, faculties, and characteristics of these domains.

Chapter 3 focuses on cognitive themes and processes features works by al-Ghazālī and al-Nābulsī with discussions on human thoughts and the factors influencing them such as Shayṭān's whisperings, as well as the significance of dreams and dream interpretation.

Chapter 4 on Emotional Themes addresses emotional well-being and the management of emotions such as sorrow, grief, fear, hope, anger, and happiness. It includes writings by al-Ghazālī, Ibn Abī al-Dunyā, Ibn Qayyim al-Jawziyya, ibn al-Jawzī, and Ibn Qādi Baalbek.

Chapter 5 on Behavioral Themes include discussions on character traits, methods of behavioral change, and the phenomenon of waswasa and behavioral compulsions, drawing from the works of Imam al-Birgivī and Mulla ʿAlī al-Qarī.

Chapter 6 focuses on general well-being, discussing topics such as recognizing and managing one's own flaws, the need for recognizing psychological symptoms, and managing and restoring mental health. The chapter includes works by Imam al-Balkhī, al-Ghazālī, and al-Rāzī.

3 Approach

The editorial and contributor team gathered these segments from classical Islamic scholarly writings and provided a translation for each segment into English. In addition to the English translation, a commentary was produced at the bottom with the following aims: (i) to explain any technical concepts that may not be readily comprehensible for someone who is not a student of the Islamic sciences, (ii) draw attention to the potential applicability and utility of such discourses to modern psychological topics, and (iii) discuss any convergences and divergences between such ideas and the modern psychological literature.

4 Aims and Target Audience

The major aim of this book is to draw out some really pertinent illustrations of psychological discussions in Islamic traditions that provides readers a taste of the Islamic literature, directly from the writings of its scholars. The need to provide a primary source was also one of the major objectives of this project. In order to fully appreciate the Islamic tradition, the team felt that a translation project was warranted in order to access the primary sources and to hear the Islamic tradition from its direct authorities, i.e., classical Islamic scholars. Even though some of the works we translated here may in fact have existing translations, we felt it was necessary to re-translate some of these works for the following two reasons:

i. We wanted to translate these works with the audience in mind and to provide a psychological commentary to help make connections between these writings and the field.
ii. The uniqueness and specialty of this book is in its extraction of some key psychological topics that exist within the larger scholarly works into one

book. For example, if a psychologist or a student of psychology wanted to find a specific topic in psychology, like cognition in Islamic traditions, they may need to spend countless hours looking through various works in order to find them. However, this work picked fruits from the garden of the Islamic scholarly literature and put them together on the bookshelf for consumption.

Having said the above, it is important to note that this is not a fully exhaustive list of Islamic scholarly works that pertain to psychology. In fact, throughout the process of this project, the editors were continuously needing to remain disciplined in attempting to keep this project small enough and not to turn it into an encyclopedia of psychological themes in Islamic traditions. It is hoped that readers will be inspired by this work enough to perhaps write an encyclopedia or be inspired by the Islamic tradition to become an avid student and consumer of its literature. Furthermore, we hope that this work will generate many potential masters, doctoral or research project ideas for students and scholars of the behavioral and social sciences.

Finally, the target audience of this particular work are those who are interested in the study of psychology in the Islamic tradition. These include students of the social, behavioral, and Islamic sciences. This book is designed with an educated and academic audience in mind.

CHAPTER 1

Epistemological Themes

1 Sources of Knowledge. *Al-Kifāya fī al-Hidāya*[1] by Imam Nūr al-Dīn al-Ṣābūnī (d. 580 AH/1184 AD)

1.1 *Author's Biography*

Imam Abū Muḥammad Aḥmad ibn Maḥmūd ibn Abī Bakr al-Bukhārī, also known as Nūr al-Dīn al-Ṣābūnī, lived during the 6th century after the Hijra. He was a prominent Ḥanafī-Māturīdī scholar from Bukhāra (in modern day Uzbekistan) and is known to have held theological debates with famous scholars from other theological schools of thought, such as Fakhr al-Dīn Al-Rāzī who represents the Ashʿarī school of theology. Imam Fakhr al-Dīn reports in his book, "*Munāẓarāt Jarāt fī Bilād ma Warā' al-Nahr*" that on his journey to Hajj at the end of his life, Imam al-Ṣābūni stopped and gave lectures at gatherings of knowledge in both Iraq and Khurasan. This is an indication toward the respect that was afforded to him for his scholarly contributions. He is most famously known for his text on the Māturīdī school of theology entitled, "Al-Bidāya fī Uṣūl al-Dīn[2]". In fact, he is often simply referred to as "Ṣāḥib al-bidāya" (The author of al-bidāya). Imam al-Ṣābūnī died in 1184 CE in Bukhara.

1.2 *Text Overview and Significance*

Al-Bidāya fī Uṣūl al-Dīn is an expansive theological text that belongs to the genre of discursive theology (*ʿilm al-kalām*), and it is considered one of the central texts representing the Māturīdī school of Islamic theology. More specifically, the text deals with a wide range of theological principles and questions and it clarifies the Māturīdī opinions in contrast to other contemporaneous opinions and theological positions. This text, like many other texts of discursive theology, starts with epistemological foundations explicating the sources of knowledge, laying the foundation for the types of proofs and sources of knowledge that are considered admissible in proving the trueness of any reality or claim. This first section which deals with epistemology is the part selected for the purposes of this book. It is then followed by 5 major sections: the first section deals with questions related to Divinity (*ilāhiyyāt*), the second

1 Al-Sābūnī, Nūr al-Dīn. *Al-Kifāya fi-l-Hidaya*. Beirut: Dār Ibn Ḥazam, 2014.
2 Al-Sābūnī, Nūr al-Dīn. *Al-Bidāya min al-Kifāya fī Uṣūl al-Dīn*. Cairo: Dār al-Mā'rif, 1969.

section deals with questions related to prophethood (*nubuwwāt*), the third section deals with questions of Imamate, the fourth section deals with questions of *taʿdīl* and *tajwīr* (imputation of justice and injustice), and the final section deals with issues pertaining to revealed and narrated traditions (*samʿiyyāt*).

The text establishes that rational, sacred, and empirical sources of knowledge can be congruous and not at odds with each other, demonstrating a multiplex epistemological framework in providing a holistic approach to understanding reality and levels of knowing that reality. This is among the most critical conversations that can be brought into the field of an Islamic psychology, providing us a foundation for understanding which sources of knowledge can be used to construct an understanding of human psychology.

1.3 *Arabic Text*

القول في مدارك العلوم

اعلم أن العلم الحادث نوعان: ضروري واكتسابي. فالضروري هو ما يُحدثه اللّٰه تعالى في نفس العالم من غير كسبه واختياره، كالعلم بوجود نفسه وتغير أحواله من الجوع والعطش واللذة والألم. واختصاصه أن لا يتمكن العالِم من دفع هذا العلم من نفسه ولا يقدر على تشكيك نفسه فيه، ويشترك في هذا النوع من العلم جميع الحيوانات. وأما الاكتسابي فهو ما يُحدثه اللّٰه تعالى بواسطة كسب العبد، وهو مباشرة أسبابه. وله أسباب ثلاثة: الحواس السليمة، والخبر الصادق، ونظر العقل.

أما الحواس السليمة فهي خمسة: السمع والبصر والشّم والذوق واللمس، وكل حاسة تختص بنوع من الـمُدرَكات إذا استُعمِلت فيها تفيد العلم. وأما الخبر الصادق فنوعان. أحدهما الخبر المتواتر، وهو ما يُسمَع من أشخاص مختلفة في أحوال مختلفة بحيث لا يُتوهم أنهم توافقوا على

الكَذِب فيه؛ وهو موجب للعلم الضروري، كالعلم بوجود الملوك الماضية والبلدان القاصية. والثاني الخبر الـمُؤيَّد بالمعجزة من الأنبياء، وهو موجب للعلم القطعي ولكن بطريق الاستدلال. وأما نظر العقل فهو سبب للعلم أيضًا، و الحاصل منه نوعان: ضروري ويُسمى بديهيًّا، وهو ما يحصل بأول النظر من غير تفكر، كالعلم بأن كل شيء أعظم من جزئه؛ واستدلالي، وهو ما يُحتاج فيه إلى ضرب تفكر ونوع تأمل، كالعلم بوجود النار عند رؤية الدخان. وحصول العلم بهذه الأسباب مُشاهَد لمن أنصف ولم يعاند.

وأنكرت السمنية والبراهمة كون الخبر من أسباب العلم، وقالت: الخبر يتنوع إلى صدق وكذب، وما يتردد بين الصدق والكذب لا يفيد العلم. قلنا: هذا الكلام خبر منكم أيضًا فلا يفيد العلم على زعمكم. ثم هذا لا يُلزِمنا فإنا عَنَيْنا الخبر الصادق وأنه لا يتنوع، ولأن

الخبر لو لم يكن سببًا للعلم كيف يعرف الإنسان والده وأخاه وعمه وخاله وسائر أقربائه، إذ لا طريق لمعرفة هؤلاء إلا بالخبر.

وأنكرت الملحدة والرافضة والمشبهة كون العقل من أسباب العلم وقالت: قضايا العقل متناقضة بدليل أن العقلاء اختلفوا فيما بينهم. وكل واحد منهم يثبت قوله بالعقل، وما تناقضت قضاياه لا يصلح أن يكون سببًا للعلم.

قلنا: بِمَ عرفتم أن العقل ليس من أسباب العلم، والأسباب محصورة في العقل والخبر والحس؟ إن قلتم: {{بالعقل}}، فقد ناقضتم حيث قلتم: علمنا بالعقل أن العقل ليس من أسباب العلم. وإن قلتم: {{بالخبر}}، فمن أخبركم أن العقل ليس من أسباب العلم وبِمَ عرفتم أن ذلك الخبر صدق أم كذب؟ وإن قلتم : {{بالحس}}، فبأي حاسة علمتم ذلك والحواس محصورة؟ ولأن العقل لو لم يكن من أسباب العلم بطل أن يكون الخبر من أسباب العلم، إذ لا يمكن التمييز بين الصادق والكاذب إلا بالعقل، وبدون التمييز لا يحصل العلم بالخبر، وقولكم: {{تناقضت قضاياه فلا يكون سببًا للعلم}}، قلنا: هذا نظر منكم بالعقل، فكيف تنفون النظر بالنظر؟ فإن قالوا: نعارض الفاسد بالفاسد، قلنا: معارضة الفاسد بالفاسد معارضة الشيء بمثله وإنه من باب العقل أيضا؛ فكيف ما كان ففيه إثبات العقل والنظر.

ثم نقول: لا تتناقض قضايا العقول ولا يجوز فيها التناقض وإن كان أقوال العقلاء متناقضة، لأن العقل حجة الله على عباده، والتناقض عن حجج الله تعالى منفيّ. وإنما وقع الاختلاف بين العقلاء إما لتقصيرهم في مراعاة شرائط النظر أو لقصورهم عن بلوغ درجة النظر، فإن للنظر شرائط تجب رعايتها ليفيد العلم. وكذا العقول متفاوتة في أنفسها، فربما قَصُرَ عقله عن معرفة ذلك فحكم بالطبع والهوى وظنّ أنه من قضيات العقل. فأما أن تختلف قضايا العقول فلأمثال ذلك إذا قيل لك: كم اثنين في اثنين؟، قلت: أربعة، وهذا من قضيات العقل لا يحتمل غير ذلك ولا يختلف فيه العقلاء كثير اختلاف. فإن قيل لك: كم ستة عشر في ستة عشر؟ قلت: مائتان وست وخمسون، ولكن يُحتاج فيه إلى زيادة تأمل واجتهاد ورعاية شروط النظر حتي يخرج ما هو المبلغ من عدد الضرب. وربما يقع الاختلاف بين العقلاء في جواب هذا السؤال. وما هو حقيقة المبلغ في قضية العقل لا يحتمل الاختلاف وإن اختلف جواب العقلاء في ذلك؛ ولكن لو راعى كل واحد من العقلاء ما هو شرط النظر لعرف أن مبلغه ما قلنا. ولو وقع الاختلاف كان الاختلاف راجعًا إلى التقصير في رعاية شرائط النظر لا إلى اختلاف قضية العقل. واعتَبِر هذا بنظر العين فإن المرئيات متنوعة، منها ما هو بديهي يحصل العلم به بأول نظرة كالنظر إلى السماء والقمر ليلة البدر لا تختلف فيه النُّظَّار، ومنها ما لا يحصل العلم إلا بنوع جهد وكلفة كالنظر إلى القطب في السماء والهلال في أول الشهر، وربما يقع الاختلاف فيه.

وهذا الاختلاف راجع إلي أحد الأمرين: إما إلى التقصير من جهة الناظر أو إلى قصور آلة النظر. والله الموفق.

1.4 *English Translation*

On the Sources of Knowledge

Know that temporal knowledge[3] is of two types: intuitive knowledge (*ḍarūrī*) and acquired knowledge (*iktisābī*). Intuitive knowledge is that which Allah the Exalted effectuates in the knower's self without their acquisition or choice, such as knowledge of one's own existence, and the [distinctive awareness] of one's varying states like hunger, thirst, pleasure, and pain. Its distinguishing attribute is that a person is incapable of repelling such knowledge from one's own self; they are furthermore unable to harbor any skepticism regarding it. All animals share this particular type of knowledge. As for acquired knowledge, it is what Allah Exalted confers via a person's undertaking [and choice], which is interaction with its occasions (*asbāb*). [This type of knowledge] has three sources: sound senses, true reports, and intellectual reasoning.[4]

3 Al-Ṣābūnī begins his concise work on discursive theology, *al-Bidāya fī Uṣūl al-Dīn*, with the following critical preface to this discussion: "Knowledge consists of two types: the eternal (*qadīm*) and the temporal (*ḥādith*). The eternal is that which is ascribed to the essence of the Creator and does not resemble the knowledge of that which is temporal. Temporal knowledge is then of two types: intuitive (*ḍarūrī*) and acquired (*iktisābī*) ..." (al-Ṣābūnī, *al-Bidāya min al-Kifāya fī Uṣūl al-Dīn*, 29).

In the above classification, al-Ṣābūnī includes true reports that are corroborated by miracles (i.e., revelation) under temporal knowledge. This is not contradictory to the belief that the Quran is in fact eternal (*qadīm*). This is because the temporal knowledge being referred to here is the knowledge of revelation which is heard through recitation or read from its written form by the believer. Although both are created forms of speech, the actuality of that knowledge is eternal in and of itself as it is the speech of Allah.

4 This establishes a very important Islamic epistemology that creates a framework for the appropriation and acceptance of both scientific knowledge and divine revelation, effectively breaking the false dichotomy that is commonly held between science and sacred traditions.

It is also important to note that all three sources of knowledge are equal in terms of their providing new knowledge, while they may not be equal in terms of sacredness. Each source is judged in accordance with the strength of its evidence, whether they are certain (*qaṭʿī*) or probabilistic (*ẓannī*). If two objective facts were to seem contradictory to one another, then there is a reconciliation process that is undertaken. The first step in this process is an attempt to reconcile both sources (*tawfīq*) so that a holistic understanding can be achieved that resolves the apparent tension between the sources. This can be seen in the section of al-Bayjūrī's discussion on the location of the 'mind' (*ʿaql*). If however a reconciliation process is unachievable, then one source may be given preference (*tarjīḥ*) over another depending

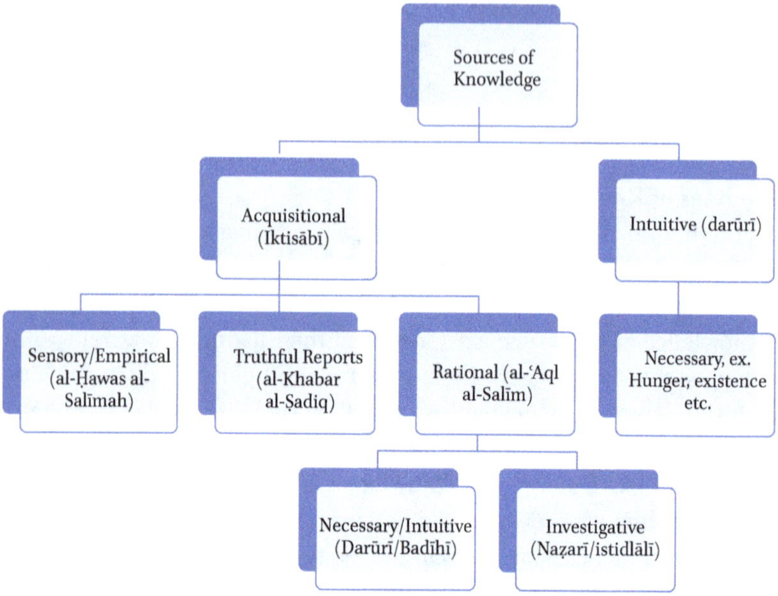

FIGURE 1

As for the sound senses, there are five: hearing, sight, smell, taste, and touch. Each sense corresponds to a specific type of perception. When each sense is utilized for [the corresponding type of perception], they will provide knowledge.[5]

As for true reports, it is of two types. The first of the two is the massively and congruently transmitted report (*khabar mutawātir*), namely that which is heard from (a multitude of) separate individuals in different states such that it is unimaginable for them to have agreed upon a falsehood within it.[6] [Such a report] establishes intuitive knowledge (*ʿilm ḍarūrī*), like the knowledge of past kings and distant lands. The second is the report[7] that is accompanied by

on the strength of its source transmission and/or the consistency and correspondence of its meaning to the principles of religion. Finally, if none of these are possible such as in the case of a verse of the Qur'an apparently conflicting with established empirical evidence then, the verse may be understood by considering another possible meaning (*taʾwīl*) for the scriptural source considering the certain (*qatiʿ*) rational or empirical evidence at hand.

5 This demonstrates that empirical data can establish certain facts. This is corroborated by al-Nasafī in his *Tabṣirat al-Adillah* (Nasafī, Tabṣirat al-adillah fī uṣūl al-dīn: 'alá ṭarīqat al-imām Abī manṣūr al-Māturīdī, ed. Muhammad al- Anwar Hamid Issa (Cairo: The Library of al Azhar, 2011), 125.). This can be extended to include the scientific method within the hard sciences, while 'soft facts' built upon qualitative, correlational, or subjective self-reports as is commonplace in the field of psychology may similarly establish only 'soft' facts.

6 A falsehood includes both an intentional lie and fabrication as well as an unintentional error.

7 What is intended here is reports of revelation being transmitted to a prophet from Allah.

a miracle from the prophets.[8] [Such a report] establishes certain (*qaṭʿī*) knowledge, however by way of inference[9] (*istidlāl*).[10]

As for intellectual reasoning, it is also a source of knowledge. In sum, it is of two types: the intuitive (*ḍarūrī*),[11] also called the self-evident (*badīhī*)[12] – which is what is obtained by preliminary reflection without [need for] any deliberation, such as knowledge that any sum is greater than its parts. [The other is] inferential (*istidlalī*) knowledge, which requires some type of deliberation and contemplation, such as knowledge of the existence of fire upon seeing smoke.

The acquisition of knowledge from these sources is an [obviously] observable affair to one who is fair and does not obstinately resist. The Śramaṇa[13]

8 In other words, the proof that the prophets' reports are undoubtedly true is that Allah granted them inimitable miracles that certify them as bearers of the truth and only the truth. Once Allah has certified them through miracles, to consider the reports of His messengers to be false is essentially akin to stating that Allah lies, which is a logical impossibility.

9 What is inferred here is that the individual (i.e., prophet) that is reporting revelation from Allah is in fact a truthful individual. This is done through investigation of their character, history, reputation, conduct, etc. Such an investigation provides evidence for the truthfulness of the individual. On top of this, when miracles are bestowed upon such an individual, their claim to prophethood is corroborated by it, leaving no doubt in the mind of the person that they are indeed transmitting revelation.

10 Reports do not need to establish certain knowledge to inform legal or scientific enquiry. In theological enquiry, however, reports need to be categorical and certain for them to establish Islamic creed, or what is necessary to believe to be considered a believer. In scientific enquiry, such as discussions of mental health principles and practices, the content of probabilistic reports is very valuable even if not categorical.

11 This contrasts with information that demands thorough investigation and careful deliberation. Badīhī knowledge is such that upon first presentation to an individual it 'clicks' and makes sense.

12 This demonstrates that according to Islamic belief, individuals are born with basic a priori knowledge which is referred to as self-evident ("*badīhī*") knowledge. Maturīdī theologians even extend this to include knowledge of some basic universal morals. That is, that individuals are born with an ability to differentiate right from wrong inherently, understand their world and surroundings and have an inborn tendency to believe in a Creator. This perspective differs from the widely accepted notion, advocated by behaviorist psychologists like Pinker, that humans are born as a 'blank slate.' (Steven Pinker, "The Blank Slate: The Modern Denial of Human Nature," *Choice Reviews Online* 40, no. 07 (March 1, 2003): 40–4305.).

13 The Sramana is an ancient religious movement in India that began as an offshoot of the Vedic religion but diverged from Vedic Hindu ritualism and the hierarchical authority of the Hindu Brahmin priesthood. Sramanas adopted the path of asceticism and self-denial and largely led monastic lives in the pursuit of spiritual liberation. The Sramana tradition gave rise to Jainism and Buddhism.

(*al-sumaniyya*) and Brahmins[14] (*al-barāhima*) deny[15] that reports are from the sources of knowledge.[16] They say: reports are categorizable into either truth or falsehood, and that which can vacillate between truth and falsehood cannot provide knowledge. We say [in response]: this statement itself is a report and as such should not establish knowledge according to your own claim. Moreover, this argument does not corner us, for our intent is a true report which does not vacillate. Furthermore, if reports are not sources of knowledge, how would mankind have knowledge of their fathers, brothers, paternal uncles, maternal uncles, and all other relatives, as there is no way of knowing them except through reports?

The heretics (*al-mulḥida*),[17] extreme Shīʿa (*al-rawāfiḍ*), and the anthropomorphists (*al-mushabbiha*) deny reason as a [certain] source of knowledge. They say: rational propositions are contradictory, evidenced by the fact that rational people differ with one another (in their conclusions), and yet each of them establishes their claim through reason.[18] Thus, that which has contradictory propositions cannot be fit to be a source of knowledge.

---

14 The Brahmins represented the priestly class of Vedic Hinduism. They were an exclusive caste of priests and teachers who were believed to be intermediaries between the supposed gods of Vedic Hinduism and common men. Brahmins guarded their exclusive access to the learning found in the Vedas.

15 This can be likened to post-modernist and social constructivist views in asserting that reports are mere beliefs and notions that individuals differ on cross culturally.

Another interesting note is that the field of psychology has evolved from the old behaviorist notion of dismissing all true reports to accepting the subjective self-report, which has led psychology to become a 'soft' science. However, a contradiction remains in doing so in that the science of psychology, despite being willing to accept these subjective self-reports that are not built upon observable realities through the senses, maintains a rejection of scripture that is massively and congruently transmitted through objective self-reports. If psychology is willing to entertain and accept self-reports, then why have they limited them only to intrapsychic experiences such as one's emotions or attitudes to make conclusions about the reality of human nature while dismissing a rigorous tradition of transmission for revelation contained within the Islamic tradition.

16 To clarify, the Sramana and the Brahmins did not deny the epistemic value of reports altogether. Rather, they believed that reports can at most establish speculative or probabilistic knowledge and cannot establish knowledge with certainty.

17 The author is referring to the Bāṭīnī sect of Shī'as.

18 This same contradiction can also be observed by social constructivists and post-modernists who dismiss objective truth and state that they are all relative or social constructions. The idea that morality, or knowledge is relative or socially constructed is established by them as a 'universal' truth, which violates its own premises of the lack of objectivity. Alternatively, an objection could be levied in that social constructivism itself can be alleged to be socially constructed.

We say: How do you know that reason is not a [certain] source of knowledge, given that the sources [of knowledge] are limited to reason, reports, and sensory perception? If you say: "[We know this] through reason", then you have contradicted yourself, since you have [essentially] stated that "we know through reason that reason is not a source of knowledge". If you state: "[We know this] through reports", then who reported to you that reason is not from the sources of knowledge, and how do you know whether that report is true or false? If you say: "[We know this] through sensory perception", then by which sense do you know that, given that the senses are limited?

Furthermore, if reason is not a source of knowledge, reports will also not be a valid source of knowledge, as discernment between a true [report] and a false [report] is not possible without reason, and without discernment, knowledge of a report is not attainable. [As for] your statement: "Its propositions are contradictory, therefore it cannot be a source of knowledge", we respond: "This is [in fact] investigation (*naẓar*) through reason! How can you deny rational investigation using rational investigation?!" If they say, "We are contradicting the invalid with the invalid", we respond: "Contradicting the invalid with the invalid is a contradiction of something with its like, which is from the category of reason as well". So however, the matter may be, in all of this is justification for [the epistemic value] reason and investigation.

Further, we say: rational prepositions are not contradictory. Contradiction is not possible in them even if the statements of people of reason are contradictory, because reason is a proof of Allah against His slaves, and there can be no contradiction in Allah the Exalted's proofs. Differences between people of reason only occur due to either their inadequate observance of the conditions of rational investigation or due to their inability to reach the level of [sound] rational investigation, as certain conditions must be observed to establish [certain] knowledge through rational investigation. Similarly, intellects are diverse in themselves. Perhaps one's intellect is deficient in recognizing that [knowledge] and thus judges based on their temperament and caprice, thinking it to be a proposition of reason. As for the [idea of] differences in rational propositions, then for examples of that [difference], [consider] if you are asked: "What is two multiplied by two?" you would say: "four". This is a rational proposition that does not carry any other possibility in which people of reason do not much differ. Then, if you are asked: "What is sixteen multiplied by sixteen?" you say: "two hundred and fifty-six". This, however, requires more deliberation, effort, and observance of the conditions of rational investigation in order for the product of the multiplication to be reached. It is perhaps in the answer to this question that a difference between the people of reason may occur. [As for] the true product according to the proposition of reason, it does not carry the possibility of a difference, even if the answers of people of reason may differ in that regard. However, if every rational person observed the conditions of rational investigation, they would realize that its total is what we stated. Even if differences were to occur the disparity therein would go back to the inadequate observance of the conditions of sound rational investigation and not to the propositions of reason. Consider this [in comparison to] ocular vision, for what is ocularly perceived (i.e., things observable with the eye) is [also] diverse, some of which is self-evident, knowledge of it being acquired upon first glance, such as seeing the sky and the moon on the night of a full moon over which viewers do not differ. Some of [those perceived things] are [such that] knowledge of them is not acquired except with some effort and difficulty, such as seeing the polestar in the sky or the new crescent moon at the beginning of the month; [in these] perhaps disparities may occur. This disparity originates in one of two things: either a deficiency from the perspective of one's ocular vision, or a deficiency in the instrument of one's vision. And Allah is the one who grants success.

2 All That the Prophet (May Allah Bless Him and Grant Him Peace) Brought from Allah Is Self-Evident (Badīhī). *The Letters of Imam Rabānnī* (*Al-Maktūbāt al-Rabbāniyya*) by Mujaddid al-Alf al-Thānī al-Imam al-Rabbanī, Aḥmad al-Sirhindī (d. 1033 AH/1624 CE)

2.1 *Author's Biography*

Shaykh Aḥmad al-Sirhindī was born on May 24 in the year 972 AH/1564 CE and is considered to be one of the most important figures of the Naqshbandī Sufī order. He is also often simply referred to as al-Imam al-Rabbānī. He was also a Hanafī scholar who hailed from the town of Sirhind in India and traced his paternal lineage to the second caliph of Islam, ʿUmar ibn al-Khattab (may Allah be pleased with him). He was given the honorific title of *Mujaddid al-alf al-Thani* (the reviver of the second Millennium) by his disciples. In fact, the disciples that follow him in the lineage of the Naqshabanī Sufi order are referred to as belonging to the mujaddidī arm of the order. He was known for his opposition to the mughal ruler of India, Akbar's innovation of a new religion known as Din-ilahi which was a synthesis of Islam and Hinduism. The period of Akbar was a time of mass confusion among the Muslim orthodoxy in the Indian subcontinent, and he is said to have made a concerted effort to contend with and single handedly reversed such trends back to the traditional understanding of Islam that was re-established under the rulership of succeeding Mughal ruler Aurangzeb. According to many contemporary historians, Sirhindī is a major figure in effecting major changes to Islam's progression in the Indian context. He died on December 10 in the year 1033 AH/1624 CE and is buried in his birthplace of Sirhind. His tomb is also referred to as the *Rawza Sharīf.*

2.2 *Text Overview and Significance*

His *Maktubat* ("Letters") is the most famous of his compilations, and it consists of letters written to his friends in India and the region north of the Amu Darya (river). It was through these letters that Shaykh Ahmad's major contribution to Islamic thought can be traced, and teachings continue. The compilation consists of 534 letters to nearly 200 people. These letters deal with a variety of subjects connected with Sufi thought, and it is through these letters that his metaphysical and mystical teachings are preserved.

The psychological significance of the selected letter in this work is due to its dealing with the notion of *fitra* in the Islamic tradition. The prophet Muḥammad (may Allah bless him and grant him peace) is reported to have said 'No child is born but that he is upon *the fitra* ....' The fitra is understood to mean the primordial inclination for spiritually connecting with God and intrinsic awareness of morality without the need for external proof. Shaykh Aḥmad Sirhindī purports that belief in God, the prophethood of the Messenger of God (may Allah bless him and grant him peace), and everything that was conveyed by him revealed to him from God are all self-evident truths (*badīhī*). Thus, purporting that human beings are in essence capable of deducing morality and acting in accordance with it. However, he stipulates that understanding morality is only self-evident to those whose inner comprehension is free of [spiritual illnesses]. To substantiate his claim, he draws upon a medical analogy of the one who is unable to taste the sweetness of honey on account of a sickness by saying: 'don't you see that a person with ageusia (*safrāwī*), for instance, so long as he suffers from ageusia (*safra'*), the sweetness of sugar and honey for him needs to be established by [external] evidence? However, after he is cured from that illness, he no longer needs any [external] evidence. Thus, there is no contradiction between his need for proof on account of the presence of a sickness and its [i.e., the reality that honey is sweet] being self-evident in its nature.' He offers that one needs to focus on curing the disease itself, not on attempting to convince the individual intellectually while his sensory perception says otherwise. Thus, Sirhindī presents a bottom-up approach to understanding reality and maintaining realistic and cognitive health. This entails the behavioral and spiritual cleansing of one's unhealthy habits and environments that serves to influence or distort one's cognitive faculties. Due to habituated habits, individuals may rationalize these unhealthy behaviors, losing their ability to see their problematic nature. Thus, instead of proposing cognitive restructuring by intellectually debating, challenging their evidence or psychoeducation, he proposes that behavioral interventions focus on removing the behavioral and environmental conditions causing these cognitive distortions of reality in the first place.

2.3 *Arabic Text*

جميع ما جاء به النبي صلى الله عليه وسلم من عند الله عز وجل بديهي:

قال رضي الله عنه أيضًا في مكتوبه إلى الشيخ فريد البخاري في بيان أن جميع ما جاء به صلى الله عليه وسلم من عند الله بديهي ما يلي:

"اعلم أن وجود الباري تعالى وتقدّس وكذلك وحدانيته سبحانه، بل نبوة محمد رسول الله ﷺ، بل جميع ما جاء به من عند الله بديهي لا يحتاج إلى فكر ودليل، على تقدير سلامة القوة المدرِكة من الآفات الرديّة والأمراض المعنوية.

والنظر والفكر فيها مقصور على زمن وجود العلة وثبوت الآفة، وأما بعد النجاة من المرض القلبي وزوال الغشاوة البصرية فلا شيء سوى البداهة، ألا ترى أن الصفراوي مثلا ما دام مبتلى بعلة الصفراء يحتاج إثبات حلاوة السكر والعسل عنده إلى الدليل، ولكن إذا تخلّص من تلك العلة لا يحتاج إلى دليل أصلا، ولا منافاة بين احتياجه إلى الدليل الناشئ عن وجود الآفة وبين بداهته يعني في ذاته، ألا ترى أن الأحول يرى الواحد اثنين ويحكم بعدم وحدته، فهو معذور في هذا الحكم، ولا يخرج حكمه هذا الناشئ من الآفة فيه وحدة ذلك الواحد من البداهة ولا يدخلها في النظرية.

ومن المحقَّق أن ميدان الاستدلال ضيق جدا وحصول اليقين من طريق الدليل والنظر والفكر متعذر، فكان فكر إزالة المرض القلبي لتحصيل الإيمان اليقيني ضروريا، كما أن إزالة علّة الصفراء في تحصيل اليقين بحلاوة السكر أشد ضرورة من إقامة الدليل على حلاوة السكر، وكيف يحصل اليقين به بإقامة الدليل عليه مع حكم وجدانه بمرارته بسبب علة الصفراء القائم به، وهكذا الحكم فيما نحن فيه، فإن النفس الأمارة منكِرة للأحكام الشرعية بالذات وحاكمة بتناقضها بالطبع، فتحصيل اليقين بحقّية هذه الأحكام الصادقة من طريق الدليل مع وجود إنكار وجدان المستدل عليه عسير جدا، فكانت تزكية النفس ضرورية لتعسر حصول اليقين اللازم الحصول بدونها (قد أفلح من زكاها. وقد خاب من دساها) (الشمس: ٩-١٠)، فتقرر أن منكِر هذه الشريعة الباهرة والملة الطاهرة الظاهرة معلول بعلة مثل منكر حلاوة السكر، ولكن:

ما ضر شمس الضحى في الأفق طالعة   أن لا يرى ضوءها من ليس ذا بصَرِ

فالمقصود من السير والسلوك وتزكية النفس وتصفية القلب هو إزالة الآفات المعنوية والأمراض القلبية المشار إليها بقوله تعالى: (في قلوبهم مرض) (البقرة: ١٠)، لتحقق حقيقة الإيمان، فإن وجد الإيمان مع وجود هذه الآفات فإنما هو بحسب الظاهر فقط؛ لأن وجدان النفس الأمارة حاكم بخلافه، وهي مصرّة على كفرها، ومَثَلُ هذا الإيمان الصوري مثل إيمان الصفراوي بحلاوة السكر في كون وجدانه حاكما وشاهدا بخلافه، فكما أن اليقين الحقيقي بحلاوة السكر إنما يحصل بعد زوال مرض الصفراء كذلك حقيقة الإيمان -يعني بحقيّة الأحكام الشرعية وصدقها- إنما تحصل بعد تزكية النفس واطمئنانها، وحينئذ يصير الإيمان وجدانيا.

وهذا القسم من أقسام الإيمان محفوظ من الزوال لقوله تعالى: (ألآ إن أولياء الله لا خوف عليهم ولا هم يحزنون) (يونس: ٦٢) صادق في شأن صاحبه، شرفنا الله سبحانه بشرف هذا الإيمان الكامل الحقيقي بحرمة النبي الأمي القرشي عليه وعلى آله من الصلوات أفضلها ومن التسليات أكملها".

2.4 *English Translation*

All that the Prophet (May Allah bless him & grant him peace) brought from Allah is Self-Evident (*Badīhī*)[19]

[Al-Imam al-Rabbānī Mujaddid al-Alf al-Thānī Shaykh Aḥmad al-Sirhindī] (may Allah be pleased with him), in his letter to Shaykh Farīd al-Bukhārī, explains that everything that Allah revealed to the Prophet (may Allah bless him and grant him peace) is self-evident (*badīhī*),[20] as follows:

---

19 Taken from the Arabic translation of the letters of Imam Aḥmad al-Sirhindī al Fārūqī's celebrated collection of correspondences on spiritual and theological topics, entitled *al-Maktūbāt* (Al-Sirhindi Al-Mirani & Senturk, 2016, 96–97). The original text is in Persian and was translated into Arabic.

20 Badīhī: self-evident, axiomatic; a priori; that which does not need any proof or reflection, as opposed to theoretical (a posteriori; *nazarī*) knowledge. Here, we see that Imam al-Sirhindī offers a *taṣawwufī* bottom-up epistemological approach. He suggests that all of revelation (including the rules of *sharī'a*) are self-evident to an unbiased mind that is free of ideological preconceptions and materialistic attachments. On the other hand, discursive theologians (*mutakallimūn*) offer a top-down approach to epistemology, stating that knowledge requires *ithbāt* (proof). This means that rational, empirical, and scriptural proofs are used to prove Islamic belief and law. Maturidi Sunni scholars go as far as to suggest that the intellect can inherently decipher the difference between universal good and evil, independent of revelation. On the other hand, they do acknowledge that the ability to realize that an action, which is not inherently evil but is evil due to external considerations (*qabīḥ lī ghayrihi*), is not possible through intellectual judgment alone (e.g., drinking a little bit of wine). In such cases revelation is required to establish its immorality

Know that the existence and oneness of the Creator – Exalted, Sanctified, and Glorified be He – as well as the prophethood of the Messenger of Allah Muḥammad (may Allah bless him and grant him peace), and even more so, everything that he conveyed from Allah is self-evident (*badīhī*) and does not require deliberation or establishment by proofs, – assuming that [a person's] faculty of comprehension (*quwwa mudrika*) is free of cognitive impairments and spiritual illnesses.[21]

The need for investigation and deliberation over [matters of revelation] is restricted to the duration of the presence of disease and determination of disorder.[22] However, after the heart is relieved of any illnesses and the curtain of the inner eye is removed, then nothing remains except self-evidence. Do you not see that a person with ageusia[23] (*ṣafrāwī*), for instance, if he suffers from

(al-Taftazānī, 2000). Whereas Imam al-Sirhindī seems to indicate that if an individual has a sound mind that is free of materialistic attachments and spiritual ailments, all of revelation would intuitively make sense to them even upon its initial presentation. It seems that a reconciliation between the two approaches may be to consider that it is important for individuals to use the intellect and proofs at the outset to accept Islam. Afterwards, however, everything else would be accepted without objection if they are free of materialistic attachments. This may be likened to the faith of Abū Bakr al-Ṣiddīq. When people, in astonishing disbelief, informed him that the Prophet (may the peace and blessings of Allah be upon him) was reported to have been transported to Jerusalem and came back in one night during what is called the Isrāʾ and Miʿrāj (the Night Journey and Ascension), Abū Bakr al-Ṣiddīq responded contrary to their expectations by exclaiming: "If Muḥammad said it, then he is speaking the truth. I have believed him regarding something even more far-fetched than that: that he receives revelation from the heavens (i.e., that an angel descends from the heavens to him). How can I not believe that he went to Jerusalem and back in a short time while these relate to occurrences on the earth." (al-Hākim, 1990, 3:81; 4407). In such an instance, he did not find the details of scripture objectionable after he had already committed and accepted the Prophet (may the peace and blessings of Allah be upon him) as the true prophet of Allah.

21 This part suggests that revelation is in accordance with what is natural and intuitive to any individual who is free of rational or spiritual ailments. For example, a person who drinks alcohol and considers its consumption normal can claim that drinking alcohol should not be forbidden unless it impairs someone's ability to avoid hurting others, questioning the dictates of the religion by way of using reason. According to this view, this person questions this prohibition as a rationalization for their spiritual sickness and habit of drinking alcohol rather than accepting it as a prohibition of Allah.

22 This demonstrates that after one has become Muslim, the continuous need for intellectual proofs and rationale is only needed for the cognitively challenged or spiritually diseased.

23 The inability to taste, particularly the loss of ability to detect sweetness. The name of this disease in Arabic is etymologically linked to the word yellow, related to the pre-modern Galenic conceptualization of this disease originating in excessive or deficient amounts of yellow bile that disturbs the balance of the four humors. Here we can see that Muslim

ageusia (*safrāʾ*) the sweetness of sugar and honey needs to be established by [external] evidence. However, after he is free from such an illness, he no longer needs any [external] evidence. There is no incompatibility between his need for proof on account of the presence of a sickness and its self-evidence in its nature (i.e., that the honey and sugar are inherently sweet in and of themselves). Do you not see that a person with diplopia[24] (*aḥwal*) sees one thing as two and judges that it is not singular? He is exempted in [making such a] judgment. This [faulty] judgment of his, arising out of the sickness in his eyes, does not remove the self-evident nature of the oneness of that singular object, nor does it place it into [the realm of] investigative (*naẓarī*) knowledge.[25]

It is clear that the domain of investigation of proofs is especially limited, and achieving true certainty (*yaqīn*) through evidence, theorization, and deliberation is near impossible. Thus, deliberating over the eradication of spiritual illnesses in order to attain conviction (*yaqīn*) is imperative, just as the elimination of the ageusia disorder in order to acquire certainty of the sugar's sweetness is more essential than providing evidence for the sugar's sweetness.[26]

How can (one) achieve certainty through the establishment of evidence for the sugar's sweetness while his sensory experiences render it bitter on account of his enduring ageusia disorder?[27] This similarly holds true for our topic of discussion, for the *nafs ammāra* inherently denies religious legal injunctions by its very being and makes judgements of contradiction in it by its very nature.

Thus, acquiring any certainty of the truthfulness of these true religious injunctions by way of intellectual proof is incredibly difficult while one's internal experience is attempting to prove otherwise. Hence, purification of the *nafs* is necessary, because reaching that certainty which is imperative to attain is impossible without it. *Successful indeed is the one who purifies their soul, and doomed is the one who corrupts it!* (Sūrat al-Shams 91:9–10). Thus, it has been established that those who deny this brilliant law and the pure,

---

scholars did not hesitate to utilize the medicinal theories of the time even if they originated in the ancient Greeks so long as they did not conflict with the Sharīʿa. Today, this sickness is referred to as ageusia (Rathee & Jain, 2023).

24 Double vision, also called diplopia, causes a person to perceive two objects as a single object (Najem & Margolin, 2023).

25 This is akin to demonstrating evidence for the binding duty of salat or prohibition of alcohol. Just as generating evidence for the sweetness of honey does not indicate that it may not be sweet in actual reality, likewise, establishing evidence by way of proof for the mandates of religion or tenants of Islamic belief does not reduce their truth value.

26 The solution cannot be providing evidence when there is a sickness which should be treated. Instead of trying to prove that sugar is sweet, one should try to cure the disease.

27 Even if he is convinced with the evidence, he cannot reach certainty by accepting it, since he internally experiences the opposite.

manifest religion suffer from an illness akin to the one who denies the sweetness of sugar.

> The morning sun risen upon the horizon remains unharmed
> if those bereft of sight cannot see its light.

The ultimate objective of traversing the spiritual path, cleansing the soul, and purification of the heart is the removal of spiritual disorders and the heart's sicknesses indicated by the Quran: *There is sickness in their hearts* (Sūrat al-Baqara 2:10), so that the reality of faith can be realized.[28] If faith is found to exist concurrently with these illnesses, then [know that] this is [only] with respect to what is apparent, since the disposition of the *nafs*[29] *ammāra* (the *nafs* that commands toward evil) is to judge in contradiction to faith while it is insistent upon disbelief. The example of this superficial faith is like the faith of the person with ageusia in the sweetness of sugar while his inner experience testifies and judges contrary to it. Just as true certainty regarding the sweetness of sugar can only occur after the elimination of ageusia, the reality of faith, that is, in the truthfulness of the rulings of divine law, is only attainable after the purification (*tazkiya*) of the self and its achieving tranquility (*iṭmi'nān*). At that point, faith becomes inherent (*wijdānī*).

This type of faith is protected from elimination, for Allah mentions: *There will certainly be no fear for the close servants of Allah, nor will they grieve* (Sūrat Yūnus 10:62) and is true for the one who holds it (type of unwavering faith). May Allah the Glorified honor us with this type of perfect, true faith through the sanctity of the unlettered Qurashyī prophet and may the best of salutations and highest degree of peace be upon him and his family.

---

28 Here we may highlight an important difference between modern schools of psychology and what is being offered here. According to Imam al-Sirhindī, cognitive distortions must also include distortions of ultimate reality as offered by scripture. This includes matters of faith. Furthermore, he is not suggesting that one merely challenges the evidence of the distortions by appealing to reason alone, since cognition can be used as a rationalizing tool by the lower ego. Since the source of the problem is the ego, and then it must be targeted and cleansed of its sickness to clear one's cognitive interpretative lens.

29 This is the lower ego that commands toward evil and that possesses excessive appetitive and aggressive drives. See the al-Ghazālī section on "An Exposition on the Meanings and Connotations of the Terms: *Nafs*, *Rūḥ*, *'Aql*, and *Qalb*".

CHAPTER 2

Ontological Themes

1 An Exposition on the Meanings of *Nafs, Rūh, ʿAql, Qalb* and What Is Intended by These Names. *The Revival of the Religious Sciences* (*Iḥyāʾ ʿUlūm al-Dīn*) by Imam Abū Ḥāmid Al-Ghazālī (d. 505 AH/1111 CE)

1.1 *Author's Biography*

Abū Ḥāmid Muḥammad ibn Muḥammad ibn Aḥmad al-Ghazālī al-Tūsī was born in Tus, Iran, in the year 450 AH/1059 CE and died in 505 AH/1111 CE. While the Imam was a young boy, his father passed away. But before his death, he had appointed a learned friend to take care of his two sons' Islamic education. Under the direction of his father's friend, the young Ghazālī studied in *madrasas* (Islamic seminaries) in Tus, Jurjan, and Nishapur (all cities within modern day Iran). When he arrived in Nishapur, Abu al-Maʿālī Abd al-Mālik al-Juwaynī, also known as Imam al-Haramayn took al-Ghazālī as his student. He managed to acquire various branches of knowledge during this time and remained in Juwaynī's company, learning from him until his death. After his death, he went to Baghdad where he was appointed by the famous Seljukī wazīr Nizām al-Mulk who had established a chain of Islamic colleges or seminaries known famously as the madrasa Nizamiyya. Imam al-Ghazālī was tasked with penning the views and positions of the *ahl al-sunna wa al-jamaʿa* and to write several treatises refuting other deviant groups. This allowed for the Seljuk dynasty, under the intellectual leadership of Imam al-Ghazali to establish a standardized and unified creed and religious positions for the public that was sponsored by the state. Given al-Ghazālī's genius and acumen, he was successfully able to write convincing treatises that demonstrated the supremacy of Sunni thought and its ability to address many modern and philosophical issues of the time. Through his relationship with Nizām al-Mulk and his work, he gained recognition and praise from the scholars. He preached to large crowds in the mosque, lecturing to over three hundred students, and giving legal opinions of great importance. Later in his life, Imam al-Ghazālī, took a long sabbatical from his teaching position in Baghdad to travel to other Muslim lands, spending years in spiritual solitude, reflection, prayer, and ascetic activities. He spent a large part of his time in the greater Sham region (Syria, Lebanon, Palestine). It is during this time that he wrote his most acclaimed work, *Iḥyāʾ ʿUlūm al-Dīn*. He later returned to his teaching position after his long journey. In sum, Imam al Ghazālī is considered by many great scholars to be the reviver of the era he lived in and recognized as one of the most important figures in the Islamic scholastic and Sufi tradition. His works continue to shape the Islamic discourse in significant ways until today.

1.2 *Text Overview and Significance*

Iḥyāʾ ʿUlūm al-Dīn (*Revival of the Religious Sciences*) is the most famous composition of Imam al-Ghazālī detailing Islamic beliefs and practices through the lens of Islamic spirituality or *tasawwuf.* The work originally spans 40 volumes, and it is divided into 4 sections, each one covering 10 subjects. The four sections are: (i) Acts of Worship (*ʿibādāt*), (ii) Social Aspects of Life (*muʿāmalāt*), (iii) Destructive actions (*muhlikāt*), and (iv) Actions that lead to ultimate Salvation (*munjiyāt*). One of the chapters contained within the third section is entitled, 'The Wonders of the Heart', which is followed by 'Disciplining the Soul'. These two chapters deal with many psychological issues such as the early nature vs nurture debates, the nature of the psyche, human drives, character, well-being, relationship between the brain and psychological processes, emotions, thoughts and their sources and relationships to actions among others. The famous traditionist, Imam Nawawī is reported to have stated about the *Ihyaʾ* that: 'were the books of Islam all to be lost, excepting only the *Ihyaʾ*, it would suffice to replace them all'. The psychological significance of the selected section in this book from the *Iḥyaʾ* addresses the ontological structure of the inner psyche or soul. In this section, Imam al-Ghazālī defines and presents the multiple meanings and usages for each of the following Islamic terms that point to aspects of the inner soul or psyche, i.e., *qalb*, *rūḥ*, *nafs*, and *ʿaql*.

1.3 *Arabic Text*

بيان معنى النفس والروح والقلب والعقل وما هو المراد بهذه الأسامي

اعلم أن هذه الأسماء الأربعة تستعمل في هذه الأبواب، ويقلٌّ في فحول العلماء من يحيط بهذه الأسامي، واختلاف معانيها وحدودها ومسمياتها، وأكثر الأغاليط منشؤها الجهل بمعنى هذه الأسامي، وباشتراكها بين مسميات مختلفة، ونحن نشرح في معنى هذه الأسامي ما يتعلق بغرضنا.

اللفظ الأول: لفظ القلب.

وهو يطلق لمعنيين:

أحدهما: اللحم الصنوبري الشكل، المودع في الجانب الأيسر من الصدر، وهو لحم مخصوص، وفي باطنه تجويف، وفي ذلك التجويف دم أسود، وهو منبع الروح ومعدنه،

ولسنا نقصد الآن شرح شكله وكيفيته؛ إذ لا تتعلق به الأغراض الدينية، وإنما يتعلق بذلك غرض الأطباء.

وهذا القلب موجود للبهائم، بل هو موجود للميت.

ونحن إذا أطلقنا لفظ القلب في هذا الكتاب.. لم نعن به ذلك؛ فإنه قطعة لحم لا قدر له، وهو من عالم المُلك والشهادة؛ إذ تدركه البهائم بحاسة البصر فضلاً عن الآدميين.

والمعنى الثاني: هو لطيفة ربانية روحانية، لها بهذا القلب الجسماني تعلق، وتلك اللطيفة هي حقيقة الإنسان، وهو المدرك العالم العارف من الإنسان، وهو المخاطب والمعاقب، والمعاتب والمطالب، ولها علاقة مع القلب الجسماني، وقد تحيرت عقول أكثر الخلق في إدراك وجه علاقته؛ فإن تعلقه به يضاهي تعلق الأعراض بالأجسام، والأوصاف بالموصوفات، أو تعلق المستعمل للآلة بالآلة، أو تعلق المتمكِّن بالمكان.

وشرح ذلك مما نتوقاه لمعنيين:

أحدهما: أنه متعلق بعلوم المكاشفة، وليس غرضنا من هذا الكتاب إلا علوم المعاملة.

والثاني: أن تحقيقه يستدعي إفشاء سر الروح، وذلك مما لم يتكلم فيه رسول الله صلى الله عليه وسلم؛ فليس لغيره أن يتكلم فيه.

والمقصود: أنا إذا أطلقنا لفظ القلب في هذا الكتاب.. أردنا به هذه اللطيفة، وغرضنا: ذكر أوصافها وأحوالها، لا ذكر حقيقتها في ذاتها، وعلم المعاملة يفتقر إلى معرفة صفاتها وأحوالها، ولا يفتقر إلى ذكر حقيقتها.

اللفظ الثاني: الروح.

وهو أيضاً يطلق فيما يتعلق بجنس غرضنا لمعنيين:

أحدهما: جسم لطيف، منبعه تجويف القلب الجسماني، وينتشر بواسطة العروق الضوارب إلى سائر أجزاء البدن، وجريانه في البدن وفيضان أنوار الحياة والحس والبصر والسمع والشم منه على أعضائه.. يضاهي فيضان النور من السراج الذي يدار في زوايا البيت؛ فإنه لا ينتهي إلى جزء من البيت إلا ويستنير به.

فالحياة مثالها النور الحاصل في الحيطان، والروح مثاله السراج، وسريان الروح وحركته في الباطن مثاله حركة السراج في جوانب البيت بتحريك محركه.

والأطباء إذا أطلقوا لفظ الروح أرادوا به هذا المعنى، وهو بخار لطيف أنضجته حرارة القلب، وليس شرحه من غرضنا؛ إذ المتعلق به غرض الأطباء الذين يعالجون الأبدان، فأما غرض أطباء الدين المعالجين للقلب حتى ينساق إلى جوار رب العالمين.. فليس يتعلق بشرح هذه الروح أصلاً.

المعنى الثاني: هو اللطيفة العالمة المدركة من الإنسان، وهو الذي شرحناه في أحد معنيي القلب، وهو الذي أراده الله تعالى بقوله: (قل الروح من أمر ربي)، وهو أمر عجيب رباني، تعجز أكثر العقول والأفهام عن درك كنه حقيقته.

اللفظ الثالث: النفس.

وهو أيضا مشترك بين معان، ويتعلق بغرضنا منه معنيان:

أحدهما: أنه يراد به المعنى الجامع لقوة الغضب والشهوة في الإنسان، على ما سيأتي شرحه، وهذا الاستعمال هو الغالب على أهل التصوف؛ لأنهم يريدون بالنفس الأصلَ الجامعَ للصفات المذمومة من الإنسان، فيقولون: (لا بد من مجاهدة النفس وكسرها)، وإليه الإشارة بقوله عليه الصلاة والسلام: "أعدى عدوٍّ لك نفسك التي بين جنبيك" (1).

المعنى الثاني: هو اللطيفة التي ذكرناها، التي هي الإنسان بالحقيقة، وهي نفس الإنسان وذاته، ولكنها توصف بأوصاف مختلفة بحسب اختلاف أحوالها، فإذا سكنت تحت الأمر، وزايلها الاضطراب بسبب معارضة الشهوات.. سميت النفس المطمئنة، قال الله تعالى في مثلها (يا أيتها النفس المطمئنة * ارجعي إلى ربك راضية مرضية)، والنفس بالمعنى الأول لا يتصور رجوعها إلى الله تعالى؛ فإنها مبعدةٌ عن الله، وهي من حزب الشيطان.

وإذا لم يتم سكونها، ولكنها صارت مدافعة للنفس الشهوانية ومعترضة عليها.. سميت النفس اللوامة؛ لأنها تلوم صاحبها عند تقصيره في عبادة مولاه، قال الله تعالى: (ولا أقسم بالنفس اللوامة).

وإن تركت الاعتراض، وأذعنت وأطاعت لمقتضى الشهوات ودواعي الشيطان.. سميت النفس الأمارة بالسوء، قال الله تعالى إخباراً عن يوسف عليه السلام أو امرأة العزيز: (وما أبرئ نفسي إن النفس لأمارة بالسوء)، وقد يجوز أن يقال: المراد بالأمارة بالسوء: هي النفس بالمعنى الأول.

فإذًا؛ النفس بالمعنى الأول مذمومة غاية الذم، وبالمعنى الثاني: محمودة؛ لأنها نفس الإنسان؛ أي: ذاته وحقيقته العالمة بالله تعالى وسائر المعلومات.

اللفظ الرابع: العقل.

وهو أيضاً مشترك لمعان مختلفة ذكرناها في كتاب العلم، والمتعلق بغرضنا من جملتها معنيان:

أحدهما: أنه قد يطلق ويراد به العلم بحقائق الأمور، فيكون عبارة عن صفة العلم الذي محله القلب.

والثاني: أنه قد يطلق ويراد به المدرك للعلوم، فيكون هو القلب؛ أعني تلك اللطيفة.

ونحن نعلم أن كل عالم فله في نفسه وجود هو أصل قائم بنفسه، والعلم صفة حالة فيه، والصفة غير الموصوف، والعقل قد يطلق ويراد به صفة العالم، وقد يطلق ويراد به محل الإدراك؛ أعني المدرِك، وهو المراد بقوله صلى الله عليه وسلم: "أول ما خلق الله العقل" (1) ؛ فإن العلم عرض لا يتصور أن يكون أول مخلوق، بل لابد وأن يكون المحل مخلوقاً قبله أو معه، ولأنه لا يمكن الخطاب معه، وفي الخبر: "أنه قال له تعالى: أقبل.. فأقبلَ، ثم قال له: أدبر.. فأدبرَ..." الحديث (2).

فإذًا؛ قد انكشف لك أن معاني هذه الأسامي موجودة، وهي القلب الجسماني، والروح الجسماني، والنفس الشهوانية، والعلوم.

فهذه أربعة معانٍ يطلق عليها الألفاظ الأربعة، ومعنى خامس؛ وهي اللطيفة العالمة المدرِكة من الإنسان، والألفاظ الأربعة بجملتها تتوارد عليها، فالمعاني خمسة، والألفاظ أربعة، وكل لفظ أطلق لمعنيين، وأكثر العلماء قد التبس عليهم اختلاف هذه الألفاظ وتواردها، فتراهم يتكلمون في الخواطر، ويقولون: هذا خاطر العقل، وهذا خاطر الروح، وهذا خاطر القلب، وهذا خاطر النفس، وليس يدري الناظر اختلاف معاني هذه الأسماء، فلأجل كشف الغطاء عن ذلك.. قدمنا شرح هذه الأسامي.

وحيث ورد في القرآن والسنة لفظ القلب فالمراد به المعنى الذي يفقهُ من الإنسان ويعرف حقيقة الأشياء، وقد يكنى عنه بالقلب الذي في الصدر؛ لأن بين تلك اللطيفة وبين جسم القلب علاقة خاصة؛ فإنها وإن كانت متعلقة بسائر البدن ومستعملة له، ولكنها تتعلق به بواسطة القلب، فتعلقها الأول بالقلب، وكأنه محلها ومملكتها، وعالمها ومطيتها.

ولذلك شبه سهل التستري القلب بالعرش، والصدر بالكرسي، فقال: (القلب هو العرش، والصدر هو الكرسي)، ولا تظنُّ به أنه يرى أنه عرش الله وكرسيه؛ فإن ذلك محال، بل أراد به أنه مملكته، والمجرى الأول لتدبيره وتصرفه، فهما بالنسبة إليه كالعرش والكرسي بالنسبة إلى الله تعالى، ولا يستقيم هذا التشبيه أيضاً إلا من بعض الوجوه، وشرح ذلك أيضاً لا يليق بغرضنا فلنتجاوزه.

1.4 *English Translation*

An Exposition on the Meanings and Connotations of the Terms: *Nafs*, *Rūḥ*, *ʿAql*, *Qalb*

Know that these four terms will be used in these chapters.[1] Few amongst even the elite scholars are those who have comprehensive knowledge of these terms, the nuances of their meanings, definitions, and denominations (i.e., the entities that are signified by them). Most misunderstandings arise out of

1 I.e., in the section on the 'Marvels of the Heart' of the *"Revival of the Religious Sciences"*.

ignorance of the meanings of these terms and their shared usages for different entities. [Here] we will [only] explain those meanings of these terms that are most relevant to our aims.

The First Term: The Word *Qalb* (Heart)

It is used for two meanings:

1) The first of them is: The piece of flesh whose shape [is like] the pinecone, situated in the left side of the chest. It is a special kind of flesh, with a cavity inside of it, and in that cavity is dark blood. It is the place of the origin (*manbaʿ*) and source (*maʿdin*) of the spirit (*rūḥ*) [of life]. At this moment, we do not intend to clarify its shape nor its mode [of functioning], since it is not relevant to religious objectives (*aghrāḍ dīniyya*), and relevant only to the objectives of the physicians.[2]

This [type of] heart is found in [all] animals; rather it is present [even] in the dead [carcass]. When we unrestrictedly mention the word *qalb* in this book, we do not intend that heart (i.e., physical heart) by it, for it is a piece of flesh with no [intrinsic] value. It [belongs to] the physical (*mulk*) and observable (*shāhada*) realm, since even animals, let alone human beings, can ocularly perceive it.

2) The second meaning [of the qalb] is: a metaphysical, divine, spiritual substance (*laṭīfa rabbāniyya rūḥāniyya*)[3] that has a connection to

2 The classical Muslim physicians who were also philosophers tended to discuss the nature of the spirit of life, as they viewed it as within the scope of their professions. Additionally, it is important to note that the physicians of that time were not pure empiricists as the science of medicine included a lot of inferences and assumptions that were not or could not be empirically validated. The physicians largely drew their foundations of medicine from Galen's humoral medicine. It is also important to note that the physicians in general were also trained in theology and discussed metaphysics in their philosophical works and alluded to some of these discussions in their works on medicine.

3 This contrasts with the first meaning of heart. This heart that he is referring to is from the metaphysical realm. Al-Ghazālī asserts that the physical heart and the first meaning of *rūh* he describes are both physical substances, though the *rūḥ* is a very gas-like subtle substance. While the rūḥ of the first meaning cannot be observed, it is part of the physical realm of existence. Whereas the second meaning of heart and all the other second meanings of the remaining terms that are discussed below are from the metaphysical realm, also referred to as the *malakūtī* world or being from the *ʿālam al-ʾamr* or divine world. According to al-Ghazālī this is a completely non-physical created thing or *jawhar mujarrad*, which is a common term used to refer to this notion in contrast to the subtly physical substance or *jism latīf.*

It is also important to note that al-Ghazālī demonstrates in the subsequent explanations that the second meaning of all the four terms are indicators of the same essence. This may be this physical heart. This metaphysical substance is the essence of man. It is the part of man that perceives, knows, and experiences gnosis, and it is that which is addressed, punished, reprimanded, and commanded (by Allah). It has a relationship with the physical heart. In attempting to understand the nature of this relationship, the minds of most of creation are perplexed, for the relationship between the two is akin to the relationship between incidents (*aʿrāḍ*) and physical objects (*ajsām*),[4] or the relationship between an attribute and the attributed, or the relationship of the user of an instrument and the instrument itself or the relationship between the occupant of a space and the space itself.

There are two reasons for our refraining from further explanation [of the metaphysical reality of this *qalb*]:

i. Firstly, because it is connected to the knowledge of mystical gnosis (*mukāshafa*) and our aim in this book is only the knowledge of social conduct (*muʿāmala*).
ii. Secondly, its investigation leads to divulging the mysteries of the soul, and that is something that the Messenger of Allah, may Allah bless him and grant him peace, did not discuss and thus is not appropriate for anyone else to discuss.

The point is that when we unrestrictedly use the term *qalb* in this book, we mean by it this metaphysical substance (*laṭīfa*). Our objective is the discussion of its attributes and states, not the discussion of its inner reality in and of itself. Moreover, the science of social conduct requires recognition of its attributes and varying states but does not require the discussion of its [inner] reality.

---

referred to as *laṭīfa rabbaniya* as he and other scholars have referred to it (see al-Bāyjūrī section). They are one unitary metaphysical essence with different expressions and contextual usages as al-Ghazālī demonstrates.

4 This is a technical concept discussed by both scholastic theologians and philosophers. A physical substance is in reference to the essential properties that make up a physical object, while incidents are those things that cannot exist independently of the physical substance. These incidents are states that are associated with their physical objects. For example, a state of movement is not an essential quality of a moving object and thus known as an 'incident'. However, physical substances too are not free from associated incidents since an object is always either in a state of rest or movement and either state is a non-essential incidental quality, subject to potential change that is affixed to the physical object (Saʿd al-Dīn Masʿūd ibn ʿUmar al-Taftāzanī, *Sharḥ al-ʿAqāʾid al-Nasafiyya* (Karachi: Maktabat al-Bushrā, 2000).

The Second Term: The *Rūh* (Soul)

Regarding the genus of our objective, this too applies to two meanings.

1) The first of the two: is the imperceptible subtle physical substance.[5] Its place of origin (*manbaʿ*) is the cavity of the physical heart, and it circulates through the medium of the veins to the rest of the parts of the body. Its flow in the body and the stream of the light of life, sensation, sight, hearing, and smell from it to the physical organs resembles the stream of light from a lantern which is taken around to the corners of a house, for it is not taken to any portion of a house except that it is enlightened by it.

So, [biological] life is like the light present within the walls, and the soul is like the lantern, and the circulation of the soul and its internal movement is akin to the movement of the lantern in the corners of the house by the mobilization of the one who moves it.

When physicians use the term "soul" unrestrictedly, this is what they intend. It is an imperceptible vapor warmed by the heart's heat. Explaining it is not our aim [here], since it is related to the aims of the physicians who treat physical bodies. As for the purposes of physicians of religion who treat [the illnesses of] the heart so that it can be drawn towards the proximity of the Lord of the cosmos, the explanation of [this intended usage of] this *rūḥ* is not at all relevant.

2) The second meaning [of the term *rūḥ*]:[6] is the knowing, perceiving, subtle faculty of man, which is what we explained as one of the meanings of the term *qalb* (i.e., the second meaning), and it is what Allah intends in His statement, *And they ask you regarding the soul. Say: the soul is one of the affairs of my Lord* (Sūrat al-Isrāʾ 17:85). It is a wonderous, divine matter that most minds and powers of comprehension are incapable of perceiving the essence of the reality of.

The Third Term: The *Nafs*

It is also a polysemic sharing several meanings, two of which are most relevant to our aims.

---

5 See above footnote.

6 This is the primordial soul i.e., *latīfa*. All human beings were once souls that stood in the court of Allah and primordially bore witness to the Oneness and existence of Allah in the covenant of Alast, where Allah asked, "Am I not your Lord" and all responded, "Indeed, we bear witness to this" (7:171). Thus, each soul has an inherent longing to return to that state of being in the presence of Allah.

1) The first of them is: a signification encompassing the appetitive (*shahwa*) and aggressive (*ghaḍab*) human drives, which will be explained. This usage is most common among the Sufis because they mean by the *nafs* the root that combines all the reprehensible qualities in human beings. Hence, they state: "It is necessary to strive against the *nafs* and break it," and there is an indication to this [usage] in the Prophetic statement: "Your greatest enemy is your *nafs* (ego) that is always with you[7]".

2) The second meaning is the aforementioned metaphysical spiritual entity [under the second meaning of *qalb* and *rūḥ*] that is the human being in reality. It is man's self and essence, but it is characterized by different attributes depending on its varying states.[8] Thus, if it becomes subjugated under the command [of reason] and the [intrapsychic] tension is removed due to resisting the appetitive drives, it is known as al-*nafs al-muṭmainna* (the tranquil self). Allah the Exalted states concerning its like: "*Oh you tranquil soul, return to your Lord, well-pleased and well-pleasing Him*" (Sūrat al-Fajr 89:27). The first meaning of the *nafs* (the ego) cannot be conceived to be returned to Allah, the Exalted (in this way), for it makes [one] distant from Allah and is from the party of the devil.

If [the *nafs*] has not yet been fully pacified but it [nevertheless] attempts to repel and obstruct the appetitive [and predatory] drives, it is referred to as *al-nafs al-lawāmma* (the blaming self), because it blames

7 Literally: "the *nafs* that is between your two sides", however the intended meaning is mentioned above given that translating it literally loses the connotations carried by the statement in the Arabic language.

This is narrated by Kharā'itī in "I'tilāl al Qulūb" (see Abū Bakr Muḥammad ibn Ja'far Kharā'iṭī, *I'tilāl al-Qulūb Fī Akhbār al-'ushshāq Wa al-Muḥibbīn*, vol. 1 (Makkah: Maktabat Bilāl Muṣṭafā al-Bāz, 2000), 26.) related by Abū Mālik al-Ash'arī from the Prophet (may Allah bless him and grant him peace). As well as by Bayḥaqī in "*Zuhd*" as a statement of ibn 'Abbas (May Allah be pleased with him). (see Abū Bakr Aḥmad ibn 'Alī al-Bayhaqī, *al-Zuhd al-Kabīr* (Beirut: Dār al-Jinān Mu'assasa al-Kutub al-Thaqāfiyya, 1987), 343.). Ḥafiz Zabīdī in his commentary on this book (*Iḥya*), entitled "*itḥāf*" criticizes the narration of Bayḥaqī in citing ibn Ḥajar. He states that ibn Ḥajar stated that there are pathways/chains for this narration other than ibn 'Abbas that is related as a statement of Anas ibn Mālik and statements of others as well for this narration (see al-Sharīf Muḥammad al-Zabīdī, *Itḥāf al-Sāda al-Muttaqīn bi-Sharḥ Iḥyā' 'Ulūm al-Dīn* (Lebanon: Dār Iḥyā' al-Turāth al- 'Arabī, 1994), 206–7.).

8 This in essence refers to the 'self' and is an indication toward the aforementioned *laṭīfa*. However, the self or one's *laṭīfa* can be at different stages based upon spiritual cleansing and purity. By graduating beyond living a completely sensual life one can eliminate the tension found within the self between the animalistic drives vs spiritual longing for connection to reach an eventual state of tranquility or reach the stage of *al-nafs al-muṭma'inna*.

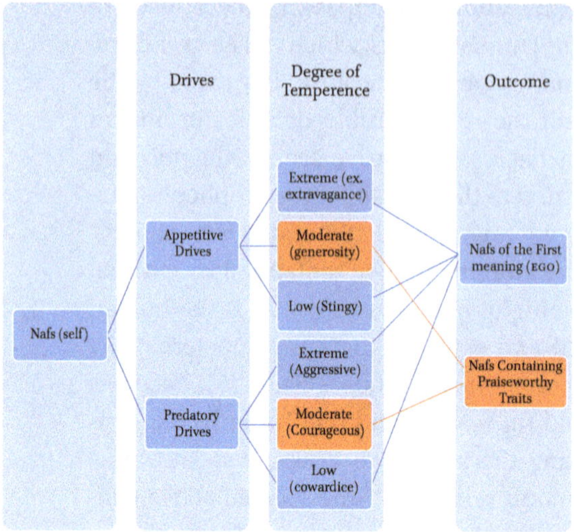

FIGURE 2 Characterizing the two meanings of *nafs*

Note: As can be seen by this diagram, the *nafs* is not evil in and of itself. Rather the appetitive drives serve as the rider and motivator of the behaviors of the human being. Similarly, aggressive drives are useful for survival and self-preservation. The ability to moderate these drives leads to the outcome of a praiseworthy *nafs* and being on either polar extreme i.e., excessive or deficiency leads to the *nafs* of the first meaning, i.e., the ego. Thus, the *nafs* evolves and can flourish based upon discipline and training. Al-Ghazālī goes into the 'how' of training this *nafs* later in this work. However, it noteworthy that this conception of self, is unlike the conception of famous psychologists, Sigmund Freud who say the human being is born essentially evil with thanos (destructive and aggressive instincts) and eros (appetitive or life producing instincts) solely needing to be tamed for socialization but not to be overly restricted for fear of repression (Sigmund Freud, "Civilization and Its Discontents," in *Princeton University Press eBooks*, 2018, 523–29). On the other hand, Carl Rogers (Jane Morgan, "On Becoming a Person (1961) Carl Rogers' Celebrated Classic in Memoriam," *Journal of Psychological Issues in Organizational Culture* 2, no. 3 (October 1, 2011): 95–105.) and other post-modernists saw the human being as inherently predisposed to good and needing to be shown 'unconditional positive regard' to flourish. Evolutionary psychologists on the other hand view the human being as a more sophisticated animal or social animal that contains these base drives for survival i.e., survival of the fittest (David M. Buss, *Evolutionary Psychology: The New Science of the Mind* (Psychology Press, 2015). Positivists and Behaviorists on the other hand say that human beings are completely blank slate (tabula rasa) and can be shaped based on reward and punishment accordingly (Burrhus Frederic Skinner, *Beyond Freedom and Dignity* (Hackett Publishing Company Incorporated, 2002).). The Islamic perspective al-Ghazālī is presenting is one that demonstrates both an inherent good disposition to know God and universal truth through the *laṭīfa rabbāniya* while also having bodily drives that have survival functions which are not reprehensible in and of themselves. Rather its over or underactivity is what leads to pathology or poor character. Thus, consistent watchful training to maintain moderation of these aggressive and appetitive drives is necessary as they have the propensity to become imbalanced if not monitored and refined, as in the analogy of the wild horse or predatory dog that Ghazali uses. By training it through the usage of the intellectual faculty that can differentiate good from bad, healthy from harmful, the human being can render both two primitive drives as their aids, in their journey and inherent need to be spiritually satiated by the Divine.

the self when it is deficient in obeying its Lord. Allah the Exalted states: "*And I swear by the blaming self*" (Sūrat al-Qiyāma 75:2).

If the soul abandons obstruction [of the appetitive and aggressive drives] and accepts and obeys the demands of the base desires and invitations of the devil, it is known as al-*nafs al-ammāra bi-l-sū'* (the soul that commands to evil). Allah the Exalted says, informing about Yūsuf, upon him be peace, or the wife of the governor [of Egypt]: "*I do not absolve myself for indeed the soul commands to evil*" (Sūrat Yūsuf 12:53). It is possible to say that what is meant by the soul commanding to evil is the *nafs* of the first meaning (i.e., the ego). If so, the *nafs* of the first meaning is completely reprehensible, whereas with the second meaning it is praiseworthy because it is [but] the human being's self, meaning: his essence and his reality that knows Allah the Exalted and all other knowable things.

The Fourth Term: The *ʿAql* (Intellect)

It too is polysemic, comprising multiple different meanings that we mentioned in the *Book of Knowledge*. Two meanings in particular are relevant to our aims.

1) The first of them is: [when] it is mentioned and what is meant by it is the knowledge of the reality of things, then [in such a case] it is an expression of the attribute of knowledge whose original locus is the *qalb* (or metaphysical heart).[9]

2) The second [meaning] is: [when] it is unrestrictedly mentioned, and what is meant by it is the faculty of conceiving knowledge. [In such a case] it is the heart, meaning that metaphysical essence (*laṭīfa*).

We know that every person of knowledge has within himself an entity (*wujūd*) that is foundational and exists independently [of other things]. [We also know that] knowledge is an attribute that exists within [the knower], and the attribute is different from the attributed. The *ʿaql* is sometimes unrestrictedly mentioned to indicate the attribute of the knower, and sometimes it is unrestrictedly mentioned to indicate the place of conception, meaning the conceiver. This [second meaning] is what is intended in the statement of the Prophet, may Allah bless him and grant him peace: "The first thing that Allah created was the *ʿaql*",[10] for knowledge is an incident (*ʿaraḍ*) that cannot be conceived as the first

9 Though al-Ghazālī seems to favor the second meaning, he mentions the usage of this term as it is a common usage of many great scholars such as his very own teacher Imam al Ḥaramayn al Juwaynī (see al-Bayjūrī section).

10 See Abū al-Qāsim Sulaymān ibn Aḥmad Ṭabarānī, *Al-Muʿjam al-Kabīr* (Cairo: Maktabat Ibn Taymiyya, 1994), 273–78.); Abū Bakr Aḥmad ibn ʿAlī al-Bayhaqī, *Kitāb Shuʿab al-Īmān*

> creation; rather, the locus (*maḥall*) must be created before it or along with it. [Moreover,] it is not conceivable that the Divine address (*khiṭāb*) be directed to the [*ʿaql* alone], while [it is mentioned] in a [portion of the previous prophetic] report: "He the Exalted said to it: 'Come', so it came. Then He said to it: 'Depart', so it departed".[11]

Thus, it has become evident to you that the meanings of these terms exist, and they are: the physical heart, the material *rūḥ or* soul, the animalistic *nafs*, and knowledge.

So, these are four meanings for which the four [aforementioned] terms are used for. [However,] there is a fifth meaning, and it is man's knowing and perceiving metaphysical faculty in the human being, and all these four terms in their totality refer to it. Thus, there are five meanings and four terms, and every term is used for two meanings. Most scholars have been confused by the variance of these terms and how they are used. So, you see them discussing *khawāṭir* (thoughts) saying things like: "This is the thought of the *ʿaql* ..." or "This is the thought of the *rūḥ* ..." or "this is the thought of the *qalb* ..." or "this is the thought of the *nafs* ...", while the examiner does not know the variance of the meanings of these terms. Therefore, to remove the confusion, we have begun with the explanation of these terms.

When the word *qalb* is used in the Qur'an and Sunna, its connotation is the entity within man that comprehends and recognizes the reality of things, and sometimes "the heart that is in the chest" is used as an allusion for it, because there is a special relationship between the physical body of the heart and the metaphysical essence (*laṭīfa*). Even though [the metaphysical heart] is linked with the rest of the body and employs it, its connection is through the intermediation of the [physical] heart. So, its primary connection is to the [physical] heart as though it is its place and dominion.

(Beirut: Maktaba Dār al-Rushd, 2003) hn. 4312.) Abū Nuʿaym al-Isfahānī, *Ḥilyat al-Awliyā' wa Tabaqāt al-Aṣfiyā'* (Cairo: Dār al-Ḥadīth, 2009), 317–18.).

11 This is a portion of the same hadith above. This is a weak *hadith* with many versions, Zabīdī, who offers a commentary on "The Revival of the Religious Sciences" discusses this hadith. (Al-Zabīdī, *Itḥāf al-Sāda al-Muttaqīn bi-Sharḥ Iḥyā' ʿUlūm al-Dīn*, 1:453.). Zabīdī also provides a more complete version of the hadith: "When Allah created the intellect He said to it, 'Come close,' and it drew near. Then He said, 'Depart,' and it left. Then He said, 'I have created nothing that I love more than you; by you I take and by you I give'."

Al-Ghazālī in his explanation is attempting to demonstrate that knowledge cannot have an independent existence of its own when the first term is intended, rather the first term must be understood considering the second term, i.e., that knowledge is an attribute of the intellect of an individual. Whereas intellect can have an independent existence that is situated within an individual, knowledge cannot and thus it needs to be an attribute or affixed to an intellect.

For this reason, Sahl al-Tustarī[12] likened the [physical] heart to the Throne (*ʿarsh*) and the chest to the Chair (*kursī*). He said, "the heart is the Throne, and the chest is the Chair".[13] It must not be assumed that he considered it Allah's Throne and His chair, for this is impossible. Rather, what he meant is the heart is its dominion and primary means for its [metaphysical heart's] activity and administration. Its [the physical heart and chest] relation to it [the metaphysical heart] is like the relation of the Throne and Chair to Allah the Exalted.[14] This metaphor is also not suitable except in some respects. However, the discussion of it is not appropriate for our aims here, so we shall pass over it.

2 The Nature of the ʿAql and Its Types. *Tuḥfat al-Murīd ʿalā Jawahart al-Tawḥid* by Ibrāhīm ibn Muḥammad al-Bājūrī (d. 1276/1860)

2.1 *Author's Biography*

Ibrāhīm ibn Muḥammad ibn Aḥmad al-Bayjurī was a Shāfī scholar, author, and teacher who was appointed as the Shaykh of al-Azhar University from 1847 CE until he passed away in 1860 CE. al-Bayjuri was born in 1784 CE in the village of Bājur which is situated in the Manufiyya province in Egypt. He began studying the traditional Islamic sciences at the age of 14 after enrolling in Al-Azhar University. Prior to that, his father taught the Holy Quran and the art of its recitation (*tajwīd*). He authored over twenty works and commentaries in sacred law, tenets of faith, Islamic estate division, scholastic theology, logic, and Arabic. He was an Ashʿarī theologian, a logician based on the methods of Fakhr al-Dīn al-Razi, and a Sufī belonging to the Naqshbandī order. Al-Bayjurī followed the scholarly tradition of giving importance to the three core sciences of law, theology, and mysticism.

2.2 *Text Overview and Significance*

Imam al-Bayjuri's *Tuḥfat al-Murīd ʿalā Jawahart al-Tawḥīd* is a commentary of *Jawharat al Tawhid*, a poem detailing the Sunni Ashʿarī creed which was originally compiled by Imam Ibrāhīm al-Laqānī. It is a work in sciences of

12 Salh al-Tustarī (or al-Tusturī) (286 AH/896 CE) was a Persian Islamic scholar and mystic. He founded the Sālimiya school of Muslim theologians named after his disciple Muḥammad ibn Sālim. He also authored a famous interpretation (tafsir) of the Quran named Tafsir al-Tustārī. He believed that mystical union (*ittiḥād*) with Allah, could be achieved through contemplation on oneself until complete consciousness was achieved.

13 See Abū Ṭālib al-Makkī, *Qūt al-Qulūb fī Muʿāmalat al-Maḥbūb*, vol. 1 (Beirut: Dār al-Kutub al- ʿIlmiyya, 2005), 885.

14 This does not mean Allah is on the Chair/Throne, rather it is the subject where Allah enacts.

discursive theology (*kalam*). Amongst the many commentaries of the aforementioned poem, Imam Bayjurī's is one of the most relied upon and accepted works among scholastic theologians.

Regarding its psychological relevance, Imam Bayjurī's commentary upon line 95 of al-Laqānī's original work has been selected due to his presentation of the nature of the intellect (ʿaql) and the various opinions related to it from Islamic scholars. He divides the *ʿaql* (*intellect*) into five types: (1) innate intelligence which is required to attain knowledge; (2) Acquired intelligence, which is acquired through interacting with intelligent people; (3) Divinely-endowed intelligence, which is the type of intelligence that Allah grants to the believers to be guided to faith; (4) the intelligence of the ascetics, through which indifference to the world is achieved; (5) Ennobled intelligence, which is in reference to the intelligence of the Prophet (May Allah bless him and grant him peace). Imam Bayjurī opines that the ʿaql is primarily responsible for cognitive processes and it can be subsumed under the broader metaphysical entity of man (*latifa rabbaniyya*) or metaphysical heart (*qalb*). Thereby establishing it separate from the brain, yet still related to it. This seems to be the position that he favors, while he mentions the position of other Islamic scholars who consider the intellect to be located within and part of the brain.

2.3 *Arabic Text*

والعقل كالروح ولكن قرروا فيه خلافا فانظرن ما فسروا

قوله: (والعقل كالروح) مبتدأ وخبر، أي: والعقل مثل الروح من حيث الخوض في بيان الحقيقة والوقف عن ذلك. واختلف كلام المصنف في الترجيح: فرجح في "هداية المريد" طريق الخوض، ورجح في "الكبير" طريق الوقف، وهو المختار؛ لأنه من المغيبات، وكل ما هو كذلك فالأولى الكف عن الخوض فيه. وهو لغة: المنع، من عقل البعير إذا منعه بالعقال، وسمي بذلك لمنعه صاحبه من العدول عن سواء السبيل.

العقل: أنواعه

واعلم أن العقل على خمسة أنواع:

الأول: غريزي، وهو غريزة يتهيأ بها لدرك العلوم النظرية كما قاله شيخ الإسلام.

والثاني: كسبي، وهو ما يكتسبه الإنسان من معاشرة العقلاء.

والثالث: عطائي، وهو ما يعطيه الله للمؤمنين ليهتدوا به إلى الإيمان.

والرابع: عقل الزهاد، وهو الذي يكون به الزهد.

والخامس: شرفي، وهو عقل نبينا ﷺ؛ لأنه أشرف العقول.

وقد اختلف في تفضيل العقل على العلم أو العكس، والراجح تفضيل العلم على العقل؛ لأن العلم من صفاته تعالى، وما يروى في فضل العقل فهو موضوع لا أصل له كما صرح به الجلال السيوطي.

قوله: (ولكن قرروا فيه خلافا) أي لكن قرر العلماء في العقل خلافا، ولا محل لهذا الاستدراك؛ لأنهم قرروا في الروح خلافا أيضا، فلعل "لكن" لمجرد التأكيد، ثم رأيت المصنف في شرحه قال: "ولكن ... إلخ" استدراك على طريقة الخائضين، فأشار إلى أنهم لم يتفقوا على حقيقة معينة، بل اختلفوا في بيانها. اهـ. فالاستدراك يشعر بانتشار الخلاف وكثرته.

العقل: تعريفه

وقول: (فانظرن ما فسروا) أي فانظر التفاسير التي ذكرها القوم في كتبهم لا في هذه المقدمة؛ لصغر حجمها. وأقوال أهل السنة متطابقة على عرضيته، فبعضهم قال: إنه من قبيل العلوم، وعرفه بأنه: العلم ببعض العلوم الضرورية، كالعلم بوجوب تحيز الجرم واستحالة عروه عن الحركة والسكون، وجواز إحراق النار وغير ذلك، وهذا القول لإمام الحرمين وجماعة، وبعضهم قال: إنه ليس قبيل العلوم، وعرفه بأنه: غريزة، أي طبيعة مغروزة، يتبعها العلم بالضروريات عند سلامة الآلات.

وعرفه الشيرازي بأنه: صفة يميز بها بين الحسن والقبيح.

وأحسن ما قيل فيه أنه: نور روحاني به تدرك النفس العلوم الضرورية والنظرية.

وقال بعضهم: إن هناك لطيفة ربانية لا يعلمها إلا اللّٰه تعالى، فمن حيث تفكرها تسمى عقلا، ومن حيث حياة الجسد بها تسمى روحا، ومن حيث شهوتها تسمي نفسا، فالثلاثة متحدة بالذات مختلفة بالاعتبار.

وقالت المعتزلة والخوارج والحكماء بجوهريته، وفسره بعضهم بأنه جوهر يدرك به الغائبات بالوسائط، والمحسوسات بالمشاهدة. ومنهم من فسره بغير ذلك. وفي كلام الغزالي أنه جوهر مجرد.

العقل: محله

واختلف في محله، والصحيح أنه محله القلب وله نور متصل بالدماغ كما ذهب إليه الإمام الشافعي والإمام مالك (رضي اللّٰه عنهما) وجمهور المتكلمين.

وقالت الحكماء وبعض الفقهاء بأن محله الدماغ لفساده بفساد الدماغ. وهذا لا يدل على ما ذكروه؛ لجواز أن تكون سلامة الدماغ شرطا لاستمراره وإن كان محله القلب.

2.4 *English Translation*

[From Imam al-Laqqānī's (d. 1041/1632) poem on Islamic theology, *Jawharat al-Tawḥīd* (the Jewel of Monotheism):]

"The intellect (ʿaql) is like the soul (rūḥ), although [scholars] maintained * a contention in this regard, so investigate what they explained."

Imam al-Bājūrī's gloss on this line of al-Laqqānī's poem in *Tuḥfat al-Murīd*:

In his (i.e., Imam al-Laqqānī) statement, "The intellect (*ʿaql*) is like the soul", [grammatically,] 'intellect' is the subject and 'soul' is the predicate [in this nominal sentence construction], meaning that the intellect is like the soul from the perspective of [the ruling pertaining to] delving deeply into the exposition of its reality or abstaining from [such an endeavor]. The statements of the author (al-Laqqānī) are inconclusive regarding which he preferred [i.e., permission or abstention from exploring its reality]. In *Hidāyat al-Murīd* (Guidance for the Seeker)[15] he prefers the course of exploration, while in [*al-Sharḥ*] *al-Kabīr*[16] he prefers the course of abstention, and [the latter] is the favored position [by the scholars] because it is from the issues of the unseen (*al-maghībāt*), and it is best to abstain from delving into all such matters.

Linguistically, it (the *ʿaql*) [denotes] restraint (*manʿ*), as in: "he restrained the camel (*ʿaqala al-baʿīr*)" when one restrains it using a rope (*ʿiqāl*).[17] The *ʿaql* is named so because it restrains its owner from straying from the straight path.

The Intellect (*ʿAql*) and its Types

Know that the intellect is of five types:[18]

1. Innate (*gharīzī*) (c.f. fluid intelligence): which is innate intelligence by which it is possible to attain investigative knowledge (*ʿulūm naẓariyya*), as Shaykh al-Islām[19] stated.
2. Acquired (*kasbī*) (c.f. crystallized intelligence): which is what humans acquire through interactions with people of intelligence.

15 This is one of three commentaries Imam Ibrāhīm al-Laqqānī wrote on his own poem: *Jawharat al-Tawḥīd*. The commentary referred to here, the *Hidāyat al-Murīd*, is the shortest of the three commentaries (Ibrāhīm al-Laqqānī, *Hidāyat al-Murīd lī-Jawhar al-Tawḥīd* (Beirut: Dār al-Kutub al-ʿIlmiyya, 2012).).

16 This is in reference to the larger commentary that the author, Ibrāhīm al-Laqqānī, composed on his original work (*Jawharat al-Tawḥīd*), entitled *ʿUmdat al-Murīd li-Jawharat al-Tawḥīd* (the Reliance of the Seeker for the Jewel of Monotheism), also commonly referred to as *al-Sharḥ al-Kabīr*, or the Large Commentary (Ibrāhīm al-Laqqānī, *ʿUmdat al-Murīd li-Jawharat al-Tawḥīd* (Beirut: Dār al-Nūr, 2016).).

17 An *ʿiqāl* is a rope with which a camel's fore shank is bound to his arm, both being folded together and bound in the middle of the arm. See Lane's Lexicon, sub *ʿa-q-l*.

18 This may be considered an alternative to Gardner's multiple intelligence theory (Howard Gardner, *Frames of mind: The theory of multiple intelligences* (New York: Basic Books, 1983) or Sternberg's Intelligence Triarchy (Robert J. Sternberg, *Beyond IQ: A Triarchic Theory of Intelligence* (Cambridge University Press, 1985).).

19 By Shaykh al-Islām, the author likely intended Zakariyyā al-Anṣārī (d. 926/1520).

3. Divinely endowed (*ʿāṭāʾī*) (c.f. spiritual intelligence): which is what Allah gives to believers so that they are guided by it to faith.
4. The intellect of the ascetics (*ʿaql al-zuhhād*) (c.f. inspired intelligence): which is (the intelligence) by which asceticism (*zuhd*) is achieved.[20]
5. Ennobled (*sharafī*) intellect: which is the intellect of our Prophet (may Allah bless him and grant him peace), because he possessed the most ennobled intelligence.

There are differences of opinion regarding the superiority of the intellect over knowledge and vice versa. The preferred position is that of the superiority of knowledge over the intellect since knowledge is an attribute of Allah the Exalted. What has been reported regarding the virtue of the intellect[21] is a baseless, fabricated report, just as Jalāl [al-Dīn] al-Suyūṭī has elucidated.[22]

[As for Imam al-Laqqānī's] statement: "although *'lākin'* [scholars] maintained a contention in this regard", it means scholars, however *'lākin'*, affirm that a contention exists regarding the intellect.

There is no place for this corrective conjunction ["although/however"] since scholars also affirm a contention regarding the soul. Perhaps [his usage of "although" is solely for emphasis. Moreover, I have seen the author in his commentary say: "although ... etc.", [this is] a corrective conjunctive [connected to] the method of those who delve [into such matters], thereby indicating that they did not all agree on a specific reality; rather, they differed in their explanations of it. Thus, the corrective conjunction [perhaps] indicates a widespread and abundant contention.

Defining the Intellect (ʿAql)

[As for] the statement: "so investigate what they explained", it means, study the explanations that people have provided in their books, not in this introductory work [on creed], due to its small size. The statements of the *Ahl al-Sunna* all correspond to it being an accident (*ʿaraḍ*). [In light of this,] some of them state,

---

20 Another conceptualization and translation of these four types of intellect could be: (1) fluid intelligence, (2) crystallized intelligence, (3) spiritual intelligence, and (4) inspired intelligence.

21 This is in reference to the hadith report, "A man has not been endowed with anything more virtuous after faith in Allah than the intellect".

22 In the aforementioned commentary, *'Umdat al-Murīd*, al-Laqqānī quotes al-Suyūṭī as stating: "Al-Jalāl al-Suyūṭī states: 'No hadith has been mentioned on the virtue of the intellect. Everything that has been transmitted on it is a forgery and a lie.' This was transmitted by the shaykh of our shaykhs al-Shams al-ʿAlqamī in his gloss on [al-Suyūṭī's] *al-Jāmiʿ al-Ṣaghīr*". Al Suyūṭī's judgment is also relevant to Imam al-Ghazālī's use of such a report in his chapter in the Iḥyā 'Ulūm al-Dīn: "An Exposition of the Meanings and Connotations of the Terms: *Nafs*, *Rūḥ*, *ʿAql*, and *Qalb*".

"It is a type of knowledge", defining it as "knowledge of some [aspects] of intuitive knowledge", such as knowledge of the necessity of a substance occupying physical space and the impossibility of it being free of movement or rest [at any given time], and [the knowledge of] the possibility of fire to burn, and the like. This is the position of Imām al-Ḥaramayn al-Juwaynī (d. 478/1085)[23] and a group [of scholars].[24] Others state that it is not a type of knowledge and define it [instead] as "an innate faculty (*gharīza*), meaning, a natural predisposition that is followed by knowledge of [logical] necessities when all of [its] faculties are sound".[25] Imam al-Shīrāzī (d. 476/1083)[26] defines it as "an attribute by which good and evil can be distinguished". The best of what has been stated regarding it is that "it is a spiritual light by which the soul can grasp intuitive (*darūrī*) and investigative (*naẓarī*) knowledge".

Some state that there exists a subtle metaphysical essence (*laṭīfa rabbāniyya*)[27] that no one knows [the reality of] except Allah the Exalted. From the perspective of cognitive processes, it is referred to as *ʿaql*; from the perspective of the life force navigating the body, it is referred to as *rūḥ* (soul); from the perspective of its appetitive drives, it is referred to as *nafs* (self). All three terms are singular in essence but divergent in consideration.[28]

---

23 Imam Ḍiyāʾ al-Dīn ʿAbd al-Mālik al-Juwaynī (d. 478/1085) is known popularly by his agnomen, Imām al-Ḥaramayn, meaning the leader of the two sanctified cities (Makkah and Medina). He was a Persian Shafiʿī jurist and scholastic theologian and is renowned for his contributions to both dialectic theology and legal theory, as was the case with his most celebrated and recognized student, Imam Abū Ḥāmid al-Ghazālī.

24 This position corresponds to the usage of the term *ʿaql* in the first meaning in al-Ghazāli's discussion of *ʿaql*.

25 Imam ʿAbd al-ʿAzīz ibn Aḥmad al-Farhārawī al-Multānī (d. 1239/1823) in *al-Nibrās* (pg. 127), a gloss on al-Taftāzānī's *Sharḥ al-ʿAqīda al-Nasafiyya*, gives the meaning of *ʿaql* as an innate disposition. He states therein: "It is an attribute placed in the attributed object from inception. The term *gharīza* connotes the recipient of the action of the root verb *gharz*, which denotes inserting a thing into another in a firmly embedded manner, such as: 'I [firmly] planted (*gharaztu*) the spear into the earth'". Imam al-Farhārawī attributes the usage of this term and its intended meaning to al-Ḥārith al-Muḥāsibī and declares it to be the preferred position of Imam Fakhr al-Dīn al-Rāzī (al-Farhārawī al-Multānī, 2012).

26 Ibrāhīm ibn ʿAlī ibn Yūsuf, Abū Isḥāq, the shaykh of the jurists of his day. He died in 476/1083. He is the author of the acclaimed Shāfiʿī legal manual *al-Muhadhdhab* as well as *al-Tabṣira* and *al-Lumaʿ* (Khayr al-Dīn al-Ziriklī, *Kitāb al-Aʿlām*, vol. 1 (Beirut: Dār al-ʿIlm al-Malāyīn, 2002), 51).

27 Imam al-Bājūrī outlines the notion of a unitary metaphysical soul, or psyche, called the *laṭīfa rabbāniyya*. This seems to indicate that the psyche is a metaphysical entity.

28 Here Imam al-Bājūrī further illustrates how there is a single unitary metaphysical entity with various manifestations and functions. He demonstrates the general dualistic approach of the discursive theologians dividing the individual into a body and soul, or physical and subtly physical essence. Just as the body is one whole entity with different parts that fulfill different functions, so too does the soul which contains the functions of cognition, human drives, and life.

The Muʿtazilites, Khawārij, and philosophers opine that it is a [nonphysical] substance.[29] Some of them elaborated that it is a non-physical entity by which unseen things are grasped through intermediaries, and sensory stimuli are perceived by way of observation. Others among them explain it differently. [The assertion that] it is an abstract non-physical essence (*jawhar mujarrad*) can be found in the statements of Imam al-Ghazālī.[30]

The Location of the *ʿAql*

The location [of the intellect] has been disputed. The correct position is that its locus is the heart, while it has a [metaphysical] light linked to the brain (*dimāgh*), just as Imam al-Shāfiʿī, Imam Mālik, and most discursive theologians propose.

[On the other hand,] the philosophers and some jurists state that its locus is the brain on account of it becoming dysfunctional because of brain

29 The discursive theologians offer that all physical beings occupy space and have some form of physicality. All matter thus is either a physical thing, i.e., *ʿayn*, or a substance that contains incidental changing qualities (*ʿaraḍ*) attached to it. These "incidents" do not have an existence of their own. For example, in the case of a black ball, the ball occupies physical existence, while the blackness is an incidental quality that is affixed to the ball. Blackness does not have an existence in and of itself. All created things have some incidental qualities attached to them and can never be free of them. For example, a ball will either be in a state of rest or movement and cannot exist without one of these incidental states. Since incidents do not have any existence of their own, they require some existent thing to be affixed to. Thus, this item must itself have a location and physicality to it. Otherwise, a contingent thing would be dependent on another contingent thing to exist, and this is impossible. To the discursive theologians, all created things exist in space and have a beginning point in which Allah created them. This includes the soul, even though the soul is subtly physical. However, Muslim philosophers did not believe that all created things must have physicality. They offered that the ʿaql, mind, soul, and angels fall into this category. This is also typically associated with their belief in the eternality (*qidam*) of the existence of the souls and cosmos, despite their being created (al-Taftāzanī, *Sharḥ al-ʿAqāʾid al-Nasafiyya*).

30 Imam al-Ghazālī offers a nuanced position. He divides the soul into two further categories (or two possible meanings/entities): (i) the animal soul or life force, which he describes as a *jism laṭīf*, or subtle body (like the discursive theologians). This soul is associated with the rest of the body and is contained within the physical heart. It simply provides the life force, and its associated survival drives of appetite and anger. The second category is what he refers to as the (ii) *latīfa rabānniya*. This is the unitary entity that is the essence of the human soul. It is completely non-physical or metaphysical and is the executive driver of a human being. Imam al-Suhrawārdī among other Sufis seems to provide a similar split between the animal soul and the heavenly soul and the need for the heavenly soul to reign supreme over the physical soul that resembles Imam al-Ghazālī's discussion of the human soul (See the translation of al-Suhrawardī's passage from *ʿAwārif al-Maʿārif*).

dysfunction.[31] However, this does not prove what they suggest, due to the possibility that the healthy functioning of the brain may be a condition for its sound operation, even if it were located in the heart.[32]

3 On Man's Recognition of the Reality of His Soul and the Spiritual Disclosures of the Sufis regarding It. *Knowledge of the Spiritually Learned* (*ʿAwārif al-Maʿārif*) by Imam Shihab al-Din al-Suhrawardī (d. 632 AH/1191 CE)

3.1 *Author's Biography*

Shihab al-Din Abū Hafs ʿUmar Al-Suhrawardī was among the foremost spiritual mentors of Baghdad during his time. He was born in the year 539 AH/1098 CE and at the age of sixteen he traveled from his hometown of Suhraward (Sohrevard in modern day Iran) to Baghdad. His uncle, Abū al-Nājid ʿAbd Al-Qādir al-Suhrawardī, was the founder of the Suhrawardī spiritual order, and it is from him that Shibab al-Dīn learned Islamic law, oratory skills, hadith, and

31 This is a demonstration of the richness of the Islamic intellectual heritage which considers multiple epistemic sources for dealing with the issue of the localization of the intellect. The question is: where is the source of cognitive functions in a human? While the Qur'an alludes to cognitive processes being in the heart (22:46), Muslim scholars did not ignore clear empirical evidence that cognitive processes also exist in the brain.

32 The position that the scholarly majority adopted here demonstrates a sophisticated reconciliation between the two positions by considering the brain an essential condition for expressions of the metaphysical mind (*ʿaql*) located in the metaphysical heart. Imam al-Farhārawī elaborates on this in *al-Nibrās* (ʿAbd al-ʿAzīz ibn Aḥmad al-Farhārawī al-Multānī, *Nibrās: Sharḥ Sharḥ al-ʿAqāʾid al-Nasafiyya* (Istanbul: Maktabat Yāsīn, 2012), 130.) stating: "The statements in revelation indicate that its location is the heart, such as His statement, exalted be He: *Have they not traveled throughout the land so their hearts may reason* (*yaʿqilūna*) (al-Ḥajj 22:46). The opinion that its location is the brain is attributed to Imam Abū Ḥanīfa (may Allah have mercy upon him) on account of the fact that if a hard strike meets the head, then one's [faculty of] reasoning becomes impaired. However, it is possible to reconcile [between these two positions] by [stating] that the acquisition of knowledge is through the medium of the faculties of the brain while it's place of settlement is the heart. The philosopher physicians posited that the place for the perception of pieces of [sensory] information is the external [five] senses and the internal senses (i.e., cognitive faculties of the brain) while the conception of universals [synthesis and analysis] is the [metaphysical] *ʿaql* that is established by the rational metaphysical soul (*nafs nāṭiqa*). The statements of Imam al-Ghazālī (known as the Proof of Islam), align with this. Amongst his positions is his proposal that the heart can generally be used [to refer to either] the 'pinecone-shaped piece of flesh' and/or the 'rational soul' (*nafs nātiqa*). This is the *nafs* that is intended by the [heart] in the statement of scripture (al-Farhārawī al-Multānī, 130.) (al-Ḥajj 22:46). Allah knows best."

Islamic spirituality (*tasawwuf*). He became an influential personality in the spiritual sciences (*tasawwuf*) through the abundance of people making a pledge of allegiance to him and adopting him as their spiritual master. He is described as someone who was humble, honest, noble, and overall well-mannered. He was also known to have no value for money and that he died leaving behind nothing of material value. Imam Suhrawardī was recognized as a pragmatic person. A disciple of his once wrote to him, inquiring about the best course of action: 'If I discontinue work I shall have no source of income, but if I continue to work, I will be filled with arrogance, so what is better [to do]?' The imam replied, 'Continue to work while you seek forgiveness for your arrogance'. And there were many examples of his pragmatic approaches to dealing with situations similar to this. He died in the year 632 AH.

3.2 *Text Overview and Significance*

His most famous work, *Awārif al Maʿārif* is a spiritual treatise and manual that outlines concepts related to Sufism in order for the seeker to understand and follow its teachings. While empirical knowledge is confined to perception via the senses, Suhrawardi purported that spiritual knowledge is perceived through the spiritual heart that is completely experiential. In this adopted excerpt from his work, Suhrawardī expounds on the differing opinions of the scholars regarding the nature of the soul. At the end, however, he concludes that there is nothing to conclusively indicate the nature of the soul and defers such conclusive knowledge to Allah alone.

However, after providing this disclaimer, he goes on to describe the nature of the soul according to his own understanding, drawing upon scriptural sources. Hc purports that the human being possesses two souls, a metaphysical soul (*rūh samāwī ʿulwi*) and an animal or life soul (*rūḥ ḥayawānī*). He offers that inherent in every individual is a tension between these two competing drives, with the animal soul wishing to live a life of hedonism, while the metaphysical soul desires connection with Allah and being freed of the shackles of materialism. He discusses the role of *ʿaql* or the intellectual as mediating between these two driving forces, attempting to service the *rūh samāwī* by helping distinguish between truth and falsehood and tame the animalistic drives.

3.3 *Arabic Text*

في معرفة الإنسان نفسه ومكاشفات الصوفية من ذلك

وحيث وجدت أقوال المشايخ تشير إلى الروح أقول: ما عندي في ذلك على معنى ما ذكرت من التأويل دون أن أقطع به؛ إذ ميلي في ذلك إلى السكوت والإمساك فأقول والله أعلم:

الروح الإنساني العلوي السماوي من عالم الأمر، والروح الحيواني البشري من عالم الخلق، والروح الحيواني البشري محل الروح العلوي ومورده، والروح الحيواني جسماني لطيف حامل لقوة الحس والحركة، ينبعث من القلب، أعني بالقلب هاهنا: المضغة اللحمية المعروفة الشكل، المودعة في الجانب الأيسر من الجسد، وينتشر في تجاويف العروق الضوارب، وهذه الأرواح لسائر الحيوانات، ومنه تفيض قوى الحواس، وهو الذى قوامه بإجراء سنة اللّٰه بالغذاء غالبا، ويتصرف بعلم الطب فيه باعتدال مزاج الأخلاط، ولورود الروح الإنساني العلوي على هذا الروح تجنس الروح الحيواني وما بين أرواح الحيوانات، واكتسب صفة أخرى فصار نفسا محلا للنطق والإلهام. قال اللّٰه تعالى: ﴿وَنَفْسٍ وَمَا سَوَّاهَا. فَأَلْهَمَهَا فُجُورَهَا وَتَقْوَاهَا﴾ فتسويتها بورود الروح الإنساني عليها، وانقطاعها عن جنس أرواح الحيوانات، فتكونت النفس بتكوين اللّٰه تعالى من الروح العلوي وصار تكون النفس التي هي الروح الحيواني من الآدمي من الروح العلوي في عالم الأمر كتكون حواء من آدم في عالم الخلق.

وصار بينهما من التألف والتعاشق كما بين آدم وحواء، وصار كل واحد منهما يذوق الموت بمفارقة صاحبه. قال اللّٰه تعالى: ﴿وَجَعَلَ مِنْهَا زَوْجَهَا لِيَسْكُنَ إِلَيْهَا﴾ فسكن آدم إلى حواء، وسكن الروح الإنساني العلوي إلى الروح الحيواني وصيره نفسا، وتكون من سكون الروح إلى النفس القلب، وأعني بهذا القلب اللطيفة التي محلها المضغة اللحمية، فالمضغة اللحمية من عالم الخلق. وهذه اللطيفة من عالم الأمر.

وكان تكون القلب من الروح والنفس في عالم الأمر كتكون الذرية من آدم وحواء في عالم الخلق، ولولا المساكنة بين الزوجين اللذين أحدهما النفس ما تكوّن القلب، فمن القلوب قلب متطلع إلى الأب الذي هو الروح العلوي ميال إليه، وهو القلب المؤيد الذي ذكره رسول ﷺ فيما رواه حذيفة رضي اللّٰه عنه قال: «القلوب أربعة: قلب أجرد فيه سراج يزهر، فذلك قلب المؤمن، وقلب أسود منكوس فذلك قلب الكافر، وقلب مربوط على غلافه فذلك قلب المنافق، وقلب مصفح فيه إيمان ونفاق، فمثل الإيمان فيه مثل البقلة يمدها الماء الطيب، ومثل النفاق فيه كمثل القرحة يمدها القيح والصديد، فأي المادتين غلبت عليه حكم له بها».

والقلب المكنوس ميال إلى «الأم» التي هي النفس الأمارة بالسوء.

ومن القلوب قلب متردد في ميله إليها، وبحسب غلبة ميل القلب يكون حكمه من السعادة والشقاوة.

والعقل جوهر الروح العلوي ولسانه والدال عليه، وتدبيره للقلب المؤيد والنفس الزكية المطمئنة تدبير الوالد للولد البار، والزوج للزوجة الصالحة، وتدبيره للقلب المنكوس والنفس

الأمارة بالسوء تدبير الوالد للولد العاق والزوج للزوجة السيئة، فمنكوس من وجه، ومنجذب إلى تدبيرهما من وجه؛ إذ لابد له منهما.

وقول القائلين واختلافهم في محل العقل؛ فمن قائل إن محله الدماغ، ومن قائل إن محله القلب، كلام القاصرين عن درك حقيقة ذلك، واختلافهم في ذلك لعدم استقرار العقل على نسق واحد، وانجذابه إلى البار تارة وإلى العاق أخرى، وللقلب والدماغ نسبة إلى البار والعاق، فإذا رؤي في تدبير العاق قيل مسكنه الدماغ وإذا رؤي في تدبير البار قيل مسكنه القلب.

فالروح العلوي يهم بالارتفاع إلى مولاه شوقا وحنوا وتنزها عن الأكوان، ومن الأكوان: القلب والنفس فإذا ارتقى الروح يحنو القلب إليه حنو الولد الحنين البار إلى الوالد، وتحن النفس إلى القلب الذي هو الولد حنين الوالدة الحنينة إلى ولدها، وإذا حنت النفس ارتقت من الأرض، وانزوت عروقها الضاربة في العالم السفلي، وانطوى هواها، وانحسمت مادته وزهدت في الدنيا، وتجافت عن دار الغرور، وأنابت إلى دار الخلود وقد تخلد النفس التي هي الأم إلى الأرض بوضعها الجبلي، لتكونها من الروح الحيواني المجنس ومستندها في ركونها إلى الطبائع التي هي أركان العالم السفلي. قال اللّٰه تعالى: ﴿وَلَوْ شِئْنَا لَرَفَعْنَاهُ بِهَا وَلَٰكِنَّهُۥٓ أَخْلَدَ إِلَى ٱلْأَرْضِ وَٱتَّبَعَ هَوَىٰهُ﴾.

فإذا سكنت النفس التي هي الأم إلى الأرض انجذب إليها القلب المنكوس انجذاب الولد الميال إلى الوالدة المعوجة الناقصة دون الوالد الكامل المستقيم.

وتنجذب الروح إلى الولد الذي هو القلب لما جبل عليه من انجذاب الوالد إلى ولده، فعند ذلك يتخلف عن حقيقة القيام بحق مولاه، وفي هذين الانجذابين يظهر حكم السعادة والشقاوة «ذلك تقدير العزيز العليم».

وقد ورد في أخبار داود عليه السلام أنه سأل ابنه سليمان: أين موضع العقل منك؟ قال: القلب؛ لأنه قالب الروح والروح قالب الحياة.

وقال أبو سعيد القرشي: الروح روحان: روح الحياة، وروح الممات؛ فإذا اجتمعا عقل الجسم وروح الممات هي التي إذا خرجت من الجسد يصير الحي ميتا، وروح الحياة ما به مجاري الأنفاس، وقوة الأكل والشرب وغيرهما.

وقال بعضهم: الروح نسيم طيب يكون به الحياة، والنفس ريح حارة تكون منها الحركات المذمومة والشهوات.

ويقال: فلان حار الرأس. وفي الفصل الذي ذكرناه يقع التنبيه بماهية النفس، وإشارة المشايخ بماهية النفس إلى ما يظهر من آثارها من الأفعال المذمومة والأخلاق المذمومة، وهي التي تعالج بحسن الرياضة إزالتها وتبديلها، والأفعال الرديئة تزال، والأخلاق الرديئة تبدل.

أخبرنا الشيخ العالم رضي الدين أحمد بن إسماعيل القزوينى، قال: أخبرنا إجازة أبو سعيد محمد بن أبي العباس الخليلي، قال أخبرنا القاضي محمد بن سعيد «الفرخزادى» قال أخبرنا أبو إسحق أحمد بن محمد بن إبراهيم قال: أخبرنا الحسين بن محمد بن عبد الله السفياني قال حدثنا محمد بن اليقطيني، قال حدثنا أحمد بن عبدالله بن يزيد العقيلي، قال حدثنا صفوان بن صالح، قال: حدثنا الوليد بن مسلم، عن أبي لهيعة عن خالد بن يزيد، عن سعيد بن أبي هلال: أن رسول الله ﷺ كان إذا قرأ هذه الآية ﴿قَدْ أَفْلَحَ مَن زَكَّاهَا﴾ وقف، ثم قال: «اللّٰهم آت نفسي تقواها أنت وليها ومولاها، وزكها أنت خير من زكاها».

وقيل: النفس لطيفة مودعة في القالب، منها الأخلاق والصفات المحمودة، كما أن العين محل الرؤية، والأذن محل السمع، والأنف محل الشم، والفم محل الذوق، وهكذا النفس محل الأوصاف المذمومة، والروح محل الأوصاف المحمودة، وجميع أخلاق النفس وصفاتها من أصلين: أحدهما الطيش، والثاني الشره، وطيشها من جهلها، وشرها من حرصها. وشبهت النفس في طيشها بكرة مستديرة على مكان أملس مصوب، لا تزال متحركة بجبلتها ووضعها. وشبهت في حرصها بالفراش الذي يلقى نفسه على ضوء المصباح، ولا يقنع بالضوء اليسير دون الهجوم على جرم الضوء الذي فيه هلاكه.

فمن الطيش توجد العجلة، وقلة الصبر، والصبر جوهر العقل، والطيش صفة النفس، وهواها وروحها لا يغلبه إلا الصبر؛ إذ العقل يقمع الهوى.

ومن الشره يظهر الطمع والحرص، وهما اللذان ظهرا في آدم حيث طمع في الخلود، فحرص على أكل الشجرة.

وصفات النفس لها أصول من أصل تكونها، لأنها مخلوقة من تراب، ولها بحسبه وصف، وقيل وصف الضعف في الآدمي من التراب، ووصف البخل فيه من الطين، ووصف الشهوة فيه من الحمأ المسنون، ووصف الجهل فيه من الصلصال

وقيل: قوله)كالفخار(فهذا الوصف فيه شيء من الشيطنة لدخول النار في الفخار، فمن ذلك: الخداع، والحيل، والحسد.

فمن عرف أصول النفس وجبلاتها عرف أن لا قدرة له عليها إلا بالاستعانة ببارئها وفاطرها.

فلا يتحقق العبد بالإنسانية إلا بعد أن يدبر دواعي الحيوانية فيه بالعلم والعدل، وهو رعاية طرفي الإفراط والتفريط ثم بذلك تتقوى إنسانيته ومعناه، ويدرك صفات الشيطنة فيه والأخلاق المذمومة.

وكمال إنسانيته يتقاضاه أن لا يرضى لنفسه بذلك، ثم تنكشف له الأخلاق التي تنازع بها الربوبية، من: الكبر والعز، ورؤية النفس، والعجب.. وغير ذلك.

فيرى أن صرف العبودية في ترك المنازعة للربوبية.

والله تعالى ذكر «النفس» في كلامه القديم بثلاثة أوصاف:

بالطمأنينة، ﴿قال يَأَيَّتُهَا النَّفْسُ الْمُطْمَئِنَّة﴾.

وسماها لوامة، قال: ﴿لَا أُقْسِمُ بِيَوْمِ الْقِيَامَةِ وَلَا أُقْسِمُ بِالنَّفْسِ اللَّوَّامَةِ﴾.

وسماها أمارة، فقال: ﴿إِنَّ النَّفْسَ لَأَمَّارَةٌ بِالسُّوءِ﴾.

وهي نفس واحدة.. ولها صفات متغايرة، فإذا امتلأ القلب سكينة خلع على النفس خِلع الطمأنينة، لأن السكينة مزيد الإيمان، وفيها ارتقاء القلب إلى مقام الروح لما منح من حظ اليقين.

وعند توجه القلب إلى محل الروح تتوجه النفس إلى محل القلب، وفي ذلك طمأنينتها. وإذا انزعجت من مقار جبلاتها ودواعي طبيعتها متطلعة إلى مقار الطمأنينة فهي لوامة، لأنها تعود باللائمة على نفسها لنظرها وعلمها بمحل الطمأنينة، ثم انجذابها إلى محلها التي كانت فيه أمارة بالسوء.

وإذا أقامت في محلها لا يغشاها نور العلم والمعرفة، فهي على ظلمتها أمارة بالسوء.

فالنفس والروح يتطاردان؛ فتارة يملك القلب دواعي الروح، وتارة يملكه دواعي النفس.

وأما السر فقد أشار القوم إليه. ووجدت في كلام القوم أن منهم من جعله بعد القلب وقبل الروح ومنهم من جعله بعد الروح وأعلى منها وألطف.

وقالوا: السر محل المشاهدة، والروح محل المحبة، والقلب محل المعرفة.

والسر الذي وقعت إشارة القوم إليه غير مذكور في كتاب الله. وإنما المذكور في كلام الله الروح والنفس وتنوع صفاتها، والقلب، والفؤاد، والعقل.

وحيث لم نجد في كلام الله تعالى ذكر السر بالمعنى المشار إليه، ورأينا الاختلاف في القول فيه، وأشار قوم إلى أنه دون الروح، وقوم إلى أنه ألطف من الروح، فنقول -والله أعلم-: الذي أسموه سرا ليس هو بشيء مستقل بنفسه، له وجود وذات كالروح والنفس..

3.4 *English Translation*

On Man's Recognition of the Reality of his Soul and the Spiritual Disclosures of the Sufis Regarding It

Since I have found statements of the scholars that point to [the meanings of] the soul, I state: I do not have from the aforementioned interpretations[33] any

33 This excerpt is only a section of the entire chapter regarding this topic. Everything that preceded what is found in this translation was a summary of the various positions of the scholars on the nature of the *rūḥ*. That entire portion was omitted in the interest

conclusive opinion on the topic, as my inclination on the subject is towards silence and abstention. I, therefore, say, and Allah knows best:

The heavenly celestial human soul (*rūḥ samāwī ʿulwī*) is from the realm of the divine command (*ʿālam al-amr*). The animalistic earthly soul (*rūḥ ḥayawānī*) is from the realm of creation.[34] The animalistic earthly soul is the locus of the heavenly celestial soul and its place of provenance. The animalistic soul is bodily, subtle, carries the faculties of sense perception and movement, and emanates from the heart. I mean by heart here the piece of flesh that is well-known in shape that is lodged in the left side of the body and flows through the hollows of the arteries. These souls exist in all animals, and from it the perceptive faculties emanate. It is that which is maintained, by the habit of Allah, predominantly through nourishment, and is regulated through medical knowledge by [maintenance of] moderation in the temperaments of its humors. Due to the emergence of the celestial human soul upon this soul, the animalistic soul is made akin to the souls of animals, and it acquires another attribute upon which it becomes a *nafs* that is suitable for speech[35] and [divine] inspiration. Allah the Exalted states: *And [by] the soul* (*nafs*) *and Him who fashioned it – and informed it with [consciousness of] its wickedness and its righteousness* (al-Shams 91:7–8). It is fashioned through the appearance

of focusing exclusively on the synthesis and position of Imam al-Suhrawardī given the diverse and complex positions regarding the reality of the soul. Imam al-Suhrawardī mentions something very important prior to beginning his explanation. He states that all that was mentioned previously by the scholars was interpretative (*taʾwīl*) and that he too does not have any conclusive proof for the position he is going to offer. This is an important epistemological point being referenced by him. The term *taʾwīl* indicates interpretations that carry possible meanings while *tafsīr* on the other hand is a much more rigorous hermeneutical process that attempts to ascertain conclusive evidence-based interpretations. In instances where there isn't strong evidence for providing an explanation to an ambiguous issue, a scholar may provide his own possible interpretations. In the usage of the word *taʾwīl*, al-Suhrawardī is demonstrating that the objective for the discussions the soul is not to provide categorical interpretations. Rather, he intends to provide useful insights and possible explanations that are derived through his own inspirations and that of the ascetics. By restricting the discussion to this process, he can justify his reason for discussing this topic, while the prohibition to delve deep into the nature and reality of the soul remains (see al-Bajūri translation). Therefore, he precedes his discussion with a disclaimer that he generally prefers to remain silent on such issues.

34 Al-Suhrawardī gives a name to the two different souls that Imām al-Ghazālī discusses in his "Exposition on the Meanings and Connotations of the Terms: *Nafs*, *Rūḥ*, *ʿAql*, *Qalb*". This corresponds to al-Ghazālī's discussion of the life spirit being situated in the physical heart, while the soul of the second usage refers to the primordial celestial soul, or *laṭīfa rabbāniyya*.

35 Or possessing the faculty of reason.

of the human soul (*rūḥ insānī*) into it and its separation from the genus of the animal souls. The soul (*nafs*) is composed from the heavenly soul by Allah the Exalted's creation, and the composition of the soul (*nafs*) – which is the animalistic soul of a human – from the heavenly soul (*rūḥ ʿulwi*) in the realm of divine command (*ʿālam al-amr*) is thus like the composition of Ḥawwāʾ (Eve) from Ādam (Adam) in the realm of creation (*ʿālam al-khalq*).[36]

Between the two (the *nafs* and the celestial soul), a union and mutual passion was formed just like between Adam and Eve, and it became so that each tastes death upon the separation of its companion. Allah the Exalted states: *And from it He made its mate, to [find] repose with her* (al-Aʿrāf 7:189). So, Adam found repose in Eve and the human celestial soul found repose in the animalistic soul and made it into a *nafs*. From the repose of the *rūḥ* with the *nafs* is the heart (*qalb*) composed. By this heart, I mean the subtle essence (*laṭīfa*) whose locus is the piece of meaty flesh. The meaty piece of flesh is from the realm of creation, and this subtle essence is from the realm of the divine command.

The composition of the *qalb* from the *rūḥ* and the *nafs* took place in the realm of the divine command similar to the composition of [Adam's] progeny from Adam and Eve in the realm of creation. If it was not for the mutual repose found amongst the two, one of which is the nafs, the qalb would not be formed.[37]

Amongst the hearts (*qulūb*) is the heart that is aware of the father that is the celestial soul and is inclined towards it. This is the reinforced heart that is mentioned by the Messenger of Allah, may Allah bless him and grant him peace, in the report narrated by Ḥudhayfa, may Allah be well-pleased with him, that he (may Allah bless him and grant him peace) said: "There are four hearts: (1) an open heart in which there is a radiant lamp; this is the heart of the believer, and (2) a black, inverted heart; this is the heart of the disbeliever, and (3) a heart that is wrapped around its cover; this is the heart of the hypocrite, and (4) a foliated heart containing [both] faith and hypocrisy. The example of faith in it is like a legume that expands with pure water. The example of hypocrisy in it

36 Upon the descent of the human being from a celestial soul that existed primordially in the heavens into the physical world, the person becomes a *nafs*, possessing both animalistic instincts and celestial instincts to do good. The *nafs* is born out of the union of the animalistic soul and celestial soul in this world, just like Eve being created from the rib of Adam.

37 The *qalb* is necessary upon the existence of the human being in the world, given that it is inclined to either turn toward the celestial instincts or the beastly desires. Depending on which direction it turns, it harbors health or spiritual pathology.

is like a sore that expands with pus and matter. Whichever of the two components overcomes it, judgment is made based on it".[38]

The inverted heart inclines heavily to "the mother" that is the *nafs* that commands to evil (*al-nafs al-ammāra bi-l-sūʾ*).[39]

Amongst the hearts is the heart that is reluctant in inclining towards any of the two, and in proportion to the dominance of the inclination of the heart will be the judgment of fortune or misfortune.

The intellect (*ʿaql*) is the essence, the tongue, and the indicator of the celestial soul. Its regulation of the reinforced heart and the purified, contented self (*nafs*) is [akin to] the regulation of the parent of the obedient child and the husband of the righteous wife. Its regulation of the inverted heart and the self that commands to evil is [akin to] the regulation of the parent of the disobedient child and the husband of the wicked wife. So, [it is] inverted from one aspect and attracted to the regulation of them both from another aspect, since it (the *ʿaql*) requires both as the presence of both is necessary.

The statements and contentions of those who hold positions on the location of the intellect: Some state that its locus is the brain, while some state that its locus is the heart. The discourses and contentions of those who are deficient in recognizing the reality of it is due to the inability of the intellect to settle upon one disposition, and [due to] its attraction to the obedient sometimes and to the disobedient at other times. The heart and the brain have an attachment to the obedient and the disobedient. Thus, when it (*ʿaql*) is seen to be in the service of the disobedient it is said that its residence is the brain, and when it is seen to be in the service of the obedient it is said that its residence is the heart.[40]

The celestial soul (*rūḥ ʿulwī*) thus seeks elevation to its Master due to an intense desire, loving affection, and attempt to detach from the universe

---

38 Abū 'Abd al-Raḥmān Ibn Mubārak, *al-Zuhd wa-l-Raqā'iq* (Amman: Dār al-Fārūq, 2022) hadith 1439; Aḥmad Ibn Ḥanbal, *Musnad al-Imām Aḥmad Ibn Ḥanbal* (Lebanon: Mu'assasat al-Risāla, 1995), 3:7; Abū Bakr Muḥammad Ibn Ibrāhīm Ibn Abī Shayba, *al-Musannaf fi-l-Aḥādīth wa-l-Āthār* (Beirut: Dār al-Tāj, 1982) 31043; Abū al-Qāsim Sulaymān ibn Aḥmad Ṭabarānī, *Muʿjam al-Ṣaghīr* (Madina: al-Maktabat al-Salafiyya, 1968) 1075; al-Isfahānī, *Ḥilyat al-Awliyāʾ wa Tabaqāt al-Aṣfiyāʾ*, 1:276 but attributed to Ḥudhayfa, may Allah be pleased with him, 4:385, with attribution to the Prophet, may Allah bless him and grant him peace, through Abū Saʿīd al-Khudrī, may Allah be pleased with him.

39 This is when the *nafs* is at a lower stage, i.e., the beastly level that seeks solely to satisfy its appetitive desires.

40 This is an interesting and unique perspective that diverges from the discussions of the location of the *ʿaql* discussed in al-Bajūrī's summary where he summarized the two major position of the scholars asserting the *ʿaql* to be either in the brain or in the metaphysical heart.

(*akwān*), and the *qalb* and *nafs* are of this universe.[41] When the soul ascends, the *qalb* develops an affection for it like a reverent, infant child does for its parent. The *nafs* feels an affection for the *qalb* – which is [like] the child – like the affection of a tender mother for her child. When the nafs feels such affection, it ascends from the earth, its participating roots (*ʿurūq ḍāriba*) withdraw into the lower realm (*ʿālam*), its caprice (*hawā*) disappears, its substance (*mādda*) terminates, and it becomes abstinent from the material world (*dunyā*). It shuns the Realm of Delusion (*dār al-ghurūr, i.e., worldly life*) and turns repentantly to the Realm of Permanence (*dār al-khulūd, i.e., the hereafter*).

Often the *nafs* – which is [likened to] the mother – clings to the earth by virtue of its natural appointment, because of its composition from the material animalistic soul, and [because] its basis is its dependence on natural dispositions that are the pillars of the lower realm.[42] Allah the Exalted states: *And if We so willed, we would have elevated him thereby; but He clung to the earth and followed his caprice* (al-Aʿrāf 7:176).

When the *nafs* – which is the mother – settles upon the earth, the inverted *qalb* is attracted to it [like] the attraction of a child who is inclined to a twisted and defective mother as opposed to the upright and perfect father. [Moreover,] The *rūḥ* is attracted to the child – which is the *qalb* – due to the naturally created attraction in the father to his child, thereby falling behind in fulfilling the rights of his Master.

It is in these two sources of attraction that the judgment of felicity (*saʿāda*) or misfortune (*shaqāwa*) becomes manifest and "*That is the determination of the All-Mighty, the All-Knowing*" (Yasīn 36:38).

It has been mentioned in the reports about Dāwūd (upon him be peace) that he asked his son Sulaymān (upon him be peace): "Where is the location of the *ʿaql* in you?" He replied: "The *qalb* (lit. that which molds), since it is what molds (*qālab*) the *rūḥ*, and the *rūḥ* is what molds life."[43]

41 al-Suhrawardī is discussing the affinity of the metaphysical celestial self to be inclined towards the Divine, while the body and animal soul is inclined to the earth and physical world.

42 Demonstrates the duality and intrapsychic conflicting drives between meeting its physical worldly needs that may be in conflict and weighing down its celestial instincts for elevation.

This is a very important in establishing a drive theory in Islam. There are opposing drives that exist within the human being that pull them toward realization of their celestial souls or pull them toward leaving a beastly and hedonistic life.

43 Transmitted by al-Hakīm al-Tirmidhī in his *Nawādir al-Uṣūl*, hadith 868, as part of a lengthy report, except for the word "brain" (*dimāgh*) in place of "the heart" (qalb).

Abū Saʿīd al-Qurashī states: "The *rūḥ* is of two types: the *rūḥ* of life, and the *rūḥ* of death.[44] When they combine, the body achieves congitive faculties (*ʿaqala al-jism*). The *rūḥ* of death is that which, when it leaves [the body], a living person dies. The *rūḥ* of life is that by which the abilities to breathe, eat, drink, etc., are carried out."[45]

Some state that the *rūḥ* is a pleasant, cool breeze by which life exists, while the [lower] *nafs* is a hot wind due to which blameworthy behaviors and desires occur.[46] It is said, for example, that so and so is hot-headed.[47]

In the chapter we have mentioned, there is an explanation (*tanbīḥ*) about the essence of the *nafs* and the indications of the shaykhs about the nature of the *nafs* towards what manifests from its effects in terms of blameworthy actions and character that are treated, through excellent spiritual exercises, for their elimination and change. Vile actions are eliminated, while vile character is exchanged [for good character].

The shaykh and scholar, Raḍī al-Dīn Aḥmad ibn Ismāʿīl al-Qazwīnī, informed us, stating: Abū Saʿd[48] Muḥammad ibn Abī al-ʿAbbās al-Khalīlī informed us through transmission-certification (*ijāza*), stating: al-Qāḍī Muḥammad ibn Saʿīd al-Farkhuzādī informed us, stating: Abū Isḥāq Aḥmad ibn Muḥammad ibn Ibrāhīm informed us, stating: al-Ḥusayn ibn Muḥammad ibn ʿAbd Allāh al-Sufyānī informed us, stating: Muḥammad ibn al-Yaqṭīnī narrated to us, stating: Aḥmad ibn ʿAbd Allāh ibn Yazīd al-ʿUqaylī narrated to us, stating: Ṣafwān ibn Ṣāliḥ narrated us, stating: al-Walīd ibn Muslim narrated to us, stating: from Ibn Lahīʿa, from Khālid ibn Yazīd, from Saʿīd ibn Abī Hilāl, that when the Messenger of Allah, (may Allah bless him and grant him peace) used to recite this verse: *the one who purifies it* (*the nafs*) *succeeds* (al-Shams 91:9), he would

44 Another indication toward the dual drives between the affinity for temporal and eternal life.

45 See Abū ʿAbd al-Raḥmān al-Sulamī, *Ḥaqāʾiq al-Tafsīr*, vol. 1 (Beirut: Dār al-Kutub al-ʿIlmiyya, 2001), 397.

46 See Abū Bakr Kalābadhī, *al-Taʿarruf li-Madhhab Ahl al-Taṣawwuf* (Beirut: Dār al-Kutub al-ʿIlmiyya, nd), 68.

47 al-Ḥakīm al-Tirmidhī, *Nawādir al-Uṣūl fī Aḥādīth al-Rasūl*, vol. 3 (Beirut: Dār al-Jīl, nd), 217.

48 The various editions of the book give the name "Saʿīd" here. The correction to "Saʿd" has been made based on what has been mentioned in *al-Taḥbīr fī al-Muʿjam al-Kabīr* (see ʿAbd al-Karīm al-Samʿānī al-Marwazī, *al-Taḥbīr fī al-Muʿjam al-Kabīr*, vol. 2 (Baghdād: Riāsāt Dīwān al-Awqāf, 1975), 69.), and *al-Muntakhab min Muʿjam Shuyūkh al-Samʿānī* (Abd al-Karīm al-Samʿānī al-Marwazī, *al-Muntakhab min Muʿjam Shuyūkh al-Samʿānī* (Riyadh: Dār ʿĀlam al-Kutub, 1996), 1370.), and *Muʿjam Shuyūkh* (see Thiqat al-Dīn Ibn ʿAsākir, *Muʿjam al-Shuyūkh*, vol. 2, (Dimashq: Dār al-Bashāir, 2000), 866.).

pause. Then he would say: "Allah! Grant my *nafs* its *taqwā*. You are its Protector and Master. Purify it! You are the best of those who purify it!"[49]

It is said that the *nafs* is a subtle substance consigned to the heart (*qālib*) from which praiseworthy character and attributes emanate. Just like the eyes are the locus of sight, the ears are the locus of hearing, the nose is the locus of smell, and the mouth is the locus of taste, the *nafs*[50] is the locus of blameworthy attributes and the rūḥ is the locus of praiseworthy attributes.[51]

All character and attributes of the *nafs* originate in two sources; one is imprudence (*ṭaysh*) and the second is gluttony (*sharah*). While its imprudence comes from its ignorance (*jahl*), its gluttony comes from its covetousness (*ḥirṣ*). The *nafs* in its imprudence is likened to a sphere placed upon a smooth, leveled place. It will continue to move on its own by virtue of its nature and placement. It is likened in its covetousness to a moth that flings itself into the lamp's light. It is not content with a dull light such that it springs toward the immensity of the light in which lies its destruction.

From imprudence, haste and lack of patience is found, and patience is the essence (*jawhar*) of the intellect. Rashness is an attribute of the *nafs*, whose desires and spirit cannot be overcome except by patience, as the intellect curbs desires.

From gluttony, greed (*ṭamaʿ*) and covetousness (*ḥirṣ*) appear, experienced by Ādam when he desired everlasting life (*khulūd*) and so coveted to eat (from) the tree.

The attributes of the *nafs* have foundational elements from the essence of its creation because it was created from dirt (*turāb*), and accordingly has its appropriate attribute. It is said that the attribute of frailty (*ḍaʿf*) in man comes from the dirt, and that the attribute of miserliness (*bukhl*) that is in him comes from the clay (*ṭīn*), and that the attribute of desire (*shahwa*) in him comes from dark foul-smelling mud (*ḥamaʾ masnūn*), and that the attribute of ignorance comes from ringing, dried clay (*ṣalṣāl*).

---

49 See Abū Isḥāq Thaʿlabī, *al-Kashf wa-l-Bayān ʿan Tafsīr al-Qurʾān*, vol. 29 (Jidda: Dār al-Tafsīr, 2015), 426–27. The report is broken-chained. It is also narrated in al-Ṭabarānī's *al-Muʿjam al-Kabīr* 11:106 from Ibn ʿAbbās (may Allah be pleased with them both) in the context of verses 7–8 in Sūrat al-Shams. Ibn Abī Ḥātim similarly transmits it in his *Tafsīr* hadith 19,339 through Abū Hurayrah, may Allah be pleased with him. Muslim transmits it in his *Ṣaḥīḥ* (hadith 2,722) from Zayd b. Arqam, may Allah be pleased with him, but not in the context of any particular verse.

50 I.e., the lower stage of the *nafs*.

51 See al-Qushayrī, *al-Risāla al-Qushayriyya*, 1: 204.

It is said about [Allah's] statement: *like pottery* (*ka al-fakhkhār*) (al-Raḥmān 55:14)[52] that this characteristic contains a satanic element due to the inclusion of fire in pottery. From it originates deceitfulness (*khidāʿ*), subterfuge (*ḥiyal*), and jealousy (*ḥasad*).

Hence, whosoever recognizes the foundations of the *nafs* and its nature also recognizes that he has no power over it except through seeking assistance from its Creator and Maker.

A slave (of Allah) is therefore not able to truly realize humanness (*insāniyya*) until he reflects – through knowledge and fairness – on the causes of animalistic tendencies (*ḥayawāniyya*) within him. This [fairness means] taking into consideration [and abstaining from] both extremes of excessiveness. By doing so his humanness and its essence are strengthened, and he can recognize satanic attributes and blameworthy character traits within himself.

The perfection of his humanness, however, demands that he not be satisfied with [just] this for himself. Rather, then the character traits that are at odds with godliness (*rubūbiyya*) become revealed to him, such as: arrogance (*kibr*), celebrity (*ʿizz*), self-absorption (*ruʾyat al-nafs*), vanity (*ʿujb*), among others.

He thus sees that unadulterated slavehood (*ʿubūdiyya*) is in abandoning any challenge to godliness.

Allah the Exalted mentions the *nafs* in his eternal speech with three attributes:

- With "contentment" (*ṭumaʾnīna*). He states: *O content nafs* (al-Fajr 89:27).
- And He called it "self-reproaching" (*lawwāma*), as He states: *I swear by the Day of Resurrection, and I swear by the self-reproaching nafs* (al-Qiyāma 75:1–2).
- And He called it "inciting" (*ammāra*), as He states: *Surely, man's nafs is oft-inciting to evil* (Yūsuf 12:53).

They are the same *nafs*, [albeit] with differing attributes. So, when the heart is filled with tranquility, it covers the *nafs* in the garb of contentment, because tranquility increases faith, and in it is the elevation of the *qalb* to the position of the *rūḥ* due to what it is apportioned of firm conviction.

When the *qalb* is directed to the place of the *rūḥ*, the *nafs* [in turn] becomes directed to the place of the *qalb*, and therein lies its contentment.

When it grows weary of the seat of its inherent nature and its natural attractions, [while being] aware of the seat of contentment, it is then self-reproaching (*lawwāma*), because it refers to itself with self-reproach because of its observation and knowledge of the place of contentment (*maqārr al-ṭumaʾnīna*), and then its attraction to its place in which it once incited to evil.

52 Referring to the 14th verse in Sūrat al-Raḥmān: "*He created mankind out of ringing, dried clay* (ṣalṣāl), *like pottery*".

When it establishes itself in its place (the place of inciting evil), the light of knowledge and gnosis do not descend upon it. It becomes thus, in its darkness, inciting towards evil.

The *nafs* and the *rūḥ* are therefore mutually repelling: sometimes the *qalb* is possessed by the callers (*dawāʿī*) of the *rūḥ*, and sometimes it is possessed by the motives of the *nafs*.[53]

As for the inner secret (*sirr*), people have given subtle indications towards it[s reality]. What I have found in people's discussions is that some have placed it following the *qalb* and preceding the *rūḥ*. Some have placed it as following the *rūḥ* and superior (*aʿlā*) to it and more subtle.

They say: the *sirr* is the locus of divine witnessing (*mushāhada*), and the *rūḥ* is the locus of divine love (*maḥabba*), and the *qalb* is the locus of divine gnosis (*maʿrifa*).

The *sirr* that people subtly indicate towards is not mentioned in the Book of Allah. What is mentioned in Allah's speech is the *rūḥ* and the *nafs* – and its various attributes – as well as the *qalb*, the *fuʾād* (heart), and the *ʿaql* (intellect). Since we do not find the mention of the *sirr* in Allah's speech with the meaning [previously] indicated towards , and we observe a difference in positions on it, and since some people indicate that it is inferior to the *rūḥ* and some indicate that it is more subtle than the *rūḥ*, we therefore state – and Allah is the Most-Knowing: What they have named the secret (*sirr*) is not something entirely independent that has a presence and essence like the *rūḥ* and *nafs*.

4 Inherent Faculties of Perception. *Al-Qānūn fī al-Ṭibb* (*The Canon of Medicine*) by Ibn Sīna (d. 428 AH/1037 CE)

4.1 *Author's Biography*

Abū ʿAlī Ḥusayn ibn Sīna, also known as Avicenna, is considered to be amongst the greatest of Muslim philosophers and physicians. He is sometimes referred to as the "prince of physicians" or the "father of early medicine." It is also said that he is "too famous to be mentioned, and his virtues are too innumerous to be recorded." Ibn Sīna's father was originally from Balkh (Afghanistan), but

53 Here is a figure illustrating the relationship between the components discussed by al-Suhrawardī. In the middle of the diagram is the heart that is pulled either toward the bodily drives found in the rūḥ hayawānī or toward the celestial soul (rūḥ samāwī). The ʿaql serves as its aid. Depending on which element becomes dominant and wins over the self, it will reflect the state of the soul (nafs) accordingly. The jasad or body is from the physical realm, while the *laṭīfa rabānniyya* is of the metaphysical realm (*malakūt/ʿālam al-ʾamr*).

moved to the village of Afshana, Bukhāra (Uzbekistan) before the birth of his prodigious son in the year 370 Hijrī. Under the tutelage of his father, Ibn Sīna completed the memorization of the Quran before the age of ten. From an early age, he demonstrated advanced reasoning coupled with an exceptional memory, having memorized Aristotle's works on metaphysics.

Throughout his life, Ibn Sīna wrote over 450 works, with many of such writings still intact today. He made significant contributions to the fields of psychology, medicine, geometry, chemistry, poetry, philosophy, and theology. Among his most famously known works are *Al-Shifā'* (The Healing), *Risāla fī al-Nafs* (Treatise on the Soul), and his *magnum opus*, al-*Qānūn fī al-Ṭibb* (The Canon of Medicine), which was used as the primary textbook in European medical schools until the sixteenth century.

Ibn Sīna's devotion to knowledge acquisition is demonstrated by his division of desire into a two-level hierarchy: one of which is physical joy, and the other is psychological or intellectual. He stated that the greatest physical pleasures may appear to come from eating and sexual gratification, but if the human being suspends these base desires in lieu of a more meaningful intellectual pursuit, then the subsequent joy supersedes the fulfillment of physical and sensual desires.

4.2 *Text Overview and Significance*

The Canon of Medicine by Ibn Sīna is referred to as "the most famous medical textbook ever written in history." Its enduring presence as a referential medical textbook in universities distinguishes it from other medical texts. In this translated excerpt, Ibn Sīna outlines and discusses the five inner cognitive faculties of the brain and their locations within the brain.

4.3 *Arabic Text*

الفصل الخامس: في القوى النفسانية المدركة

والقوة النفسانية تشتمل على قوتين هي كالجنس لهما: إحداهما قوة مدركة، والأخرى قوة محركة. وَالْقُوَّة المدركة كالجنس لقوتين: قُوَّة مدركة فِي الظَّاهِر وَقُوَّة مدركة فِي الْبَاطِن. وَالْقُوَّة المدركة فِي الظَّاهِر هِيَ الحسية، وَهِي كالجنس لقوى خمس عِنْد قوم وثمان عِنْد قوم. وَإِذا أخذت خَمْسَة كَانَت قُوَّة الإبصار وَقُوَّة السّمع وَقُوَّة الشم وَقُوَّة الذَّوْق وَقُوَّة اللَّمْس. وَأما إِذا أخذت ثَمَانِيَة فالسبب فِي ذَلِك أَن أَكثر المحصلين يرَوْنَ أَن اللَّمْس قوى كَثِيرَة، بل هُوَ قوى أَربع. ويخصون كل جنس من الملموسات الْأَرْبَع بِقُوَّة على حِدة، إِلَّا أَنَّهَا مُشْتَركَة فِي الْعُضْو الحساس كالذوق واللمس فِي اللِّسَان والإبصار، واللمس فِي الْعين،

وَتَحْقِيق هَذَا إِلَى الفيلسوف. وَالْقُوَّة المدركة فِي الباطن أعني الحيوانية هي كالجنس لقوى خمس:

إِحْدَاهَا: الْقُوَّة الَّتِي تسمى الْحس الْمُشْتَرك والخيال: وَهِي عِنْد الْأَطِبَّاء قُوَّة وَاحِدَة، وَعند المحصلين من الْحُكَمَاء قوتان. فالحس الْمُشْتَرك هُوَ الَّذِي يتَأَدَّى إِلَيْهِ المحسوسات كلهَا وينفعل عَن صورها ويجتمع فِيهِ. والخيال هُوَ الَّذِي يحفظها بعد الِاجْتِمَاع، ويمسكها بعد الغيبوبة عَن الْحس، وَالْقُوَّة الْقَابِلَة مِنْهُمَا غير الحافظة. وَتَحْقِيق الْحق فِي هَذَا هُوَ أَيْضا على الفيلسوف. وَكَيف كَانَ فَإِن مسكنهما ومبدأ فعلهمَا هُوَ الْبَطن الْمُقدم من الدِّمَاغ.

وَالثَّانِيَة: الْقُوَّة الَّتِي تسميها الْأَطِبَّاء مفكرة: والمحققون تَارَة يسمونها متخيلة، وَتارَة مفكرة، فَإِن استعملتها الْقُوَّة الوهمية الحيوانية الَّتِي نذكرها بعد أَو نهضت هِيَ بِنَفسِهَا لفعلها سَموهَا متخيلة، وَإِن أَقبلت عَلَيْهَا الْقُوَّة النطقية وصرفتها على مَا ينْتَفع بِهِ سَمّهَا سميت مفكرة. وَالْفرق بَين هَذِه الْقُوَّة وَبَين الأولى كَيفَ مَا كَانَت: أَن الأولى قَابِلَة أَو حافظة لما يتَأَدَّى إِلَيْهَا من الصُّور المحسوسة، وَأما هَذِه فَإِنَّهَا تتصرف على المستودعات فِي الخيال تصرفاتها من تركيب وتفصيل فتستحضر صوراً على نَحْو مَا تأدى من الْحس، وصوراً مُخَالفَة لَهَا كإنسان يطير وجبل من زمرد. وَأما الخيال فَلَا يحضرهُ إِلَّا للقبول من الْحس. ومسكن هَذِه الْقُوَّة هُوَ الْبَطن الْأَوْسَط من الدِّمَاغ. وَهَذِه الْقُوَّة هِيَ آلَة لقُوَّة هِيَ بِالْحَقِيقَةِ المدركة الْبَاطِنَة فِي الْحَيَوَان وَهِي الْوَهم، وَهُوَ الْقُوَّة الَّتِي تحكم فِي الْحَيَوَان بِأَن الذِّئْب عَدو، وَالْولد حبيب، وَأَن المتعهد بالعلف صديق لَا ينفر عَنهُ على سَبِيل غير نطقي. والعداوة والمحبة غير محسوسين لَيْسَ يدركهما الْحس من الْحَيَوَان فَإِذن إِنَّمَا يحكم بهما ويدركهما قُوَّة أُخْرَى، وَإِن كَانَ لَيْسَ بالإدراك النطقي، إِلَّا أَنه لَا محَالة إِدْرَاك مَا غير النطقي. وَالْإِنْسَان أَيْضا قد يسْتَعْمل هَذِه الْقُوَّة فِي كثير من الْأَحْكَام وَيجْرِي فِي ذَلِك مجْرى الْحَيَوَان غَيْر النَّاطِق. وَهَذِه الْقُوَّة تفارق الخيال؛ لِأَن الخيال يستثبت المحسوسات وَهَذِه تحكم فِي المحسوسات بمعان غير محسوسة، وتفارق الَّتِي تسمّى مفكرة ومتخيلة بِأَن أَفعَال تِلْكَ لَا يتبعهَا حكم مَا، وأفعال هَذِه يتبعهَا حكم مَا، بل هِيَ أَحْكَام مَا وأفعال تِلْكَ تركيبات فِي المحسوسات، وَفعل هَذِه هُوَ حكم فِي المحسوس من معنى خَارج عَن المحسوس. وكما أَن الْحس فِي الْحَيَوَان حَاكم على صور المحسوسات كَذَلِك الْوَهم فِيهَا حَاكم على مَعَاني تِلْكَ الصُّور الَّتِي تتأدى إِلَى الْوَهم وَلَا تتأدى إِلَى الْحس، وَمن النَّاس من يتجوز ويسمي هَذِه الْقُوَّة تخيلاً، وَله ذَلِك إِذْ لَا مُنَازعَة فِي الْأَسْمَاء، بل يجب أَن يفهم الْمعَانِي والفروق، وَهَذِه الْقُوَّة لَا يتَعَرَّض الطَّبِيب لتعرفها؛ وَذَلِكَ أَن مضار أفعالها تَابِعَة لمضار أَفعَال قوى أُخْرَى قبلهَا مثل الخيال والتخيّل وَالذكر الَّذِي سنقوله بعد. والطبيب إِنَّمَا ينْتَظر فِي القوى الَّتِي إِذا لحقها مضرَّة فِي أفعالها كَانَ ذَلِك مَرضا فَإِن كَانَت المضرّة تلْحق فعل قُوَّة بِسَبَب مضرَّة لحقت فعل قبلهَا وَكَانَت تِلْكَ الْمضرَّة تتبع سوء مزاج أَو فَسَاد

تركيب فِي عُضْو مَا فيكفيه أَن يعرف لُحُوق ذَلِك الضَّرَر بِسَبَب سوء مزاج ذَلِك الْعُضْو أَو فَسَاده حَتَّى يتداركه بالعلاج أَو يتحفظ عَنهُ. وَلَا عَلَيْهِ أَن يعرف حَال الْقُوَّة الَّتِي إِنَّمَا يلْحقهَا مَا يلْحقهَا كَمَا أَن الخيال خزانَة لما يتَأَدَّى إِلَى الْحس من الصُّورَة المحسوسة بِوَاسِطَة إِذْ كَانَ قد عرف حَال الَّتِي يلْحقهَا بِغَيْر وَاسِطَة.

وَالثَّالِثَة مِمَّا يذكر الْأَطِبَّاء -وَهِي الْخَامِسَة أَو الرَّابِعَة عِنْد التَّحْقِيق- وَهِي الْقُوَّة الحافظة والمذّكرة وَهِي خزانَة لما يتَأَدَّى إِلَى الْوَهم من معَان فِي المحسوسات غير صورها المحسوسة، وموضعها الْبَطن الْمُؤخر من بطُون الدِّمَاغ. وَهَهُنَا مَوضِع نظر حكمي فِي أَنه هَل الْقُوَّة الحافظة والمتذكرة المسترجعة لما غَابَ عَن الْحِفْظ من مخزونات الْوَهم قُوَّة وَاحِدَة أم قوتان؟ وَلَكِن لَيْسَ ذَلِك مِمَّا يلْزم الطَّبِيب إِذا كَانَت الْآفَات الَّتِي تعرض لأيهما كَانَ هِيَ الْآفَات الْعَارِضَة للبطن الْمُؤخر من الدِّمَاغ، إِمَّا من جنس المزاج وَإِمَّا من جنس التَّرْكِيب.

وَأما الْقُوَّة الْبَاقِيَة من قوى النَّفس المدركة فَهِيَ الإنسانية الناطقة. وَلما سقط نظر الْأَطِبَّاء عَن الْقُوَّة الوهمية لما شرحناه من الْعلَّة فَهُوَ أسقط عَن هَذِه الْقُوَّة بل نظرهم مَقْصُور على أَفعَال القوى الثَّلَاث لَا غير.

4.4 *English Translation*

Regarding the Inherent Faculties of Perception[54]

The basic innate faculties are comprised of two categorically distinct capabilities; the first is the faculty of perception, and the second is locomotion.

The faculty of perception is classified as having an external [component] as well as an internal [one]. Its external aspect includes the [physical] senses,

---

54 The branch of psychology that is concerned with the subject matter of sensation and its translation into perception is known as cognitive psychology. It delves into the complexities of human cognition, encompassing the processing of sensory information received from external stimuli, its internal translation into perceptions, and its subsequent storage and retrieval within the brain for various cognitive functions. Sensory information perceived by our senses is converted into neural signals in the brain, where it is encoded as mental representations. These representations are initially stored in our working memory, allowing us to manipulate and process them in our mental workspace or mind. If the information is practiced or associated with emotions, it may then be further encoded into long-term memory for retention (E. Bruce Goldstein *Cognitive Psychology: Connecting Mind, Research, and Everyday Experience* (Cengage Learning, 2017), 4th ed.). Although the localization of the five faculties of human perception to specific parts of the brain, as described by Ibn Sīnā and other pre-modern physicians, has been proven largely inaccurate with the advent of modern brain imaging technologies, it is nonetheless remarkable how closely his description of the cognitive process aligns with the explanations of human perception in modern cognitive psychology.

which are divided into five [faculties] according to some,[55] and eight according to others. Thus, according to the first view, the five faculties are: sight, hearing, smell, taste, and touch.

However, regarding [the other view that] lists [the faculties] as eight, it is because most proponents of that view regard [the sense of] touch to include multiple faculties within itself; [in their view,] touch consists of four aspects, and they classify each one to be a distinct faculty given that [various] senses are jointly perceived through [more than one particular] body part. To elucidate, the tongue [experiences] both taste and touch. Likewise, the eye [perceives] sight and touch. This [view] is supported overall by the philosophers.

The innate internal faculty of perception consists of five composite faculties.

The first of them is termed the faculty of sensory integration (*ḥiss mushtarak*) and perceptual recall (*khayāl*). According to physicians, it is one singular faculty, but the erudite philosophers classify it as two faculties.

The faculty of sensory integration (*ḥiss mushtarak*) is defined as the section [of the brain] in which all sensations are processed; such are separated from their [external] forms and reconstructed therein. The perceptual recall faculty (*khayāl*) is that which retains everything after it is gathered [in the brain]; it stores the perception [of the stimuli] after the stimuli is separated from sensory awareness. In considering both faculties, that which receives the sensations is distinct from that which retains them. The final verdict on this matter [i.e., whether they are considered as one or two faculties] is determined by the philosophers.[56] Regardless of how they [may] be [classified], both [faculties] are located and operate [in the] inner anterior of the brain.[57]

The second faculty is termed by doctors as [the] cogitative [faculty] (*mufakkira*). Some researchers occasionally refer to it as [the faculty of] imagination (*mutakhayyala*), although they [can also] refer to it as [the] cogitative faculty at times. If this faculty is employed by the sensorial intuitive faculties that we

55 It is important to note that ibn Sīnā among other physicians had adopted the notion of five internal faculties of perception from Aristotle and the ancient Greeks.

56 At face value, Ibn Sīna seems to suggest that classifying these faculties as one unit or as separate faculties is the realm of the philosophers and their discipline. Accordingly, the onus is upon the philosopher to determine the final verdict considering all that is known regarding these cognitive faculties and how they work together in various capacities. However, it is possible and perhaps even more likely that Ibn Sīna is referring to Aristotle, as it was his habit to refer to Aristotle as "the philosopher" in many of his writings.

57 According to modern cognitive neuroscience, the switchboard for all incoming sensory information that gets relayed to the other parts of the cerebral cortex is the part of the brain known as the thalamus, which is a paired gray matter structure located near the center of the brain. It is above the midbrain and contains neural pathways connecting to all the various parts of the cerebral cortex.

will discuss later, or if is activated involuntarily as per its function, then such is termed imaginative (*mutakhayyala*). However, if the faculty of intellect is further used to direct it advantageously, it is termed cogitative (*mufakkira*).

The [main] difference between this faculty and the aforementioned [faculty of integration] goes back to how each [of them] function. The initially [discussed] faculty [of integration] (*ḥiss mushtarak*) receives and retains the sensory input that is channeled to it. As for this faculty, it draws upon that [same] information stored in the perceptual recall faculty (*khayāl*), utilizing their composition and details to create mental images similar to that which may be perceived physically as well as that which defies reality, like a flying human or an emerald mountain. As for the perceptual recall faculty (*khayāl*), it is not capable of recalling other than that which it has [already] received through the senses.

This [imaginative] faculty is situated in the middle part of the brain.[58] And this faculty is a tool for the intuitive faculty, which, in reality, is [part of] the inner perceptual capabilities [found] within all animals. And it is this instinctual faculty within an animal that adjudges a wolf to be a threat,[59] a suckling to be precious, and the one committed to feeding [them] a trusted friend rather than someone to flee from.

58 According to modern cognitive neuroscience, the imaginative faculties of humans are situated within the neocortex and the thalamus. The thalamus relays sensory information that is then manipulated by the neocortex to form imagination. The neocortex is the largest part of the cerebral cortex, and it is essentially the sheet of neural tissue that makes up the outer surface of the brain. It comprises all four major lobes of the cortex given the involvement of multiple areas of the brain in the forming of imagination. The limbic system is also activated during the imagination processes given the important role of memory and emotions in relation to imagination.

59 In cognitive psychology, previous learning as well as biological survival instincts like emotions interact with the nature of the perception of stimuli. For example, if an individual has been previously exposed to a threatening person or animal, then such learned information stored within the cerebral cortex would serve to inform or modulate the interpretation of new stimuli observed later on, consequently adjudging it to be either threatening or affable. Similarly, if an individual were to see an animal snarling, they may interpret this animal as threatening even in cases wherein there was no previous learning, on account of predisposed biological survival instincts, according to evolutionary and emotion theory. At this particular juncture, Ibn Sīna is suggesting that the qualities attributed to the stimuli are on account of an inferential faculty contained within the brain. It would be supposed that such a faculty, simply labeled 'perception' in cognitive psychology, would be the result of an interplay between the actual physical sensory input and previously learned reactions and emotions that come together to formulate the ultimate interpretation of sensory inputs.

Now, both hostility and affinity are [physically] imperceptible; basic sensory perception cannot detect them. As such, it must be that they are perceived and governed by another faculty altogether. If such is not perceivable through deductive faculties, then we can [at least] say definitively that it is a type of acuity that is [intuitive,] not logically deductive. Although human beings may also employ this faculty in various [cognitive] judgements, this functionality [in particular] is carried out instinctively by all animals.

This faculty is separate from the perceptual recall faculty (*khayāl*), as the perceptual recall faculty interprets physical stimuli, whereas this [faculty] infers qualities that are beyond the physical representation [of the stimuli]. It is also different from what is termed the cogitative faculty (*mufakkira*) and imagination (*mutakhayyala*), as their functions do not correspond to any [of the] inferences [of the inferential faculty]. Their abstractions are formulated on account of sensory inputs, whereas this [faculty] adjudges sensory stimuli using information [sourced] beyond sensory input. Moreover, just as sensory perception interprets the forms of physical sensory inputs, this inferential [faculty] (*al-wahm*) abstracts [additional] meanings associated with these [physical] forms, leading to inference as opposed to [mere] sensation.

Now, there are some people who conflate this faculty, [simply] referring to it as imagination (*takhayyul*); and this is tolerable, as there [should be] no disputation regarding semantic differences so long as the meanings [of each] and their distinct differences are [clearly] understood.

This faculty [in and of itself] is not something that a physician would monitor or diagnose, because the harms [that may arise from its] functions [typically] coalesce with the detriments of other prominent faculties, like the perceptual recall faculty (*khayāl*), imagination (*takhayyul*), and memory (*dhikr*), which we shall discuss later. Normally, a physician only examines the faculties that cause sickness when they are dysfunctional. If the functionality of any given faculty is negatively affected by an infirmity in a more prominent faculty that then results in temperamental disequilibrium or the impaired function of any given organ, then it is sufficient to diagnose the issue as an imbalance of humors afflicting or impeding that particular organ. Based on that, one may prescribe a remedy or monitor it [accordingly]. As such, it is not necessary for a physician to know the condition of the faculty that has merely been affected by that which would [typically] affect it. Afterall, the perceptual recall faculty (*khayāl*) is merely a perceptive repository that uses a medium to process sensory input through the senses. Thus, without intervention, a physician would commonly know what afflicts the perceptual recall faculty (*khayāl*).

The third faculty that physicians mention – which, in actuality is the fourth or fifth – is the capacity to retain (*ḥāfiẓa*) and recall (*mudhakkira*) [information]. It is a repository for the ideas interpreted by the inferential faculty (*wahm*) – not merely mental images. It is located in the innermost, lower back portion of the brain.[60]

Here, personal discretion [is to be used] regarding the question of whether [or not] the faculty of retention (*ḥāfiẓa*) and memory recall (*mudhakkira*) for that which is stored in the inferential faculty (*wahm*) is one [singular] faculty, or two [separate] faculties. Again, [determining] this is not necessary for the physician to ascertain, [especially] if the unhealthy conditions that affect either faculty are the same as those stemming from the lower back portion of the brain. Such are either viewed as related to [one's] predisposition or [physical] composition.

As for the remaining faculty from amongst the [various] faculties of perception, such is [inherently] unique to human beings. Given that physicians have [largely] overlooked the inferential faculty (*wahm*) as per the reasons we have already explained, this [last] faculty is even further disregarded; their attention to it is restricted to the functionality of only three of the senses [in that category], and nothing more.

5 An Elucidation of the Malleability of Character Traits through Spiritual Exercises. *Iḥyā' 'Ulūm al-Dīn* by Imam Abu Hamid Al-Ghazali (d. 1111 AD)

5.1 *Author's Biography*

See Author Biography under section 1.

5.2 *Text Overview and Significance*

In this section, Imam al-Ghazālī asserts that character can indeed be developed and acquired contrary to some of the views of some contemporary philosophers of his day. He contends that a person's character is influenced by a combination of nature and nurture and that one's behavior is not biologically predetermined. While biological temperamental predispositions influence character development, good character is something that can be acquired through the management and moderation of one's biological drives. This

60 According to modern cognitive neuroscience, the faculty of short-term or working memory lies within the hippocampus, which is part of the limbic system of the brain underneath the cerebral cortex. Once short-term information is retained within the hippocampus, it becomes transferred and stored within various parts of the cerebral cortex if practiced or deliberated upon.

finding is quite remarkable given that psychologists have only in the 20th century concluded upon the role of both environment and biology in influencing human psychological processes and behaviors.

Furthermore, Al-Ghazālī outlines that good character is a byproduct of the moderation of one's primary drives of appetite (*shahwa*) and survival (*ghaḍab*). Thus, praiseworthy traits in Islam are those that are balanced and between the two polar extremes. For example, he says that generosity is praiseworthy because it is a trait that is between the extremes of extravagance and stinginess. He also draws attention to the important role of a shaykh or a mentor to help one achieve such moderation in one's drives, and that such a mentor should make sure to point out disdainful behaviors when a seeker displays any extremes in their character traits. Such discussions regarding the role may be meaningful for psychologists to consider their role in bringing about equilibrium in any given problematic character trait in their patients.

5.3 *Arabic Text*

بيان قبول الأخلاق للتغيير بطريق الرياضة

فرد الغضب والشهوة إلى حد الاعتدال، بحيث لا يقهر واحد منهما العقل ولا يغلبه، بل يكون العقل هو الضابط لهما والغالب عليهما ممكن، وهو المراد بتغيير الخُلُق؛ فإنه ربما تستولي الشهوة على الإنسان بحيث لا يقوى عقله على دفعها عن الانبساط إلى الفواحش، وبالرياضة تعود إلى حد الاعتدال، فدل أنّ ذلك ممكن، والتجربة والمشاهدة تدل على ذلك دلالة لا شك فيها.

والذي يدل على أن المطلوب هو الوسط في الأخلاق دون الطرفين أنّ السخاء خلق محمود شرعاً، وهو وسط بين طرفي التبذير والتقتير، وقد أثنى الله تعالى عليه فقال: "والذين إذا أنفقوا لم يسرفوا ولم يقتروا وكان بين ذلك قواما"، وقال تعالى: "ولا تجعل يدك مغلولة إلى عنقك ولا تبسطها كل البسط".

وكذلك المطلوب في شهوة الطعام الاعتدال دون الشره والخمود، قال الله تعالى: "وكلوا واشربوا ولا تسرفوا إنه لا يحب المسرفين".

وقال في الغضب: "أشداء على الكفار رحماء بينهم".

وقال صلى الله عليه وسلم: "خير الأمور أوساطها".

وهذا له سر وتحقيق، وهو أن السعادة منوطة بسلامة القلب عن عوارض هذا العالم، قال الله تعالى: "إلا من أتى الله بقلب سليم"، والبخل من عوارض الدنيا، والتبذير أيضاً من عوارض الدنيا، وشرط القلب أن يكون سليماً منهما؛ أي: لا يكون ملتفتاً إلى المال، ولا يكون حريصاً على إمساكه ولا على إنفاقه، فإن الحريص على الإنفاق مصروف القلب

إلى الإنفاق، كما أن الحريص على الإمساك مصروف القلب إلى الإمساك، فكان كمال القلب أن يصفو عن الوصفين جميعاً، وإذا لم يكن ذلك في الدنيا طلبنا ما هو الأشبه بعدم الوصفين وأبعد عن الطرفين، وهو الوسط، فإن الفاتر لا حار ولا بارد، بل هو وسط بينهما، فكأنه خال عن الوصفين؛ فكذلك السخاء بين التبذير والتقتير، والشجاعة بين الجبن والتهور، والعفة بين الشره والخمود، وكذلك سائر الأخلاق، فكلا طرفي قصد الأمور ذميم، هذا هو المطلوب، وهو ممكن.

نعم، يجب على الشيخ المرشد للمريد أن يقبح عنده الغضب رأسا، ويذم إمساك المال رأساً، ولا يرخص له في شيء منه؛ لأنه لو رخص له في أدنى شيء اتخذ ذلك عذراً في استبقاء بخله وغضبه، وظنّ أنه القدر المرخص فيه، فإذا قصد قطع الأصل وبالغ فيه لم يتيسر له إلا كسر سورته، بحيث يعود إلى الاعتدال، فالصواب له أن يقصد قلع الأصل حتى يتيسّر له القدر المقصود، فلا يكشف هذا السر للمريد؛ فإنه موضع غرور الحمقى، إذ يظنّ بنفسه أن غضبه بحق، وأنّ إمساكه بحق.

5.4 *English Translation*

An Elucidation of the Malleability of Character Traits Through Spiritual Exercises

It is possible to bring aggressive and appetitive drives to the point of moderation, such that neither one of them overpowers nor overcomes the mind, but rather the mind is the one that regulates and subdues them.[61,62] This is what is

61 Imam al-Ghazālī is answering the objections of those who assert that character cannot be developed and that human beings are ultimately driven by biological or predisposed drives. Though Imam al-Ghazālī acknowledges differences in the biological composition of individuals, he draws an important distinction between character development and inherent personality dispositions. He says for example in *Iḥyā' 'Ulūm al-Dīn* (Revival of the Religious Sciences), "the causes of being overcome by appetitive or aggressive drives may be on account of: (i) inherent dispositions or (ii) habituation and social modeling. Sometimes an individual may be born with a preparedness for [releasing] anger such that their face naturally appears angry". This demonstrates the sophisticated approach of al-Ghazālī in describing inherent dispositions toward some characteristics, while they are most certainly possible to bring within the path of moderation such that they do not become pathological nor pathways to immorality. While all individuals possess underlying aggressive and appetitive drives, the degree and specific inclinations vary from person to person based upon their inherent predispositions and personality compositions. In fact, Mulla Alī Qārī, a traditionist and *Ḥanafī* jurist cites the hadith, "If you hear of a mountain moving from its place, then certainly believe it, however, if you hear that a man has changed his character then do not believe it, for he will [behave] in correspondence to what he has been predisposed to do" in his commentary on the *Mishkāt al-Maṣābīḥ*, entitled *Mirqāt al-mafātīḥ*. Mulla Alī Qārī provides an explanation to this ḥadīth that

intended by "modification of character"; for perhaps a person might be overcome by his lower appetitive ambitions such that his mind cannot repel the urges to engage in immorality, but through [spiritual] exercises it returns to the point of moderation, proving that [modification of character] is indeed

---

seems to apparently contradict with other ahadith that instruct Muslims to perfect and develop their characters. However, he outlines that there is no real contradiction in that this hadith is simply demonstrating that changing one's character especially for those whose predisposed tendencies contravene prosocial traits can be difficult. He goes as far as to say that the inherent dispositions that an individual experiences can never be fully eradicated even if they have been able to train their actions to act in accordance with moral injunctions. For example, if an individual possesses miserliness on account of an inherent risk aversive personality disposition, then generously spending or donating to charities may always serve as a challenge for him. However, through training and self-discipline he most certainly can develop the characteristic of generosity even if he may continually feel some inner pain or anxiety upon giving. Psychologists too highlight that habituation through practiced goal directed behavior overtime, can generate an ability to ingrain these habituated actions such that they emerge automatically later without conscious deliberation or exertion (Nancy E. Snow, *Virtue as Social Intelligence: An Empirically Grounded Theory* (New York: Routledge, 2010), 14; 39–62; Helen Y. Weng et al., "Compassion Training Alters Altruism and Neural Responses to Suffering" 24, no. 7 (2013): 1171–80.).

Al-Ghazālī also maintains that social modeling plays an important role in explaining human behaviors in his saying, "to mingle with a [social] group that prides themselves of releasing their anger and obeying their aggressive impulses. They consider this to be bravery and masculinity." Thus, through a process of social modeling, individuals may adopt unhealthy aggression. This bears resemblance to the role of social modeling discussed by Albert Bandura (Albert Bandura, *Social learning theory* (Englewood Cliffs, NJ: Prentice Hall, (1977).).

62 In contrast, the nature versus nurture debate is still one of the most enduring in the field of psychology. While those who support nature in this debate attach all importance to heredity, those that favor nurture give all credit to the environment. Nativists take the position that all or most behaviors and characteristics are the results of inheritance, while humanistic psychologists tend to favor the environment or nurture (Abraham H. Maslow, "A Theory of Human Motivation," *Psychological Review* 50, no. 4 (1943): 370–96; Carl R. Rogers, *On Becoming a Person: A Therapist's View of Psychotherapy* (Boston: Houghton Mifflin, 1961).). Similarly, behaviorists believed that all behavior could be traced to environmental conditions as exemplified by the famous statement John Watson, "Give me a dozen healthy infants, well-formed, and my own specified world to bring them up in and I'll guarantee to take any one at random and train him to become any type of specialist I might select – doctor, lawyer, artist, merchant-chief and, yes, even beggar-man and thief, regardless of his talents, penchants, tendencies, abilities, vocations, and race of his ancestors" (John B. Watson, *Behaviorism* (London: Kegan Paul, Trench, Trubner & Co., Ltd., 1930), echoing his predecessor John Locke, who asserted that human beings are born as a blank slate (*tabula rasa*).

possible. Both observation and experience provide indisputable proof that [it is possible].[63]

The evidence that what is required is moderation in character, and not the two extremes, is that generosity is a praiseworthy trait according to religion, and generosity is the middle point between the two polar extremes of extravagance (*tabdhīr*) and miserliness (*taqtīr*). Allah the Exalted has praised this trait where He said: *They are those who are neither wasteful nor miserly when they spend but keep to a just balance* (al-Furqān 25:67), And He the Exalted said: *And do not keep your hand tied to your neck, nor spread it out fully* (al-Isrā' 17:29).

This is also what is required in [regard to] the craving for food: moderation without gluttony nor lethargy. Allah the Exalted said: *and eat and drink [as We have permitted] but do not be extravagant: God does not like extravagant people* (al-Aʿrāf 7:31).

And He said concerning anger: [*Those who follow the Prophet*] *are harsh towards the disbelievers and compassionate towards each other* (al-Fatḥ 48:29), and [The Prophet] may Allah bless him and grant him peace said: *The best of affairs are the ones done in moderation.*[64]

There is a truism and a subtle [reality] that [true] happiness is linked to the preservation of the heart from the defects of this world. Allah the Exalted said: *Only those who come before Allah with a pure heart ⸢will be saved* (al-Shuʿarā' 26:89). Stinginess is from the defects of the world. Extravagance is also from the defects of the world. The condition of [purification of] the heart is to be free from them, meaning one should not be attracted to money, neither too eager to collect it nor to spend it. For the heart of the one who fervently spends is inclined to spending limitlessly, just as the heart of the one who is adamant upon saving money is drawn toward withholding wealth. Therefore, the perfection of the heart is for it to be purified from both of these two [extreme] characteristics altogether. [However], since this state of complete purification is not achievable in the temporal world, then at the least we seek the closest

63 This is a clear demonstration of the holistic epistemological approach of Islamic scholars. Prior to even citing revelation to substantiate his claims, he used both rational and empirical evidence to prove his argument.

64 Ibn 'Abd al-Barr states in *istidhkār*, that this is from the statements of the philosopher physicians and not authentically transmitted from the Prophet, may Allah bless him and grant him peace (see Abū 'Umar Ibn 'Abd al-Barr, *al-Istidhkār*, vol. 2 (Beirut: Dār al-Kutub al-ʿIlmiyya, 2000), 524.). Hafidh al-ʿIrāqī stated in his investigation of the ahadith of Imam al-Ghazālī's *Revival of the Religious Sciences* that this hadith has been transmitted by Bayḥaqī in the chapter "branches of faith" wherein it is a narration of Maṭraf bin 'Abdullah that is consecutively missing two narrators within the chain (*muʿḍal*) (see Abū al-Faḍl 'Irāqī, *Al-Mughnī 'an Ḥaml al-Asfār* (Lubnān: Dār Ibn Ḥazm, 2005), 1064.).

thing to the absence of the two traits and the furthest thing from both extremes, which is the middle path. As an example, [something] lukewarm is neither hot nor cold, it is the middle in between; as if it is free of both characteristics [of the extremes]. So is generosity (*sakhā'*) between extravagance and miserliness, courage (*shajā'a*) between cowardliness and recklessness, and chastity (*'iffa*) between gluttony and lethargy, and so on with all character traits. Thus, both extremes are despised. This is the goal, and it is possible [to attain].

Indeed, a shaykh (spiritual guide) who guides a disciple must wholly declare the repugnance of anger and miserliness altogether. He should not permit even for the existence of any amount [irrespective of how small it is], because if he allows even the slightest amount, [the disciple] will use that as an excuse to maintain his stinginess and anger and will consider it to be the permitted amount to possess.[65] [As for] when [the disciple] intends to remove its roots and exaggerates in doing so, he [still] won't be able to [eradicate it completely] except to decrease its intensity such that it remits back [to the path] of moderation. Therefore, the correct thing to do is to intend to uproot it completely so that the intended amount is made accessible.

This is a secret that [the *shaykh*] should not reveal to his disciple; as it is where fools are deceived by themselves, thinking that their anger and stinginess are justified.

6 Types of Insanity (*Aqsām al-Junūn*). *Durar al-Ḥukkām Sharḥ Majallat al-Aḥkām* by Imam Ali Haydar Efendi (d. 1380 AH/1960 CE)

6.1 *Author's Biography*

Born on April 24, 1853, CE in Batumi, Imam 'Alī Haydar Efendī was born into a family with a strong sense of traditional scholarship. His father, Dardaganzāde Mehmed Amīn Efendī, was a teacher in Istanbul for many years and was part of the committee that drafted the first *Qānūn al-Asāsī*, or foundational law of the Ottoman Empire. His father likewise served as a judge (*qāḍī*) in Mecca, regent (*nāib*) of Izmir, and Anatolian judge of the army (*qāḍī 'askar*).

Imam 'Alī Haydar Efendī completed his primary education in Batumi. He then traveled to Istanbul and took lessons from Ḥāfiz Rashīd Efendī, the Imam

65 This principle is consistent with the concept of reciprocal inhibition whereby one attempts to replace an undesired response to a situation with a more desirable one through counterconditioning. Thus, the alternative response needs to be trained and conditioned until it becomes internalized and automated (Wolpe Joseph, *Psychotherapy by Reciprocal Inhibition* (California: Stanford University Press, 1958).).

of Hünkār, receiving scholarly authorizations (*ijāza*) from him. He graduated from the School of Judges (*Madrasa al-Quḍāt*) in 1877 CE, thereafter, serving as the judge (*qāḍī*) of Burdur, Uşak and Denizli. During this time, he also served as a lecturer at the Islamic law school and held various legal posts. He taught the *mejelle*, *aḥkām al-awqāf*, and *qawānīn* for twelve years at the School of Civil Service (*Mulkiya*), five years at the Madrasa al-Quḍāt (School of Judges), and thirty years at the school of law. He became a consultant (*amīn*) for religious edicts (*fatwā*) in 1914 CE. It was Imam Alī Haydar Efendī who announced the religious edict for the Muslims to enter the first World War known as the *al-jihād al-akbar*, pronounced on November 14, 1914, CE, at the Fātiḥ Mosque. In 1916, he was appointed Rumeli judge of the army (*qāḍī ʿaskar*) and retired within the same year. Between November 11, 1918, and January 21, 1919, he briefly served as the minister of justice under the second leadership of Tevfik Pasha. After leaving this job, he busied himself with writing books at home until his death on September 14, 1935, CE. He was married twice and had four sons and three daughters. Two of his sons became jurists like him, including Ahmet Esat Arsebük, who became a faculty member at the Ankara Law School.

In addition to *Durar al-Ḥukkām fī sharḥ Majallat al-Aḥkām*, he wrote *Mirqāt al-Majalla*, *Sharḥ al-Jadīd li-qānūn al-ʿarāḍī*, *Tertīb al-Ṣunūf fī aḥkām al-wuqūf*, *Tawḍīḥ al-mushkilāt fī aḥkām al-īntiqālāt* and *Tashīl al-farāiḍ*.

6.2 *Text Overview and Significance*

This text delves into the types of insanity that are legally recognized within the framework of Islamic law. Furthermore, it illustrates the comprehensive nature of Islamic law, which has built-in mechanisms for considering the mental status of legal subjects in the adjudication of their legal cases. In modern practice, this intersection of Islamic law and psychology is referred to as forensic psychology. The translated text below, penned by Imam ʿAli Haydar Efendī, is part of a commentary of the famous Ottoman *Mejelle*, which is the codification and standardization of Ḥanafī-based Islamic law for application by the Ottoman courts. Accordingly, within the Ottoman legal system, those who fit into the various categories of legal insanity on account of mental illness would be given different disability accommodations and would not be held liable for their actions.

As per the text, Islamic law broadly categorizes the insane person into two types: the one whose insanity manifests at all times, and the one whose insanity is intermittent. Both of these broad categories have other more specific subcategories. In the work, Imam ʿAli Haydar Efendī also discusses the cases of those who do not meet the threshold of legal insanity but whose reasoning may still be deficient, resulting in disorders like impulsive spending. He also outlines the legal implications for such individuals who possess compromised mental faculties. In the bigger picture, this text serves as a primer for forensic psychology in Islamic law. It introduces readers to the legal issues that can be implicated due to mental illness and may pique the interest of those who may attempt to explore the further utility of such categories of insanity in Islamic law to contemporary clinical disorders.

6.3 *Arabic Text*

[(مَادَّةُ 944) الْمَجْنُونُ عَلَى قِسْمَيْنِ]

أَحَدُهُمَا: الْمَجْنُونُ الْمُطْبِقُ وَهُوَ الَّذِي يَسْتَوْعِبُ جُنُونُهُ جَمِيعَ أَوْقَاتِهِ، وَالثَّانِي: الْمَجْنُونُ غَيْرُ الْمُطْبِقِ وَهُوَ الَّذِي يَكُونُ فِي بَعْضِ الْأَوْقَاتِ مَجْنُونًا وَيُفِيقُ فِي بَعْضِهَا.

الْمَجْنُونُ قِسْمَانِ وَلِكُلٍّ تَعْرِيفٌ فِيمَا يَأْتِي وَلَيْسَ كَمَا يَقُولُ صَاحِبُ الدُّرَرِ فِي بَحْثِ سَجْدَةِ التِّلَاوَةِ: إنَّ الْمَجْنُونَ ثَلَاثَةُ أَقْسَامٍ: وَالْقِسْمَانِ الْمَذْكُورَانِ فِي التَّقْسِيمِ الْمُعْتَمَدِ آنِفًا هُمَا:

الْقِسْمُ الْأَوَّلُ: الْمَجْنُونُ الْمُطْبِقُ وَهُوَ الَّذِي يَسْتَوْعِبُ جُنُونُهُ جَمِيعَ أَوْقَاتِهِ.

وَالْجُنُونُ هُوَ زَوَالُ الْعَقْلِ وَاخْتِلَالُهُ وَيَمْنَعُ الْأَفْعَالَ وَالْأَقْوَالَ أَنْ تَجْرِيَ عَلَى نَهْجٍ مُسْتَقِيمٍ. (الْمَجَامِعُ) وَيَنْشَأُ الْجُنُونُ إمَّا عَنْ نَقْصٍ فِطْرِيٍّ فِي الْعَقْلِ أَوْ رَدَاءَةِ مِزَاجِ الدِّمَاغِ وَاسْتِيلَاءِ التَّخَيُّلِ الْفَاسِدِ (فُصُولُ الْبَدَائِعِ) وَلَا يُقْصَدُ فِي الْجُنُونِ هُنَا أَنْ يَكُونَ الْمَجْنُونُ مَجْنُونًا فِي جَمِيعِ الْأَوْقَاتِ كُلَّ عُمْرِهِ أَوْ فِي جَمِيعِ أَوْقَاتِهِ بَعْدَ طُرُوءِ الْجُنُونِ؛ لِأَنَّ الْمَجْنُونَ الْمُطْبِقَ إنَّمَا يَتَحَقَّقُ كَوْنُ جُنُونِهِ مُطْبِقًا بَعْدَ وَفَاتِهِ وَلَا يُقْطَعُ قَبْلَ الْمَوْتِ بِكَوْنِ جُنُونِهِ مُطْبِقًا أَوْ غَيْرَ مُطْبِقٍ.

وَعَلَيْهِ فَمَنْ يَقْضِي أَيَّامَ حَيَاتِهِ مَجْنُونًا لَا تَعْتَرِيهِ إفَاقَةٌ أَصْلًا وَيَأْتِيهِ الْمَوْتُ وَهُوَ عَلَى هَذِهِ الصُّورَةِ يُعَدُّ مَجْنُونًا مُطْبِقًا كَمَا أَنَّهُ يُعَدُّ مَجْنُونًا مُطْبِقًا بِالِاتِّفَاقِ مَنْ يَقْضِي سَنَةً وَهُوَ مَجْنُونٌ كَمَا سَيَأْتِي إيضَاحُهُ وَعَلَيْهِ فَلَوْ أُرِيدَ بِجَمِيعِ الْأَوْقَاتِ الْمَعْنَى الْمَذْكُورُ فَلَا يَكُونُ جَامِعًا لِأَفْرَادِهِ وَلِذَلِكَ فَلَفْظُ (جَمِيعِ أَوْقَاتِهِ) بِمَعْنَى جَمِيعِ أَوْقَاتِهِ فِي سَنَةٍ كَامِلَةٍ أَوْ شَهْرٍ كَامِلٍ وَبِذَلِكَ تَكُونُ خُلَاصَةُ التَّعْرِيفِ كَمَا يَأْتِي: الْمَجْنُونُ الْمُطْبِقُ عَلَى قَوْلٍ هُوَ مَنْ يَسْتَوْعِبُ جُنُونُهُ جَمِيعَ أَوْقَاتِهِ فِي سَنَةٍ وَعَلَى قَوْلٍ آخَرَ جَمِيعَ أَوْقَاتِهِ فِي شَهْرٍ.

وَالْآنَ فَلْنُدَقِّقْ الْوَقْتَ الَّذِي يَلْزَمُ لِيُعَدَّ الْجُنُونُ فِيهِ جُنُونًا مُطْبِقًا.

وَيَكُونُ لَفْظُ الْمُطْبِقِ إذَا جَاءَ صِفَةً لِلْجُنُونِ بِكَسْرِ الْبَاءِ وَإِذَا جَاءَ صِفَةً لِلْمَجْنُونِ يَكُونُ بِفَتْحِهَا.

فِي الْجُنُونِ الْمُطْبِقِ أَرْبَعَةُ أَقْوَالٍ:

الْقَوْلُ الْأَوَّلُ: الْجُنُونُ الْمُطْبِقُ هُوَ الَّذِي يَمْتَدُّ إلَى سَنَةٍ كَامِلَةٍ؛ لِأَنَّ الْمَجْنُونَ إذَا تَقَلَّبَتْ عَلَيْهِ الْفُصُولُ الْأَرْبَعَةُ وَلَمْ يُفِقْ مِنْ جُنُونِهِ عُلِمَ أَنَّ جُنُونَهُ مُسْتَحْكِمٌ، وَالْفَتْوَى فِي حَقِّ

التَّصَرُّفَاتِ عَلَى تَقْدِيرِ الْجُنُونِ لِمُدَّةِ سَنَةٍ (حَاشِيَةُ الْأَشْبَاهِ لِلْغَزِّيِّ) وَقِيلَ (حَقُّ التَّصَرُّفَاتِ)؛ لِأَنَّ مُدَّةَ الْجُنُونِ فِي حَقِّ الْعِبَادَاتِ قَدْ حُدِّدَتْ بِصُورَةٍ أُخْرَى وَتُوجَدُ التَّفْصِيلَاتُ فِيهَا فِي أُصُولِ الْفِقْهِ.

الْقَوْلُ الثَّانِي، الْجُنُونُ الْمُطْبِقُ لِمُدَّةِ شَهْرٍ أَيْ: الْجُنُونُ الَّذِي يَمْتَدُّ شَهْرًا كَامِلًا وَقَدْ رُجِّحَ هَذَا الْقَوْلُ بِقَوْلِ (وَبِهِ يُفْتَى) وَأَشْعَرَ قَوْلُ الْخَانِيَّةِ (وَعَلَيْهِ الْفَتْوَى) رُجْحَانَ هَذَا الْقَوْلِ أَيْضًا (رَدُّ الْمُحْتَارِ).

الْقَوْلُ الثَّالِثُ: هُوَ كَالْجُنُونِ الَّذِي يَمْتَدُّ أَكْثَرَ مِنْ سَنَةٍ.

الْقَوْلُ الرَّابِعُ: هُوَ الْجُنُونُ الَّذِي يَسْتَوْعِبُ أَكْثَرَ مِنْ يَوْمٍ وَلَيْلَةٍ.

إِلَّا أَنَّ هَذَا الْقَوْلَ الرَّابِعَ يُخَالِفُ ظَاهِرَ الرِّوَايَةِ كَمَا جَاءَ فِي الْخَانِيَّةِ وَيُقَالُ لِلْمَجْنُونِ الْمُطْبِقِ الْمَجْنُونُ الْمَغْلُوبُ أَيْضًا.

وَقَدْ ذُكِرَ حُكْمُ الْجُنُونِ الْمُطْبِقِ فِي الْمَادَّةِ (979).

الْقِسْمُ الثَّانِي هُوَ الْمَجْنُونُ غَيْرُ الْمُطْبِقِ وَهُوَ الَّذِي يَكُونُ فِي بَعْضِ الْأَوْقَاتِ مَجْنُونًا وَيُفِيقُ فِي بَعْضِهَا كَالْمَصْرُوعِ (التَّنْقِيحُ، وَالْهِنْدِيَّةُ فِي الْحَجْرِ).

وَيَصْدُقُ تَعْرِيفُ الْمَجْنُونِ غَيْرِ الْمُطْبِقِ هَذَا عَلَى الْمَجْنُونِ الْمُطْبِقِ أَيْضًا؛ لِأَنَّهُ إِذَا بَقِيَ أَحَدٌ مَجْنُونًا سَنَةً كَامِلَةً أَوْ شَهْرًا كَامِلًا ثُمَّ بَعْدَ أَنْ رَجَعَ إِلَى عَقْلِهِ عَادَ فَجُنَّ أَيْضًا مُدَّةَ سَنَةٍ كَامِلَةٍ أَوْ شَهْرٍ كَامِلٍ فَيُعَدُّ مَنْ كَانَ حَالُهُ كَذَلِكَ مَجْنُونًا غَيْرَ مُطْبِقٍ أَيْضًا.

وَعَلَيْهِ فَيَكُونُ الْمَجْنُونُ غَيْرَ الْمُطْبِقِ هُوَ الَّذِي يَكُونُ مَجْنُونًا أَقَلَّ مِنْ سَنَةٍ عَلَى قَوْلٍ أَوْ أَقَلَّ مِنْ شَهْرٍ عَلَى قَوْلٍ آخَرَ.

وَقَدْ ذُكِرَ فِي أُصُولِ الْفِقْهِ أَنَّ بَعْضَ الْأَحْكَامِ الشَّرْعِيَّةِ تَخْتَلِفُ بِاخْتِلَافِ مُدَّةِ الْجُنُونِ وَقَدْ يَتَّحِدُ الْمَجْنُونُ الْمُطْبِقُ وَغَيْرُ الْمُطْبِقِ فِي بَعْضِ الْأَحْكَامِ وَذَلِكَ كَتَصَرُّفَاتِ الْمَجْنُونِ الْمُطْبِقِ وَالْمَجْنُونِ غَيْرِ الْمُطْبِقِ الْقَوْلِيَّةِ فِي حَالِ جُنُونِهِمَا يَعْنِي: مَثَلًا بَيْعُهُمَا وَشِرَاؤُهُمَا وَإِيجَادُهُمَا وَاسْتِئْجَارُهُمْ وَصَيْرُورَتُهُمَا مَحَالًا لَهُمَا أَوْ عَلَيْهِمَا أَوْ كَفَالَتُهُمَا أَوْ رَهْنُهُمَا وَارْتِهَانُهُمَا وَإِيدَاعُهُمَا وَاسْتِيدَاعُهُمَا وَهِبَتُهُمَا وَاتِّهَابُهُمَا فَهَذِهِ التَّصَرُّفَاتُ كُلُّهَا بَاطِلَةٌ.

وَقَدْ مَرَّتْ التَّفْصِيلَاتُ الْمُتَعَلِّقَةُ بِهَذَا فِي شَرْحِ الْمَوَادِّ الْمَخْصُوصَة وَإِذَا أَفَاقَ الْمَجْنُون الْمُطْبَق وَالْمَجْنُون غَيْر الْمُطْبَق وَعَادَ إِلَيْهِمَا الْعَقْل تَامًّا تَصِحّ تَصَرُّفَاتهمَا الْقَوْلِيَّة الْمَذْكُورَة وَتَجُوز.

وَيَخْتَلِف الْمَجْنُون الْمُطْبَق وَغَيْر الْمُطْبَق فِي بَعْض الْأَحْكَام وَذَلِكَ أَوَّلًا إِذَا جن الْوَكِيل أَوْ الْمُوَكَّل جُنُونًا مُطْبَقًا تَبْطُلُ الْوَكَالَة وَعَلَيْهِ فَلَا يَبْقَى حُكْم لِلْوَكَالَةِ وَلَوْ أَفَاقَ بَعْد ذَلِكَ يَلْزَم تَجْدِيدهَا أُنْظُرْ الْمَادَّة (1530) وَإِذَا جن جُنُونًا غَير مُطْبَق لَا تَبْطُلُ الْوَكَالَة فَلِلْوَكِيلِ أَنْ يُوفِي الْوَكَالَة إِلَى أَنْ يُجَنَّ الْمُوَكَّل جُنُونًا مُطْبَقًا كَمَا أَنَّ لَهُ الْقِيَام بِهَا لَوْ جن هُوَ نَفْسه جُنُونًا غَير مُطْبَق بِدُونِ حَاجَة إِلَى تَجْدِيدهَا؛ لِأَنَّ الْجُنُون غَيْر الْمُطْبَق هُوَ بِمَثَابَةِ إِغْمَاء فَكَمَا أَنَّ الْوَكَالَة لَا تَبْطُلُ بِالْإِغْمَاءِ فَلَا تَبْطُلُ بِالْجُنُونِ الْقَلِيل.

ثَانِيًا: وَإِذَا جن أَحَد الشُّرَكَاء جُنُونًا مُطْبَقًا تَنْفَسِخ الشَّرِكَة كَمَا هُوَ مُبِين فِي الْمَادَّة (1352) بِخِلَافِ مَا لَوْ جن جُنُونًا غَيْر مُطْبَق فَلَا تَنْفَسِخُ.

وَفِي هَذِهِ الْحَالَة إِذَا جن أَحَد الشُّرَكَاء تَبْقَى الشَّرِكَة إِلَى أَنْ يُصْبِح الْجُنُون مُطْبَقًا وَمَتَى تَمَّ الْإِطْبَاق تَنْفَسِخ الشَّرِكَة فِي الْحَال (الْوَاقِعَات) وَقَدْ تَوَضَّحَ ذَلِكَ فِي شَرْح الْمَادَّة (1652) .

ثَالِثًا، تَنْفَسِخ الْمُضَارَبَة كَمَا هُوَ مُبِين فِي الْمَادَّة (1429) إِذَا جن رَبّ الْمَال أَوْ الْمُضَارِب جُنُونًا مُطْبَقًا أَمَّا إِذَا كَانَ جُنُونهمَا غَيْر مُطْبَق فَلَا تَنْفَسِخ.

رَابِعًا: إِذَا جن الْمَأْذُون جُنُونًا مُطْبِقًا أصبح مَحْجُورًا.

أَمَّا إِذَا جن جُنُونًا غَيْر مُطْبَق فَلَا (الْهِنْدِيَّة فِي الْبَاب الْخَامِس) .

وَسَيَأْتِي فِي الْمَادَّة (980) بَيَان حُكْم الْجُنُون غَيْر الْمُطْبَق.

[(مَادَّةُ 945) الْمَعْتُوهُ هُوَ الَّذِي اخْتَلَّ شُعُورُهُ]

(مَادَّةُ 945) الْمَعْتُوهُ هُوَ الَّذِي اخْتَلَّ شُعُورُهُ بِأَنْ كَانَ فَهْمُهُ قَلِيلًا وَكَلَامُهُ مُخْتَلِطًا وَتَدْبِيرُهُ فَاسِدًا.

الْمَعْتُوهُ لُغَةً نَاقِصُ الْعَقْلِ وَشَرْعًا هُوَ الَّذِي اخْتَلَّ شُعُورُهُ بِأَنْ كَانَ قَلِيلَ الْفَهْمِ مُخْتَلِطَ الْكَلَامِ فَاسِدَ التَّدْبِيرِ. وَلَكِنَّهُ لَا يَشْتُمُ وَلَا يَضْرِبُ كَالْمَجْنُونِ. بَلْ يَكُونُ كَلَامُهُ مُخْتَلِطًا فَبَعْضُهُ يُشْبِهُ كَلَامَ الْعُقَلَاءِ وَبَعْضُهُ يُشْبِهُ أَلْفَاظَ الْمَجَانِينِ.

وَإِنْ وَقَعَ اخْتِلَافٌ فِي تَفْسِيرِ الْمَعْتُوهِ فَالْمُخْتَارُ هَذَا التَّعْرِيفُ (رَدُّ الْمُحْتَارِ، التَّنْقِيحُ) وَعَلَيْهِ فَالْعَاقِلُ هُوَ الَّذِي تَكُونُ أَقْوَالُهُ وَأَفْعَالُهُ مُسْتَقِيمَةً (الْبَهْجَةُ)

[(مَادَّةُ 946) السَّفِيهُ هُوَ الَّذِي يَصْرِفُ مَالَهُ فِي غَيْرِ مَوْضِعِهِ]

(مَادَّةُ 946) السَّفِيهُ هُوَ الَّذِي يَصْرِفُ مَالَهُ فِي غَيْرِ مَوْضِعِهِ وَيُبَذِّرُ فِي مَصْرُوفَاتِهِ وَيُضِيعُ أَمْوَالَهُ وَيُتْلِفُهَا بِالْإِسْرَافِ وَالَّذِينَ لَا يَزَالُونَ يَغْفُلُونَ فِي أَخْذِهِمْ وَإِعْطَائِهِمْ وَلَمْ يَعْرِفُوا طَرِيقَ تِجَارَتِهِمْ وَتَمَتُّعِهِمْ بِحَسَبِ بَلَاهَتِهِمْ وَخُلُوِّ قُلُوبِهِمْ يُعَدُّونَ أَيْضًا مِنْ السُّفَهَاءِ. السَّفِيهُ مَأْخُوذٌ مِنْ السَّفَهِ، وَالسَّفَهُ لُغَةً خِفَّةُ الْعَقْلِ، وَالسَّفِيهُ هُوَ مَنْ كَانَ فِي عَقْلِهِ خِفَّةً، أَمَّا شَرْعًا فَهُوَ الَّذِي يَصْرِفُ مَالَهُ فِي غَيْرِ مَوْضِعِهِ يَعْنِي خِلَافًا لِمَا يَقْتَضِيهِ الشَّرْعُ وَالْعَقْلُ وَيُبَذِّرُ فِي مَصْرُوفَاتِهِ وَيُضِيعُ أَمْوَالَهُ وَيُتْلِفُهَا بِالْإِسْرَافِ.

وَالْفَرْقُ بَيْنَ الْإِسْرَافِ وَالتَّبْذِيرِ هُوَ أَنَّ التَّبْذِيرَ صَرْفُ الشَّيْءِ فِي غَيْرِ مَحَلِّهِ اللَّائِقِ أَمَّا الْإِسْرَافُ فَهُوَ صرفُ الشَّيْءِ فِي مَحَلِّهِ اللَّائِقِ زِيَادَةً عَنْ اللَّازِمِ (رَدُّ الْمُحْتَارِ فِي الْفَرَائِضِ) فَعَلَى ذَلِكَ التَّبْذِيرُ هُوَ تَجَاوُزُ مَوْضِعِ الْحَقِّ وَجَهْلٌ بِمَوَاضِعِ وَمَوَاقِعِ الْحُقُوقِ أَمَّا الْإِسْرَافُ فَهُوَ تَجَاوُزٌ فِي الْكَمِّيَّةِ وَجَهْلٌ فِي مَقَادِيرِ الْحُقُوقِ.

6.4 *English Translation*

Types of Insanity[66]

There are two types of insane[67] persons (*majnūn*):

i. Non-remittent (*majnūn muṭbaq*): A person whose insanity manifests at all times.

---

66 Forensic psychology is the discipline of psychology that explores the intersection between legal insanity and mental status. The American Board of Forensic Psychology defines it as, "the application of the science and profession of law to questions and issues relating to psychology and the legal system." Islamic law, despite its comparatively distant origins, has long established that the legal status of an individual with regards to rights and responsibilities may change on account of their mental condition. This is exemplified by the tradition of the Prophet, may Allah bless him and grant him peace, "The pen has been lifted from three: (i) the insane one until he recovers ..." (cf. Abū Dāwūd al-Sijistānī, *Sunan Abī Dāwūd* (Lebanon: Dār al-Risāla al-ʿĀlamiyya, 2009), 4398). Thus, the determination of whether or not some clinical syndromes impact the legal obligations or rights of Muslims is instrumental to their societal, communal, familial, and personal lives. While forensic psychology, within a secular context, typically only covers criminal and civil issues, the scope of forensic psychology in an Islamic context is much wider. This is because even the personal religious obligations of Muslims may be impacted by their mental status, including issues of whether individuals are liable for performing their prayers, fasting, etc. For example, those with severe expressions of Obsessive Compulsive Disorders (OCD) may not be held liable even if the patient did not wash a particular limb properly, made a pronouncement of divorce incidentally (that typically nullifies his marriage), or missed an aspect of prayer, as they may be exempted on account of severe clinical dysfunction (Hooman Keshavarzi et al., eds., *Applying Islamic Principles to Clinical Mental Health Care: Introducing Traditional Islamically Integrated Psychotherapy*, 1st ed. (Routledge, 2020).). Thus, this section translated above provides a good overview of the major legal categories of insanity that have various implications on the rights and responsibilities of Muslims.

67 It is crucial to note that a prerequisite for accountability in Islamic law is mental competence (*ahliyya*). One who does not properly possess such, as indicated by, (i) conception (*idrāk*), (ii) willful intent (*irāda*), (iii) volition (*ikhtiyār*), (iv) appreciation of the consequences of one's actions, (v) presence of mind (*aql*) or awareness of one's actions, is effectively not liable (*ghayr mukallaf*) under Islamic law (Hooman Keshavarzi and Bilal Ali, "Forensic Psychology in Islamic Jurisprudence," in *Oxford Encyclopedia of Islamic Bioethics*, 2016.).

It is also important to note that insanity is not a clinical term, but a legal one. The central interest of the courts and the legal system is to determine responsibilities, rights, and liabilities, whereas clinical categories are created in order to differentiate the type of mental dysfunction one is afflicted with in the interest of treatment and recovery. This is why there are a plethora of clinical categories, whereas in legal settings there are comparably only a few; such are primarily concerned with the question of whether or not an individual was of sound mind when engaging in a particular legal or illegal behavior irrespective of what that may be referred to as in clinical settings. In sum, it is to cast a judgement on someone, not to determine the course of treatment.

ii. Intermittent (*majnūn ghayr muṭbaq*): One who is insane at times, and sensible at other times.

The insane person is of two types, and each has a definition [that will be elucidated] in what is to follow. It is not what the author of *al-Durar* asserts in his discussion on the prostration of recital (*sajdat al-tilāwa*).[68] [He purports] the one afflicted with insanity (*majnūn*) is of three types. The two types mentioned in the aforementioned categorization are [as follows]:

The first type, *majnūn muṭbaq*, is one whose insanity manifests at all times. Insanity (*junūn*) refers to the loss and disturbance of one's mind; such inhibits one's actions and speech from their proper manner of functioning (*al-Majāmiʿ*).[69]

Insanity can stem from a pre-disposed deficiency of the intellect, or a deterioration of the temperateness of the brain coupled with overwhelming delusions[70] (*Fuṣūl al-Badāʾiʿ*).[71]

Here, "insanity" is not intended to imply that the afflicted person has been perpetually insane throughout his entire life, nor that he is permanently insane [and has been] from the onset of his intermittent insanity. This is because the insanity of one who is *majnūn muṭbaq* can only be verified as such after his death; before death it is not possible to determine with certainty whether his insanity is [categorized as] non-intermittent (*muṭbiq*) or intermittent (*ghayr muṭbiq*). Thus, [if] someone is afflicted with insanity throughout his entire life without regaining his sensibility at all, then in this scenario, it is [only] when death approaches that they would they be adjudged *majnūn muṭbaq*. Similarly, one who is afflicted with insanity for [only] a year, is also considered *majnūn muṭbaq* by consensus; further clarification regarding this is forthcoming.

On this basis, if "at all times" denoted the aforementioned, meaning [the duration of one's life,] it would not be inclusive of all of its instances.[72]

---

68 This is in reference to Muhammad ibn Farāmarz's (d. 886/1454) renowned work *Durar al-Hukkām Sharḥ Gharaz al-Aḥkām*.

69 The author is referencing Muhammad al-Khadimi's (d. 1176/1763) *Majāmiʿ al-Ḥaqāʾiq*, which is an authoritative work in the principles of jurisprudence according to the Ḥanafī school of Islamic law.

70 This may also simply include impaired reality testing, such as when one falsely perceives or interprets reality.

71 The author is referencing Mullā Shams al-Dīn al-Fenārī's (d. 863/1431) work on Ḥanafī legal theory, *Fuṣūl al-Badāʾiʿ fī Uṣūl al-Sharāʾiʿ*. Mullā al-Fenārī was one of the most renowned early representatives of the Ottoman scholarly legacy.

72 Here, the author is providing an explanation of what is intended by the earlier statement, "a *majnūn muṭbaq* is one whose insanity remains at all times." Since continuity cannot encompass an entire lifetime, as this would be exceedingly difficult to apply, and just saying "remains all the time" does not provide a specific time frame, the author is clarifying

Accordingly, the expression “at all times” [is taken to] mean at all times within a complete year or a complete month. By this [consideration], the summary definition of *majnūn muṭbaq* would be, “one whose insanity encompasses all moments for the duration of a [n entire] year.” Or, according to another opinion, “... for the duration of a [whole] month.”

We shall now examine the time period for insanity to be considered *muṭbiq*.

[It shall also be pointed out that] the word *muṭbaq* is used to describe the insane person, while *muṭbiq* is used to refer to [non-remittent] insanity itself.

There are four views regarding non-remittent insanity (*junūn muṭbiq*):

i. Non-remittent insanity is that which extends for an entire year. This is due to [the fact that] when a cycle of the four seasons passes without one having regained his sensibility, it is [clearly] known that his insanity is acute. The legal opinion (*fatwā*) in respect to the right of engaging in contracts (*ḥaqq al-taṣarrufāt*) is in accordance with the consideration of a measure of one year's duration of insanity.[73]

As for responsibilities related to worship (*ḥaqq al-ʿibādāt*), the duration of insanity is defined differently; the particulars of which are discussed within the realm of legal theory (*uṣūl al-fiqh*).

ii. Non-remittent insanity is for the duration of a month, meaning insanity that lasts an entire month. This position has been preferred as per the wording “and it is given as a verdict (*fatwā*)”. The statement of *al-Khāniyya*,[74] “and upon it is the legal ruling,” also indicates its preference (*Radd al-Muḥtār*).[75]

iii. It is when the insanity extends beyond a year.

iv. It is when [one's] insanity encompasses more than [a combined period of] one day and one night. However, this view contradicts the clearly transmitted opinions (*ẓāhir al-riwāya*),[76] as is stated in *al-Khāniyya*.

---

the potential legal thresholds required to qualify for this category as outlined by the authoritative legal manuals.

73 Meaning, if the insanity has extended beyond one year, then the individual can no longer independently initiate or fulfill legally binding contracts. If they were to do so, such would be considered null and void.

74 This is in reference to *Fatāwā Khāniyya*, which is a collection of the legal edicts of the renowned Ḥanafī jurist Fakhr al-Dīn Ḥasan al-Farghānī, more famously known as Qāḍī Khān (d. 592/1160).

75 *Radd al-Muḥtār* is one of the most commonly cited jurisprudential works of the Ḥanafī school, cataloguing the collection of responses to practical legal issues. It is authored by the Syrian scholar Muḥammad Amīn ibn ʿĀbidīn (d. 1268/1836).

76 Also called the *Uṣūl* or *Masāa'il al-Uṣūl*, this collection of the rulings of the Ḥanafī school is contained in five books of Imam Muḥammad ibn al-Ḥasan al-Shaybānī. Ibn ʿĀbidīn lists them as:

The one afflicted with non-remittent insanity (*majnūn muṭbaq*) is also referred to as one who is overwhelmed [by his insanity] (*majnūn maghlūb*). The ruling of non-remittant insanity (*junūn muṭbiq*) has been mentioned under article 979.

The second type, *majnūn ghayr muṭbaq*, refers to a person who is insane at times, yet regains his senses at other times, much like an epileptic.[77] Furthermore, it is conceivable to describe the one afflicted with non-remittent insanity (*majnūn muṭbaq*) as also being afflicted with intermittent insanity (*majnūn ghayr muṭbaq*). This would be so if a person is insane for an entire year, or an entire month, and thereafter regains his sensibility only to relapse back to being insane for [another] year or month; a person in such a state would also be classified as being afflicted with intermittent insanity (*majnūn ghayr muṭbaq*).[78]

In light of this [potential contradiction], one afflicted with intermittent insanity (*majnūn ghayr muṭbaq*) [should be defined as] a person who is insane

1. *al-Jāmiʿ al-Kabīr.*
2. *al-Jāmiʿ al-Saghīr.*
3. *al-Siyar al-Kabīr.*
4. *al-Siyar al-Ṣaghīr.*
5. *al-Mabsūṭ* (also called *al-Aṣl*).
6. *al-Ziyādāt.*

Some Ḥanafī scholars did not include the two *Siyar* collections listed above amongst the books classed as *ẓāhir al-riwāya*, meaning that which is narrated from Imam Muḥammad through numerous reliable narrators and clearly established mass-transmitted or well-known chains. The *ẓāhir al-riwāya* primarily serve as a compendium of the legal opinions of the three preeminent *imams* of the Ḥanafī school (*aṣḥāb al-madhhab*), namely Abū Ḥanīfa, Abū Yūsuf, and Muhammad. However, the books do not limit themselves to the rulings of these three; they include the legal opinions of other eminent scholars both within the framework of the Ḥanafī school, and beyond it as well.

77 This may include manic episodes of bipolar, temporary psychotic episodes, or features associated with other similar mental health conditions.

78 Given that non-remittent insanity is assumed to be lifelong, and it is difficult to definitively predict whether an individual will be insane for their entire lifetime, scholars have outlined specific thresholds of time that once met, allow for such an individual to be categorized as being afflicted with non-remittent insanity. This is in the interest of having clearly defined categories based on objective evaluations of time. However, if such an individual recovers from the seemingly "permanent" non-remittent insanity, they will find themselves in two categories at the same time; being ruled previously to be in the category of non-remittent insanity and then later impermanent or intermittent insanity on account of their unexpected recovery. All in all, the author is merely pointing out some of the potential problems of leaving intermittent insanity (*junūn ghayr muṭbiq*) undefined without a time frame.

for a period spanning less than a year, according to one opinion. Or, less than a month, according to another [view].[79]

It is mentioned in legal theory (*uṣūl al-fiqh*) that some legal rulings (*aḥkām shar'iyya*) differ depending on the duration of insanity. However, the one afflicted with non-remittent insanity (*majnūn muṭbaq*) as well as the one with intermittent insanity (*ghayr muṭbaq*) may sometimes be undifferentiated in certain rulings, like the verbal transactions of both, whilst they are in a state of insanity. Such, for example, includes their buying, selling, and disposing of assets; their acquisition and renting; their guaranteeing, giving, or receiving collateral; their entrusting and deposits; their gift-giving and receiving; all such transactions are invalid [for both of them]. A detailed explanation of this subject has preceded under its specific articles. Notably, when either the one with non-remittent insanity (*majnūn muṭbaq*) or the one facing intermittent insanity (*ghayr muṭbaq*) regains lucidity, and their reason has been completely restored, then engaging in the aforementioned verbal transactions are deemed valid and permissible.

In various other rulings, however, the *majnūn muṭbaq* and the *ghayr muṭbaq* are distinctly different. These are [as follows]:

Firstly, if the agent (*wakīl*) or the commissioner (*muwakkal*) is afflicted with non-remittent insanity (*junūn muṭbiq*), his agency (*wakāla*) becomes invalid, and the ruling of agency no longer remains. If he regains his lucidity thereafter, there must be a renewal [of the contract]. Refer to article 1530.

However, if he is afflicted with insanity [that is] intermittent (*ghayr muṭbiq*), his agency (*wakāla*) is not voided. [In such a case,] the agent (*wakīl*) shall continue to fulfill his role up until the insanity of the commissioner (*muwakkal*) is deemed to be non-remittent (*muṭbiq*), just as he, [the agent,] is allowed to fulfill his agency if he himself were to be afflicted with intermittent insanity (*ghayr muṭbaq*), without a need to renew [the agency]. This is because insanity [that is] intermittent (*ghayr muṭbiq*) is comparable to fainting; just as fainting does not invalidate agency (*wakāla*), slight insanity does not invalidate it either.

Secondly, if the insanity of a partner in a business partnership is non-remittent (*muṭbiq*), the partnership is voided, as has been clarified in article

79 In order to avoid this overlap, the author is stating that the definitions or thresholds that are adopted should be mutually exclusive of the other. For example, in contractual dealings, if more than one year is adopted as the threshold at which to categorize someone as suffering from non-remittent insanity, (*junūn muṭbiq*), then intermittent insanity (*junūn ghayr mutbiq*) should be defined to be less than one year.

1352. [This is as opposed to] if the insanity of the partner is intermittent (*ghayr muṭbiq*), in which case the partnership is not voided. In such a case, when any one partner becomes insane, the partnership remains [valid] until the insanity is deemed non-remittent (*muṭbiq*). Once it is ascertained to be non-remittent (*muṭbiq*), the partnership is voided immediately. These details have been clarified in article 1652.

Thirdly, the profit-sharing partnership (*muḍāraba*) is voided when the insanity of either the financier (*rabb al-māl*) or the entrepreneur (*muḍārib*) is classified as non-remittent (*muṭbiq*). However, if their insanity is intermittent (*ghayr muṭbiq*), such is not voided.

Fourthly, if the insanity of an authorized transactor (*ma'dhūn*) is deemed as non-remittent (*muṭbiq*), he is interdicted (*maḥjūr*). However, such would not be interdicted if the insanity is intermittent (*ghayr muṭbiq*)[80] (*al-Hindiyya*, Chapter 5).

Rulings related to non-remittent insanity (*junūn ghayr muṭbiq*) shall be clarified in article 980.

[Article 945]
The Mentally Impaired (*Maʿtūh*) is One Whose Sensibility is Marred:
The mentally impaired (*maʿtūh*) is someone whose cognitive faculties of conception are disturbed, in that his comprehension is inadequate, his expressions are confused, and his coordination is unsound. Lexically, the *maʿtūh* is someone who is deficient in their reasoning. Legally, such is someone whose perception is defective, in that they have inadequate comprehension, confused expressions, and unsound coordination.[81] However, unlike the insane person (*majnūn*), he is neither vile nor violent. His speech varies; it is occasionally comparable to those who are reasonable, and at times [more] like those who are insane.

This is the description that shall be referenced if there is a disagreement concerning the definition of the *maʿtūh* (*Radd al-Muḥtār; al-Tanqīḥ*). Correspondingly, the sane (*ʿāqil*) is one whose speech and actions are sound (*al-Bahja*).

80 This is particularly relevant to mental health settings, wherein all contractual arrangements pertaining to a patient suffering from non-remittent insanity will thus be handed over to a guardian who will assume responsibility for the patient's transactions and dealings.

81 Clinically, this is most likely in reference to one who possesses intellectual deficiency (ID), or what used to be called mental retardation.

[Article 946]
The Spendthrift (*safīḥ*) is Someone Whose Spending is Misplaced

The spendthrift (*safīh*) is one who spends their wealth inappropriately; such are extravagant in their expenditures, squandering their wealth and wasting it.[82] Furthermore, such are continuously heedless of their giving and taking. Those who are unaware of their business practices and consumption due to their fatuousness and inattention are likewise counted as spendthrifts.

The term *safīh* is derived from *safah*, which linguistically means feeble-mindedness. Thus, the *safīh* is one who has weakness in their intellect. Legally, however, the *safīh* is one who spends his wealth inappropriately; meaning, in a manner that is against Islamic Law (*sharīʿa*) and [basic] reason. Instead, they recklessly squander their wealth and waste it by being excessive.

The difference between excessiveness (*isrāf*) and squandering (*tabdhīr*) is that the former is spending excessively in what is permissible, whereas the latter relates to spending on that which is inappropriate (*Radd al-Muḥtār*). Thus, squandering (*tabdhīr*) is the trespassing of the rightful bounds to spend irresponsibly, and ignorance of the [correct] areas of [expenditure]. As for excessiveness (*isrāf*), it is exceeding the amount of rightful [spending],[83] and ignorance of the [correct] amounts of [expenditure].

82 This can include those with mild intellectual deficiency, or, more generally, impulse control disorders.

83 Thus, his deficiency is in not knowing the appropriate amount to spend.

CHAPTER 3

Cognitive Themes

1 An Exposition of Shayṭān's Influence over the Heart through Subtle Whisperings (*Waswasa*), the Significance of *Waswasa*, and the Means through Which It Takes Hold [of a Person]. *Iḥyā' 'Ulūm al-Dīn* by Imam Abu Hamid Al-Ghazali (d. 1111 AD)

1.1 *Author's Biography*

See Author Biography under section 1 of Chapter 2.

1.2 *Text Overview and Significance*

This section's relevance to psychological discourse is very evident in that it deals with the issues of thoughts and ruminations. In this section, Imam al-Ghazālī outlines his thought-action theory, discussing the nature of thoughts and their origins. He mentions that one's inner thoughts are influenced by what one experiences via the external five senses, through one's imaginations, appetitive drives, survival instincts or simply predisposed inherent inclinations. He also outlines a model that describes the processes involved in the initial conception of a thought until one performs an action. He then categorizes thoughts into two types: those that stimulate motivation toward evil and thoughts that stimulate motivation toward good. He terms the former as *waswasa* originating in the metaphysical whispers of Satan and the latter as *ilhām* originating in the metaphysical influences of the angel upon man. The significance of this text can be appreciated by recognizing the potential for such a model to provide a religious explanatory framework for Muslims for the origins of thoughts, where CBT or ACT therapies stop short. By making a distinction between one's mental actions of beliefs and mere cognitive processes that are external to the self (i.e., whisperings of shaytan), patients may be able to better diffuse and distance themselves from the influences of these thoughts and from their turning into compulsions in the case of obsessive compulsive disorders (OCD) or other anxiety disorders.

1.3 *Arabic Text*

بيان تسلط الشيطان على القلب بالوساوس ومعنى الوسوسة وسبب غلبتها

اعلم أن القلب كما ذكرناه مثل قبة مضروبة لها أبواب، تنصب إليه الأحوال من كل باب.

ومثاله أيضاً مثال هدف تنصب إليه السهام من الجوانب.

أو هو مثال مرآة منصوبة تجتاز عليها أصناف الصور المختلفة، فتتراءى فيها صورة بعد صورة، ولا تخلو عنها.

أو مثال حوض تنصب فيه مياه مختلفة من أنهار مفتوحة إليه، وإنما مداخل هذه الآثار المتجددة في القلب في كل حال إما من الظاهر فالحواس الخمس، وإما من الباطن فالخيال والشهوة والغضب والأخلاق المركبة في مزاج الإنسان، فإنه إذا أدرك بالحواس شيئاً.. حصل منه أثر في القلب، وكذلك إذا هاجت الشهوة مثلاً بسبب كثرة الأكل، أو بسبب قوة في المزاج.. حصل منها في القلب أثر، وإن كف عن الإحساس.. فالخيالات الحاصلة في النفس تبقى، وينتقل الخيال من شيء إلى شيء، وبحسب انتقال الخيال ينتقل القلب من حال إلى حال آخر.

والمقصود: أن القلب في التغير والتأثر دائماً إنما هو من هذه الأسباب.

وأخص الآثار الحاصلة في القلب هي الخواطر، وأعني بالخواطر: ما يعرض فيه من الأفكار والأذكار، وأعني به: إدراكاته علوماً إما على سبيل التجدد، وإما على سبيل التذكر؛ فإنها تسمى خواطر من حيث إنها تخطر بعد أن كان القلب غافلاً عنها.

والخواطر هي المحركات للإرادات؛ فإن النية والعزم والإرادة إنما تكون بعد خطور المنوي بالبال لا محالة، فمبدأ الأفعال الخواطر، ثم الخاطر يحرك الرغبة، والرغبة تحرك العزم، والعزم يحرك النية، والنية تحرك الأعضاء.

والخواطر المحركة للرغبة تنقسم:

إلى ما يدعو إلى الشر؛ أعني: إلى ما يضر في العاقبة.

وإلى ما يدعو إلى الخير؛ أعني: إلى ما ينفع في الدار الآخرة.

فهما خاطران مختلفان، فافتقرا إلى اسمين مختلفين، فالخاطر المحمود يسمى إلهاماً، والخاطر المذموم – أعني: الداعي إلى الشر – يسمى وسواساً.

ثم إنك تعلم أن هذه الخواطر حادثة، ثم إن كل حادث فلا بد له من محدث، ومهما اختلفت الحوادث.. دل ذلك على اختلاف الأسباب.

هذا ما عرف من سنة الله تعالى في ترتيب المسببات على الأسباب، فمهما استنارت حيطان البيت بنور النار، وأظلم سقفه واسود بالدخان.. علمت أن سبب السواد غير سبب الاستنارة، وكذلك لأنوار القلب وظلمته سببان مختلفان فسبب الخاطر الداعي إلى الخير يسمى ملكاً، وسبب الخاطر الداعي إلى الشر يسمى شيطانا، واللطف الذي يتهيأ به القلب لقبول إلهام الخير يسمى توفيقا، والذي به يتهيأ لقبول وسواس الشيطان يسمى إغواء وخذلاناً؛ فإن المعاني المختلفة تفتقر إلى أسامي مختلفة.

والملك: عبارة عن خلق خلقه الله تعالى، شأنه إفاضة الخير، وإفادة العلم، وكشف الحق، والوعد بالخير، والأمر بالمعروف، وقد خلقه وسخره لذلك.

والشيطان: عبارة عن خلق شأنه ضد ذلك، وهو الوعد بالشر، والأمر بالفحشاء، والتخويف عند الهم بالخير بالفقر.

فالوسوسة في مقابلة الإلهام، والشيطان في مقابلة الملك، والتوفيق في مقابلة الخذلان، وإليه الإشارة بقوله تعالى: {ومن كل شيء خلقنا زوجين}، فإن الموجودات كلها متقابلة مزدوجة إلا اللّٰه تعالى؛ فإنه فرد لا مقابل له، بل هو الواحد الحق، الخالق للأزواج كلها.

فالقلب متجاذب بين الشيطان والملك، وقد قال صلى اللّٰه عليه وسلم: "في القلب لمتان: لمة من الملك، إيعاد بالخير، وتصديق بالحق، فمن وجد ذلك.. فليعلم أنه من اللّٰه سبحانه، فليحمد اللّٰه، ولمة من العدو، إيعاد بالشر، وتكذيب بالحق، ونهي عن الخير، فمن وجد ذلك.. فليستعذ باللّٰه من الشيطان الرجيم" ثم تلا قوله تعالى: (الشيطان يعدكم الفقر ويأمركم بالفحشاء...) (أخرجه الترمذي والنسائي).

وقال الحسن: "إنما هما همان يجولان في القلب، هم من اللّٰه تعالى، وهم من العدو، فرحم اللّٰه عبدا وقف عند همه، فما كان من اللّٰه تعالى.. أمضاه، وما كان من عدوه.. جاهده)" (قوت القلوب).

ولتجاذب القلب بين هذين المتسلطين قال رسول اللّٰه صلى اللّٰه عليه وسلم: "قلب المؤمن بين إصبعين من أصابع الرحمن"، واللّٰه يتعالى عن أن يكون له إصبع مركبة من لحم ودم وعصب، منقسمة بالأنامل، ولكن روح الإصبع سرعة التقليب، والقدرة على التحريك والتغيير، فإنك لا تريد إصبعك لشخصه، بل لفعله في التقليب والترديد، كما أنك تتعاطى الأفعال بأصابعك، واللّٰه تعالى إنما يفعل ما يفعله باستسخار الملك والشيطان، وهما مسخران بقدرته في تقليب القلوب، كما أن أصابعك مسخرة لك في تقليب الأجسام مثلا.

والقلب بأصل الفطرة صالح لقبول آثار الملك ولقبول آثار الشيطان صلاحاً متساوياً، ليس يترجح أحدهما على الآخر، وإنما يترجح أحد الجانبين باتباع الهوى، والإكباب على الشهوات، أو الإعراض عنها ومخالفتها.

فإن اتبع الإنسان مقتضى الغضب والشهوة.. ظهر تسلط الشيطان بواسطة الهوى، وصار القلب عش الشيطان ومعدنه؛ لأن الهوى هو مرعى الشيطان ومرتعه، وإن جاهد الشهوات، ولم يسلطها على نفسه، وتشبه بأخلاق الملائكة عليهم السلام.. صار قلبه مستقر الملائكة ومهبطهم.

ولما كان لا يخلو قلب عن شهوة وغضب، وحرص وطمع وطول أمل، إلى غير ذلك من صفات البشرية المتشعبة عن الهوى.. لا جرم لم يخل قلب عن أن يكون للشيطان فيه جولان بالوسوسة، ولذلك قال صلى اللّٰه عليه وسلم: "ما منكم من أحد إلا وله شيطان"، قالوا: وأنت يا رسول اللّٰه؟ قال: "وأنا، إلا أن اللّٰه أعانني عليه فأسلم، فلا يأمر إلا بخير" (رواه مسلم).

وإنما كان هذا لأن الشيطان لا يتصرف إلا بواسطة الشهوة، فمن أعانه الله على شهوته حتى صارت لا تنبسط إلا حيث ينبغي وإلى الحد الذي لا ينبغي.. فشهوته لا تدعو إلى الشر، فالشيطان المتدرع بها لا يأمر إلا بالخير.

ومهما غلب على القلب ذكر الدنيا بمقتضيات الهوى.. وجد الشيطان مجالا فوسوس، ومهما انصرف القلب إلى ذكر الله تعالى.. ارتحل الشيطان وضاق مجاله، وأقبل الملك وألهم.

1.4 *English Translation*

An Exposition of Shayṭān's Influence over the Heart Through Subtle Whisperings (*Waswasa*), the Significance of *Waswasa*, and the Means Through Which it Takes Hold [of a Person]

Know that the heart, as we have mentioned, is like a domed tent pitched up with many doors; the [outside] elements can penetrate through [any and] all doors. It is also similar to a target towards which arrows flit from all directions. Or it can be compared to an affixed mirror upon which a variety of different images are casted; it ceaselessly reflects one image after another. Likewise, [the heart] may also be compared to a body of water formed by the channeling of various small streams that originate from different rivers.[1]

At any given time, recurring influences that penetrate the heart are either external, like the five senses, or internal, including the conceptual faculties, appetitive drives, protective instincts, and character traits rooted in personal proclivity.[2] For indeed, if one were to apprehend something through sensory perception, the heart would [necessarily] be affected by it. Similarly, if

1 Imām al-Ghazālī is pointing out that one can never be free of influences that shape the thoughts occurring within the heart or mind. Thus, the mind can never fully be quieted as it is always active, with a multitude of different thoughts passing through it all the time. Notably, the initial thought-stopping interventions in cognitive behavioral therapy (CBT) aimed at addressing unpleasant thoughts lacked substantial empirical support, underscoring the inherent difficulty in completely halting thoughts (Amelia Aldao, Susan Nolen-Hoeksema, and Susanne Schweizer, "Emotion-Regulation Strategies across Psychopathology: A Meta-Analytic Review," *Clinical Psychology Review* 30, no. 2 (March 1, 2010): 217–37.). Such research and experimentation have led to third-wave cognitive theories like Acceptance and Commitment Therapy (ACT), which asserts that while a person cannot stop one's thoughts, they could determine which particular thoughts they wanted to focus on and thus which ones they would allow to have a greater influence over the self (Steven C. Hayes PhD, *A Liberated Mind: How to Pivot Toward What Matters* (National Geographic Books, 2020).

2 Here, al-Ghazālī is highlighting the multiple inner sources of influence upon the human heart or psyche. He demonstrates that individuals may be driven to particular behaviors based upon their inner biologically predisposed temperaments, personality dispositions, or

the appetitive drives were aroused due to excessive eating or on account of a humoral imbalance, then there will [inevitably] be some sort of effect on the heart through that.

Furthermore, if one could avoid all [forms of] external stimulation, the imaginative faculties would remain functional within the psyche (*nafs*), [mentally] switching from one thing to another. On account of the mind alternating [between ideas], the heart likewise shifts from one state to another. The point is: the continual changing and impressibility of the heart is exclusively via these avenues.

The most distinct influences that occur within the heart are thoughts. What I mean by "thoughts" are the cogitations and memories that occur within it. Particularly, I am referring to the acquisition of various types of knowledge, either by way of [receiving] new information or by way of recollecting [stored memories]. Such are termed *khawāṭir* since they become present in the heart after the heart was previously unaware of them.[3]

Thoughts are the mobilizers of personal will. Invariably, intentions, resolve, and will can only arise after the intended [action] occurs as a thought in the mind. Accordingly, the beginning of all actions are thoughts. Next, such thoughts incite motivation. Thereafter, motivation fosters a firm resolve. Such resolve then develops into an intention, which finally mobilizes the body [to act].[4]

Thoughts that incite motivation can be classified into:

i. That which invokes evil; meaning that which results in harmful outcomes.
ii. That which incites goodness, meaning that which benefits in the afterlife.[5]

---

fantasies that strongly contribute to the arousal of particular emotions, or one's appetitive and or aggressive drives.

3 Thoughts (*khawāṭir*), from the Arabic trilateral root kh-ṭ-r, is a literal reference to revealed things. The word in its various morphological forms is used to convey that which occurs or becomes apparent.

4 This can be seen as al-Ghazālī's thought-action model of behavior. Here, he outlines a model for the sequence of events that occurs from thoughts that ultimately lead to action. He demonstrates that thoughts stimulate emotions and motivations that then lead to a commitment to perform that action, followed by the formation of a deliberate intention, and finally the carrying out of the action. The first two stages out of the five can be considered to be non-volitional, while the subsequent two may be considered volitional "mental actions" that precede the behavior itself.

5 Delayed gratification is the ability to resist a temptation in the hope of obtaining a valuable and long-lasting reward in the long-term. It is the ability to postpone an immediate reward for the sake of more distant long-term gains, which requires cognitive control. It is theorized that the ability to choose distant long-term goals over immediate reward is under the control of the cognitive-affective personality system (CAPS) (Walter Mischel and Yuichi Shoda, "A Cognitive-Affective System Theory of Personality: Reconceptualizing Situations,

These two types of thoughts are categorically different and thus, they require two different terms. Thoughts that are praiseworthy are called inspiration (*ilhām*), whereas thoughts that are reprehensible, meaning those that urge towards evil, are termed subtle whisperings (*waswās*).

Moreover, you are surely aware that these thoughts are emergent,[6] and everything that is emergent must necessarily have an initiator. Whenever there are different emergent events, such indicates that there are various causes.

This is what is known from the system of Allah, the Exalted, in the arrangement of causes and their effects. As such, whenever the walls of a house are illuminated by the light of a fire, and the roof becomes darkened and blackened with smoke, you know that the cause of the blackening is something other than the cause of illumination.

Similarly, the illumination and darkening of the heart occur on account of two different causes. Accordingly, the cause of thoughts that call towards goodness is referred to as an angel (*malak*), and the cause of thoughts that call towards evil is referred to as a devil (*shayṭān*). [Furthermore,] the grace by which the heart is prepared to receive inspiration for [doing] good is referred to as divine enablement (*tawfīq*), and that by which it is prepared to receive *waswās* from the devil is referred to as divine deprivation (*ighwāʾ wa khidhlān*). [We provided these terms] because different meanings require different terms.

The [term] "angel" is used to express a type of creation that Allah the Exalted has created [that is] consigned for the [purposes of] bestowing goodness, transmitting knowledge, revealing truth, promising good, and commanding towards virtue. Indeed, Allah, the Exalted, has created and subjugated such [solely] for those [noble purposes].

Conversely, the [term] "devil" denotes a creature whose endeavors are the exact opposite of such; [inherently] foreboding, they urge [towards] shamelessness, and induce a fear of loss when one intends to do good.

Thus, subtle whisperings (*waswasa*) are in contradistinction to inspiration (*ilhām*); the devil (*shayṭān*) is likewise in contradistinction to the angel (*malak*); and divine enablement (*tawfīq*) is in contradistinction to divine deprivation (*khidhlān*). There is a [subtle] indication to this in the statement of Allah, the Exalted: *and we have created everything in pairs* (Al-Dhāriyāt 51:49). For every existing thing there is a corresponding opposite, excepting Allah, the

---

Dispositions, Dynamics, and Invariance in Personality Structure," *Psychological Review* 102, no. 2 (1995): 246–68.) or according to al-Ghazālī, the cognitive element (*ʿaql*) of the metaphysical heart (*qalb*).

6 In other words, thoughts are inherently created as opposed to being eternal.

Exalted; He is singular with no opposite at all. Indeed, He is the Sole Reality and the Creator of all pairs.

Moreover, the heart is [predisposed to be] influenced by both devils and angels. Indeed, the Prophet, may Allah bless him and grant him peace, stated, "There are two types of intimations [that arise] within the heart. [Firstly,] intimations from the angels; such are glad tidings of goodness and affirmations of truth. Whosoever experiences this should recognize that it is from Allah, the Exalted, and should consequently praise Him. [The second type of] intimations [are] from the enemy, foreboding evil, falsifying truth, and dissuading from [that which is] good. Whosoever detects this within their heart should seek refuge in Allah from the accursed shayṭān." Next, the Prophet, may Allah bless him and grant him peace, recited Allah's statement: *shayṭān promises you poverty and urges towards lewdness* (al-Baqara 2:268).[7]

[Imam] Ḥasan al-Baṣrī once said, "There are two kinds of impulses that traverse through the heart: impulses from Allah, and impulses from the mortal enemy [shayṭān]. May the mercy of Allah be upon one who gives [due] consideration to his thoughts such that. whatever comes from Allah, he embraces it, and whatever is from his enemy, he resists it".[8]

In relation to the susceptibility of the heart to these two opposing forces, the Messenger of Allah, may Allah bless him and grant him peace, said, "The heart of the believer is between two of the many fingers of the Most Merciful."[9] [Note that] Allah is exalted and completely above having fingers made up of flesh, bones, blood, and nerves that are divided into phalanges. Rather, the essence of "fingers" [here] is the immediacy of altering as well as the power of mobilizing and changing [something]. For [in utilizing this kind of language,] you do not intend your fingers in and of themselves, but the functions of flipping and rotating just as you do things with your fingers. Allah, the Exalted, enacts what He does through the medium of angels and devils, as they are both subjected to His power in changing the hearts, just like your fingers are subjected to you in the movement of physical objects, for example.[10]

---

7 Al-Tirmidhī 2914; al-Nasā'ī, 10985.

8 al-Makkī, *Qūt Al-Qulūb fī Mu'āmalat al-Maḥbūb*, 1:200.

9 Muslim 2654; Ibn Māja 199, 3834; Ahmad 6569.

10 While modern psychology typically largely considers the internal sources of thoughts like personal history, preoccupations, social experiences etc., a more holistic Islamic approach further considers external sources of thinking that arise on account of satanic and angelic inspirations and influences. This can be particularly useful in providing an explanatory source for the presence of negative thoughts in the treatment of some forms of anxiety disorders such as Obsessive Compulsive Disorders (OCD) by effectively dissociating or externalizing negative thoughts to satanic whispers and differentiating

The heart, by default, is predisposed to equally accept both the influences of angels as well as the effects of the devil;[11] one is not [inherently] stronger than the other. The only way in which one of the two forces becomes predominant is by following one's base desires and implacably satisfying the appetitive drives, or [in converse,] resisting and opposing them. If a person follows the dictates of his appetitive and aggressive drives, the dominance of the devil emerges through the medium of carnal desires and the heart subsequently becomes his nest and abode. [This is] because the carnal desires are [like] breeding grounds or fertile soil for the devil. However, if a person opposes their appetitive drives and does not allow such to become dominant, and if one emulates the characteristics of the angels, upon them be peace, such a person's heart will [effectively] become a stronghold and [ennobled] place of descent for the angels.[12]

Since the heart is never fully devoid of appetitive and aggressive drives, greed, gluttony, whimsical aspirations, and other human traits driven by desire, it is no wonder that the heart is never fully free of shayṭān's vagrant insinuations.[13] For this reason, the Prophet, may Allah bless him and grant him peace, stated, "Not a single one from amongst you is exempted from having a devil with them". [His companions] inquired, "Even you, O Messenger of Allah?" He replied, "Even me. However, Allah has helped me against him and he has thus become Muslim, so he does not urge towards anything other than goodness."[14]

---

them from personal values or beliefs (A. Yusuf and H. Elhaddad, "The Use of the Intellect (*'aql*) as a Cognitive Restructuring Tool in an Islamic Psychotherapy," in *Applying Islamic Principles to Clinical Mental Health Care: Introducing Traditional Islamically Integrated Psychotherapy*, 1st ed. (Routledge, 2020), 209–35.).

11 This highlights al-Ghazālī's Islamic understanding of what contemporary discourse refers to as the ontology of human nature. Accordingly, he asserts that a human child is neither born with an inclination to do good nor bad. While al-Ghazālī acknowledges the inherently good disposition (*fiṭra*) of the human being, there are nonetheless various competing drives within the human being. Human beings possess an inclination towards excessive egocentric appetitive drives that the devil attempts to exploit, yet simultaneously, human beings also possess a conscience with angelic suggestions and an inherent desire for divine connection and upright moral conduct. Thus, the dominating inclination within each person is contingent upon their training and upbringing; the greater habituation towards good or bad will automate a propensity to act accordingly.

12 By allowing restraining one's impulses for immediate gratification, a greater sense of self-control not only allows one to be in line with religious values but will lead to positive consequences in this life and the Hereafter.

13 This normalizes negative thinking in human beings since all are inescapably influenced by devilish influences.

14 Muslim, 2814.

Again, this is only because shayṭān cannot operate except through the medium of the appetitive desires. Therefore, whoever Allah has assisted against his appetitive drives such that they are only actuated to the extent that is appropriate without exceeding propriety, then such a person's appetite does not incite towards evil. In that case, the devil is restricted, and cannot enjoin anything other than goodness.[15]

Otherwise, so long as the preoccupation with worldly things takes hold within the heart on account of carnal desire, the devil will find some avenue [or another] to subtly whisper. Yet, so long as the heart turns to the remembrance of Allah, the Exalted, the devil will flee and his avenues [of influence] will become constricted; allowing angels to approach and provide positive inspiration (*ilhām*).

2 An Introduction to Dream Interpretation (*Taʿbīr al-Manām*). *Taʿṭīr al-Anām fī Taʾbīr al-Manām* (*Dream Interpretation*) by Imam ʿAbd al-Ghanī al-Nābulsī (d. 1143 AH/1730 CE)

2.1 *Author's Biography*

Imam ʿAbd al-Ghanī al-Nabulsī was an astute Islamic scholar, skilled poet, and an accomplished Sufi. His lineage traces back to the second caliph of Islam, ʿUmar ibn al-Khattāb, may Allah be pleased with him; his family was famously known for their piety and knowledge in Damascus during the Ottoman era. Upon migrating to Nablus, they adopted the affiliated family surname al-Nabulsī. At the tender age of five, Imam al-Nabulsī memorized the Holy Quran under the tutelage of his father. By the time he was ten years old, he had memorized the many Islamic primer texts such as *Alfiyya bin Mālik* in Arabic grammar, *al-Kanza* in Islamic jurisprudence, *al-Shātibiyya* in the variant Quranic readings, and *al-Jazariyya* in the rules of recitation. Even though his father passed away when the Imam was only twelve years old, he continued his Islamic studies under the care of his widowed mother.

15 Thus, one can never completely eliminate negative or undesirable thoughts. Rather, one can indirectly influence their intensity and frequency, by working on strengthening and addressing one's underlying vulnerabilities. If one has underlying fears of poverty, low self-esteem, addictions, or excessive inclinations related to material gain, the devil will more easily place negative thoughts and suggestions in such a heart. However, by virtue of working on strengthening oneself, a person can indirectly reduce such thoughts even though they are not actively working on eliminating or stopping such thoughts from occurring.

At the age of twenty, al-Nabulsī became a teacher at the Umayyad Mosque in Damascus. Thereafter he shifted to various locations for different work-related and educational purposes. By the year 1090 AH, he had successfully written approximately fifty books of varying sizes and subject matters. After he reached the age of forty, he opted to seclude himself from people except for the purposes of teaching students and writing. This was on account of his struggle with melancholia for a period of seven years in which he would only leave his house out of extreme necessity. Nonetheless, he continued his teaching activities as there were over twenty correspondences with him on religious matters throughout the Ottoman empire. When he emerged from his seclusion, overcoming his depression, the general public warmly welcomed him back into the community, revering him for his depth of knowledge and noteworthy contributions. Despite his status as a scholarly figure in the public eye, many Islamic jurists expressed skepticism of his scholarship on account of his adopting many of Ibn ʿArabī's controversial Sufi teachings.

2.2 *Text Overview and Significance*

The significance of dreams and their interpretation in the Islamic tradition and human experience overall makes any mainstream text on this topic noteworthy. Even in the early development of modern psychology, the role of dreams was given considerable attention as is evident in Sigmund Freud's popular book entitled *The Interpretation of Dreams*. While dreams may have waned as a topic in psychology during the latter part of the twentieth century, psychologists have, in the past twenty years, rediscovered their importance in understanding human psychology. In fact, there is now an International Association for the Study of Dreams (IASD).

Again, dreams have always held significant importance in the Islamic tradition. In the Qu'ran, one of the most central themes in the story of Prophet Yūsuf, upon him peace, is dream interpretation. As a child, he dreamt of the sun, the moon, and eleven stars prostrating towards him. This dream later materialized when he became the ruler of Egypt, and his parents and brothers bowed before him. The Islamic scholarly tradition reflects the significance attributed to dreams, with over sixty works dedicated to dream interpretation written within the first five centuries of Islam. Additionally, there are more than 171 manuscripts on this topic that have been preserved and remain in manuscript form (Fahd, 1959). Imam al-Nabulsī's text is thus one of many written works on dreams. However, his work uniquely provides a good synthesis of the dream manuals and writings that precede his time. In his work, Imam al-Nabulsī, details the different categories of dreams that must be recognized before an interpretation of it can be considered. He also expounds on the necessity of the interpreter to be keenly aware of the context of the dreamer in order to give a befitting interpretation. It is noteworthy that while Freud saw dreams as "the royal road to the subconscious" (Sigmund Freud, *The Interpretation of Dreams* (Courier Dover Publications, 2015).), the Islamic tradition acknowledges in part that dreams can and often do represent the inner wishes and psychological worlds of people, but it further views dreams as a "royal road to the metaphysical world" as well. Islamic dream interpreters have long recognized the vital significance of distinguishing between psychological elements that align with the inner worlds and contexts of the dreamer, and those that signify divine or metaphysical unveilings. This discernment carries profound implications for the interpretations offered and aids in understanding the psychological conditions and states of the dreamer. By differentiating between these aspects, interpreters gain deeper insights into the dreams, enabling a more nuanced understanding of their symbolic meanings and the messages they convey.

2.3 *Arabic Text*

قال اللّٰه تعالى: ﴿لهم البشرى في الحياة الدنيا وفي الآخرة﴾ (يونس: 64). قال بعض المفسرين: يعني الرؤيا الصالحة يراها الإنسان أو تُرى له في الدنيا، وفي الآخرة رؤية اللّٰه تعالى.

وقال -عليه الصلاة والسلام-: "من لم يؤمن بالرؤيا الصالحة لم يؤمن باللّٰه ولا باليوم الآخر"، وقالت عائشة -رضي اللّٰه عنها-: أول ما بدئ به رسول اللّٰه صلى اللّٰه عليه وسلم من الوحي الرؤيا الصالحة في النوم، فكان لا يرى رؤيا إلا جاءت مثل فلق الصبح.

وروي عنه -عليه الصلاة والسلام- أنه قال لأبي بكر الصديق -رضي اللّٰه عنه-: "يا أبا بكر! رأيت كأني أنا وأنت نرقى في درجة فسبقتك بمرقاتين". فقال: يا رسول اللّٰه يقبضك اللّٰه تعالى إلى رحمته وأعيش بعدك سنتين ونصفاً.

وروي أنه -عليه الصلاة والسلام- قال له: "رأيت كأنما تبعني غنم سود وتبعتها غنم بيض" فقال أبو بكر -رضي اللّٰه عنه-: "تتبعك العرب وتتبع العرب العجم".

وقد منّ اللّٰه تعالى على يوسف -عليه الصلاة السلام- بعلم الرؤيا فقال تعالى: ﴿وكذلك يجتبيك ربك ويعلمك من تأويل الأحاديث﴾ (يوسف:6) يعني به علم الرؤيا، وهو العلم الأول منذ ابتداء العالم لم يزل عليه الأنبياء والرسل صلوات اللّٰه عليهم يأخذون به ويعملون عليه حتى كأن نبواتهم بالرؤيا وحي من اللّٰه عز وجل إليهم في المنام، وما كان قبل النبي صلى اللّٰه عليه وسلم من علوم الأوائل أشرف من علم الرؤيا.

وقد قال بإبطال الرؤيا قوم من الملحدين يقولون إن النائم يرى في منامه ما يغلب عليه من الطبائع الأربعة فإن غلبت عليه السوداء رأى الأحداث والسواد والأهوال والأفزاع، وإن غلبت عليه الصفراء رأى النار والمصابيح والدم والمعصفرات، وإن غلبت عليه البلغم رأى البياض والمياه والأنهار والأمواج، وإن غلب عليه الدم رأى الشراب والرياحين والمعازف والمزامير.

وهذا الذي قالوا نوع من أنواع الرؤيا وليست الرؤيا منحصرة فيه، فإنا نعلم قطعاً أن منها ما يكون من غالب الطبائع كما ذكروا، ومنها ما يكون من الشيطان، ومنها ما يكون من حديث النفس، وهذه أصح الأنواع الثلاثة، وهي الأضغاث، وإنما سميت أضغاثاً لاختلاطها فشبهت بأضغاث النبات، وهي الحزمة مما يأخذ الإنسان من الأرض فيها الصغير والكبير والأحمر والأخضر واليابس والرطب؛ ولذلك قال الله تعالى: ﴿وخذ بيدك ضغثاً فاضرب به ولا تحنث﴾ (ص:44).

وقال بعضهم: الرؤيا ثلاثة: رؤيا بشرى من الله تعالى، وهي الرؤيا الصالحة التي وردت في الحديث، ورؤيا تحذير من الشيطان، ورؤيا مما يحدث به المرء نفسه. فرؤيا تحذير الشيطان هي الباطلة التي لا اعتبار لها، وفي الحديث الصحيح أن النبي صلى الله عليه وسلم أتاه رجل فقال: يا رسول الله رأيت كأن رأسي قطع وأنا أتبعه فقال: "لا تتحدث بتلاعب الشيطان بك في المنام". وأما الرؤيا التي من همة النفس فمثل أن يرى الإنسان مع من يحب قلبه، أو يخاف من شيء فيراه، أو يكون جائعاً فيرى أنه يأكل، أو ممتلئاً فيرى أنه يتقايأ، أو ينام في الشمس ويرى أنه في نار يحترق، أو في أعضائه وجع ويرى أنه يعذب.

والرؤيا الباطلة سبعة أقسام:

الأول: حديث النفس والهم والتمني والأضغاث.

والثاني: الحلم الذي يوجب الغسل لا تفسير له.

والثالث: تحذير من الشيطان وتخويف وتهويل ولا تضره.

والرابع: ما يريه سحرة الجن والإنس فيتكلفون منها مثل ما يتكلفه الشيطان.

والخامس: الباطلة التي يريها الشيطان ولا تعد من الرؤيا.

والسادس: رؤيا تريها الطبائع إذا اختلفت وتكدرت.

والسابع: الوجع وهو أن يرى الرؤيا صاحبها في زمن هو فيه وقد مضت منه عشرون سنة.

وأصح الرؤيا البشرى. وإذا كان السكون والدعة واللباس الفاخر والأغذية الشهية الشافية صحت الرؤيا، وقلت: الأضغاث.

والرؤيا الحق خمسة أقسام:

الأول: الرؤيا الصادقة الظاهرة، وهي جزء من النبوة لقوله تعالى: ﴿لقد صدق الله رسوله الرؤيا بالحق لتدخلن المسجد الحرام إن شاء الله آمنين﴾ (الفتح: 72) وذلك أن رسول الله

صلى اللّٰه عليه وسلم لما سار إلى الحديبية رأى في المنام أنه دخل هو وأصحابه رضي اللّٰه عنهم مكة آمنين غير خائفين يطوفون بالبيت وينحرون ويحلقون رءوسهم ويقصرون فبشر صلى اللّٰه عليه وسلم في المنام بشارة من اللّٰه من غير صنع ملك الرؤيا ولا تفسير لها، مثل رؤيا إبراهيم عليه السلام في المنام في ذبح ولده كما حكى اللّٰه تعالى عنه بقوله: ﴿يا بني إني أرى في المنام أني أذبحك﴾ (الصافات:102). وقال بعضهم: طوبى لمن رأى الرؤيا صريحاً لأن صريح الرؤيا لا يريه إلا الباري تعالى دون واسطة ملك الرؤيا.

والثاني: الرؤيا الصالحة، بشرى من اللّٰه تعالى. كما أن المكروهة زاجرة يزجرك اللّٰه بها. قال صلى اللّٰه عليه وسلم: "خير ما يرى أحدكم في المنام أن يرى ربه أو نبيه أو يرى أبويه مسلمين". قالوا: يا رسول اللّٰه! وهل يرى أحد ربه؟ قال: "السلطان والسلطان هو اللّٰه تعالى".

والثالث: ما يريكه ملك الرؤيا، واسمه صديقون على حسب ما علمه اللّٰه تعالى من نسخة أم الكتاب وألهمه من ضرب أمثال الحكمة لكل شيء من الأشياء مثلاً معلوماً.

والرابع: الرؤيا المرموزة وهي من الأرواح، ومثالها أن إنساناً رأى في منامه ملكاً من الملائكة قال له: إن امرأتك تريد أن تسقيك السم على يد صديقك فلان، فعرض له من ذلك أن صديقه هذا زنى بامرأته، وإنما دلت رؤياه على أن الزنا مستور كما أن السم مستور.

والخامس: الرؤيا التي تصح بالشاهد ويغلب الشاهد عليها فيجعل الشر خيراً والخير شراً، كمن يرى أنه يضرب الطنبور في المسجد فإنه يتوب إلى اللّٰه تعالى من الفحشاء والمنكر، ويفشو ذكره، وكمن رأى أنه يقرأ القرآن في الحمام أو يرقص فإنه يشتهر في أمر فاحش أو بِعَوَر لأن الحمام موضع كشف العورات ولا تدخله الملائكة كما أن الشيطان لا يدخل المسجد. ورؤيا الحائض والجنب تصح لأن الكفار والمجوس لا يرون الغسل. وقد عبر يوسف عليه السلام رؤيا الرجل في السجن وهو كافر، ورؤيا الصبيان تصح لأن يوسف عليه السلام كان ابن سبع سنين فرأى رؤيا فصحت. وقال دانيال عليه السلام: اسم الملك الموكل بالرؤيا صديقون ومن شحمة أذنه إلى عاتقه مسير سبعمائة عام، فهو الذي يضرب الأمثال للآدميين فيريهم بضياء اللّٰه تعالى من علم غيبه في اللوح المحفوظ ما هو كائن من خير أو شر، ولا يشتبه عليه شيء من ذلك، ومثل هذا الملك كمثل الشمس إذا وقع نورها على شيء أبصرت ذلك الشيء به، كذلك يعرفك هذا الملك بضياء اللّٰه تعالى معرفة كل شيء، ويهديك ويعلمك ما يصيبك في دنياك وآخرتك من خير أو شر، ويبشرك بخير قدمته أو تقدمه، وينذرك بمعصية قد ارتكبتها أو تريد ارتكابها، فإذا أراك رؤيا منذرة فإنها تخرج في وقت تراها لئلا تكون مغموماً، وإذا أراك رؤيا حسنة فإنها تخرج بعد ذلك بأيام لتكون في نعمة وسرور.

وأصدق الرؤيا ما كان بالأسحار، وأصدق الرؤيا بالنهار، وقال جعفر الصادق رضي الله عنه: أصدقها القيلولة.

وقال المعبرون من المسلمين: الرؤيا يراها الإنسان بالروح ويفهمها بالعقل. ومستقر الروح نقطات دم في وسط القلب، ومستقر القلب في رسوم الدماغ، والروح معلق بالنفس، فإذا نام الإنسان امتد روحه مثل السراج أو الشمس فيرى بنور الله وضيائه تعالى ما يريه ملك الرؤيا، وذهابه رجوعه إلى النفس مثل الشمس إذا غطاها السحاب الكثيف وانكشف عنها، فإذا عادت الحواس باستيقاظها إلى أفعالها ذكر الروح ما أراه ملك الرؤيا وخيل له.

وقال بعضهم إن الحس الروحاني أشرف من الحس الجسماني؛ لأن الروحاني دال على ما هو كائن، والجسماني دال على ما هو موجود.

واعلم أن تربة كل بلد تخالف غيرها من البلاد لاختلاف الماء والهواء والمكان، فلذلك يختلف تأويل كل طائفة من المعبرين من أهل الكفر والإسلام لاختلاف الطبائع والبلدان، كالذي يرى في بلاد الحر ثلجاً أو جليداً أو برداً فإنه يدل على الغلاء والقحط، ثم إن رأى هذا الرائي في بلد من بلاد البرد فإن ذلك لهم خصب وسعة، والطين والوحل لأهل الهند مال، ولغيرهم محنة وبلاء وبلية، كما أن الضرطة عندهم بشارة وسرور، ولغيرهم كلام قبيح، والسمك في بعض البلاد عفونة، وفي بعضها من واحد إلى أربعة تزويج، ولليهود مصيبة.

واعلم أن الإنسان قد يرى الشيء لنفسه، وقد يراه بنفسه وهو لغيره من أهله وأقاربه أو شقيقه أو والده أو شبيهه أو سميه أو صاحب صنعته أو بلدته أو زوجته أو مملوكه كأبي جهل بن هشام رأى في المنام أنه قد دخل في دين الإسلام وبايع رسول الله صلى الله عليه وسلم فكان ذلك لابنه، وأن أم الفضل أتت النبي صلى الله عليه وسلم قالت: يا رسول الله رأيت أمراً فظيعاً، فقال عليه السلام: "خيراً رأيت"، فقالت: يا رسول الله رأيت بضعة من جسدك قد قطعت ووضعت في حجري، فقال رسول الله صلى الله عليه وسلم متبسماً: "ستلد فاطمة غلاماً وتأخذيه في حجرك"، فأتت فاطمة رضي الله عنها من ابن عمها بالحسن رضي الله عنهم وأخذته أم الفضل في حجرها.

ومن أراد أن تصدق رؤياه فليحدث الصدق ويحذر الكذب والغيبة والنميمة، فإن كان صاحب الرؤيا كذاباً ويكره الكذب من غيره صدقت رؤياه، وإن كذب ولم يكره الكذب من غيره لم تصدق رؤياه.

ويستحب للرجل أن ينام على الوضوء لتكون رؤياه صالحة، والرجل إذا كان غير عفيف يرى الرؤيا ولا يذكر شيئاً منها لضعف نيته وكثرة ذنوبه ومعاصيه وغيبته ونميمته.

وينبغي للمعبر إذا قصت عليه الرؤيا أن يقول: "خيراً رأيت، وخيراً نلقاه، وشراً نتوقاه، خيراً لنا، وشر لأعدائنا، الحمد لله رب العالمين اقصص رؤياك"، وأن يكتم على الناس عوراتهم، ويسمع السؤال بأجمعه، ويميز بين الشريف والوضيع، ويتمهل ولا يعجل في رد الجواب، ولا يعبر الرؤيا حتى يعرف لمن هي، ويميز كل جنس وما يليق به، وليكن العابر عالماً فطناً

ذكياً تقياً نقياً من الفواحش، عالماً بكتاب الله تعالى وحديث النبي صلى الله عليه وسلم ولغة العرب وأمثالها وما يجري على ألسنة الناس، ولا يعبر الرؤيا في وقت الاضطرار وهي ثلاثة: طلوع الشمس، وغروبها، وعند الزوال.

وإذا سأل سائل عن رؤيا عناد ولم يكن رآها فلا يترك المعبر سؤاله بغير جواب فإنه إن كان خيراً فمصروف إلى المعبر، وإن كان شراً فمصروف إلى المعاند لأنه مخذول، والمجيب منصور على أعدائه، كما ورد في قصة يوسف عليه السلام حين سأله الفتيان في السجن عناداً فقال ﴿أحدهما إني أراني أعصر خمراً وقال الآخر إني أراني أحمل فوق رأسي خبزاً تأكل الطير منه﴾ (يوسف:36) فقال لهما يوسف عليه السلام: ﴿أما أحدكما فيسقي ربه خمراً وأما الآخر فيصلب فتأكل الطير من رأسه قضي الأمر الذي فيه تستفتيان﴾ (يوسف:41). وإن عبر المعبر رؤياه عناداً على سبيل الاعوجاج فإنه إن كان خيراً فهو للسائل وإن كان شراً فهو للمعبر.

ولا يقص الرائي رؤياه إلا على عالم أو ناصح ولا يقصها على جاهل أو عدو. والرؤيا على رجل طائر ما لم يحدث بها فإذا حدث وقعت، ولا يقص أحد رؤياه على معبر وفي مصره أو إقليمه معبر أحذق منه؛ لأن فرعون يوسف لما قص رؤياه على معبري بلده فقالوا أضغاث أحلام لم تبطل رؤياه، وسأل عنها يوسف عليه السلام فعبرها له فخرجت. وإذا اشتبهت الرؤيا على المعبر ولم يعرف لها تأويلاً فليأمر صاحبها إذا خرج من بيته يوم السبت أول النهار أن يسأل أي شخص يلقاه عن اسمه فإن كان اسمه حسناً كأسماء الأنبياء والصالحين فالرؤيا حسنة وإن كان غير ذلك فالرؤيا غير حسنة.

ويحترز من الكذب فيها فقد روي عن رسول الله صلى الله عليه وسلم أنه قال: "من كذب في الرؤيا كلف يوم القيامة عقد شعيرة ومن كذب على عينيه لا يجد رائحة الجنة وإن أعظم الفرية أن يفتري الرجل على عينيه يقول رأيت ولم ير شيئاً".

وقال بعضهم إن الكاذب في رؤياه مدعي النبوة كاذباً؛ لأنه ورد في الحديث كما قدمناه أن الرؤيا جزء من أجزاء النبوة، ومدعي الجزء كمدعي الكل.

وقال بعض العلماء ينبغي أن يعبر الرؤيا المسئول عنها على مقادير الناس ومراتبهم ومذاهبهم وأديانهم وأوقاتهم وبلدانهم وأزمنتهم وفصول سنتهم. والتعبير يكون بالمعنى وباشتقاق الأسماء. والميت في دار حق فما قاله في المنام حق، وكذلك الطفل الذي لا يعرف الكذب، وكذلك الدواب وسائر الحيوانات والطيور إذا تكلمت في المنام فقولها حق.

.....

وللمعبرين طرق كثيرة في استخراج التأويل، وذلك غير محصور بل هو قابل للزيادة باعتبار معرفة المعبر وكمال حذقه وديانته والفتح عليه بهذا العلم.

والله يهدي من يشاء إلى صراط مستقيم.

2.4 *English Translation*

Allah, the Exalted, states, *"for them is good news in this worldly life and in the Hereafter"* (Yūnus 10:64). Some exegetes interpreted this [good news] as good dreams that are seen by the person or seen on their behalf in this [temporal] life. Or, as seeing Allah, the Most Exalted, in the Hereafter. Additionally, the Prophet, may Allah bless him and grant him peace, said, "Whoever does not believe in righteous dreams does not believe in Allah or in the Hereafter."[16]

ʿĀ'isha, may Allah be pleased with her, also said, "The commencement of Divine revelation to Allah's Messenger, may Allah bless him and grant him peace, was in the form of righteous dreams in his sleep. He never had a dream except that it manifested to him like the break of dawn."[17]

It was additionally narrated from the Prophet, may Allah bless him and grant him peace, that he said to Abū Bakr al-Ṣiddīq, may Allah be pleased with him, "Abu Bakr! I saw [in a dream] that we were both ascending[18] a staircase, and I came two steps ahead of you." Abū Bakr said, "Messenger of Allah! Allah will take you back to His mercy and I will live on for two and a half years after you."[19]

It was also narrated that the Prophet, may Allah bless him and grant him peace, told Abū Bakr, "I saw [in a dream] as though I was followed by black sheep, and they were followed by white sheep." Abū Bakr[20] replied, "The Arabs will follow you, and the non-Arabs will follow the Arabs."[21]

---

16 Al-Suyūṭī, *al-Jāmiʿal-Kabīr*, 23829.

17 Therefore, true dreams were both experienced and described by the Prophet, may Allah bless him and grant him peace. In other narrations, true dreams are deemed as a forty-sixth part of prophecy (cf. al-Bukhārī, 6988; Aḥmad, 14681).

18 When analyzing the recounting of dreams in both the Quran and prophetic Sunna, an intriguing observation pertains to the prevalent usage of the present-tense verb. This linguistic choice creates a sense of immediacy and active engagement, enhancing the immersive experience of narrating a dream. Additional investigation and scholarly inquiry are required to explore potential correlations between the language employed in dream narratives and the processes of dream recall and interpretation.

19 Muḥammad Ibn Sa'd, *al-Ṭabaqāt al-Kubrā*, vol. 3 (Cairo: Maktabat al-Khanjī, 2001), 167; Aḥmad Ibn Ḥanbal, *Faḍāil al-Ṣaḥāba*, vol. 1 (Beirut: Muassasat al-Risāla, 1983), 423.

20 The illustrious Abū Bakr al-Ṣiddīq, may Allah be pleased with him, is reported to have engaged in dream interpretation numerous times in the presence of the Prophet, may Allah bless him and grant him peace, as well as in his absence. In one incident, a dream was presented to the Prophet, may Allah bless him and grant him peace, and Abū Bakr requested to offer his own interpretation, seeking to ascertain his interpretative accuracy. The Prophet may Allah bless him and grant him peace, then told him that he had interpreted a part of the related dream correctly, but he had also erred in interpreting part of it (cf. Muslim, 2269).

21 Abū Bakr Muḥammad Ibn Ibrāhīm Ibn Abī Shayba, *al-Muṣannaf*, vol. 17 (Riyadh: Dār Kunūz Ishbiliyya li-l-nashr wa-l-tawzīʿ, 2015), 70, ḥadīth 32501.

Allah, the Exalted, granted Yūsuf, upon him be peace, knowledge of dream interpretation. Accordingly, Allah states, "As *such your Lord will choose you,* ⌜Yūsuf⌝, *and teach you the interpretation of dreams* (*ta'wīl al-aḥādīth*)" (Yūsuf 12:6).

[Ta'wīl al-aḥādīth] refers to knowledge of dream [interpretation], which was the first science since the inception of the universe; it has always been acquired and applied by the prophets and messengers, upon them be Allah's blessings. Not only that, but prophetic dreams were also a form of revelation from Allah Almighty, conferred upon them during sleep. There is no preliminary science predating the Messenger, may Allah bless him and grant him peace, that is more noble than the science of dream interpretation.

A group of heretics denied [the truthfulness of] dreams. They state that dreams seen by someone asleep purely reflect the dominance of the four bodily humors. If one is dominated by black bile, they will see events characterized by darkness, panic, and terror. If yellow bile prevails, they will see fire, lamps, blood, and things which are reddish in color. If they are overcome by phlegm, they will see whiteness, water, rivers, and waves. Finally, if blood prevails, they will see beverages, aromatic plants, musical instruments, and flutes.[22] These dreams [reflecting the biological underpinnings] are indeed one category of different types of dreams. However, not all dreams are confined to this type. We know with certainty that some dreams are caused by the dominant bodily humors as they mentioned, whereas some are caused by shayṭān, and some

---

Altogether, these narrations accentuate the status of dreams from an Islam viewpoint; instead of being dismissed as meaningless or practically irrelevant, in a particular context, they are deemed central matters of faith. True dreams received by the Prophets are a form of revelation and can serve as a criterion to distinguish believers from disbelievers. Other dreams unveil hidden realities, whereas some even foretell the onset of future events and circumstances. These transmitted accounts are only a few examples of the dreams that were interpreted and discussed by the Prophet, may Allah bless him and grant him peace, and his Companions. Numerous other examples can be found in well-known Hadith collections and compendiums, which typically include a dedicated chapter for narrations that are solely related to dreams and dream interpretation.

22 This paragraph addresses a reductionist approach to dreams, which reduces their origin and occurrence to purely biological humoral influences. Across civilizations, humoral theory of this nature dominated the understanding of human physiology, pathology, and psychology for centuries. Such assumed that for the body to function normally, a balance should exist between the four main bodily humors: blood, yellow bile, black bile, and phlegm. Although the prevalence of humoral theory declined in the eighteenth and nineteenth century, a biological mechanism underpinning dreams is still considered to be a potential origin of dreams. Nonetheless, al-Nabulsī importantly asserts that dreams cannot be reduced solely to their biological origins; the Islamic perspective is further nuanced in that it does not limit the basis of dreams to one's intrapsychic conflicts and unconscious desires or wishes.

stem from one's inner thoughts (self-talk). The latter is the truest of all types and is referred to as *aḍghāth* given its jumbled nature, in the same way the *aḍgāth* of plants refers to a bunch of plants pulled from the ground together that include small and large, red, and green, as well as dry and moist plants. Thus, Allah, the Exalted, says [to Prophet Ayyūb], *Take in your hand a bundle of grass* (*ḍighth*) *and strike with it, and do not break your oath*, (Ṣāḍ 38:44).

Yet another tripartite classification of dreams was given by some [scholars]: Dreams can be glad tidings from Allah, the Exalted, which is the "righteous dream" referenced in the prophetic reports. Secondly, dreams may be caused by the menacing of shayṭān. Finally, dreams can reflect one's self-talk. Satanic nightmares are illegitimate and are not to be given any [real] consideration, as it was authentically narrated that a person came to the Prophet, may Allah bless him and grant him peace, and told him, "I saw in a dream that my head was cut off and I was following it around." The Prophet, may Allah bless him and grant him peace, replied, "Do not speak [to others] about how shayṭān manipulates you in dreams."[23] On the other hand, examples of dreams which reflect one's preoccupations include seeing oneself with a person who is dear to one's heart; seeing something of which one is afraid; seeing food whilst one is hungry; or seeing that they are vomiting when they feel full; seeing that they are burning in fire whilst they are sleeping under the sun; seeing that they are being tortured when they are suffering from severe bodily pain.

Meaningless dreams[24] are [divided into] seven categories:

1. [Dreams generated by] inner self-talk, anxiety, yearning, and muddled thoughts.
2. [Erotic] dreams that necessitate a purificatory bath; they have no interpretation.
3. [From the] foreboding, terrorizing, and distressing of shayṭān; such are all harmless.

---

23 Muslim, 2268; Abū Dāwūd 5022; Ibn Mājah, 3912.

This narration emphasizes that certain dreams should not be recounted or narrated. Rather, the best way to deal with them is to disregard them and to avoid becoming overly occupied with them or their potential ramifications. The Prophet, may Allah bless him and grant him peace, is reported to have advised anyone who sees an upsetting dream to seek refuge with Allah from shayṭān, "for it [the dream] will not harm him," (cf. al-Bukharī, 6985).

24 The seven categories of dreams listed here refer to ordinary dreams, which do not require any interpretation, in contrast to true dreams. Here, al-Nābulsī primarily focuses on the origins of such dreams rather than the qualities through which one can identify them. However, he does make some subtle references, including reflecting over one's preoccupations, trauma, and distress; dreams that are sexual in nature; and nightmares that evoke feelings of fear and distress.

4. That which human and jinn sorcerers conjure, effectuating similar to what is incited by shayṭān.
5. Illusory visions simulated by shayṭān; such are not even counted as dreams.
6. Dreams occasioned by the changing or sullying of the bodily humors.
7. Trauma [-induced dreams], wherein a person sees a dream in the present of something that transpired twenty years ago.

The truest of dreams are glad tidings. And if such were to contain [a sense of] tranquility, ease, elegant clothing, or delectable and healthful foods, then the dream [could be considered] true. However, I opine [that such mostly indicate] jumbled dreams.

True dreams[25] are [divided into] five categories:

1. Manifest and true visions, which are [considered to be] part of prophecy, as Allah the Exalted says: *With profound certainty, Allah has confirmed His Messenger's vision. You shall indeed enter the Sacred Mosque, by the will of Allah, in full security,* (al-Fatḥ 48:27). When the Messenger of Allah, may Allah bless him and grant him peace, was on his way to al-Ḥudaybiyya he saw in a dream that he had entered Mecca with his Companions in full security without any fear, and that they were circumambulating around the Kaʿba, performing their ritual slaughter, and shaving their heads or shortening their hair. In this dream, the Messenger, may Allah bless him and grant him peace, received glad tidings directly from Allah without the intermediation of the angel of dreams or any [required] interpretation. This was similarly the case in the dream of Ibrāhīm, upon him be peace, in which he saw himself sacrificing his son, as Allah, the Exalted, relates when he says, *Dear son! I have seen in a dream that I ⸢must⸣ sacrifice you,* (Al-*Ṣāffāt* 37:102). Accordingly, some [scholars of dream interpretation] said, "Blessed is he who sees a vivid dream, for such comes directly from Allah Almighty, without the intermediation of the angel of dreams."
2. Righteous dreams which are glad tidings from Allah, the Exalted. Similarly, [certain] unpleasant dreams which are sent to you by Allah as a deterrent. The Messenger, may Allah bless him and grant him peace, said, "The best of dreams are the ones where you see your Lord, your prophet,

25 Here, al-Nābulsī lists five types of true dreams with some elaboration on their nature, origin, source, and function. While literal true dreams are possible, as elucidated in the first category above, some true dreams are symbolic in nature, such as in categories #4 and #5. Symbolic dreams usually necessitate an interpretation which is sometimes the opposite of the dream symbol as the author clarifies in his discussion of #5. Examples of symbolic true dreams from the Quran are those mentioned in Sura Yūsuf.

or [you see] your parents in a state of Islam." Someone asked: "Messenger of Allah, can one in fact see his Lord?" He replied: "The Sultan [represents Allah in one's dream]. The Sultan [symbolizes] Allah the Most Exalted."[26]

3. Dreams that are shown to you by the angel of dreams. His name is *Ṣiddīqūn*, as per what Allah, the Exalted, has taught him from the Inscribed Record, further inspiring him with parables of wisdom for each and every thing in a conceivable symbolic form.
4. Figurative dreams, which are from the [world of] the souls. An example of such would be that a person sees an angel in his dream, who says to him, "Indeed, your wife wishes for you to ingest poison at the hands of your friend!" Through this, he may deduce that his friend has committed adultery with his wife. His dream would have correlated the two because adultery is secretive just as poison is [administered] secretively.
5. Dreams that are deemed true based on a dominating reference that determines [the interpretation of] it. Accordingly, one could interpret the [seemingly] bad as good, and the [seemingly] good as bad. For example, if one were to dream that they are banging on a drum in the mosque, then [it could mean] they are going to repent to Allah Most High from that which is vulgar and wrong, propagating His remembrance. Similarly, if one sees that they are reciting the Quran in the washroom or dancing, then one [may] become well-known for something obscene or become blind. This is because the washroom is a place in which peoples' private parts are uncovered, and angels do not enter it just as shayṭān does not enter the mosque.

Furthermore, [it is possible for] the dream of a menstruating woman or someone who is in a sexually defiled state to be true, considering that fire-worshipers and other non-Muslims do not even view purificatory ritual bathing [as necessary], and Yūsuf, upon him be peace, interpreted the dream of the non-Muslim man in prison. The dreams of children may also be deemed as valid, as Yūsuf, upon him be peace, was only seven years old when he saw a dream that proved to be true.

Prophet Danyāl, upon him be peace, once stated:

> The name of the angel appointed for dreams is *Ṣiddīqūn*; the distance between his earlobe and shoulder is that of seven hundred years. He is the one who draws parables for human beings, effectively using Allah's [divine] light to show them [both] that which is good and bad from the

26 Abū Bakr Ibn Abī ʿĀṣim, *Al-Sunna*, vol. 1 (Beirut: al-Maktaba al-Islāmiyya, 1400), 215 (488).

> knowledge of the unseen as transcribed in the Protected Tablet; nothing of such is obscured to him. The example of this angel is like that of the sun; when its light shines on something, it makes it visible. In that sense, this angel employs Allah's light to make you cognizant of everything, guiding you, and enlightening you with regards to what good or evil will afflict you in your worldly affairs as well as in the afterlife. He graces you with glad tidings for good that you have sent forth or have yet to fulfill; he likewise warns you of sins that you have perpetrated or are intent upon committing. As such, if he were to show you a dream as a warning, then it would be at a time that you would see it [clearly] so that you do not become dejected [by committing that sin]. Contrarily, if he were to show you a good dream, then it would [typically] occur later on, after a few days have passed, so you may blissfully rejoice.

The truest dreams are seen before dawn or during the daytime. Jaʿfar al-Ṣādiq, may Allah be pleased with him, said that the truest dream is [seen during] the midday nap.[27]

Muslim dream interpreters stipulated that dreams are seen by the soul and are comprehended by the mind. The soul resides within certain blood vessels at the center of one's heart, while the functions of the heart are dictated by one's brain. Moreover, the soul is connected to the self, so when a person falls asleep, his soul extends like [the rays of light from] a lamp or the sun. He then sees, through the effulgent light of his Lord the Exalted, what the angel of dreams reveals to him. The departure of the soul from the body and its return to it are like the sun being covered behind thick clouds and reappearing thereafter. When one's senses return through wakefulness, one may remember, through his soul, what the angel of dreams has shown him and made him envision.[28]

---

27 This is a discretionary matter of scholarly deduction (*ijtihād*); some scholars deliberated on the signs that distinguish true dreams from ordinary dreams.

28 Al-Alūsī, a famous exegete, relates the following Quranic verse: *⸢It is⸣ Allah ⸢Who⸣ calls back the souls ⸢of people⸣ upon their death as well as ⸢the souls⸣ of the living during their sleep. Then He keeps those for whom He has ordained death and releases the others until ⸢their⸣ appointed time. Surely in this are signs for people who reflect.* (al-Zumar 39:42) He then relates a conversation that took place between ʾUmar ibn al-Khaṭṭāb and ʿAlī ibn Abī Ṭālib, may Allah be pleased with them: "ʿAlī explained, 'Allah takes all of the souls when they sleep. Whatever [dreams] they see while they are with Him in the heavens are true visions and whatever they see when they are sent back to their bodies are false dreams'" (see Shihāb al-dīn al-Ālūsī, *Rūḥ al-Maʿānī*, vol. 12 (Beirut: Dār al-Kutub al-ʿIlmiyya, 1415), 263.).

Some [scholars] state that [a person's] spiritual sense is more virtuous than [one's] physical sense, as spiritual feelings allow perception of the entire existent universe, whereas physical feelings can only recognize what is [currently physically] present.

It should be known that soil is different from one land to another because of the difference in location and in the quality of water and air in each. Consequently, the dream interpretations for unbelievers will differ when compared to believers given the variation in [their] temperaments and the lands [in which they live]. To explain, if one who lives in a hot country and sees snow, ice, or hail in his dream, it means rising prices or drought. On the other hand, if one lives in a cold country and sees snow, rain, or hail, it means fruitfulness and prosperity. In India, for example, seeing mud and mire means wealth, while for another country it may mean adversity, affliction, and calamity. Similarly, for them, flatulence indicates glad tidings and happiness, but for others it is odious discourse. Likewise, fish, in some lands, represents putridity, yet in others it indicates marrying from one to four [spouses]; but for Jews, [the same imagery] indicates tribulation.[29]

It is also necessary to know that a person can see something related to their own self or they can see something that relates to others, such as members of his household, his relatives, his siblings, his parents, his business partners, his town, his spouse, his servant, or someone who looks like him or has the same name. For example, Abū Jahl ibn Hishām saw himself in a dream accepting Islam and pledging allegiance to Allah's Messenger, may Allah bless him and grant him peace. However, [Abū Jahl died as an unbeliever and] it was his son that fulfilled the dream.

Another example is the dream of Umm al-Faḍl who once came to the Prophet, may Allah bless him and grant him peace, and said, "Messenger of Allah! I had a frightening dream." He replied, "It is but good that you saw." She continued, "I saw a piece of your flesh cut off and put in my lap!" The Messenger, may Allah bless him and grant him peace, smiled, and said, "[My daughter] Fāṭima will beget a son, and you shall take him into your lap." The dream later came true when Fāṭima, may Allah be pleased with her, gave birth to al-Ḥasan, may Allah be pleased with him, by the son of her uncle (her cousin and husband, ʿAlī ibn Abī Ṭalib). Thereafter, Umm al-Faḍl cradled him in her lap.

---

29 Here, al-Nābulsī alludes to a critical element in dream interpretation: When interpreting dreams, consideration should be given to understanding the social context of the dreamer and the meanings associated with different symbols in different cultures. Thus, dream interpretation is an ever-evolving, highly nuanced science and art.

And whosoever wishes to experience true dreams should speak truthfully and carefully avoid lying, backbiting, and gossip. If a compulsive liar who dislikes others lying were to have a dream, such could be true; but if a liar does not dislike others lying, then their dreams are [typically] not true.[30]

Furthermore, it is recommended for a person to sleep in a purified state (wuḍū') so as to [better] ensure [he experiences] a righteous dream. If a person is unchaste and they see a dream, they will [likely] not remember anything of it given their weak resolve coupled with their abundance of sins, including backbiting and gossip.

When someone relates a dream, it is imperative for the dream interpreter to [first] say, "May it be goodness that you have seen, and goodness that we are encountering; may we be protected from evil, with your dream being good for us, and ominous for our enemies. All praises belong to Allah, the Lord of the worlds – now relate your dream."[31]

Also, an interpreter should conceal peoples' private affairs; fully listen to all inquiries; adeptly differentiate between the noble and insignificant; and deliberate without responding too hastily. One should not interpret a dream unless one knows who has seen it and can navigate between each category appropriately. An interpreter must be scholarly, intuitive, clever, religiously cautious, and abstinent from all obscenities. [He should also be] knowledgeable of Allah's Book, the Prophetic *ḥadīth* sciences, and the Arabic language along with its allegory. [He must also be familiar] with common parlance and colloquialism. One should not attempt to interpret dreams at any of the three detrimental times, which are during the rising of the sun, at sunset, and at midday.

Now, if a person [misleadingly] inquiries regarding a dream to test [the interpreter], but they have not actually seen any dream, then the interpreter should not leave them without a response. This is because if there is goodness [in the response], then it would be bestowed upon the interpreter. However, if

30 al-Nābulsī is emphasizing the role of personal qualities and morals and their subsequent correlation to the veracity of their dreams. As reiterated by the author himself, it is important to note that true dreams can be seen by believers, non-believers, righteous people, and non-righteous people alike.

31 This emphasizes the importance of being attuned to the psychological impact of dreams and their interpretations; the interpreter should use gentle positive hope-instilling words and strategies when individuals relate their dreams. An example of such is the remark made by the Prophet, may Allah bless him and grant him peace, when 'Abdullah Ibn 'Umar narrated a dream in which he saw the Hellfire, and people from Quraysh were being tormented therein. The Prophet, may Allah bless him and grant him peace, remarked, "What an excellent man 'Abdullah is – if only he would observe the night prayer." (cf. al-Bukhari, 1121; Muslim, 2479).

there is evil associated with it, then it would fall upon the person inquiring as they are depraved, plus the interpreter is [divinely] aided against his adversaries. This has been illustrated in the story of Yūsuf, upon him be peace, when the two youth in prison insidiously queried, *one of them said, "Indeed, I dreamt that I was pressing ⌜grapes for⌝ wine." And the other stated, "I dreamt that I was carrying bread on my head, from which some birds were eating."* (Yūsuf 12:36). Yūsuf, upon him be peace, thus replied to both of them, *⌜The first⌝ one of you will serve wine to his master. As for the other, he will be crucified, and the birds will then eat from his head. The matter about which you are inquiring has ⌜indeed⌝ been determined.* (Yūsuf, 12:41).[32] However, if the interpreter [himself] deliberately puts forth a twisted interpretation, then if there is goodness [in it], such would be allotted to the one inquiring. However, if there is evil [in it], then such [falls back] upon the interpreter.

Anyone who sees a dream should not relate it to anyone other than a scholar or a genuine well-wisher. Likewise, one should [certainly] not relate it to someone who is ignorant or antagonistic. The [truth of] dreams are suspended for a person so long as they do not speak of it; it is when one mentions it that it becomes manifest. As such, no one should relate their dreams to someone for interpretation when there is a more adept interpreter present in their locality. This is because when the Pharaoh at the time of Yūsuf narrated his dream to local interpreters, they dismissed it as jumbled dreams, but that did not delegitimize his dream at all. Rather, after inquiring about it with Yūsuf, upon him be peace, he interpreted for him, and it manifested accordingly.

If a dream is obscure, and the interpreter does not know the [appropriate] interpretation, then he should instruct the person who saw the dream to step out of his house in the early part of the day on a Saturday and ask any [arbitrary] person that they come across what their name is. If their name happens to be good, like one of the names of the prophets or other pious personalities, then [they can assume the meaning of] the dream is good. If their name is not as such, then the dream would not be [considered as] good.[33]

---

32 al-Nābulsī is referring to a lesser-known valid scholarly interpretation of this verse which suggests that the prisoners that approached Yūsuf, upon him peace, fabricated their so-called dreams to challenge and test his knowledge. This opinion was recorded by Imam al-Ṭabarī in his famous multi-volume exegesis. It should be duly noted, however, that the majority of Quranic exegetes hold the opinion that the dreams recounted by the two prisoners were in fact true dreams.

33 Dream interpretation manuals are replete with opinions that are based on interpretative knowledge and the personal expertise of their respective authors more than on clear textual evidence or references. Readers should understand that such writings are mere tools to assist with certain aspects of dream interpretation, and they are not meant to

Additionally, a person must be wary of lying with regards to dreams, as it has been narrated that the Messenger of Allah, may Allah bless him and grant him peace, warned, "Whosoever lies regarding dreams will be ordered on the Day of Resurrection with the [impossible] task of [tying] a grain of barley in a knot. Indeed, whoever lies about what they see, will not even sense the fragrance of Paradise. Verily, one of the most serious [forms] of lying is for a person to falsely claim [something] regarding what they have witnessed, saying 'I have seen,' when they have not [actually] seen anything."[34] Some scholars have similarly stated that the one who lies regarding their dreams is making a false claim of prophethood. As mentioned previously, this is because it has been narrated in the ḥādīth [literature] that dreams are a part of the various portions of prophethood;[35] as such, one who claims a portion [of something] is [indirectly] claiming its totality.

Some scholars state that the interpreter, when asked to interpret a dream, must take into consideration people's status, ranks, social customs, religious norms, habits, countries, eras, and seasons.[36] The interpretation must depend on the meanings of words and the derivation of names.

A deceased person is in an abode of truth. Therefore, whatever a deceased person [seen in a dream] says in the dream is true. Similarly, [it is considered true whatever is spoken in a dream by] children, who by nature do not lie. Also, animals, birds, and other living creatures, if seen to be speaking in a dream, their statements are true.

Interpreters have a multitude of ways to derive interpretations. Their interpretive abilities are bettered through stronger interpretive knowledge and skills, a stronger commitment to religion, and through Allah's bestowed favor. Indeed, Allah guides whom He wills to the Straight Path.

---

be utilized in the same way that conventional reference works in other fields are typically used.

34 Aḥmad, 5711; al-Bukhārī, 7043.

35 Al-Bukhārī, 7017; Muslim, 2263.

36 The same way the interpreter should consider the socio-cultural context as highlighted above, the psycho-social-spiritual circumstances of the dreamer should be taken into account when interpreting dreams. Dream interpretation manuals are replete with examples of differential interpretations of symbols based on the psycho-social-spiritual status of the dreamer.

CHAPTER 4

Emotional Themes

1 Repelling Excess Sorrow. *Al-Ṭibb al-Ruhānī* (*Psycho-Spiritual Medicine*) by Imam ʿAbd al-Raḥmān Abū al-Faraj ibn al-Jawzī (d. 597 AH/1184 CE)

1.1 *Author's Biography*

Imam ʿAbd al-Raḥmān ibn ʿAlī ibn Muḥammad Abū al-Faraj ibn al-Jawzī, more famously known as Ibn al-Jawzī, is reported to have been born in Baghdad in the year 519 or 520 hijri/1107 CE. His lineage traces back to the first caliph of Islam, Abū Bakr, may Allah be pleased with him. From a young age, he received an excellent primary education which continued and developed into an entire lifetime of seeking and propagating Islamic knowledge. Ibn al-Jawzī became an adept scholar of the Ḥanbalī school of Islamic jurisprudence; his fame further increased when al-Mustaḍī, who was a proponent of the Hanbali school, rose to political power as the Abbasid caliph. Through the caliph's influence, Imam Ibn al-Jawzī was given a significant scholarly platform to teach and preach to the masses. He gained widespread acclaim for his leadership in various educational institutions and the spread of his highly influential written works. Ibn al-Jawzī was and is still recognized as one of the most prolific Islamic polymaths; his valuable written works cover a range of key topics and focuses within the Islamic tradition. Imam al-Dhahabī writes about him, saying, "I have not known anyone amongst the scholars to have written as much as [Ibn al-Jawzī] did ..." (al-Dhahabī, Siyar A'lām al-Nubalāʾ, 21:384). Ibn al-Jawzī was also a proponent of Sufism, regarding it as a branch of the Islamic sciences. This is evident through his support for Imam al-Ghazālī; he seems to have adopted many of his ideas and discussions in his own works. Ibn al-Jawzī died on the 12th of Ramadan in the year 597 AH/1184 CE at the age of 84; his tomb is located in Baghdad.

1.2 *Text Overview and Significance*

Imam Ibn al-Jawzī's treatise Al-Ṭibb al-Rūhānī focuses on character development and virtue acquisition. Some of the subsections of this particular work include virtues of the intellect, the regulation of one's desires, virtues and their acquisition, self-discipline, raising children, family relations and others. In the selected excerpts below, Ibn al-Jawzī discusses excessive sorrow, grief, depression, and anxiety. After defining such terms, he explores their excesses as well as how to bring about a balance with regards to each of these states. Whilst delving into various spiritual causes and cures for imbalance, he further suggests that internal physiological states could also contribute to some of these imbalances as well.

1.3 *Arabic Text*

الباب الثامن عشر

في دفع فضول الحزن

اعلم أن العاقل لا يخلو من الحزن؛ لأنه يتفكر في سالف ذنوبه فيحزن على تفريطه، وفيما قال العلماء والصالحون فيحزن لفوته.

بسنده إلى مالك بن دينار قال: إن القلب إذا لم يكن فيه حزن خرب، كما أن البيت إذا لم يسكن خرب.

وبسنده إلى إبراهيم بن عيسى قال: مارأيت أطول حزنًا من الحسن وما رأيته قط إلا حسبته حديث عهد بمصيبة.

وبسنده إلى مالك بن دينار قال: بقدر ما تحزن للدنيا كذلك يخرج هم الآخرة من قلبك.

وإذ قد تبين أن الحزن لا يزال ملازما قلوب المتقين فينبغي أن يتقى إفراطه لأن الحزن إنما يكون على الفائت وقد عرفنا طريق الاستدراك.

وجاء في الحديث: "بقية عمر المؤمن لا قيمة له يستدرك فيه ما فات" فإن كان المحزون عليه لا يمكن استدراكه لم ينفع الحزن، وإن كان دينا فينبغي أن يقاومه برجاء الفضل والرحمن ليعتدل الحال، فأما إذا كان الحزن لأجل الدنيا وما فات منها فذلك الخسران المبين، فليدفعه العاقل عن نفسه. وأقوى علاجه أن يعلم أنه لا يرد فائتًا وإنما يضم إلى المصيبة فتصير اثنتين، والمصيبة ينبغي أن تخفف عن القلب وتدفع، فإذا استعمل الحزن والجزع زادت ثقلًا. قال ابن عمرو: إذا استأثر اللّٰه بشيء فالهَ عنه ((أي إذا نهى عن شيء فاتركه)) ثم في الخلف عن الفائت ما يسلي، فإن عدم ما يسلى اجتهد في صرف ذلك عن قلبه، وليعلم أن الداعي إلى الحزن الهوى لا العقل؛ لأن العقل لا يدعو إلى مالا ينفع، وليعلم أنه سيسلو بعد حين، فليجتهد في تقديم المؤخر، وليرتح ما بين الزمانين، ومما يمحق الحزن العلم بأنه لا يفيد، والإيمان بالثواب، ويذكر من أصابه أكثر من مصيبته.

الباب التاسع عشر

في دفع فضول الغم والهم

الغم يكون للماضي، والهم للمستقبل، فمن اغتم لما مضى من ذنوبه نفعه غمه على تفريطه، لأنه يثاب عليه، ومن اهتم بعمل خير نفعته همته، فأما إذا اغتم لمفقود من الدنيا

فالمفقود لا يرجع، والغم يؤذي، فكأنه أضاف إلى الأذى أذى، كما قلنا في الحزن. وينبغي للحازم أن يحترز مما يجلب الغم، وجالبه فقد المحبوب، فمن كثرت محبوباته كثر غمه، ومن قللها قل غمه، فإن قال قائل إذا لم أجد محبوبًا اغتممت، قيل له صدقت، ولكن لا يبلغ غمك بالعدم معشار عشر غم من فقد الحبوب، ألا ترى أن من لا ولد له يغتم، ولكن لا كغم من أصيب بولده، ثم إن الإنسان كلما طال ألفه لما يحبه واستمتاعه به تمكن من قلبه، فإذا فقده أحس من مر التألم في لحظة فقده بما يزيد على لذات دهره المتقدم، وهذا لأن المحبوب ملائم للنفس كالصحة فلا تجد النفس لذتها إلا عند وجودها، وفقدها مناف لها، ولذلك تألم بالفقد مالا تفرح بالموجود لأنها ترى وجود المحبوب كالحق الواجب لها، فينبغي للعاقل تقليل الألفة، فإن اضطر إلى جوالب الغم فأثمرت الغم فعلاجه في الأول الإيمان بالقدر، وأنه لابد مما قضى، ثم يعلم أن الدنيا موضوعة على الكدر، فالبناء إلى النقض، والجمع إلى التفرق، ومن رام بقاء ما لا يبقى كان كمن رام وجود ما لا يوجد، فلا ينبغي أن يطلب من الدنيا ما لم توضع عليه، كما قال الشاعر:

طبعت على كدر وأنت تريدها صفوًا من الإيذاء والأكدار

ثم يتصور مانزل به مضاعفا فيهون عليه حينئذ ماهو فيه، ومن عادة الحمال الحازم أن يترك فوق حمله شيئا ثقيلا، ثم يمشي خطوات، ثم يولى به فيخف الأمر عنه، ثم ليرتقب زمن العافية هجوم البلاء، فإذا هجم ما يكرهه، وليتمثل كلما يتصور نزوله نازلا، فإذا نزل بعض ذلك كان ربحًا مثل أن يتصور أن يؤخذ ماله كله، فإذا أخذ البعض عد الباقي غنيمة، ويتصور أن يعمى، فإذا رمد سهل الأمر، وكذلك جميع المضرات. قال الشاعر:

يمثل ذو اللب في نفسه مصائبه قبل أن تنزلا
فإن نزلت بغتة لم ترعه لما كان في نفسه مثلا
وذو الجهل يأمن أيامه وينس مصارع من قد خلا
فإن بدهته صروف الزمان ببعض مصائبه أعولا
ولو قدم الحزم في أمره لعلمه الصبر حسن البلا

قال بعض السلف: رأيت امرأة فتعجبت من نضارتها، فقلت هذا وجه ما طرقه حزن، فقالت لا تقل هذا، فما أعرف من ناله ما نالني؛ كان لي زوج، فاشترى أضحية فذبحها، وله ولدان، فقال الأكبر للأصغر تعال حتى أريك كيف ذبح أبي الشاة، فذبحه، فلما طلبناه هرب، فخرج
الأب في طلبه فهلكا، فقلت وكيف حزنك، قالت لو وجدت في الحزن دركا لاستعملته.

1.4 *English Translation*

Countering Excessive Sadness

Realize [even] rational people are not exempted from [experiencing] sadness. [This is] because an individual reflects on their past sins and thus feels remorse for their lack of restraint. One also [contemplates] that which the scholars and righteous people have mentioned [of virtue and wisdom], feeling saddened for falling short.[1]

Mālik ibn Dīnār[2] once said, "If the heart is devoid of sadness, it will be ruined just as a house, if uninhabited, becomes ruined."

Ibrāhīm ibn ʿĪsā once noted, "I have not seen a more sorrowful person than al-Ḥasan. Never did I see him except that I presumed a calamity had just befallen him."[3]

Mālik ibn Dīnār also stated, "The amount of grief you feel over a worldly matter is proportionately related to the [amount of] concern for the afterlife that escapes your heart."

It is clear that sorrow characteristically abides within the hearts of the righteous. Thus, it is the excess of it that should be avoided.

Sorrow occurs after missing out on something that we know we could have attained.

The following comes in a hadith: "The remainder of a believer's life is valueless, [unless,] during it, he realizes what he has missed."

If the thing about which one is saddened is not attainable, then such sadness is not of any benefit. If one's sorrow concerns a religious matter, then it must be countered with hope for divine grace and mercy[4] till one's state is

1 The author first starts with discussing the adaptive utility of sadness, as something that enhances functioning. Similarly, emotion theorists postulate that emotions are adaptive to the extent that they produce the required actions needed to meet personal needs (Leslie S. Greenberg, *Changing Emotion with Emotion: A Practitioner's Guide*. American Psychological Association, 2021). This is indicated by an orientation to the past such that an individual reflects upon something that they lost or committed an action that they regretted leading to feelings of shame. This feeling of shame thus becomes a source of motivation to not repeat the same mistake in the future.

2 The statement of the author "with his chain of transmission to …" is omitted throughout the translated excerpt for the sake of flow.

3 Being in a state of sadness and sorrow is an indication of taking one's life and religion seriously.

4 The published edition of the work says, "the All-Merciful" (*al-Raḥmān*) which is one of Allah's unique names. However, it is possible that this is a typographical error and that the correct

[properly] balanced.[5] As for sorrow on account of worldly matters, such is a manifest loss; an intelligent person should really protect himself from [falling into] it.

The most potent remedy for [excessive] sorrow is to know that the past is simply irreversible, and that sorrow only adds to the initial calamity, thus producing two problems [instead of one]. Really, one should [try to] de-escalate calamities by mitigating them within the heart. Ruminating over sadness and anxiety only makes the calamities [that cause them] feel heavier.

Ibn ʿAmr[6] said, "If Allah repossesses something that you once held, then turn your attention away from it." It [also] means that one should [totally] avoid what Allah has prohibited. Whatever one [supposedly] misses [out on] should be palatably substituted by something, [as] a distraction. If a suitable diversion is unavailable, one should effortfully keep the heart away from focusing on the [apparent] loss. Also, one must realize that sorrow is caused by emotion rather than the intellect; the rational mind does not attend to something devoid of benefit. Furthermore, a person should recognize that with the passing of time, one will [inevitably] forget [and move on]. Let him then look forward to that moment and be in a state of serenity sooner rather than later.[7] What additionally serves to curtail sorrow are the following:

---

word is "mercy" (*raḥma*). To support this, *Sharḥ al-Fayḍ al-Raḥmānī* also mentions the word "mercy" instead of "the All-Merciful" in the text provided.

5 Here, the author demonstrates the other end of the spectrum where sadness can be maladaptive. This can occur because it is excessive and thus one becomes too emotionally dysregulated to be able to derive any meaning or benefit from such sadness. Such may be the case of clinical depression where the sadness produces a type of numbing effect, leading an individual to feel hopeless and more dysfunctional as they seemingly drown in their emotions as is consistent with the hopelessness theory of depression (see Lyn Y. Abramson, Gerald I. Metalsky, and Lauren B. Alloy, "Hopelessness Depression: A Theory-Based Subtype of Depression.," *Psychological Review* 96, no. 2 (April 1989): 358–72.).

Another maladaptive expression of sadness is directly tied to one's attachments with the world. This is consistent with other Islamic literature that lists sorrow (*ḥuzn*) as a vice; such works typically describe it as an indication of an excessive attachment to the temporal world, the loss of which results in feelings of grief and sorrow. Within this context, sadness is understood to be a spiritual illness that must be remedied. In order to ward off excessive sadness and the potential for hopelessness regarding religious matters, Ibn al-Jawzī suggests what is termed in modern discourse as cognitive reframing by relying on Divine mercy with hope in Allah.

6 The attribution here is likely to Ibn ʿUmar and not ibn ʿAmr, and it is likely a typographical error.

7 In cognitive behavioral therapy (CBT), this is known as the "time machine" technique. The purpose of the technique is to help patients put their emotions into perspective by encouraging them to think about how they would likely feel about their troubling circumstances in

Knowing that sorrow is devoid of benefit; having faith in [heavenly] compensation; and remembering the One who has enabled such tribulations to occur rather than [focusing on] their [mere] occurrence.

Dealing with Grief and Anxiety

Grief is tied to the past, whereas anxiety relates to the future. Whoever is grieved because of his past sins, his sadness, even if excessive, will benefit him as he will be rewarded for it. As for one who is concerned regarding the performance of [a] good [deed], such concern will likewise benefit him. As for the one who is grieved by a worldly loss, then what passed is forever gone, and feeling depressed only adds to the loss. This is similar to what we have said regarding sorrow.

The prudent person is [one who is] duly cautious of all that may foment grief. Losing that which is cherished fosters grief, so whoever has a multitude of attachments [is likely to] experience more grief. Inversely, whoever has less attachments [is likely to] experience less grief. Now, if someone says, "When I have nothing to cherish, I feel grief," then his point is valid. However, we say to him that your grief due to a lack of attachment does not reach even one-tenth of the level of one who has lost someone [or something] dear. Do you not see the childless one grieve? Yet, such [pain] is incomparable to the grief of a person who is tested by [losing] their child.

Next, the longer a person bonds with and enjoys that which they love, the deeper it takes root in their heart. And when they suddenly lose it, they experience bitter pain in that moment of loss; such pain is [seemingly] greater than all other pleasures previously experienced in their life. This is because that which is beloved is [naturally] congenial to one's soul. Just as health is [in relation to the body], the soul finds no enjoyment except when the beloved is present; hence, losing the beloved is, [naturally,] unfavorable. This is why the soul is pained by the loss of that which is beloved to an extent that is much greater than the joy [felt] when it was present; one considers the presence of that which is beloved as if it was their indispensable right.

a week, a month, a year, and up to five years from now. This technique practically increases one's sense of awareness of their negative emotions' temporary nature. As the patient becomes more adept in this regard, such proves to be a valuable tool as they may consciously bring this to mind whenever they face feelings of overwhelm and therefore alleviate much of their inner suffering (Laura R. Silberstein et al., "Mindfulness, Psychological Flexibility and Emotional Schemas," *International Journal of Cognitive Therapy* 5, no. 4 (December 2012): 406–19.).

As such, an intelligent person ought to minimize their attachments. If one becomes driven towards that which provokes sadness, which thereafter develops into grief, then its primary cure is to inculcate a firm belief in destiny; what has transpired was inevitably meant to be. Next, one should know that the temporal world was inherently meant to be sullied; all that is built up ultimately crumbles; all that is amassed is eventually squandered.[8] Whoever expects that which is temporary to last forever is just like someone who hopes to get something out of nothing; it is not befitting to seek from the world that for which it was not inherently designed. Relevantly, a poet once said: "[This world] was made to be murky, yet you want it without misery or muck."

Moreover, a person can imagine [how it would be if] their situation was radically worse, which [would] effectively mitigate whatever [difficulty] he is dealing with in the moment.

Characteristically, those who are resolute and forbearing [at first] tend to leave off things that are beyond their capacity and [are thus] too arduous to

---

8 The passage's thoughts align with a historical continuum of philosophical and psychological ideas. Stoic philosophy, rooted in ancient wisdom, encourages individuals to accept the natural order, acknowledge the impermanence of external things, and cultivate resilience. This view on detachment from external circumstances finds support in the passage, where minimizing attachments and recognizing the transient nature of the temporal world are central themes.

In the Islamic Golden Age, al-Kindī (c. 801–873 CE), the first of the Islamic peripatetic philosophers, and a renowned polymath made substantial contirbutions to this idea. In his *Epistle on the Device for Dispelling Sorrows* (*Risāla fi al-ḥīla li-daf' al-aḥzān*), he emphasized that in the world of generation and decay, it is impossible to attain everything one desires or be safe from losing things they love . He suggested focusing on the intelligible world of the intellect, which offers stable, unchanging objects of desire. Al-Kindī warns against seeking permanence in a temporal world and, like Stoicism, encourages accepting things as they are and modifying wants and desires accordingly (Peter S. Groff, "Al-Kindi and Nietzsche on the Stoic Art of Banishing Sorrow," *The Journal of Nietzsche Studies* 28, no. 1 (January 1, 2004): 139–73.).

Further in history, existentialists, and existential psychologists advocated for confronting the fundamental issues of human existence, including freedom, responsibility, and the inevitability of death. (See Irvin D. Yalom, *Existential Psychotherapy* (London, England: Basic Books, 1980; Irvin D. Yalom, *Staring at the sun: Overcoming the terror of death* (San Francisco: Jossey-Bass, 2008.). These existential concerns are supported by the passage's invitation to accept life's uncertainties and find meaning in the midst of existential difficulties.

Additionally, the passage's thoughts are in line with dialectical behavior therapy (DBT)'s principle of radical acceptance. Radical acceptance, a central tenet of DBT, promotes accepting and embracing reality without resistance or denial. Minimizing attachments is consistent with this acceptance of the unpredictable nature of events, and embracing the inherent flaws in the temporal World (see Marsha Linehan, *Skills Training Manual for Treating Borderline Personality Disorder* (New York: Guilford Press, 1993.).

endure. They progressively advance, step-by-step, and thereafter take on such matters. This [approach] makes one's affairs [much] more manageable. Next, they picture themselves to soon be worry-free as a way to tackle the difficulty at hand. Plus, if a person confronts what he dislikes by imagining himself in the worst [possible] scenario, then for only a portion of that to [actually] occur, such is [easy to handle, like] a breeze. For example, if he were to envision that all of his wealth was stolen when only a portion was [actually] taken, then what remains would be counted as a gain. Another example is to imagine himself to be [completely] blind when he is [merely] experiencing eye pain; such becomes easier [to bear]. All other difficulties can be dealt with similarly.[9]

A poet once said:

> The wise one prepares for his [share of] calamities before they happen;
> When they suddenly descend, such does not startle him,
> Given what he has [already] anticipated from within.
> Whereas the fool passes his days feeling safe,
> Forgetting the downfalls of those who have previously passed on.
> When the vicissitudes of time and disasters suddenly strike, he cries out.
> If only he were to have prepared [with] prudence in his affairs,
> Patience would have taught him [how to] handle adversity well.[10]

---

9 This is a resilience development tactic designed to get the individual to consider a condition that is considerably worse than the one that they are currently experiencing. By focusing one's attention on the possibility of things being worse, one can cognitively reframe their suffering, consequently viewing their tragedy as a blessing. Such a person can then be grateful for all that they have as opposed to feeling distressed over what was lost. A similar technique is used in cognitive behavioral therapy (CBT), which postulates that when people are anxious about something, they fixate on the worst possible outcome even though the worst outcome is usually not the likely outcome. As a result, people can needlessly overwhelm themselves with anxiety. Thus, while encouraging their patient to think of the worst-case scenario in relation to their anxiety-provoking situation, a CBT therapist asks them to come up with ways to cope with that theoretical scenario. This technique helps put difficult matters into perspective, effectively making it feel much more manageable in the eyes of the patient (Laura R. Silberstein et al., "Mindfulness, Psychological Flexibility and Emotional Schemas," *International Journal of Cognitive Therapy* 5, no. 4 (December 2012): 406–19.).

Furthermore, this approach can be combined with the belief in destiny and divine will, recalling the belief that there are hidden blessings in every tragedy that one may not always be able to fully perceive; only an all-Merciful and all-Powerful Lord knows what is best, and He has full control.

10 As per Borkovec et al., individuals frequently experience anxiety when attempting to evade distressing mental images or thoughts. They invest considerable cognitive energy in preventing the occurrence of these terrifying events (Thomas D. Borkovec, Oscar M.

A person from amongst the pious predecessors said, "I once saw a woman, and noticed a unique radiance on her [face]. I said to her, 'This face [of yours]! It [seems] to have never been stricken by any sorrow!' She replied, 'Do not say that. I do not know anyone who has gone through what I have faced. I had a husband who once purchased a sacrificial animal, which he slaughtered. Then, the older of his two sons said to the younger one, 'Come, I will show you how our father slaughtered the sheep.' He then slaughtered his younger brother [instead]. When we went after him, he ran away. His father set out to find him, and both of them perished.' When I asked about her grief, she said, 'Had I found a limit to grief, I would have made use of it.'"

2 The Station of Grief. *Madārij al-Sālikīn Bayn Manāzil Iyyāka Naʿbud wa-Iyyāka Nastaʿīn* (*Stations of the Seekers*) by Imam Ibn Qayyim al-Jawziyya (d. 751 AH/1351 CE)

2.1 *Author's Biography*

Shams al-Dīn Abū ʿAbd Allah Muḥammad ibn ʿAlī Bakr ibn Ayyūb al-Zurʿi al-Dimashqī, more famously known as Ibn al-Qayyim, is famously recognized as the most prominent student under the tutelage and mentorship of Ibn Taymiyya. He is known as Ibn al-Qayyim – which literally means "the son of the principal," – due to his father's role in serving as the headmaster of the renowned *Jawziyya* seminary college in Damascus. Imam Ibn al-Qayyim was a true polymath, having mastered the Islamic sciences while also demonstrating proficiency in the natural sciences. Throughout his sixty years of life, he has produced over one hundred written works in a diverse range of fields, including the Quranic sciences, jurisprudence, ḥadīth, medicine, and psychology. Ibn al-Qayyim posited that meditation, reflection, and introspection are necessary for striving towards inner contentment, drawing upon the oft-quoted statement, "the righteous among our predecessors used to say that mindful

Alcaine, and Evelyn Behar, "Avoidance Theory of Worry and Generalized Anxiety Disorder" *Generalized Anxiety Disorder: Advances in Research and Practice*, January 1, 2004, 77–108). However, avoidance is counterproductive and potentially useless in alleviating anxiety. Building on this idea, Robert L. Leahy who is a clinical psychologist and leading figure in the field of cognitive-behavioral therapy (CBT) introduced the Feared Fantasy Worry, a paradoxical flooding technique aimed at assisting patients in reducing anxiety to a more manageable level. This technique encourages individuals to deliberately prolong their contemplation of their most intense fears. Over time, this exposure leads to habituation, rapidly diminishing the preceding worry (Robert L. Leahy, *Cognitive Therapy Techniques, Second Edition: A Practitioner's Guide* (Guilford Publications, 2017).

reflection for an hour is better than worshiping for sixty years." He passed away in the year 1350 CE and is buried in the famous Bāb al-Ṣaghīr cemetery of Damascus, Syria.

2.2 *Text Overview and Significance*

Ibn al-Qayyim's book *Madārij al-Sālikīn*, is based upon a book written by Abū Isma'īl al-Ansārī al-Ḥarāwī (d. 482 AH/1089 CE) entitled *Manāzil al-Sā'irīn* (Stations of the Wayfarers). This original work outlines one hundred various stations that seekers of the spiritual path traverse on their reformative spiritual journey. Although it could be read as an independent work, Ibn al-Qayyim's *Madārij al-Sālikīn* serves as a commentary of *Manāzil al-Sā'irīn*; it is brilliant in providing details of the different spiritual stations, replete with injunctions and valuable advice to the seekers of spiritual reformation.

The selected section translated below is taken from a segment in *Madārij al-Sālikīn* that explores the topic of grief. Ibn al-Qayyim outlines that it is a station that every seeker inevitably has to experience and pass through. However, albeit natural and necessary, he does not consider grief to be praiseworthy in and of itself. Rather, he indicates that one must retreat from this station, which seemingly contradicts other scholars like that of Ibn Abī Dunyā who discusses the value of grief. While it ostensibly appears that Ibn al-Qayyim discredits grief, upon reading the text closely, one comes to understand that he merely views grief as an indication of what one values. In other words, he sees the feeling of grief as more utilitarian and not of value in and of itself; thus, it is a gateway to identify that which is more practically important. For example, if a person experiences grief for religious reasons like missing prayer, then it can prove to be quite valuable. However, grief that indicates an excessive attachment to the temporal world is a clear spiritual disorder. To elucidate, Ibn al-Qayyim cites a segment of the Quran that recounts an incident in which a group of the companions of the Prophet, may Allah bless him and grant him peace, returned with tears flowing after they were told that they cannot partake in a military expedition. Ibn al-Qayyim explains that their pious desire to partake in a noble deed is an indication of faith; thus, the associated grief is praiseworthy. Furthermore, in traversing the spiritual path, one gradually reduces their attachment to the ephemeral world; such transformative detachment from materialistic desires necessarily comes with feelings of grief. Ibn al-Qayyim therefore sees it as a necessary station of spiritual growth; and the more swiftly a person can pass through it, the better it is overall.

While providing a unique perspective regarding grief and its utility, some of the strategies he employs and insights Ibn al-Qayyim offers somewhat resemble cognitive theories. Both place emphasis on the underlying beliefs and thoughts as one of the most central aspects to consider; thus, emotions are rendered as mere byproducts of these underlying beliefs.

2.3 *Arabic Text*

فَصْلٌ مَنْزِلَةُ الْحُزْنِ

وَمِنْ مَنَازِلِ ﴿إِيَّاكَ نَعْبُدُ وَإِيَّاكَ نَسْتَعِينُ﴾ [الفاتحة: 5] مَنْزِلَةُ الْحُزْنِ.

وَلَيْسَتْ مِنَ الْمَنَازِلِ الْمَطْلُوبَةِ، وَلَا الْمَأْمُورِ بِنُزُولِهَا، وَإِنْ كَانَ لَا بُدَّ لِلسَّالِكِ مِنْ نُزُولِهَا. وَلَمْ يَأْتِ "الْحُزْنُ" فِي الْقُرْآنِ إِلَّا مَنْهِيًّا عَنْهُ، أَوْ مَنْفِيًّا.

فَالْمَنْهِيُّ عَنْهُ كَقَوْلِهِ تَعَالَى ﴿وَلَا تَهِنُوا وَلَا تَحْزَنُوا﴾ [آل عمران: 139] وَقَوْلِهِ: ﴿وَلَا تَحْزَنْ عَلَيْهِمْ﴾ [الحجر: 88] فِي غَيْرِ مَوْضِعٍ، وَقَوْلِهِ: ﴿لَا تَحْزَنْ إِنَّ اللَّهَ مَعَنَا﴾ [التوبة: 40] وَالْمَنْفِيُّ كَقَوْلِهِ: ﴿فَلَا خَوْفٌ عَلَيْهِمْ وَلَا هُمْ يَحْزَنُونَ﴾ [البقرة: 38].

وَسِرُّ ذَلِكَ أَنَّ "الْحُزْنَ" مُوقِفٌ غَيْرُ مُسَيِّرٍ، وَلَا مَصْلَحَةَ فِيهِ لِلْقَلْبِ. وَأَحَبُّ شَيْءٍ إِلَى الشَّيْطَانِ أَنْ يَحْزَنَ الْعَبْدُ لِيَقْطَعَهُ عَنْ سَيْرِهِ، وَيُوقِفَهُ عَنْ سُلُوكِهِ، قَالَ اللَّهُ تَعَالَى: ﴿إِنَّمَا النَّجْوَى مِنَ الشَّيْطَانِ لِيَحْزُنَ الَّذِينَ آمَنُوا﴾ [المجادلة: 10]. وَنَهَى النَّبِيُّ صَلَّى اللَّهُ عَلَيْهِ وَسَلَّمَ الثَّلَاثَةَ أَنْ يَتَنَاجَى اثْنَانِ مِنْهُمْ دُونَ الثَّالِثِ، لِأَنَّ ذَلِكَ يُحْزِنُهُ. فَالْحُزْنُ لَيْسَ بِمَطْلُوبٍ، وَلَا مَقْصُودٍ، وَلَا فِيهِ فَائِدَةٌ، وَقَدِ اسْتَعَاذَ مِنْهُ النَّبِيُّ صَلَّى اللَّهُ عَلَيْهِ وَسَلَّمَ فَقَالَ «اللَّهُمَّ إِنِّي أَعُوذُ بِكَ مِنَ الْهَمِّ وَالْحَزَنِ» فَهُوَ قَرِينُ الْهَمِّ. وَالْفَرْقُ بَيْنَهُمَا أَنَّ الْمَكْرُوهَ الَّذِي يَرِدُ عَلَى الْقَلْبِ إِنْ كَانَ لِمَا يُسْتَقْبَلُ أَوْرَثَهُ الْهَمَّ، وَإِنْ كَانَ لِمَا مَضَى أَوْرَثَهُ الْحُزْنَ، وَكِلَاهُمَا مُضْعِفٌ لِلْقَلْبِ عَنِ السَّيْرِ، مُفَتِّرٌ لِلْعَزْمِ.

وَلَكِنَّ نُزُولَ مَنْزِلَتِهِ ضَرُورِيٌّ بِحَسَبِ الْوَاقِعِ، وَلِهَذَا يَقُولُ أَهْلُ الْجَنَّةِ إِذَا دَخَلُوهَا ﴿الْحَمْدُ لِلَّهِ الَّذِي أَذْهَبَ عَنَّا الْحَزَنَ﴾ [فاطر: 34] فَهَذَا يَدُلُّ عَلَى أَنَّهُمْ كَانَ يُصِيبُهُمْ فِي الدُّنْيَا الْحَزَنُ، كَمَا يُصِيبُهُمْ سَائِرُ الْمَصَائِبِ الَّتِي تَجْرِي عَلَيْهِمْ بِغَيْرِ اخْتِيَارِهِمْ.

وَأَمَّا قَوْلُهُ تَعَالَى ﴿وَلَا عَلَى الَّذِينَ إِذَا مَا أَتَوْكَ لِتَحْمِلَهُمْ قُلْتَ لَا أَجِدُ مَا أَحْمِلُكُمْ عَلَيْهِ تَوَلَّوْا وَأَعْيُنُهُمْ تَفِيضُ مِنَ الدَّمْعِ حَزَنًا أَنْ لَا يَجِدُوا مَا يُنْفِقُونَ﴾ [التوبة: 92] فَلَمْ يُمْدَحُوا عَلَى نَفْسِ الْحَزَنِ، وَإِنَّمَا مُدِحُوا عَلَى مَا دَلَّ عَلَيْهِ الْحَزَنُ مِنْ قُوَّةِ إِيمَانِهِمْ، حَيْثُ تَخَلَّفُوا عَنْ رَسُولِ اللَّهِ صَلَّى اللَّهُ عَلَيْهِ وَسَلَّمَ لِعَجْزِهِمْ عَنِ النَّفَقَةِ، فَفِيهِ تَعْرِيضٌ بِالْمُنَافِقِينَ الَّذِينَ لَمْ يَحْزَنُوا عَلَى تَخَلُّفِهِمْ، بَلْ غَبَطُوا نُفُوسَهُمْ بِهِ.

وَأَمَّا قَوْلُهُ صَلَّى اللَّهُ عَلَيْهِ وَسَلَّمَ فِي الْحَدِيثِ الصَّحِيحِ «مَا يُصِيبُ الْمُؤْمِنَ مِنْ هَمٍّ وَلَا نَصَبٍ وَلَا حَزَنٍ إِلَّا كَفَّرَ اللَّهُ بِهِ مِنْ خَطَايَاهُ» فَهَذَا يَدُلُّ عَلَى أَنَّهُ مُصِيبَةٌ مِنَ اللَّهِ يُصِيبُ بِهَا الْعَبْدَ، يُكَفِّرُ بِهَا مِنْ سَيِّئَاتِهِ، لَا يَدُلُّ عَلَى أَنَّهُ مَقَامٌ يَنْبَغِي طَلَبُهُ وَاسْتِيطَانُهُ.

وَأَمَّا حَدِيثُ هِنْدِ بْنِ أَبِي هَالَةَ فِي صِفَةِ النَّبِيِّ صَلَّى اللَّهُ عَلَيْهِ وَسَلَّمَ: "إِنَّهُ كَانَ مُتَوَاصِلَ الْأَحْزَانِ" فَحَدِيثٌ لَا يَثْبُتُ، وَفِي إِسْنَادِهِ مَنْ لَا يُعْرَفُ.

وَكَيْفَ يَكُونُ مُتَوَاصِلَ الْأَحْزَانِ وَقَدْ صَانَهُ اللَّهُ عَنِ الْحُزْنِ عَلَى الدُّنْيَا وَأَسْبَابِهَا، وَنَهَاهُ عَنِ الْحُزْنِ عَلَى الْكُفَّارِ، وَغَفَرَ لَهُ مَا تَقَدَّمَ مِنْ ذَنْبِهِ وَمَا تَأَخَّرَ؟ فَمِنْ أَيْنَ يَأْتِيهِ الْحُزْنُ؟

بَلْ كَانَ دَائِمَ الْبِشْرِ، ضَحُوكَ السِّنِّ، كَمَا فِي صِفَتِهِ: "الضَّحُوكُ الْقَتَّالُ" صَلَوَاتُ اللَّهِ وَسَلَامُهُ عَلَيْهِ.

وَأَمَّا الْخَبَرُ الْمَرْوِيُّ: «إِنَّ اللَّهَ يُحِبُّ كُلَّ قَلْبٍ حَزِينٍ» فَلَا يُعْرَفُ إِسْنَادُهُ، وَلَا مَنْ رَوَاهُ، وَلَا تُعْلَمُ صِحَّتُهُ.

وَعَلَى تَقْدِيرِ صِحَّتِهِ فَالْحُزْنُ مُصِيبَةٌ مِنَ الْمَصَائِبِ الَّتِي يَبْتَلِي اللَّهُ بِهَا عَبْدَهُ، فَإِذَا ابْتَلَى بِهِ الْعَبْدَ فَصَبَرَ عَلَيْهِ أَحَبَّ صَبْرَهُ عَلَى بَلَائِهِ.

وَأَمَّا الْأَثَرُ الْآخَرُ: «إِذَا أَحَبَّ اللَّهُ عَبْدًا نَصَبَ فِي قَلْبِهِ نَائِحَةً، وَإِذَا أَبْغَضَ عَبْدًا جَعَلَ فِي قَلْبِهِ مِزْمَارًا» فَأَثَرٌ إِسْرَائِيلِيٌّ، قِيلَ: إِنَّهُ فِي التَّوْرَاةِ، وَلَهُ مَعْنًى صَحِيحٌ، فَإِنَّ الْمُؤْمِنَ حَزِينٌ عَلَى ذُنُوبِهِ، وَالْفَاجِرَ لَاهٍ لَاعِبٌ، مُتَرَنِّمٌ فَرِحٌ.

وَأَمَّا قَوْلُهُ تَعَالَى عَنْ نَبِيِّهِ إِسْرَائِيلَ: ﴿وَابْيَضَّتْ عَيْنَاهُ مِنَ الْحُزْنِ فَهُوَ كَظِيمٌ﴾ [يوسف: 84] فَهُوَ إِخْبَارٌ عَنْ حَالِهِ بِمُصَابِهِ بِفَقْدِ وَلَدِهِ، وَحَبِيبِهِ، وَأَنَّهُ ابْتَلَاهُ بِذَلِكَ كَمَا ابْتَلَاهُ بِالتَّفْرِيقِ بَيْنَهُ وَبَيْنَهُ.

وَأَجْمَعَ أَرْبَابُ السُّلُوكِ عَلَى أَنَّ حُزْنَ الدُّنْيَا غَيْرُ مَحْمُودٍ إِلَّا أَبَا عُثْمَانَ الْحِيرِيَّ، فَإِنَّهُ قَالَ: الْحُزْنُ بِكُلِّ وَجْهٍ فَضِيلَةٌ، وَزِيَادَةٌ لِلْمُؤْمِنِ، مَا لَمْ يَكُنْ بِسَبَبِ مَعْصِيَةٍ، قَالَ: لِأَنَّهُ إِنْ لَمْ يُوجِبْ تَخْصِيصًا، فَإِنَّهُ يُوجِبُ تَمْحِيصًا.

فَيُقَالُ: لَا رَيْبَ أَنَّهُ مِحْنَةٌ وَبَلَاءٌ مِنَ اللَّهِ، بِمَنْزِلَةِ الْمَرَضِ وَالْهَمِّ وَالْغَمِّ، وَأَمَّا إِنَّهُ مِنْ مَنَازِلِ الطَّرِيقِ فَلَا، وَاللَّهُ سُبْحَانَهُ أَعْلَمُ.

فَصْلٌ

قَالَ صَاحِبُ الْمَنَازِلِ: الْحُزْنُ تَوَجُّعٌ لِفَائِتٍ، وَتَأَسُّفٌ عَلَى مُمْتَنِعٍ. يُرِيدُ أَنَّ مَا يَفُوتُ الْإِنْسَانَ قَدْ يَكُونُ مَقْدُورًا لَهُ، وَقَدْ لَا يَكُونُ، فَإِنْ كَانَ مَقْدُورًا تَوَجَّعَ لِفَوْتِهِ، وَإِنْ كَانَ غَيْرَ مَقْدُورٍ تَأَسَّفَ لِامْتِنَاعِهِ. قَالَ: وَلَهُ ثَلَاثُ دَرَجَاتٍ، الْأُولَى: حُزْنُ الْعَامَّةِ، وَهُوَ حَزَنٌ عَلَى التَّفْرِيطِ فِي الْخِدْمَةِ، وَعَلَى التَّوَرُّطِ فِي الْجَفَاءِ، وَعَلَى ضَيَاعِ الْأَيَّامِ. التَّفْرِيطُ فِي الْخِدْمَةِ عِنْدَهُمْ فَوْقَ التَّفْرِيطِ فِي الْعَمَلِ وَتَضْيِيعِهِ، بَلْ هَذَا الْحُزْنُ يَكُونُ مَعَ الْقِيَامِ وَالْعَمَلِ، فَإِنَّ الْخِدْمَةَ عِنْدَهُمْ مِنْ بَابِ الْأَخْلَاقِ وَالْآدَابِ، لَا مِنْ بَابِ الْأَفْعَالِ، وَهِيَ حَقُّ الْعُبُودِيَّةِ، وَأَدَبُهَا وَوَاجِبُهَا، وَصَاحِبُ هَذَا الْحُزْنِ بِالْأَوْلَى: أَنْ يَحْزَنَ لِتَضْيِيعِ الْعَمَلِ.

وَأَمَّا التَّوَرُّطُ فِي الْجَفَاءِ فَهُوَ أَيْضًا أَخَصُّ مِنَ الْمَعْصِيَةِ بِارْتِكَابِ الْمَحْظُورِ لِأَنَّهُ قَدْ يَكُونُ لِفَقْدِ أُنْسٍ سَابِقٍ مَعَ اللَّهِ، فَإِذَا تَوَارَى عَنْهُ تَوَرَّطَ فِي الْجَفْوَةِ، فَإِنَّ الشَّيْخَ ذَكَرَ الْحُزْنَ فِي قِسْمِ الْأَبْوَابِ وَهُوَ عِنْدَهُ مِنْ قِسْمِ الْبِدَايَاتِ.

وَأَمَّا تَضْيِيعُ الْأَيَّامِ فَنَوْعَانِ أَيْضًا: تَضْيِيعُهَا بِخُلُوِّهَا عَنِ الطَّاعَاتِ، وَتَضْيِيعُهَا خُلُوِّهَا عَنْ مَوَاجِيدِ الْإِيمَانِ، وَذَوْقِ حَلَاوَتِهِ، وَالْأُنْسِ بِاللَّهِ، وَحُسْنِ الصُّحْبَةِ مَعَهُ. فَكُلُّ وَاحِدٍ مِنَ الثَّلَاثَةِ نَوْعَانِ لِأَهْلِ الْبِدَايَةِ، وَلِلسَّالِكِينَ الْمُتَوَسِّطِينَ. وَكَلَامُهُ يَعُمُّ النَّوْعَيْنِ، وَإِنْ كَانَ بِالثَّانِي أَخَصَّ.

قَالَ: الدَّرَجَةُ الثَّانِيَةُ حُزْنُ أَهْلِ الْإِرَادَةِ، وَهُوَ حُزْنٌ عَلَى تَعَلُّقِ الْقَلْبِ بِالتَّفْرِقَةِ، وَعَلَى اشْتِغَالِ النَّفْسِ عَنِ الشُّهُودِ، وَعَلَى التَّسَلِّي عَنِ الْحُزْنِ. تَعَلُّقُ الْقَلْبِ بِالتَّفْرِقَةِ: هُوَ عَدَمُ الْجَمْعِيَّةِ فِي الْحُضُورِ مَعَ اللَّهِ، وَتَشْتِيتُ الْخَوَاطِرِ فِي أَوْدِيَةِ الْمُرَادَاتِ. وَأَمَّا اشْتِغَالُ النَّفْسِ عَنِ الشُّهُودِ فَهُوَ نَوْعَانِ: اشْتِغَالُهَا عَنِ الذِّكْرِ الَّذِي يُوجِبُ الشُّهُودَ وَيُثْمِرُهُ بِغَيْرِهِ. وَالثَّانِي: اشْتِغَالُهَا عَنِ الشُّهُودِ، لِضَعْفِ الذِّكْرِ، أَوْ لِضَعْفِ الْقَلْبِ عَنِ الشُّهُودِ، أَوْ لِمَانِعٍ آخَرَ، وَلَكِنْ إِذَا قَهَرَ الشُّهُودُ النَّفْسَ لَمْ تَتَمَكَّنْ مِنَ التَّشَاغُلِ عَنْهُ إِلَّا بِقَاهِرٍ يَقْهَرُهَا عَنْهُ.

وَأَمَّا التَّسَلِّي عَنِ الْحُزْنِ فَيَعْنِي أَنَّ وُجُودَ الْحُزْنِ فِي الْقَلْبِ دَلِيلٌ عَلَى الْإِرَادَةِ وَالطَّلَبِ، فَفَقْدُهُ وَالتَّسَلِّي عَنْهُ نَقْصٌ، فَيَحْزَنُ عَلَى فَقْدِ الْحُزْنِ، كَمَا يَبْكِي عَلَى فَقْدِ الْبُكَاءِ، وَيَخَافُ مِنْ عَدَمِ الْخَوْفِ، وَهَذَا فِيهِ نَظَرٌ، وَإِنَّمَا يُحْمَدُ الْحُزْنُ عَلَى فَقْدِ الْحُزْنِ، أَمَّا إِذَا اشْتَغَلَ عَنِ الْحُزْنِ بِفَرَحٍ مَحْمُودٍ وَهُوَ الْفَرَحُ بِفَضْلِ اللَّهِ وَرَحْمَتِهِ فَلَا مَعْنَى لِلْحُزْنِ عَلَى فَوَاتِ الْحُزْنِ.

قَالَ صَاحِبُ الْمَنَازِلِ: وَلَيْسَتِ الْخَاصَّةُ مِنْ مَقَامِ الْحُزْنِ فِي شَيْءٍ، لِأَنَّ الْحُزْنَ فَقْدٌ، وَالْخَاصَّةَ أَهْلُ وِجْدَانٍ. وَهَذَا إِنْ أَرَادَ بِهِ أَنَّهُ لَا يَنْبَغِي لَهُمْ تَعَمُّدُ الْحُزْنِ فَصَحِيحٌ، وَإِنْ أَرَادَ بِهِ لَا يَعْرِضُ لَهُمْ حُزْنٌ فَلَيْسَ كَذَلِكَ، وَالْحُزْنُ مِنْ لَوَازِمِ الطَّبِيعَةِ، وَلَكِنْ لَيْسَ هُوَ بِمَقَامٍ.

قَالَ: الدَّرَجَةُ الثَّالِثَةُ مِنَ الْحُزْنِ التَّحَزُّنُ لِلْمُعَارِضَاتِ دُونَ الْخَوَاطِرِ وَمُعَارِضَاتُ الْقُصُودِ، وَاعْتِرَاضَاتُ الْأَحْكَامِ.

هَذِهِ ثَلَاثَةُ أُمُورٍ، بِحَسَبِ الشُّهُودِ وَالْإِرَادَةِ.

الْأَوَّلُ: حُزْنُ الْمُعَارِضَاتِ، فَإِنَّ الْقَلْبَ يَعْتَرِضُهُ وَارِدُ الرَّجَاءِ مَثَلًا، فَلَمْ يَنْشَبْ أَنْ يُعَارِضَهُ وَارِدُ الْخَوْفِ، وَبِالْعَكْسِ، وَيَعْتَرِضُهُ وَارِدُ الْبَسْطِ، فَلَمْ يَنْشَبْ أَنْ يَعْتَرِضَهُ وَارِدُ الْقَبْضِ، وَيَرِدُ عَلَيْهِ وَارِدُ الْأُنْسِ، فَيَعْتَرِضُهُ وَارِدُ الْهَيْبَةِ، فَيُوجِبُ لَهُ اخْتِلَافُ هَذِهِ الْمُعَارِضَاتِ عَلَيْهِ حُزْنًا لَا مَحَالَةَ. وَلَيْسَتْ هَذِهِ الْمُعَارِضَاتُ مِنْ قَبِيلِ الْخَوَاطِرِ، بَلْ هِيَ مِنْ قَبِيلِ الْوَارِدَاتِ الْإِلَهِيَّةِ، فَلِذَلِكَ قَالَ "دُونَ الْخَوَاطِرِ" فَإِنَّ مُعَارِضَاتِ الْخَوَاطِرِ غَيْرُ هَذَا. وَعِنْدَ الْقَوْمِ هَذَا مِنْ آثَارِ الْأَسْمَاءِ وَالصِّفَاتِ، وَاتِّصَالِ أَشِعَّةِ أَنْوَارِهَا بِالْقَلْبِ، وَهُوَ الْمُسَمَّى عِنْدَهُمْ بِالتَّجَلِّي.

وَأَمَّا مُعَارِضَاتُ الْقُصُودِ فَهِيَ أَصْعَبُ مَا عَلَى الْقَوْمِ، وَفِيهِ يَظْهَرُ اضْطِرَارُهُمْ إِلَى الْعِلْمِ فَوْقَ كُلِّ ضَرُورَةٍ، فَإِنَّ الصَّادِقَ يَتَحَرَّى فِي سُلُوكِهِ كُلِّهِ أَحَبَّ الطُّرُقِ إِلَى اللَّهِ، فَإِنَّهُ سَالِكٌ

بِهِ وَإِلَيْهِ، فَيَعْتَرِضُهُ طَرِيقَانِ لَا يَدْرِي أَيُّهُمَا أَرْضَى لِلَّهِ وَأَحَبَّ إِلَيْهِ، فَمِنْهُمْ مَنْ يُحَكِّمُ الْعِلْمَ بِجُهْدِهِ اسْتِدْلَالًا، فَإِنْ عَجَزَ فَتَقْلِيدًا، فَإِنْ عَجَزَ عَنْهُمَا سَكَنَ يَنْتَظِرُ مَا يَحْكُمُ لَهُ بِهِ الْقَدَرُ، وَيُخْلِي بَاطِنَهُ مِنَ الْمَقَاصِدِ جُمْلَةً. وَمِنْهُمْ مَنْ يُلْقِي الْكُلَّ عَلَى شَيْخِهِ، إِنْ كَانَ لَهُ شَيْخٌ.

وَمِنْهُمْ مَنْ يَلْجَأُ إِلَى الِاسْتِخَارَةِ وَالدُّعَاءِ، ثُمَّ يَنْتَظِرُ مَا يَجْرِي بِهِ الْقَدَرُ. وَأَصْحَابُ الْعَزَائِمِ يَبْذُلُونَ وُسْعَهُمْ فِي طَلَبِ الْأَرْضَى عِلْمًا وَمَعْرِفَةً، فَإِنْ أَعْجَزَهُمْ قَنِعُوا بِالظَّنِّ الْغَالِبِ، فَإِنْ تَسَاوَى عِنْدَهُمُ الْأَمْرَانِ، قَدَّمُوا أَرْجَحَهُمَا مَصْلَحَةً.

وَلِتَرْجِيحِ الْمَصَالِحِ رُتَبٌ مُتَفَاوِتَةٌ، فَتَارَةً تَتَرَجَّحُ بِعُمُومِ النَّفْعِ، وَتَارَةً تَتَرَجَّحُ بِزِيَادَةِ الْإِيمَانِ، وَتَارَةً تَتَرَجَّحُ بِمُخَالَفَةِ النَّفْسِ، وَتَارَةً تَتَرَجَّحُ بِاسْتِجْلَابِ مَصْلَحَةٍ أُخْرَى لَا تَحْصُلُ مِنْ غَيْرِهَا، وَتَارَةً تَتَرَجَّحُ بِأَمْنِهَا مِنَ الْخَوْفِ مِنْ مَفْسَدَةٍ لَا تُؤْمَنُ فِي غَيْرِهَا. فَهَذِهِ خَمْسُ جِهَاتٍ مِنَ التَّرْجِيحِ، قَلَّ أَنْ يَعْدِمَ وَاحِدَةً مِنْهَا.

فَإِنْ أَعْوَزَهُ ذَلِكَ كُلُّهُ تَخَلَّى عَنِ الْخَوَاطِرِ جُمْلَةً، وَانْتَظَرَ مَا يُحَرِّكُهُ بِهِ مُحَرِّكُ الْقَدَرِ ، وَافْتَقَرَ إِلَى رَبِّهِ افْتِقَارَ مُسْتَنْزِلٍ مَا يُرْضِيهِ وَيُحِبُّهُ، فَإِذَا جَاءَتْهُ الْحَرَكَةُ اسْتَخَارَ اللَّهَ، وَافْتَقَرَ إِلَيْهِ افْتِقَارًا ثَانِيًا، خَشْيَةَ أَنْ تَكُونَ تِلْكَ الْحَرَكَةُ نَفْسِيَّةً أَوْ شَيْطَانِيَّةً، لِعَدَمِ الْعِصْمَةِ فِي حَقِّهِ، وَاسْتِمْرَارِ الْمِحْنَةِ بِعَدُوِّهِ، مَا دَامَ فِي عَالَمِ الِابْتِلَاءِ وَالِامْتِحَانِ، ثُمَّ أَقْدَمَ عَلَى الْفِعْلِ. فَهَذَا نِهَايَةُ مَا فِي مَقْدُورِ الصَّادِقِينَ.

وَلِأَهْلِ الْجِهَادِ فِي هَذَا مِنَ الْهِدَايَةِ وَالْكَشْفِ مَا لَيْسَ لِأَهْلِ الْمُجَاهَدَةِ، وَلِهَذَا قَالَ الْأَوْزَاعِيُّ وَابْنُ الْمُبَارَكِ: إِذَا اخْتَلَفَ النَّاسُ فِي شَيْءٍ فَانْظُرُوا مَا عَلَيْهِ أَهْلُ الثَّغْرِ، يَعْنِي أَهْلَ الْجِهَادِ، فَإِنَّ اللَّهَ تَعَالَى يَقُولُ ﴿وَالَّذِينَ جَاهَدُوا فِينَا لَنَهْدِيَنَّهُمْ سُبُلَنَا وَإِنَّ اللَّهَ لَمَعَ الْمُحْسِنِينَ﴾ [العنكبوت: ٦٩].

وَأَمَّا اعْتِرَاضَاتُ الْأَحْكَامِ فَيَجُوزُ أَنْ يُرِيدَ بِالْأَحْكَامِ الْأَحْكَامَ الْكَوْنِيَّةَ، وَهُوَ أَظْهَرُ، وَأَنْ يُرِيدَ بِهَا الْأَحْكَامَ الدِّينِيَّةَ، فَإِنَّ أَرْبَابَ الْأَحْوَالِ يَقَعُ مِنْهُمُ اعْتِرَاضَاتٌ عَلَى الْأَحْكَامِ الْجَارِيَةِ عَلَيْهِمْ بِخِلَافِ مَا يُرِيدُونَهُ، فَيَحْزَنُونَ عِنْدَ إِدْرَاكِهِمْ لِتِلْكَ الِاعْتِرَاضَاتِ عَلَى مَا صَدَرَ مِنْهُمْ مِنْ سُوءِ الْأَدَبِ. وَتِلْكَ الِاعْتِرَاضَاتُ هِيَ إِرَادَتُهُمْ خِلَافَ مَا جَرَى لَهُمْ بِهِ الْقَدَرُ، فَيَحْزَنُونَ عَلَى عَدَمِ الْمُوَافَقَةِ، وَإِرَادَةِ خِلَافِ مَا أُرِيدَ بِهِمْ.

وَإِنْ كَانَ الْمُرَادُ بِهِ الْأَحْكَامَ الدِّينِيَّةَ فَإِنَّهُمْ تَعْرِضُ لَهُمْ أَحْوَالٌ لَا يُمْكِنُهُمُ الْجَمْعُ بَيْنَهَا وَبَيْنَ أَحْكَامِ الْأَمْرِ كَمَا تَقَدَّمَ فَلَا يَجِدُونَ بُدًّا مِنَ الْقِيَامِ بِأَحْكَامِ الْأَمْرِ، وَلَا بُدَّ أَنْ يَعْرِضَ لَهُمُ اعْتِرَاضٌ خَفِيٌّ أَوْ جَلِيٌّ، بِحَسَبِ انْقِطَاعِهِمْ عَنِ الْحَالِ بِالْأَمْرِ، فَيَحْزَنُونَ لِوُجُودِ هَذِهِ الْمُعَارَضَةِ، فَإِذَا قَامُوا بِأَحْكَامِ الْأَمْرِ، وَرَأَوْا أَنَّ الْمَصْلَحَةَ فِي حَقِّهِمْ ذَلِكَ، وَحَمِدُوا عَاقِبَتَهُ حَزِنُوا عَلَى تَسَرُّعِهِمْ عَلَى الْمُعَارَضَةِ. فَالتَّسْلِيمُ لِدَاعِي الْعِلْمِ وَاجِبٌ، وَمُعَارَضَةُ الْحَالِ مِنْ قَبِيلِ الْإِرَادَاتِ وَالْعِلَلِ، فَيَحْزَنُ عَلَى نَفْيِهِمَا فِيهِ، وَاللَّهُ أَعْلَمُ.

2.4 *English Translation*

The Station of Grief

The station of grief is one of the [various] stations of *You alone we worship, and You alone we ask for help* (al-Fātiḥa 1:6).[11] It is not a desirable station nor is it condoned, even though every seeker must inevitably pass through it. Indeed, grief does not appear in the Quran except that it is either prohibited or preceded by a negative particle. As for its prohibition, Allah the Exalted says, *Do not worry and do not grieve* (Āl ʿImrān 3:139). He also says, *Do not grieve over them* (al-Naḥl 16:127), which is [repeated] in numerous instances [throughout the Quran].[12] Furthermore, Allah says, *And do not grieve, indeed Allah is with us* (al-Tawba 9:40). As for negation, He mentions, *No fear will be upon them, nor shall they grieve* (al-Baqara 2:38).

The reality is that grief is an impediment and not a facilitator [along the spiritual journey]. There is no benefit in it for the heart. The most beloved thing to Shayṭān is to inflict grief upon the seeker so as to cut them off from their [spiritual] path and impede all progress. Allah the Exalted states: *Verily the whispers of Shayṭān are to make those who believe grieve.* (al-Mujādila 58:10). The Prophet, may Allah bless him and grant him peace, forbade, "that two should have a private conversation when sitting with a third, for it will make him feel sad."[13]

Essentially, grief should not be sought; it is not a [desirable] objective, and there is no utility in it. In fact, the Prophet, may Allah bless him and grant him peace, sought refuge from it, supplicating, "Oh Allah, I seek refuge in you from worry and grief."[14] Indeed, it is closely associated with worry. The difference between the two is [gauged by the following]: If the disliked matter that occurs in the heart concerns a future matter, it results in worry. If it concerns a matter of the past, it results in grief. Both of them, however, weaken the heart and diminish one's resolve.

---

11 Meaning, by endeavoring to embody the prayer recited in Sūrat al-Fātiḥa, one who strives to grow closer to Allah and undergo spiritual reformation will inevitably encounter occasions of grief along the way. Some Sūfis describe this grief as "*qabḍ*," which is the sense of feeling constrained (Suhrawardī, *ʿAwārif al-Maʿārif*, 1:250–252). As one struggles to rid themselves of their worldly attachments, unlock their spiritual potential, and develop a stronger affinity for the divine, they inevitably experience grief from losing their old worldly habits and preoccupations as they progress.

12 Cf. al-Ḥijr 15:88; al-Naḥl 16:127; al-Naml 27:70.

13 Al-Bukhārī, 5932; Muslim, 2184.

14 Al-Bukhārī, 6008.

Nonetheless, as [practical] reality dictates, one must inevitably traverse through this station. It is because of this that the people of Paradise will say upon entering it, *All praise is due to Allah who has removed all grief from us* (al-Fāṭir 35:34). This indicates that they were afflicted by grief in this world, just like all other afflictions that would have befallen them involuntarily.

As for His saying, *Likewise, there is no [blame] on those who, when they came to you so that you might provide them with a conveyance [for jihād] you told them, "I have no conveyance to give to you". They turned back whilst their eyes were flowing with tears from grief, as they had nothing that they could spend* (al-Tawba 9:92). In this instance, they were not praised for the feeling of grief itself. Rather, they were praised for what their grief [clearly] indicated: their strong faith. They [were saddened because they] could not join the Messenger of Allah, may Allah bless him and grant him peace, as they did not have the financial means to afford it. This is in critical contrast to the hypocrites who did not grieve because of their remaining behind; instead, they relished it.[15]

Now, considering the authentically transmitted statement of the Prophet, may Allah bless him and grant him peace, "The believer is not afflicted with worry, discomfort, or grief except that Allah expiates his sins through it."[16] This indicates that it is an affliction through which Allah tests His servants and expiates their sins. It does not indicate that it is a station that must be sought out or attained.[17]

And as for Hind bin Abī Hāla's transmitted description of the Prophet, may Allah bless him and grant him peace, [mentioning] "He was perpetually in a state of grief," the report is not [adequately] substantiated, as there is someone unrecognized in the chain of transmission. How could he perpetually grieve when Allah safeguarded him from the grief of the world and its [various]

15 This statement contextualizes the basis of Ibn al-Qayyim's view regarding grief, which seems to depict it as an inherently and entirely bad thing. It should be noted that this view, with due respect for its merit and integrity, contradicts the perspectives offered by other leading classical Islamic scholars who view grief positively, like Ibn Abī Dunya. Here, Ibn al-Qayyim demonstrates that the underlying source of grief can be either praiseworthy or blameworthy. As such, grief merely reveals what an individual is attached to and believes to be valuable; one thus naturally feels sad upon its loss. Opposedly, a hypocrite's absence of sadness in such a scenario is reprehensible; not because of a lack of tears per se, but a lack of value or concern that which is deemed good and valuable in Islam.

Again, in and of itself, sadness is not praiseworthy according to Ibn al-Qayyim, especially if it is due to one's attachment to the ephemeral world, as this is considered maladaptive.

16 Al-Bukhārī, 5318; Muslim, 2573.

17 This further reinforces his view that the feeling of sadness and grief is not a pleasant experience to be sought but rather something that one needs to bear and persevere through.

means; He prohibited him, may Allah bless him and grant him peace, from grieving over the disbelievers; and He [primordially] forgave him for all [potential] past and future errors? So then from what angle could grief have possibly come to him? Rather, he was always cheerful and smiling,[18] As it comes in his description that he was "a smiling warrior."

As for the transmitted report, "Allah loves every grieving heart," its chain is not known, thus those who narrate it [are unknown]. Accordingly, its authenticity is not verified.

Nonetheless, assuming the report's soundness, [we purport that] grief is one of many afflictions through which Allah tests his servants. If one is patient when Allah tests them with it, He consequently loves his patience[19] in the face of affliction.[20]

And as for the other narration, "When Allah loves a slave, He places a lamenting wailer in his heart. If He despises a slave, He places a flute[21] in his heart." This is an Israelite report which is said to be found in the Torah. [In any case,] its meaning is sound. For verily a believer is sorrowful over his sins whereas the transgressor is frivolous, [inappropriately] joyful, musical,[22] and overly pleased.

In consideration of what Allah, the Exalted says regarding His prophet Isrāʾīl (Yaʿqūb), *His eyes turned white with sorrow, suppressing [grief]* (Yūsuf: 84), this simply provides information regarding his [state of] grief from losing his beloved son.[23] Allah was merely testing him with grief just as he was testing him by separating both of them from each other.

Masters of the spiritual path unanimously agree that the grief of this world is not praiseworthy. The [only] exception is that of Abū ʿUthmān al-Harīrī; he states, "Grief, in every form, is virtuous and a [means of] elevation for the believer so long as it is not the result of transgression. He continues, "because,

18 The author seems to express a disapproval of portraying the Prophet, may Allah bless him and grant him peace, as constantly engulfed in sorrow. He does not consider it appropriate for the Prophet, may Allah bless him and grant him peace, to be overwhelmed by worldly events or the condition of disbelievers. As previously discussed, it is evident that experiencing excessive grief over worldly matters is a flaw and it signifies an excessive attachment to material possessions; all of which is completely unbefitting for any prophet, let alone the Best of Allah's Creation, may Allah bless him and grant him peace.

19 In other words, Allah loves the act of exercising patience when the heart is grieving.

20 The adaptive expression of grief is indicated by one's ability to remain patient and attain the pleasure of Allah by it.

21 The Arabic term "*mizmār*" is a flute or a similar type of woodwind musical instrument that uses a reed.

22 Meaning inclined to melody when he should be sorrowful.

23 I.e., that it is simply a descriptive statement, not a prescriptive one.

even if it does not necessitate elevation intrinsically, it leads to it through the expiation of sins".[24]

To conclude, it has been said, "There is no doubt that grief is a trial and tribulation from Allah, similar in status to sickness, stress, and worry. As for [the idea that] it is from amongst the [requisite] stations of the spiritual path, this is [certainly] not the case.

Section:
The Degrees of Grief (*Ḥuzn*)

The author[25] of *Manāzil*, may Allah have mercy upon him, states, **"Grief (ḥuzn) is the feeling of pain (*tawajju'*) caused by missing out on [certain] things, or the feeling of regret (*ta'assuf*) due to deprivation."**

The author means that which escapes an individual was either [practically] attainable by him or unattainable. If it was within his capacity [to attain it], then not [actually] doing so pains him. If it was not [practically attainable], then he regrets having to forfeit it.

He [then continues,] saying, **"Grief has three levels. The first is the grief of the common people, which entails sadness for inadequately serving [others], being involved in something inappropriate, and the wastage of time."**

For the average person, [one who is saddened because of their] inadequate service is at a higher level than [one who merely] falls short or messes up in the performance of good deeds, as such consequent grief is [atleast] associated with doing something good. From their perspective, service is part of good character and manners and is thus separate from doing good deeds. Service is considered to be an inherent responsibility of servanthood [to Allah]; it is [inescapably a part of] its requisite etiquettes and obligations. Accordingly, the one who carries this grief [of deficiency in service] is all the more likely to be grieved by the lack of performance of a good deed altogether.

---

24 Ibn al-Qayyim acknowledges the validity of Ibn Harīrī's assertion that grief can lead to spiritual elevation and forgiveness, implying that there may be certain indirect benefits associated with it. Thus, Ibn al-Qayyim, whilst presenting his own perspective, nonetheless accepts that grief is a complex state with both positive and negative aspects. However, he firmly maintains and reiterates that grief should not be actively sought after or considered inherently praiseworthy. Instead, it is seen as a natural occurrence that inevitably arises in life, and its potential benefits are contingent upon exercising patience. By quoting Ibn Harīrī after offering his own viewpoint, Ibn al-Qayyim skillfully provides a level of reconciliation between the two approaches in understanding grief as a spiritual station.

25 Abū Isma'īl al-Ansārī al-Ḥarāwī (d. 482 AH/1089 CE) who authored *Manāzil al-Sā'irīn* (Stations of the Wayfarers), of which this work serves as a commentary, as mentioned previously.

Likewise, [the one who regrets] engaging in something inappropriate is also considered to be at a higher [spiritual] level as compared to [one who grieves after] disobeying [Allah] by committing a prohibited act. This is because feeling grief [from acting inappropriately] conceivably stems from the loss of a previously experienced closeness with Allah, the Exalted. When a person drifts away from Him, they [can] get tangled up in improper acts.[26] The Shaykh (al-Ḥarāwī) mentions "grief" in the [ten-fold] category of chapters, because according to him, it is from the category of "the beginnings."[27]

As for the wastage of one's time, this is also of two categories: that which involves the absence of worshipful deeds, and that which entails a lack of spiritual experiences pertaining to faith, which includes tasting the sweetness of faith, proximity to Allah, and [having] an intimate presence with Him. Additionally, each of these three categories are of two types: [That which is] for beginners, and also for those intermediate seekers on the [spiritual] path. [Al-Harāwī's aforementioned] discussion is addressed to both groups, while he places special emphasis on the second group [of intermediate seekers].

[Next,] al-Harāwī says, "The second level is the grief of the people of sincere resolve (*irāda*).[28] It is grief due to the heart's experiencing [spiritual] separation; the soul's distraction from witnessing [the divine]; and the inability to [appropriately] feel grief."

The heart's experiencing [spiritual] separation is the absence of wholeness in [one's complete] presence with Allah and scattered thoughts with [one's] fixations.

As for the soul's distraction from [divine] witnessing, it is of two types. [Firstly,] its being distracted from the remembrances [or litanies] that lead to [divine] witnessing, bringing it into fruition through other means. Secondly, its distraction from [divine] witnessing due to a weakness in [one's] remembrances, or a weakness of the heart in respect of witnessing, or [even] due to

26 Engagement in something inappropriate involves committing an act that is not technically prohibited or sinful. Feeling grief for this is an indication of a higher spiritual status than that of one who engages in transgression. Regarding the comparison of spiritual levels, there is a highly relevant and oft-quoted Arabic proverb that translates as, "the good deeds of the righteous are the shortcomings of the ascetics." While doing good deeds is important, there is a higher standard for the ascetics who habitually engage in that which is superior; thus, their descent into a state in which they perform mere good deeds of the average person is a type of spiritual demotion.

27 This is in reference to al-Ḥarawī's division of the spiritual stations; he lists ten categories, and each distinct category is comprised of ten separate stations.

28 What is meant by "the people of sincere resolve" or *irāda*, is the advanced seekers of spiritual progress, reformation, and proximity as opposed to the average believer.

some other preventative cause. However, when [divine] witnessing overcomes the soul, it cannot become preoccupied by anything else unless another overwhelming force distracts it.

Regarding the lack of [ability to feel] grief: the feeling of grief in the heart is an indication of [strong] will and yearning [for proximity to Allah]. To lose or to be unable to feel grief is [thus] a [spiritual] deficiency. As such, a person may grieve because he cannot grieve, just as he may cry over the inability to cry or may feel afraid due to the absence of fearfulness.

This is, however, debatable. Sadness caused by the inability to [feel] grief is only praiseworthy if it [functionally] preoccupies a person from rejoicing inappropriately. Contrarily, if one is distracted from sadness on account of praiseworthy joyousness [stemmed in] relishing the bounties and mercy of Allah, then there is no utility in grieving over the absence of sad feelings.[29]

[Al-Harāwī] says, "The [spiritually] adept (*khāṣa*) has nothing to do with the [spiritual] station of sadness at all, as grief is [caused by] absence whereas such distinguished people are ever-present."

If he intended by this that it is not fitting for them to force grief upon themselves, then this is correct. However, if he meant that grief never besets them, then such is not the case because [feeling] grief is naturally commonplace, even though it is not considered to be a [spiritual] station.

[Al-Harāwī] states, "Whereas the third level of grief is to feel unsettled by: inward incongruities [that are] distinct from passing thoughts; compunction [regarding] future endeavors; and objections against [divine] order." These are three matters that correspond to [one's state of divine] witnessing and sincere desire.

Firstly, [with regards to feeling] unsettled by inward incongruities: [When] the heart experiences rays of hope, for example, it cannot [concurrently] experience fear and vice-versa. Similarly, the heart, [when] experiencing [spiritual] jubilance, cannot [simultaneously] experience [spiritual] constriction, and vice-versa. Or whilst [the heart] experiences [divine] amity, then [divine] reverence contradicts it. These varying contradictions necessarily cause him [some form of] grief. These contradictions are not mere passing thoughts. Rather, they are the result of celestial emanations. Accordingly, he said, "that are distinct from passing thoughts," for contradicting thoughts are different from these. Some [spiritual masters] proffer that they come from the effects of [Allah's] names and attributes and the [inherent] connection of their various

29 Again, the author is reiterating that grief is not praiseworthy in and of itself; in his view, whether or not it is commendable or blameworthy is determined by what is associated with it or by what induces it.

rays of light to a person's heart. According to them, this is termed as "divine manifestation" (*tajallī*).[30]

As for compunction regarding future endeavors, it weighs heaviest upon seekers; [when] dealing with it, a seeker's urgent need for knowledge over all [other] necessities come to light. Indeed, throughout the entire course of his spiritual journey, a sincere seeker carefully endeavors [to tread] the most beloved of paths to Allah; he is constantly traversing towards Him on it. Suddenly, [he may] encounter two opposing paths, not knowing which of them is most pleasing and beloved to Allah. Some will make a judgment call on the basis of their knowledge that they draw upon for direction; and if a person is incapable of doing this, then he will follow the authority of someone else. If, perchance, he is unable to do either of these, he will patiently wait for what destiny decides for him, inwardly purging himself of all potential biases. Others may hand the entire matter over to their Shaykh, if one has a Shaykh. Others still, will resort to *istikhāra*[31] and supplication, and thereafter wait for divine decree to take its course.

The people of higher [spiritual] resolve [always] put forth everything in their capacity to seek that which is most pleasing [to Allah, on the basis of] knowledge and gnosis. However, if they are rendered incapable, then they will be content [accepting] the predominant assumption. If two matters are [seemingly] equivalent, then they will prefer that which is most likely to be the most beneficial.

In order to determine that which is most beneficial, there are various levels of consideration: At times, it is determined by that which has a wider reach. Sometimes, that which leads to an increase of faith is given precedence. Frequently, that which opposes the lower ego is prioritized. Occasionally, preference is accorded to that which brings about other benefits that would otherwise not be attainable. Lastly, one may opt to safeguard a benefit out of fear of [potential] harm that may arise should an alternate benefit be preferred. These are five reasons [used] in the prioritization process; rarely is any one of them left out.[32]

---

30 These 'seeming' thoughts do not originate in volitional thinking, but they are spiritual experiences that occur as the spiritual seeker traverses the spiritual path.

31 *Istikhāra*, is a well-known practice that literally entails "*seeking goodness*," in which a person presents their decision to Allah, supplicating for the best outcome. Although doing so is still considered to be *istikhāra*, the term, by default, denotes a formal, transmitted supplication preceded by two units of a specifically intended supererogatory prayer (cf. al-Bukhari, 6019).

32 This is a very effective decision-making process model that Ibn al-Qayyim outlines. At its core, it is methodically carried out with a deep sense of prioritization, thoroughly

If all else fails, the seeker will totally ignore all thoughts and wait for destiny to take its course, with full reliance on his Lord to cause what He loves and is pleased with to descend. If an [inclination towards any sort of] action comes to him then he will resort to *istikhāra* with full reliance upon Allah yet again, with concern that his inclinations may be egocentric or devilish considering he is not free from sin and is continuously tested by shayṭān so long as he dwells in this world of trials and tribulations. Then at last, he will proceed to act. This is the extent of the ability [to exercise caution] for the sincere seekers.[33]

And the people who ardently combat (*jihād*) [their egos] possess [special] guidance and unveilings that the people who strive (*mujāhada*) do not have. For this reason, [Imams] al-Awzāʿī and Ibn al-Mubārak stated, "If people disagree regarding a matter, then look to what the people of the frontline are upon," meaning, the people of *jihād*. Indeed, Allah the Exalted says, *and those who effortfully struggle for Our sake, we shall surely guide them along Our ways*, (al-ʿAnkabūt 29:69).

Now, as for "objections against [divine] order," [causing grief], it is possible that he meant "worldly decrees," as this is most apparent. It is also possible that he is referring to religious decrees. The [advanced] spiritual masters [who are]

considering that which is most beneficial as defined by what is most beloved to Allah, as opposed to what is self-serving. By surrendering one's will over to Allah in this way, the seeker is able to interact with the divine, being able to open up his spiritual senses to signs that direct him via his prayers and *istikhāra*.

The five possibilities outlined above specify and define the parameters for what is most beneficial, providing enough flexibility in determining what is best based upon the individual state or circumstances of the seeker. It is noteworthy that prayers and beseeching Allah for help in making a decision does not contradict seeking the counsel of a righteous guide.

After undergoing this exhaustive process of decision-making that includes relying upon knowledge, spiritual intuition, expert counsel, and a five-factor personal and contextual analysis, one can easily accept the outcome and consequences of one's decisions. Such a decision-making process can help produces an overall feeling of contentment in one's choices, minimizing regrets.

33 This places a great emphasis on limiting overconfidence and overreliance upon oneself; rather, it is the development of Allah-reliance that is being emphasized in this approach. One must necessarily have a higher degree of self-scrutiny, skepticism, and personal interrogation of one's motives so as not to mistake divine intuition with satanic or egocentric whispers and inclinations. Such personal skepticism should not be mistaken for an excessive or unhealthy degree of self-debasement that leads to low self-esteem, but rather the combination of recognizing one's God-given abilities and weakness combined with an ultimate reliance on Allah is critical to psychological and spiritual well-being and consistent with living the Islamically good life. This self-critical approach is in stark contrast to theories of self-psychology in modern psychological theories that overemphasizes a need for self-confidence and self-reliance to the point of self-admiration.

overtaken by [powerful] states sometimes unintentionally have objections to decreed judgements, leading them to feel grief-stricken once they come to know of their objections and thus the unideal etiquette that had emanated from them.[34] Such objections are their wishes that were in contradistinction with what destiny willed for them; so, they become saddened on account of the absence of correspondence [between their desire and divine will] and for having a will other than that which has been ordained for them [by Allah].

If what was intended here [by Al-Harāwī] is religious judgments, then [some] people experience [overwhelming] spiritual states wherein they are unable to reconcile between their experience[s] and [certain] divine commands, as mentioned earlier. Inevitably, they find no way to avoid establishing what is commanded; they thus experience a type of inward or outward [feeling of] contradiction relative to how detached they are from the command due to their spiritual state. They thus grieve on account of this contradiction as submission to the call of [scriptural] knowledge is compulsory and opposing it because of the likes of spiritual states [ineluctably] arises from [personal] will and [spiritual] ailments. One feels saddened by the remnants of such incohesiveness within themselves, and Allah knows best.

3 Worry and Sorrow. *Al-Hamm wa-l-Ḥazan* (*Worry and Sorrow*) by Imam Ibn Abī al-Dunyā (d. 281 AH/882 CE)

3.1 *Author's Biography*

Abū Bakr ʿAbdullah ibn Muḥammad bin ʿUbayd ibn Sufyān ibn Qays al-Qurayshī, famously known as Ibn Abī al-Dunyā, was born in the year 208 AH/806 CE in the city of Baghdad. There, he learned from many prominent scholars, subscribing to the Ḥanbali school of Islamic jurisprudence. He was renowned as an ascetic, pious scholar who inspired people towards righteous actions through his trustworthiness, truthfulness, indifference to the world, and inclination towards worship. He wrote on many subjects, authoring over 180 works throughout his lifetime. Amongst his most esteemed teachers were Imam al-Bukharī and Imam Zuhayr ibn Ḥarb. Imam Ibn Abī al-Dunyā was considered a reliable hadith narrator of his time. He was also known to have tutored the famous Abbasid caliphs, al-Muʿtadid and his son, al-Muktafī.

34 It is to hold tentative plans for oneself and not create an insistent fixation on what one thinks is the best course of action, thereby leaving room for divine decree to determine otherwise.

3.2 *Text Overview and Significance*

In sharp contrast to Ibn al-Qayyim's section pertaining to grief, this excerpt from Ibn Abī al-Dunyā's writings views grief in a very positive light. Grief is portrayed as something with the potential to be praiseworthy and even encouraged, in a sense; various supportive narrations and related stories value it as an indication of goodness from Allah, akin to what common parlance would describe as a "blessing in disguise." The perspectives and quotations proffered in this section can be very uplifting for those who struggle with excessive grief and sadness, as many may sometimes wonder whether such is an indication of distance from Allah or perhaps even a type of punishment. However, in his spiritually enriching scholarly style, Ibn Abī al-Dunyā adeptly frames sadness as an opportunity for a potential increase in connection with Allah.

3.3 *Arabic Text*

بسم الله الرحمن الرحيم

سند الكتاب

أخبرنا الشيخ الصالح أبو الفتح محمد بن عبد الباقي بن أحمد بن سلمان – رحمه الله – قراءة عليه، وأنا أسمع يوم الأربعاء تاسع عشر من جمادى الآخرة سنة ثلاث وستين وخمسمائة قيل له:

أنبأك أبو الحسين عاصم بن الحسن بن محمد بن علي قال: أخبرنا أبو الحسين علي بن محمد بن عبد الله بن بشران المعدل قراءة عليه فأقر به قال: أخبرنا أبو علي الحسين بن صفوان البرذعي في المحرم سنة أربعين وثلثمائة قال: حدثنا أبو بكر عبد الله بن محمد بن عبيد بن سفيان القرشي قال:

متواصل الأحزان دائم الفكرة

حدثنا سفيان بن وكيع بن الجراح بن مليح الرواسي قال: حدثنا جميع بن عم العجلي قال: حدثني رجل من بني تميم يكنى أبا عبد الله عن ابنٍ لأبي هالة التميمي عن الحسن بن علي – عليه السلام – عن خاله هند بن أبي هالة قال: «كان رسول الله صلى الله عليه وسلم متواصل الأحزان، دائم الفكرة، ليست له راحة، طويل السكت، لا يتكلم في غير حاجة.»

هل يحب الله كل قلب حزين؟

ثنا الحسن بن مهدي البصري قال: ثنا عبد القدوس بن الحجاج الحمصي عن أبي بكر بن أبي مريم عن ضمرة بن حبيب عن أبي الدرداء – رضي الله عنه – أن رسول الله صلى الله عليه وسلم قال: «إن الله يحب كل قلب حزين».

الهم والحزن يكفران الذنوب

حدثنا إسحاق بن إسماعيل قال: ثنا الحسين بن علي العجلي عن زائدة عن ليث عن مجاهد عن عائشة – رضي اللّٰه عنها – عن النبي صلى اللّٰه عليه و سلم، قال: «إذا كثرت ذنوب العبد، ولم يكن له ما يكفرها، ابتلاه اللّٰه بالحزن ليكفرها عنه».

حديث آدم عليه السلام عن الهم والحزن

حدثني محمد بن الحسين قال: حدثني عبد اللّٰه بن الفرج العابد عن فتح الموصلي قال: قال آدم عليه السلام: «كنا نسلا من الهم والحزن في الجنة، أما إلى الدنيا، فليس لنا فيها إلا الهم والحزن حتى نرد إلى الدار التي خرجنا منها».

حدثني محمد بن الحسين قال: حدثني عبد اللّٰه بن الفرج فتح الموصلي قال: قال آدم عليه السلام: «بني طال حزني على أخرج منها أبوك لزهقت نفسك»

صور من أحزان يعقوب على يوسف عليهما السلام

حدثني عبد اللّٰه بن رجاء قال: حدثني أحمد بن بشير عن هشام عن الحسن قال: «كان (منذ خرج يوسف عليه السلام من عند) يعقوب – عليهما السلام – إلى أن رجع ثمانين سنة فما فارق الحزن قلبه، ومازال يبكي حتى ذهب بصره».

قال الحسن: «واللّٰه إن كان على الأرض يومئذ بشر أكرم على اللّٰه – عز وجل – من يعقوب».

حدثني سفيان بن وكيع قال: ثنا ابن عيينة عن محمد بن سوقة عن العلاء بن عبد الرحمن قال: قال علي بن أبي طالب – رضي اللّٰه عنه-: «ما اكتحل رجل بمثل ملمول الحزن».

القلب الخالي من الحزن خراب

ثنا عبيد اللّٰه بن عمر بن ميسرة الجشمي، ونعيم بن هيصم وغيرهما قالوا: ثنا جعفر بن سليمان، قال: سمعت مالك بن دينار قال: «إن القلب إذا لم يكن فيه حزن خرب، كما أن البيت إذا لم يسكن خرب».

الدنيا والآخرة ضرتان

ثنا محمد بن يزيد بن رفاعة قال: ثنا أبو الحسين العكلي، ثنا سميل بن عبد اللّٰه قال: سمعت مالك بن دينار يقول: «حزنك على الدنيا للدنيا يذهب بحلاوة الآخرة من قلبك، وفرحك بالدنيا للدنيا يذهب بحلاوة الآخرة من قلبك».

حدثني أحمد بن العباس النميري قال: حدثني محمد بن طفيل قال: قال فضيل بن عياض: «فرحك بالدنيا للدنيا يذهب بحلاوة العبادة، وهمك بالدنيا يذهب بالعبادة كلها».

حدثني الحسين بن عبد الرحمن الفزاري قال: سمع الحسن رجلا يقول: واحزناه على الحزن، فقال له الحسن: «ياهذا فهلا على ما سلف من علمه فيك».

قل واحزناه على الحزن

ثني أبو بكر الصيرفي قال: سمعت أبي قال: سمع ابن السماك رجلا يقول: واحزناه، فقال: «قل واحزناه على الحزن، ألا أكون من أهله، وهل رأيت محزونا».

قال: وبلغني عن حامد بن عمر البكراوي قال: سمعت عبد اللّٰه بن ثعلبة يقول لسفيان بن عيينة: «يا أبا محمد، واحزناه على الحزن». فقال سفيان بن عيينة: «هل حزنت قط لعلم اللّٰه فيك». قال عبد اللّٰه: تركتني لا أفرح.

حدثني عياش القطان قال: حدثني قاسم الخواص، قال: قال محمد بن رافع: «أبكاك قط سابق علم اللّٰه فيك».

الأحزان في الدنيا ثلاثة

حدثني الحسين بن عبد الرحمن عن عبد اللّٰه بن صالح بن مسلم العجلي قال: «كان يقال: الأحزان في الدنيا ثلاثة: خليل فارق خليله، ووالد ثكل ولده، ورجل افتقر بعد غنى».

هل الدعاء يستجاب عند الأحزان ؟

حدثني عبد الرحمن بن صالح قال: حدثنا أبو النضر عن صالح المري عن يزيد الرقاشي قال: «الدعاء المستجاب الذي تهيجه الأحزان، ومفتاح الرحمة التضرع».

أحزان على ضياع صلاة الجماعة

ثني الحسن بن الصباح قال: ثنا زيد بن الحباب عن مرجي عن غالب القطان عن بكر بن عبد اللّٰه «في الرجل يخرج إلى الصلاة فتفوته في الجماعة، فإذا حزن لذلك أعطاه اللّٰه فضل الجماعة».

حدثني هاشم بن القاسم أبو محمد، قال: حدثني أبي قال: حدثني محمد بن هانئ قال: حدثنا يوسف بن أسباط عن وهيب بن الورد قال: «من توضأ في بيته وأسبغ الوضوء، ثم خرج يريد الصلاة في جماعة، فاستقبلهم منصرفين فأحزنه ذلك أعطاه اللّٰه أجرين، أجرا لحزنه، وأجرا لما فاته من الجماعة».

الحزن جلاء القلوب:

حدثني محمد بن الحسين قال: حدثني جعفر بن جسر بن فرقد قال: حدثني حماد بن واقد قال: سمعت أبا عبيدة الخواص يقول: «الحزن جلاء القلوب، به تستلين مواضع الفكرة ثم بكى».

من أقوال الصالحين عن الحزن

حدثنا أحمد بن بجير عن أبي إسحاق الطالقاني عن عبد الله بن المبارك عن سفيان الثوري قال: «كان يقال الحزن على قدر البصر».

حدثنا أحمد بن حاتم الطويل قال: ثنا يحيى بن يمان عن سفيان عن يونس بن عبيد عن الحسن قال: «ما عبد الله بمثل طول الحزن».

حدثنا عاصم بن عمر بن علي عن حفص بن قرير قال: «كان رجل منا يجالس الحسن قال: سمعت الحسن يقول: إن أكثر ما يرى للعبد في صحيفته يوم القيامة مما يسر به الهم والحزن».

هل الهم والحزن يزيدان الحسنات؟

حدثني أبو الحارث سريح بن يونس عن خلف بن خليفة عن منصور بن زاذان قال: «الهم والحزن يزيدان في الحسنات، والأشر والبطر يزيدان في السيئات».

حدثنا أبو عبد الله أحمد بن إبراهيم عن بشر بن سلم الكوفي عن مسعر عن بكير أو أبي بكير عن إبراهيم التيمي قال: «ينبغي لمن لم يحزن أن يخاف ألا يكون من أهل الجنة؛ لأنهم قالوا ﴿الحمد لله الذي أذهب عنا الحزن﴾. وينبغي لمن لم يشفق أن يخاف ألا يكون من أهل الجنة؛ لأنهم قالوا ﴿إنا كنا قبل في أهلنا مشفقين﴾».

حديث القرآن عن الحزن

حدثني المثنى بن معاذ العنبري عن معاذ بن هاشم عن أبيه عن عمرو بن مالك عن أبي الجوزاء عن ابن عباس: ﴿الحمد لله الذي أذهب عنا﴾قال: حزن النار.

حدثني الخليل بن عمرو عن عبد الله بن إدريس عن أبيه عن عطية: ﴿الحمد لله الذي أذهب عنا الحزن﴾. قال: الموت.

حدثني محمد بن ناصح قال: ثنا بقية بن الوليد عن مجاشع بن عمرو عن من حدثه عن سعيد بن جبير: ﴿الحمد لله الذي أذهب عنا الحزن﴾. قال: هم الخبز في الدنيا.

3.4 *English Translation*

In the name of Allah, the Most Gracious, the Most Merciful.

The Treatise's Chain of Transmission

The righteous Shaykh Abū al-Fatḥ Muḥammad ibn ʿAbd al-Bāqī ibn Aḥmad ibn Salmān, may Allah have mercy on him, informed us, while[35] I was listening

35 This particular expression implies that the hadith report that the teacher narrated was being read to him by a student for checking while others present were listening and transcribing the transmissions in their own notes.

[attentively] during a [ḥadīth] reading session with him held on Wednesday the 19th of Jumādā al-Ākhira, in the year 563 AH, that it was said to him:

> Abū al-Ḥusayn ʿĀṣim ibn al-Ḥasan ibn Muḥammad ibn ʿAlī narrates to you that Abū al-Ḥusayn ʿAlī ibn Muḥammad ibn ʿAbd Allah ibn Bishrān al-Muʿaddil transmitted [a report] that was read to him, and he [subsequently] validated that Abū ʿAlī al-Ḥusayn ibn Ṣafwān al-Bardhaʿī informed us, in Muḥarram of the year 340 AH, that Abū Bakr ʿAbd Allah ibn Muḥammad ibn ʿUbayd ibn Sufyān al-Qurashī detailed [the following]:

Continuous Grief and Persistent Preoccupation

Sufyān ibn Wakīʿ ibn al-Jarrāḥ ibn Malīḥ al-Rawāsī narrated to us, stating that Jamīʿ ibn ʿAmm al-ʿIjlī related:

> A man from Banū Tamīm, called Abū ʿAbd Allāh, narrated from the son of Abū Hāla al-Tamīmī, through al-Ḥasan ibn ʿAlī, upon him be peace, from his uncle, Hind ibn Abī Hāla who said, "The Prophet, may Allah bless him and grant him peace, was continuously in grief[36] and was constantly

36 Mulla ʿAlī al-Qārī mentions in his famous ḥadīth commentary *Mirqāt al-Mafātīḥ* that the word for grief (*ḥuzn*) is simply the opposite of the word for happiness (*surūr*). He provides this explanation of grief in his description of the grief that the Prophet, may Allah bless him and grant him peace, experienced when there was a moratorium on his receiving of revelation (cf. ʿAlī al-Qārī, *Mirqāt al-Mafātīḥ*, vol. 9 (Lebanon: Dār al-Kutub al-ʿIlmiyya, 2001), 731.). This is further elucidated by the ḥadīth wherein the Prophet, may Allah bless him and grant him peace, mentioned, "Woe be to the hoarding slave; if Allah reduces the value [of his commodities] he becomes sad (*ḥazina*), but if He raises them in value, he becomes happy." (cf. ʿAlī al-Qārī, *Mirqāt al-Mafātīḥ*, vol. 5 (Lebanon: Dār al-Kutub al-ʿIlmiyya, 2001), 952.). Mulla ʿAlī Qārī also cites additional explanations of ḥuzn and hamm (worry) in saying that they occur on account of the loss of something beloved. He states that some scholars also mention that *ḥuzn* occurs due to a loss in the past whereas *hamm* occurs due to an anticipated fear of a loss in the future (cf. ʿAlī al-Qārī, *Mirqāt Al-Mafātīḥ*, vol. 3 (Lebanon: Dār al-Kutub al-ʿIlmiyya, 2001), 128.).

However, with a slight variation to the vowelling of the word, *ḥazn* connotes a close yet distinct meaning of harshness or roughness. It can be used to refer to a harsh, hard, and barren land. It is the opposite of the word that denotes ease (*sahl*) and can similarly be used to refer to lush, soft, and fertile land. Mulla ʿAli Qārī provides the aforementioned explanation under the narration wherein a man named Ḥazn came to the Prophet, may Allah bless him and grant him peace; Upon learning his name, the Prophet, may Allah bless him and grant him peace, changed it to Sahl in order to inculcate the good virtues of softness and gentleness in him (cf. ʿAlī al-Qārī, *Mirqāt Al-Mafātīḥ*, vol. 7 (Lebanon: Dār al-Kutub al-ʿIlmiyya, 2001), 3000.).

[engrossed] in contemplation. He had no rest. His silence was prolonged, and he did not speak except when necessary."[37]

Does Allah Love Each and Every Saddened Heart?

Al-Ḥasan ibn Mahdī al-Baṣrī related to us that Abd al-Quddūs ibn al-Ḥajjāj al-Ḥimṣī narrated through Abū Bakr ibn Abī Maryam, from Ḍamra ibn Ḥabīb, on the authority of Abū al-Dardā, may Allah be pleased with him, that the Messenger of Allah, [may Allah bless him and grant him peace,] said, "Allah loves every saddened[38] heart."[39]

Worry and Sorrow Remove Sins

Isḥāq ibn Ismāʿīl narrated to us, stating that al-Ḥusayn ibn ʿAlī al-ʿIjli transmitted from Zā'ida, through Layth, then Mujāhid, on the authority of ʿĀ'isha, may Allah be pleased with her, that the Prophet, may Allah bless him and grant him peace, said, "When a man's sins are numerous and he has no good deeds wherewith to atone for them, Allah afflicts him with sorrow so as to remove them from him."

---

37 This narration provides great consolation to those who experience any form of chronic sadness or grief that is not on account of worldly attachments. It provides a humane portrait of the Prophet, may Allah bless him and grant him peace, that normalizes the natural human experience of worry and sadness.

38 Indirectly drawing on other related texts, Imam al-Ṣan'ānī comments on this narration, explaining, "[Meaning] the heart that is saddened on account of one's misdeeds and the resultant distance from one's Lord; not the heart that is saddened due to some kind of worldly displeasure or loss." (see Muḥammad b. Ismāʿīl Sanʿānī, *al-Tanwīr Sharḥ al-Jāmiʿ al-Ṣaghīr*, vol. 3 (Riyadh: Maktabat Dār al-Salām, 2011), 381.). He further mentions, "It is said that a believer's happiness appears on his face, whereas his sadness is entrenched in his heart. As such, the heart was specifically mentioned [in the narration] as it behooves a believer to maintain a cheerful, smiling face instead of a persistently gloomy one," (Ibid).

39 One can see a stark contrast between the collection of narrations employed by Ibn Abī al-Dunyā and the discussion of grief offered by Ibn al-Qayyim. Ibn Abī al-Dunyā brings together a series of narrations that provide a positive portrait of grief and sadness, whereas Ibn al-Qayyim seems to view grief as rewarding or blameworthy in correspondence to the beliefs and values that underlie it. Ibn al-Qayyim does not see sadness as intrinsically rewarding, rather the belief that underlies and leads to the emotions is what is either rewarding or blameworthy.

A potential reconciliation can be made between both scholars' viewpoints by considering that while Ibn Abī al-Dunyā appears to favor the idea that grief is a natural emotion that is generally and inherently positive for a believer; for Ibn al-Qayyim, this would hold true only for believers for whom it would be assumed that their sadness is indicative of sound and desirable beliefs.

The Narration of Adam, upon him be peace, Pertaining to Worry and Sorrow

Muḥammad ibn al-Ḥusayn narrated to us, saying that ʿAbd Allāh ibn al-Faraj al-ʿĀbid narrated from Fatḥ al-Mawṣilī, who related, "Prophet Adam, upon him be peace, said, 'We were without worry or sadness in Paradise. However, in the temporal world, we have nothing but worry and sadness until we return to our home from which we left.'"[40]

Muḥammad ibn al-Ḥusayn also transmitted [a report], saying that ʿAbd Allah ibn al-Faraj al-ʿĀbid narrated from Fatḥ al-Mawṣilī, who said, "Ādam, upon him be peace, said to his son, 'By Allah, my grief over the abode from which I departed is long-drawn; if you were to experience such, you would surely lose yourself.'"

Illustrations of Yaʿqūb's Grief for Yūsuf, Upon Them Be Peace

Narrating to me, ʿAbd Allah ibn Rajāʾ stated that Aḥmad ibn Bashīr related through Hishām from al-Ḥasan, who said, "From the time in which Yūsuf, upon him be peace, left [his home] until he returned eighty years later, grief never left the heart of Yaʿqūb, upon him be peace; he continued to weep until he lost his eyesight."

Al-Ḥasan further said, "By Allah, at that time there was no human being on earth dearer to Allah than Yaʿqūb."

Sufyān ibn Wakīʿ narrated to me, saying that Ibn ʿUyayna narrated from Muḥammad ibn Sūqa, through al-ʿAlāʾ ibn ʿAbd al-Raḥmān, who said that ʿAlī ibn Abī Ṭālib, may Allah be pleased with him stated, "There is no antimony that a man can apply [to his eyes] better than sadness."

Ruined is the Heart that is Devoid of Sadness

ʿUbayd Allāh ibn ʿUmar ibn Maysara al-Jushamī, Naʿīm ibn Hayṣam, and others narrated to us, saying that Jaʿfar ibn Sulaymān related, "I heard Mālik ibn Dīnār say, 'If the heart is devoid of sadness, it will be ruined just as a house, if uninhabited, becomes ruined.'"

The World and the Hereafter are Co-wives

Muḥammad ibn Yazīd ibn Rifāʿa narrated to us, saying that Abū al-Ḥusayn al-ʿUkalī related from Sumayl ibn ʿAbd Allāh who mentioned, "I heard Mālik ibn Dīnār say, 'Your sadness over the temporal world on account of worldly matters disappears from your heart by the utter sweetness of the Hereafter.

40 This is consistent with the writings of other scholars indicating that this ephemeral world is one of trials and tribulations (*dār al-ibtilāʾ*), by divine design.

Similarly, your happiness in the temporal world on account of worldly matters disappears from your heart by the sweetness of the hereafter.'"[41]

Aḥmad ibn al-ʿAbbās al-Namīrī narrated to me that Muḥammad ibn Ṭufayl said, "Fuḍayl ibn ʿIyāḍ said, 'Your happiness in the world on account of worldly matters gets obliterated by the [sheer] sweetness of worship. Also, your worries pertaining to the world are eradicated by worship in its totality.'"

Al-Ḥusayn ibn ʿAbd al-Raḥmān al-Fazārī narrated to me, stating that al-Ḥasan heard a man exclaiming, "How agonizing is it to grieve!" Al-Ḥasan retorted, "Hey you! Shouldn't you say that for what has preceded of His knowledge about you?"

Say: How Agonizing is it to Grieve!

Abū Bakr al-Ṣayrafī narrated to us, saying, "I heard my father saying that Ibn al-Sammāk overheard a man exclaiming, 'Ah, such sadness pains [me]!' So, he then told him to say, 'How agonizing is it to grieve!' [He further added,] 'And [I hope] that I am not one of such people. Have you [ever] seen a grieving man?'"

He [further] states, "It has reached me through Ḥāmid ibn ʿUmar al-Bakrāwī, who said, "I heard ʿAbd Allāh ibn Thaʿlaba saying to Sufyān ibn ʿUyayna, 'O Abū Muḥammad, how agonizing is it to grieve!' Sufyān ibn ʿUyayna replied, 'Have you ever felt any [real] grief given what Allah knows of you?' ʿAbd Allāh said, 'You left me to never feel joy [again].'

ʿAyyāsh al-Qaṭṭān narrated to me, saying that Qāsim al-Khawwāṣ transmitted that Muḥammad ibn Rāfiʿ said, "Did knowing that Allah has prior knowledge of your states ever make you weep?"

There are Three Forms of Grief in the World

Al-Ḥusayn ibn ʿAbd al-Raḥmān related to me from ʿAbd Allāh ibn Ṣāliḥ ibn Muslim al-ʿIjlī who said, "It used to be said that grief in this world is three: [when] two close friends are separated; [when] a parent who loses their child; and [when] a man is impoverished after [having been] rich."

Are Supplications Answered in a State of Grief?

ʿAbd Allāh ibn al-Raḥmān ibn Ṣāliḥ transmitted that Abū-l-Naḍr narrated from Ṣāliḥ al-Murrī that Yazīd al-Raqāshī said, "The prayer that is [readily] answered is that which emanates from [deep] sadness, as the key to mercy is [in] earnestly and humbly beseeching [Allah]."

41 This provides a demarcation between adaptive sadness that is associated with religious affairs contrasted by maladaptive sadness that is associated with worldly attachments.

Grief Due to Missing the Congregational Prayer

Al-Ḥasan ibn al-Ṣabāḥ narrated to me, saying that Zayd ibn al-Ḥubāb transmitted from Marjī, through Ghālib al-Qaṭṭān from Bakr ibn ʿAbd Allāh [the following]: "If a man leaves to attend the congregational prayer but misses it and consequently feels sad, then Allah gives him the [same] rewards of the congregational prayer."

Hāshim ibn al-Qāsim Abū Muḥammad narrated to me, stating, "My father narrated to me that Muḥammad ibn Hānī mentioned that Yūsuf ibn Asbāt related from Wuhayb ibn al-Ward, who said, 'Whoever performs the ritual ablution at home with excellence, and then leaves for the congregational prayer, but thereafter sees people departing [from the prayer] and is saddened by this, Allah will give him two rewards; a reward for his grief, and a reward for the congregational prayer that he missed.'"

Grief Polishes the Hearts

Muḥammad ibn al-Ḥusayn narrated to me, saying, "Jaʿfar ibn Jisr ibn Farqad told me that Ḥammād ibn Wāqid said, 'I heard Abū ʿUbayda al-Khawwāṣ saying that grief polishes the hearts. Through it, hearts are softened for [clearer] contemplation.' Thereafter, he wept."

Sayings of the Righteous Regarding Grief

Aḥmad ibn Jubayr narrated from Abū Isḥāq al-Ṭaliqānī through ʿAbd Allāh al-Mubārak on the authority of Sufyān al-Thawrī, who said, "It used to be said that [one's] sorrow corresponds to the degree of [their] foresight."

Aḥmad ibn Ḥātim al-Ṭawīl narrated to us, stating that Yaḥyā ibn Yamān related through Sufyān, on the authority of Yunus ibn ʿUbayd, from al-Ḥasan, who said, "Allah is not worshiped with anything better than long-drawn sorrow."

ʿĀṣim ibn ʿUmar ibn ʿAlī narrated from Ḥafṣ ibn Qarīr, who said, "A man amongst us accompanied al-Ḥasan, who said that he heard al-Ḥasan saying, 'Of all that a person will see in their record [of deeds] on the Day of Judgment, there will be nothing more pleasing than [their] worries and sorrows.'"

Does Worry and Grief Increase One's Rewards?

Abū al-Ḥārith Surayḥ ibn Yūnus related to me through Khalaf ibn Khalīfa, from Manṣūr ibn Zādhān, who stated, "Worry and grief increase one's rewards, whereas frivolity and carelessness increase one's bad deeds."

Abū ʿAbd Allāh Aḥmad ibn Ibrāhīm narrated to us, saying that Bishir ibn Salam al-Kūfī transmitted from Misʿar through Bukayr or Abū Bukayr, that Ibrāhīm al-Taymī once said, "The one who does not experience sadness should fear not being [included] amongst the people of Paradise, as they will exclaim [therein], 'All praise be to Allah Who has removed all grief from us.' Likewise, one who does not feel genuine concern should [also] be afraid of not being amongst the people of Paradise. This is because they will say, 'Verily, before [this] we used to be so worried amongst our people!'"

The Quran's Discussion on Grief

Al-Muthannā ibn Muʿādh al-ʿAnbarī narrated to us from Muʿādh ibn Hāshim, through his father, from ʿAmr ibn Mālik, [who transmitted] from Abū al-Jawzāʾ that Ibn ʿAbbās had said, "All praise be to Allah Who has saved us from …" He [then] continued, "… the joylessness of the Hellfire."

Al-Khalīl ibn ʿAmr narrated to us through ʿAbd Allāh ibn Idrīs [who related] from his father from ʿAṭiyya [who said], "All praise be to Allah who has kept away from us all [causes of] grief." He said, "[Meaning] death."

Muḥammad ibn Nāṣiḥ narrated to us, stating that Baqiyya ibn al-Walīd transmitted from Mujāshiʿ ibn ʿAmr from someone who related to him from Saʿīd ibn Jubayr [that he said], "All praise be to Allah who has kept away from us all [causes of] grief," He [further] explained, "[Meaning] concern about [earning] daily bread in this world."

4 Between Fear and Hope. *Mukhtaṣar Iḥyāʾ ʿUlūm al-Dīn* by Imam Abū Ḥāmid Muḥammad al-Ghazālī (d. 505 AH/1111 CE)

4.1 *Author's Biography*

See Author Biography under section 1 of Chapter 2.

4.2 *Text Overview and Significance*

This excerpt is taken from the condensed, summarized version of *Iḥyāʾ ʿUlūm al-Dīn* that Imam al-Ghazālī wrote himself towards the end of his lifetime. This particular selection highlights the importance of being in a state of balance between both fear and hope, as opposed to being overly consumed by either of the two. Such a discussion is important in the realm of psychological discourse due to the considerable influence each state has over one's thinking processes and accompanying behaviors. Fear propels future-oriented safety seeking behaviors, increasing one's need for control to avoid a potential harm in the future, whereas hope mediates safety-seeking behaviors by relinquishing control in anticipation of a positive future outcome. Imam al-Ghazālī proffers that healthy or balanced fear is attained when an individual sufficiently fears Allah to the extent that it drives them to act in a goal-oriented manner, purposefully preparing for the afterlife through the performance of good deeds and the abandonment of evil deeds. By nature, fear induces a state of control and strengthens one's sense of responsibility that effectively motivates behavior towards purposeful goals. However, fear needs to be counterbalanced with sufficient hope that allows a person to surrender control after they have exhausted their efforts, relying upon Allah's mercy and His facilitation of ultimately good outcomes. Imam al-Ghazālī provides prescriptive approaches utilizing Quranic cognitive therapy to promote this balance. First, he outlines the harms of each state when imbalanced, characterizing an individual with excessive fear as someone who may be unhealthily scrupulous, which can eventually lead to despondency. On the other hand, an individual with too much hope and too little fear risks becoming languid in their worship and religious commitment, delusionally relying on Allah's gifting them with good outcomes, despite their inaction.

In order to counterbalance between these states, Imam al-Ghazālī employs what cognitive psychologists refer to as bibliotherapy – which, in an Islamic context is more aptly termed *Quranotherapy*. Such entails the utilization of religious scripture to cognitively reframe and engender a healthy psychological orientation to life. More specifically, al-Ghazālī advises the one who suffers from excessive fear to read and reflect upon the mercy of Allah, while the one who is overly hopeful should read about the punishments of Allah. Such reflection will mediate their excessive fear or hope, leading them to act with a better-balanced cognitive orientation in striving towards achieving their religious goals.

Towards the end of the chapter, al-Ghazālī cautions spiritual masters to be wary of randomly employing interventions or mass-assigning certain verses of the Quran for all their disciples to reflect upon. Rather, the spiritual master must tailor their approach to the corresponding state of each unique individual in order to provide the most effective interventions. As supportive evidence, he cites the statement of Alī ibn Abī Ṭālib, may Allah be pleased with him, "The scholar is the one who neither causes people to despair from the mercy of Allah, nor feel spared from the punishment of Allah; rather they are the ones who employ what is most fitting for each person."

4.3 *Arabic Text*

الباب الثالث والثالثون
في الرجاء والخوف

اعلم أن الرجاء من مقامات السالكين وأحوال الطالبين، وإنما يسمى الوصف حالا ما دام يعرض ويزول، ويسمى مقامًا إذا ثبت، فيقول: اعلم أن المنتظر فيما بعد إذا كان مما يتألم به القلب سمي خوفا.

وإذا كان مما يفرح به القلب سمي رجاء، فإذًا الرجاء ارتياح القلب لانتظار ما هو محبوب، ولكن ذلك المحبوب لابد وأن يكون له سبب، فإن كان قد حصل أكثر أسبابه فيصدق اسم الرجاء عليه، وإن كان انتظارا مع انخرام أسبابه فاسم الغرور عليه أصدق، وإن تعادل طرفا حصول الأسباب وانتفائها كان اسم التمني عليه أصدق.

وقد علم أرباب القلوب أن الدنيا مزرعة الآخرة، القلب كالأرض والإيمان كالبذر فيه، والطاعات جارية مجرى سقي الماء وقلب الأرض وإمدادها بما يقويها، والقلب المستتر بالدنيا المستغرق بها كالأرض السبخة التي لا ينمو فيها البذر، ويوم القيامة يوم الحصاد ولا يحصد أحد إلا ما زرع، ولا ينمو زرع إلا من بذر الإيمان، وقلما ينمو الإيمان مع خبث القلب وسوء أخلاقه.

كما لا ينمو بذر في الأرض السبخة، فمن استجمعت له الأسباب من الأرض الطيبة والماء والمدد وتطهير الأرض كما سبق وألقى فيها بذاراً جيداً ثم انتظر على الحصاد راجياً من فضل الله تعالى دفع الصواعق والآفات المفسدة فهذا له وجه يسمى رجاء. وإن بث البذر في الأرض الصلبة السبخة التي لا ماء لها وانتظر الحصد فهذا يسمى غرورا.

وإن بث البذر في أرض طيبة ولكن لا ماء لها وانتظر الحصاد اعتماداً على ماء المطر فهذا يسمى تمنياً. فقد تبين لك أن من زرع الإيمان في قلبه وسقاه بماء الطاعات وطهر القلب عن الخبائث كما تطهر الأرض من الشوك والحشيش فله أن يرجو.

وما دون ذلك فتمن أو غرور، وإليه الإشارة بقوله عليه الصلاة والسلام: «الكيس من دان نفسه وعمل لما بعد الموت، والأحمق من أتبع نفسه هواها وتمنى على الله الأماني»، وقد أخبر الله سبحانه وتعالى عن مثل ذلك فقال تعالى: ﴿فخلف من بعدهم خلف ورثوا الكتاب يأخذون عرض هذا الأدنى ويقولون سيغفر لنا﴾ بين أن هذا الرجاء لا أصل له إذا لم يتقدم عليه ما ينبغي أن يتقدم.

ويدل عليه أيضاً ما روي عن زيد الخيل أنه قال لرسول الله صلى الله عليه وسلم: ”جئت لأسألك عن علامة الله فيمن يريد وعلامته فيمن لا يريد، فقال: كيف أصبحت قال: أصبحت ألحظ الخير وأهله وإذا قدرت على شيء منه سارعت إليه أيقنت بثوابه، وإن فاتني شيء منه حزنت عليه وحننت إليه، فقال: هذا علامة الله فيمن يريد ولو أرادك للأخرى هيأك لها، ثم لا يبالي في أي أوديتها هلكت“ فقد ذكر علامة من أريد به الخير ويحصل منه الرجاء.

بيان فضيلة الرجاء والترغيب فيه:

اعلم أن العمل على الرجاء أعلى منه على الخوف، لأن أقرب العباد إلى الله تعالى أحبهم إليه، والحب يغلب بالرجاء.

فإن رجاء الخير يقرب ويحبب، والخوف موجب للهرب، وإليه الإشارة بقوله عليه الصلاة والسلام: ”لا يموت أحدكم إلا وهو يحسن الظن بالله“، ودخل على رجل وهو في النزع

فقال: "كيف تجدك؟ فقال: أجدني أخاف ذنوبي وأرجو رحمة ربه" فقال: "ما اجتمعا في قلب عبد في هذا الموطن إلا أعطاه الله تعالى ما رجا وآمنه مما يخاف".

فصل

اعلم أن من غلب عليه اليأس حتى أورثه القنوط، أو غلب عليه الخوف حتى أضر بنفسه وأهله، فهذان يحتاجان إلى المعالجة بالمداواة. وأما من غلب عليه الأماني فأسباب الرجاء سم قاتل في حقه فهو كالعسل فيه شفاء لمن غلبت عليه البرودة، فإن تناوله المحرور هلك. فمن غلب عليه التمني وأسرف في المعاصي فهو جدير بأن يعالج بما يورث الخوف. فهما (الخوف والرجاء) شطران يسقى بكل واحد منهم من له حالة مخصوصة.

قال علي رضي الله عنه: إنما العالم الذي لا يقنط الناس من رحمة الله، ولا يؤمنهم من مكر الله. ولما كان العلماء ورثة الأنبياء؛ كانوا أطباء القلوب، واستعملوا ما كان لائقاً بحال كل مريض. ومن الدواء النافع في جلب الرجاء أن يتأمل الإنسان فيما أنعم الله تعالى به عليه من صحة البدن وسلامة الأعضاء، ثم بعثه الأنبياء لهدايته، ثم خلق الأطعمة والأشربة والأدوية لإصلاحه.

ومما يقوي أسباب الرجاء ما قاله سبحانه وتعالى: "يا عبادي الذين أسرفوا على أنفسهم لا تقنطوا من رحمة الله، إن الله يغفر الذنوب جميعاً". وقال تعالى: "والملائكة يسبحون بحمد ربهم ويستغفرون لمن في الأرض". وقال تعالى: "من فوقهم ظلل من النار ومن تحتهم ظلل ذلك يخوف الله به عباده"، بين أنه يخوف المؤمنين إلا أنها للكافرين لأنها خلقت لهم.

وقد روى أبو موسى الأشعري أنه قال: "أمتي أمة مرحومة لا عذاب عليها في الآخرة"، والآيات والأخبار الواردة في هذا الباب أكثر من أن تحصى.

وقد ورد في حديث طويل عن أنس: أن الأعرابي لما قال لرسول الله صلى الله عليه وسلم يا رسول الله من يلي حساب الخلق يوم القيامة قال:"الله عز وجل" فقال: "هو بنفسه". قال: "نعم"، فتبسم الأعرابي، فقال رسول الله صلى الله عليه وسلم: "مم ضحكت يا أعرابي؟". فقال: "إن الكريم إذا قدر عفا، وإذا حاسب سامح". قال النبي صلى الله عليه وسلم: "صدق الأعرابي ألا ولا كريم أكرم من الله تعالى وهو أكرم الأكرمين". ثم قال صلى الله عليه وسلم: "فقه الأعرابي". وقال صلى الله عليه وسلم: "قال الله تعالى" سبقت رحمتي غضبي".

الشطر الثاني في الخوف وقد بينا معنى الخوف:

اعلم أن الخوف والرجاء زمامان يقاد بهما من لم يظهر لقلبه جمال الحق، فمن شاهد بقلبه ذلك الجمال ترقى عن الخوف أو الرجاء. إليه الإشارة بقول الواسطي: الخوف حجاب بين الله وبين العبد، وقال أيضاً: إذا ظهر الحق على السرائر لا يبقى فيها فضيلة لا لرجاء ولا لخوف.

وعلى الجملة إذا وصل المحب إلى جمال المحبوب، فالتفاته إلى خوف الفراق مضيع للوصال، ولكنا نتكلم في أوائل المبدأ فعند هذا نقول دواء جلب الخوف أن ينظر و يتأمل في الآيات الواردة في شدة العذاب والحساب، والأخبار الواردة في ذلك، ويتأمل أيضاً حال نفسه بالنسبة إلى جلال الله وعظمته. وقوله تعالى هؤلاء في الجنة ولا أبالي وهؤلاء في النار ولا أبالي، ويعلم أنه بجنايته وتركه أوامر الله وارتكابه المناهي مستحق للعقاب الأليم.

والله تعالى لو أهلك العالمين فهو لا يبالي وهذا المسكين قد ارتكب الجرائم والآثام، فهو أولى بأن يخاف، فإنه إن أهلك لم يبال به، فكيف وسيد المرسلين يقول: "أنا أعلمكم بالله وأخشاكم لله"، وأوحى الله تعالى إلى داود عليه السلام: يا داود خفني كما تخاف السبع الضاري، وحقيقة السبع أنه مهلكك ولا يبالي.

وقد قال صلى الله عليه وسلم: "من خاف من الله خافه كل شيء ومن خاف غير الله خاف من كل شيء". وقالت عائشة رضي الله عنها: "قلت يا رسول الله ﴿الذين يؤتون ما آتوا وقلوبهم وجلة﴾ أهو الرجل يسرق ويزني قال: "لا بل يصوم ويتصدق ويصلي ويخاف أن لا يقبل منه"". وقال النبي صلى الله عليه وسلم: "ما من عبد مؤمن يخرج من عينه دموع وإن كانت مثل رأس الذباب من خشية الله تعالى ثم يصيب شيئًا وقت خروجه إلا حرمه الله على النار".

بيان أحوال الأنبياء في الخوف:

روت عائشة رضي الله عنها أن رسول الله صلى الله عليه وسلم كان إذا تغير الهواء وهبت ريح عاصفة يتغير وجهه ويقوم ويتردد في الحجرة ويدخل ويخرج كل ذلك خوفاً من عذاب الله تعالى، وقرأ عليه السلام آيات في سورة الحاقة فصعق.

وقال تعالى: ﴿وخر موسى صعقاً﴾، ورأى رسول الله صلى الله عليه وسلم صورة جبريل في الأبطح فصعق. وقال صلى الله عليه وسلم: ما جاءني جبريل قط إلا وهو يرعد خوفا من الجبار جل جلاله. وقيل لما ظهر على إبليس ما ظهر طفق جبريل وميكائيل عليهما السلام يبكيان فأوحى الله تعالى إليهما "ما لكما تبكيان كل هذا البكاء؟"، فقالا "يا رب ما أمنا من مكرك"، فقال تعالى: "هكذا كونا لا تأمنا مكري".

قال أبو الدرداء: كان يسمع أزيز قلب خليل الرحمن عليه السلام إذا قام في الصلاة من مسيرة ميل خوفا من ربه. وقال مجاهد رضي الله عنه: بكى داود عليه السلام أربعين يوما ساجداً لا يرفع رأسه حتى نبت المرعى من دموعه، وحتى غطى رأسه فنودي يا داود أجائع أنت فتطعم، أم ظمآن فتسقى، أم عار فتكسى، فتنفس الصعداء، فاحترق العود من حر جوفه، فأنزل الله تعالى عليه التوبة والمغفرة، فقال: يا رب اجعل خطيئتي في كفي فصارت خطيئته في كفه مكتوبة فكان لا يبسط كفه لطعام ولا لشراب ولا لغيرهما إلا رآها فأبكته.

قال وكان يؤتى بالقدح ثلثاه ماء فإذا تناوله أبصر خطيئته فلا يضعه على شفته حتى يفيض من دموعه.

وروي عنه عليه السلام أنه ما رفع رأسه إلى السماء حتى مات حياء من اللّٰه تعالى، وكان يقول في مناجاته: إلهي إذا ذكرت خطيئتي ضاقت علي الأرض برحبها، وإذا ذكرت رحمتك ارتدت إلي روحي، سبحانك إلهي أتيت أطباء عبادك ليداووا خطيئتي فكلهم عليك يدلني فبؤسًا للقانطين من رحمتك.

وقال الفضيل رحمة اللّٰه عليه بلغني أن داود عليه السلام ذكر ذنبه ذات يوم فوثب صاعقًا واضعًا يده على رأسه حتى لحق بالجبال، فاجتمعت إليه السباع فقال: ارجعوا فلا أريدكم إنما أريد كل بكاء على خطيئته فلا يستقبلني إلا باكيًا. ومن لم يكن ذا خطيئة فما يصنع بداود الخطاء، وكان يعاقب في كثرة البكاء، فيقول: دعوني أبكي قبل خروج يوم البكاء قبل تحرق العظام واشتعال الحشا وقبل أن يؤمر في ملائكة غلاظ شداد لا يعصون اللّٰه ما أمرهم ويفعلون ما يؤمرون.

وقال عمر بن عبد العزيز: لما أصاب داود الخطيئة نقص صوته فقال: إلهي بح صوتي في صفاء أصوات الصديقين.

وروي أنه عليه السلام لما طال بكاؤه ولم ينفعه ذلك ضاق ذرعه واشتد غمه، قال: يا رب أما ترحم بكائي؟ فأوحى اللّٰه تعالى إليه يا داود نسيت ذنبك وذكرت بكاءك فقال: إلهي وسيدي كيف أنسى ذنبي وكنت إذا تلوت الزبور كف الماء الجاري عن جريه، وسكن هبوب الريح، وأظلني الطير على رأسي، وأنست الوحوش إلى محرابي، إلهي وسيدي فما هذه الوحشة التي بيني وبينك، فأوحى اللّٰه تعالى إليه: يا داود ذلك أنس الطاعة وهذه وحشة المعصية، يا داود آدم خلق من خلقي خلقته بيدي، ونفخت فيه من روحي، وأسجدت له ملائكتي، وألبسته ثوب كرامتي وتوجته بتاج وقاري، وشكى إلي الوحدة فزوجته بحواء أمتي، وأسكنته جنتي، فلما عصاني طردته من جواري عريانًا ذليلًا. يا داود اسمع مني والحق أقول أطعتنا فأطعناك وسألتنا فأعطيناك وعصيتنا فأمهلناك، وإن عدت إلينا على ما كان منك قبلناك.

وقال يحيى بن بكير بلغنا أن داود عليه السلام كان إذا أراد أن يخرج مكث قبل ذلك سبعا لا يأكل الطعام ولا يشرب الشراب ولا يقرب النساء، فإذا كان قبل ذلك بيوم أخرج له منبر إلى البرية فيأمر سليمان أن ينادي بصوت يستقرى البلاد وما حولها من الغياض والآكام والبراري، وتأتي السباع من الغياض وتأتي الهوام من الجبال وتأتي الطير من الأوكار، وتأتي العذارى من خدورهن وتجتمع الناس لذلك اليوم. ويأتي داود عليه السلام حتى يرقي على المنبر ويحيط به بنو إسرائيل وكل صنف على حدته محيطون به، وسليمان عليه السلام قائم على رأسه فيأخذ في الثناء على ربه فيضجون بالبكاء والصريخ، ثم يأخذ في

ذكر الجنة فيموت الهوام وطائفة من الوحوش والسباع، ثم يأخذ في أهوال يوم القيامة وفي النياح على نفسه فيموت من كل نوع طائفة، فإذا رأى سليمان كثرة الموتى قال يا أبتاه قد مزقت المستمعين كل مزق، وماتت طوائف من بني إسرائيل ومن الوحوش والهوام فيأخذ في الدعاء، فبينما هو كذلك، إذ ناداه بعض عباد بني إسرائيل يا داود عجلت بطلب الجزاء على ربك، قال فخر داود مغشيا عليه فلما نظر سليمان عليه السلام إلى ما أصابه أتي بسرير فحمله عليه، ثم أمر مناديًا ينادي ألا من كان له مع داود قريب أو حميم فليأت بسريره فليحمله عليه فإن الذين كانوا معه قد قتلهم ذكر الجنة والنار. وكانت المرأة تأتي بالسرير وتحمل قريبها، وتقول يا من قتله ذكر الجنة يا من قتله خوف الله تعالى، ثم أفاق داود عليه السلام، ووضع يده على رأسه ودخل بيت عبادته وأغلق بابه وقال يا إله داود أغضبان أنت على داود، ولا يزال يناجي، حتى يأتي سليمان عليه السلام، ويقعد على الباب ويستأذن ثم يدخل ومعه قرص شعير، ويقول: يا أبتاه تقو بهذا على ما تريد. فيأكل من ذلك القرص ما شاء الله تعالى. ثم يخرج إلى بني إسرائل فيحكم بينهم.

وقال يزيد الرقاشي خرج داود ذات يوم للناس يعظهم ويخوفهم فخرج في أربعين ألفًا فمات ثلاثون ألفًا وما رجع إلا في عشرة آلاف وكان له جاريتان اتخذهما، حتى إذا جاءه الخوف وسقط فاضطرب قعدتا على صدره ورجليه مخافة أن تتفرق أعصاؤه.

وقال أبو بكر رضي الله عنه لطير ليتني كنت مثلك يا طير، ولم أخلق بشرًا، وقال أبو ذر وددت أني شجرة تعضد. وقال عثمان رضي الله عنه: وددت أني إذا مت لم أبعث. وقالت عائشة رضي الله عنها: وددت أني لو كنت نسيًا منسيًا. وكان في وجه عمر رضي الله عنه خطان أسودان من الدموع. وقال عمر رضي الله عنه: من خاف الله لم يشف غيظه، ومن اتقى الله لم يصنع ما يريد، ولولا يوم القيامة لكان غير ما ترون.

قال علي رضي الله تعالى عنه ذات يوم وقد سلم من صلاة الفجر، وقد علاه كآبة وهو يقلب يده: لقد رأيت أصحاب محمد ﷺ فلم أر اليوم شيئًا يشبههم، لقد كانوا يصبحون صفرًا شعثًا غبرًا بين أعينهم أمثال ركب المعزى، قد باتوا لله سجدًا وقيامًا يتلون كتاب الله يزاوجون بين جباههم وأقدامهم، وإذا أصبحوا وذكروا الله مادوا كما تميد الشجر في يوم الريح وهملت أعينهم بالدموع حتى تبل ثيابهم. والله كأني بأقوام باتوا غافلين. ثم قال: فما رؤي بعد ذلك ضاحكًا حتى ضربه ابن ملجم.

وكان عمر رضي الله تعالى عنه إذا سمع آية من القرآن يسقط من الخوف مغشيًا عليه فكان يعاد أيامًا وأخذ يومًا تبنة من الأرض فقال يا ليتني كنت هذه التبنة يا ليتني لم أك شيئًا مذكورًا يا ليتني لم تلدني أمي يا ليتني كنت نسيًا منسيًا.

وكان علي بن الحسين رضي الله عنه إذا توضأ اصفرَّ لونه فيقول له أهله ما هذا الذي يعتادك عند الوضوء، فيقول أتدرون بين يدي من أريد أن أقوم؟

وروي أن الفضيل رضي اللّٰه عنه رؤي يوم عرفة والناس يدعون وهو يبكي بكاء الثكلى المحترقة، حتى إذا كادت الشمس تغرب قبض على لحيته ثم رفع رأسه إلى السماء، فقال واسوأتاه منك وإن غفرت لي ثم انقلب مع الناس.

وسئل ابن عباس رضي اللّٰه عنه عن الخائفين فقال: قلوبهم من الخوف قريحة وأعينهم باكية يقولون كيف نفرح والموت وراءنا، والقبر أمامنا والقيامة موعدنا، وعلى جهنم طريقنا، وبين يدي ربنا موقفنا. وكان حماد بن عبد ربه إذا جلس جلس مستوفزًا على قدميه فيقال له لو اطمأننت، فيقول تلك جلسة الآمنين وأنا غير آمن إذا عصيت اللّٰه عز وجل.

وقال عمر بن عبد العزيز إنما جعل اللّٰه تعالى هذه الغفلة رحمة في قلوب عباده كيلا يموتوا من خشية اللّٰه تعالى، وروي أن فتى من الأنصار دخلته خشية من النار فدخل النبي ﷺ فاعتنقه فخر ميتًا فقال ﷺ: "جهزوا صاحبكم فإن الفرق فتت كبده" فافهم تغنم واللّٰه أعلم بالصواب وإليه المرجع والمآب.

4.4 *English Translation*

Between Hope and Fear

Understand that hope is one of the [various] ranks of a spiritual wayfarer and one of the states of a spiritual seeker. An attribute (*waṣf*) is labeled a "state" (*ḥāl*) when it comes and goes; it is termed a "station" (*maqām*) when it becomes [an] ingrained [trait].

They say one should know that if something is anticipated to occur in the future and such pains the heart, then it is called "fear" (*khawf*). However, if such brings joy to the heart, then it is called "hope" (*rajāʾ*). As such, hope is that which brings comfort to the heart in anticipating [the attainment of that which is] cherished. However, there must be a [practical] means for [attaining] that beloved [thing]; if one is [capable] of securing more avenues [towards] it then the term "hope" is rightfully applicable. Whereas if one is awaiting [positive outcomes] while the [requisite] means have ceased to exist, then "delusion" (*ghurūr*) is a more appropriate term. If both securing the means and their privation are equally likely, then the label "wish" (*tamannī*) is most befitting.

Verily, the masters of the heart know that the ephemeral world (*dunyā*) is a cultivating field for the Hereafter. The heart is like soil, and faith (*īmān*) is like the seeds [planted] therein. Acts of obedience [to Allah] are the running water which irrigates the earth and sustains it with nutrients. A heart that is immersed in the *dunyā* and obscured by it is like swampy earth in which seeds cannot grow. The Day of Recompense will be the day of harvest in which no one will reap [anything] other than that which they have sowed. No crops will grow except for the ones [that sprout] from the seeds of faith. Indeed, faith is seldomly cultivated when paired with a vile heart and an evil character.

Whilst seeds do not sprout in a swamp, a person who amasses the [correct] means (including pure soil, water, care, and fertilizer, as was previously mentioned) and then places a good seed therein, awaiting the harvest with hope for Allah's grace, and for [His] prevention of storms and natural disasters, then it is warranted for one to call this hope. If one scatters seeds in barren, desolate land that has no water, and [thereafter] anticipates a harvest, then this is called delusion (*ghurūr*). If one sprinkles seeds in pure soil without any water, and then anticipates a harvest by relying [solely] on rainwater, then this is called wishful thinking (*tamannī*).

It should thus be clear to you that the one who cultivates faith in his heart, irrigating it with the water of righteous deeds, and purifying it from [spiritual] impurities in the same way that land is cleared of thorns and weeds, is [rightfully] entitled to have hope. Anything other than that is wishful thinking or delusion,[42] towards which there is an indication in the Prophet's saying, may Allah bless him and grant him peace, "The intelligent one is he who subdues his carnal self and works for that which comes after death; the foolish one is he who follows his carnal desires with false hopes in Allah."[43] Verily Allah, the Exalted, has mentioned something similar to this in His statement: *Then, a generation came after them that inherited the Book, opting for the temporal goods of this world, saying, "We shall be forgiven,"* (Al-Aʿrāf 7:169). He clarifies that this [type of] hope has no basis when that which should rightfully precede it does not precede it.

What bolsters this further is what has been reported by Zayd al-Khayl [may Allah be pleased with him], who said to the Messenger of Allah, may Allah bless him and grant him peace, "'I have come to ask you regarding the signs for those whom Allah wants [goodness] and the signs for those whom He does not want [goodness].' He responded [may Allah bless him and grant him peace], 'In what state did you awaken this morning?' He answered, 'I awoke recognizing goodness and its people, and if I was capable of performing any of such, then I hastened towards it with firm conviction of its reward. If, perchance, any of it escaped me, I grieved over it and I yearned for it.' So, he [may Allah

---

42 This is a unique feature of Islamic traditional thought as exemplified by Imam al-Ghazālī, wherein even "positive" feelings or traits such as happiness or hopefulness must be tempered, as an excess of such can also be maladaptive.

43 Al-Tirmidhī, 45; Ibn Māja, 161.
In his *Takhrīj Minhāj al-Qāṣidīn*, Shuʿayb al-Arnaʾūt has graded this ḥadīth to be weak (*ḍaʿīf*) on account of the presence of a weak narrator in the chain, Abū Bakr al-Ghaṣānī (p. 298). Furthermore, most of the variations of this ḥadīth mention the word, "The incapacitated one" (*ʿĀjiz*) instead of "the foolish one" (Aḥmaq).

bless him and grant him peace] said, 'This is the sign of Allah for whomsoever he wants [goodness]. And if He had wanted other than that for you, He would have propelled you towards it without any care for which valley you perished in thereafter.'"[44] Thus he, [may Allah bless him and grant him peace,] mentioned the signs of those whom He wants good for, due to which one may become hopeful.

An Elucidation of the Virtues of Hope and Its Encouragement

Realize that deeds performed out of hope are superior to [deeds rooted] in fear. This is because the closest servants to Allah, the Exalted, are the most beloved to Him, and [it is] love [that] embodies hope.

Indeed, hope for good [naturally] draws one near and makes one beloved, whereas fear inherently incites one to run away. There is an indication towards this in the statement of the Prophet, may Allah bless him and grant him peace, "None of you should die without thinking well of Allah."[45] Additionally, when visiting a person on the verge [of death], he, may Allah bless him and grant him peace, asked, "How do you find yourself?" He answered, "I dread my sins whilst I [also] have hope in the Mercy of my Lord." He, may Allah bless him and grant him peace, said, "These two [characteristics] do not converge in the heart of a [believing] slave in such a moment except that Allah, the Exalted, grants him what he hopes for and saves him from that which he fears."[46]

Section One:

Realize that one who is overcome by hopelessness such that it makes him [totally] disheartened, as well as a person who is overcome with fear to the extent that it harms himself and his family,[47] are both in need of treatment[48]

44 Ḥāfiẓ al-ʿIrāqī grades this ḥadīth as weak. He states that it has been narrated in al-Tabrani's collection called, "al-Kabīr" (see ʿIrāqī, *al-Mughnī ʿan Ḥaml al-Asfār*, 149.).

45 Muslim, 2877.

46 Ibn Māja, 4261; al-Tirmidhī, 983.

47 In moderation, fear is thought to have adaptive functions in terms of both cognitive and behavioral responses. From the perspective of evolutionary psychologists, fear, in its adaptive form, allows for the aversion of danger. In its maladaptive form, however, it can lead to anxiety disorders and depression (John D. Teasdale, Zindel Segal, and J. Mark G. Williams, "How Does Cognitive Therapy Prevent Depressive Relapse and Why Should Attentional Control (Mindfulness) Training Help?," *Behaviour Research and Therapy* 33, no. 1 (January 1995): 25–39.).

In the above section, al-Ghazālī highlights that excessive anxiety can lead to dysfunction that is indicated by personal, familial, and social functioning. This is quite similar to the Diagnostic and Statistical Manual of Mental Disorders (DSM) criteria for considering something to have met the clinical threshold of being considered a disorder (American Psychological Association, 2013).

48 Modern psychological perspectives struggle to determine the adaptiveness of emotion regulation as researchers assume that it is adaptive to down-regulate all negative

with corresponding [positive] opposites.[49] As for the one who is overrun by vain hopes, the means [that incite] hope is like a fatal poison for him; they are like honey in which there is cure for the one experiencing excessive [inner] coolness [in their body]. If someone with excessive heat were to consume it, they would perish. As for the one who is engulfed by false hope and inordinately engages in sin, it is especially necessary for him to be treated with that which induces fear.[50] Both fear and hope are proportionately correlated; each should be [appropriately] induced in accordance with the specific state of every individual.

ʿAlī, may Allah be pleased with him, once stated, "The scholar is one who does not cause people to despair of Allah's mercy; he likewise does not let them feel [overly] secure regarding the plans of Allah. Since the scholars are the inheritors of the prophets, they are doctors of the [spiritual] heart; they administer that which appropriately suits the condition of each [and every] patient."[51]

---

emotions and up-regulate all of the positive ones (cf. Drew Westen and Pavel S. Blagov, "A Clinical-Empirical Model of Emotion Regulation: From Defense and Motivated Reasoning to Emotional Constraint Satisfaction," in *Handbook of Emotion Regulation* (The Guilford Press, 2007), 374.). For example, Westen and Blagov define emotion regulation as "... procedures people use to try to maximize pleasant and minimize unpleasant feelings, emotions, and moods," (Westen and Blagov, "A Clinical-Empirical Model of Emotion Regulation: From Defense and Motivated Reasoning to Emotional Constraint Satisfaction."). However, to truly determine the adaptiveness of emotion regulation, one must study the emotion in its cultural-religious context by taking into consideration short-term and long-term goals, and other motivators behind the regulation process. As outlined above, as well as throughout the vast heritage of classical literature, Islamic perspectives view emotions as processes involving the demands of the religion.

49 The Arabic term *mudāwā* indicates and includes treatment with the opposite states. This approach was and is commonplace in traditional humoral medicine whereby an individual afflicted with too much heat in their body would be regulated through the consumption of cooling foods and activities. This analogy is extended to psycho-spiritual conditions by many traditionally trained spiritual practitioners, whereby they attempt to treat an extreme manifestation of an emotional or spiritual state with its opposite state in order to establish equilibrium within the patient. In this case, too much fear is then treated through cognitive reframing in order to engender a hopeful psychological orientation via the usage of Quranic verses as al-Ghazali describes in this text.

50 Adaptive anxiety leads an individual to be concerned with fears of adverse consequences; such serves as a motivator to desist from engaging in sins for fear of punishment from Allah. Conversely, someone immersed in sin who does not put forth any significant effort to improve on account of a misplaced hope for the forgiveness of Allah needs to have their false hopes countered through reminders of Allah's wrath.

51 This underscores a very important principle describing psycho-spiritual treatment as a very nuanced process. Similar to cognitive therapies, al-Ghazālī suggests that a spiritual guide should adopt an approach that is based on an assessment of the patient's particular needs, working to induce and adjust their states accordingly. The philosophy of unique treatment elucidated here entails the referencing of scripture in order to cognitive

One of the [most] effective remedies [used] to inculcate hope involves the patient closely reflecting over the blessings that Allah has bestowed upon him; this includes his bodily health and the soundness of his limbs; the commission of prophets for the sake of his guidance; the creation of various foods, drinks, and medicinal cures for his betterment.

Something else that reinforces the means for [increasing] hope is in what He, the Exalted, says: *O My servants who have exceeded the limits against their souls! Do not lose hope in Allah's mercy, for Allah certainly forgives all sins* (Al-Zumar 39:53). He also states: ... *and the angels proclaim the purity and praise of their Lord, seeking forgiveness for those on the earth* (Al-Shūrā 42:5). Additionally, he mentions: *Above them are canopies of fire as well as canopies underneath them. That is the thing against which Allah warns His servants* (Al-Zumar 39:16). Even though He strikes fear within the believer [here], such is actually directed towards the disbelievers for whom [the fire] was created.

Abū Mūsā al-ʾAshʿarī, may Allah be pleased with him, reported that the Prophet, may Allah bless him and grant him peace, said, "My nation is a privileged nation; it will not be punished in the hereafter."[52] Indeed, there are innumerable verses and prophetic reports to support this.

It also appears in a long hadith [narrated] by Anas, may Allah be pleased with him, that a bedouin once asked the Messenger of Allah, may Allah bless him and grant him peace, "who will preside over the accounts of the entire creation on the Day of Judgment?" He [may Allah bless him and grant him peace] replied, "Allah, the Honored and Majestic." The bedouin further asked, "Him, and Him alone?" He [may Allah bless him and grant him peace] answered, "Yes." Thereafter, the bedouin smiled, and the Messenger of Allah, may Allah bless him and grant him peace, asked him, "O Bedouin, what makes you smile?" He responded, "Verily, the Most Kind. When He enumerates, He forgives, and when He calls to account, He overlooks." The Prophet, may Allah bless him and grant him peace, affirmed, "The bedouin has spoken the truth. Truly, there is no one more kind than Allah, the Exalted – He is the most benevolent of all." He, may Allah bless him and grant him peace, then said, "This Bedouin has understood [well]."[53] He, may Allah bless him and grant him peace, also said, "Allah, the Exalted, has proclaimed, 'My mercy supersedes my wrath.'"[54]

---

reframe or induce the opposite emotional state that the patient is experiencing, thereby engendering psychospiritual equilibrium.

52 Abū Dāwūd, 4278.

53 Bayḥaqī has narrated a similar ḥadīth with slightly different wording in Shuʿāb al-Īmān, vol. 1, p. 421. However, Bayḥaqī classifies this ḥadīth as a fabrication (*mawḍūʿ*). (See al-Bayhaqī, *Kitāb Shuʿab al-Īmān*, 1:421.)

54 Muslim, 2751.

Section Two: Regarding Fear

Note: the meaning of fear has been explained in the aforementioned section.

One should realize that both fear and hope are two lead reins that drive the one in whose heart the beauty of truth has not become [fully] manifest. Whosoever beholds such beauty with his heart transcends [the need for] fear or hope. This is elucidated by the saying of [Imam] al-Wāsiṭī, "Fear is a veil between Allah and His servant." He likewise said, "When the truth is made manifest within the hearts, they no longer retain any [other] motive – [actions are no longer] driven by fear or hope."

Generally, if a lover is engulfed by the splendor of His beloved, then [even] turning his attention towards the fear of separation will detract from the union [between them]. Nonetheless, we are [only] speaking about the preliminary basics of this phenomenon. At this juncture, we assert that the remedy to incite fear entails looking over and reflecting upon the [Qurʾānic] verses that mention the severity of divine punishments and the [Day of] Judgment as well as related prophetic narrations. One should also reflect upon the condition of their own self in relation to the Majesty and Grandeur of Allah, alongside His statement [in a ḥadīth qudsī], "These people are in paradise and it makes no difference to Me, plus these are in the Hellfire and it makes no difference to Me."[55] Furthermore, a person must realize that they are deserving of a painful retribution on account of one's transgressions, disregard for the commands of Allah, and their perpetration of forbidden deeds.

If Allah, the Exalted, were to destroy the entire world, it would make no difference to Him at all. Whereas this deprived person has committed crimes and sins and is thus most deserving of being in [a state of] fear. If he were to be destroyed, then Allah would not be affected by such. And how [can one not worry] when the Leader of all Messengers, [may Allah bless him and grant him peace], said, "I am the most knowledgeable amongst you regarding Allah; I am also the most fearful of Allah."[56] Also, Allah revealed to Dawūd [upon him be peace], "Dawūd! Fear me just as you fear a menacing predator." And the reality of [the nature of] a predatory beast is that it will readily devour you without any concern.

---

55 Muḥammad Ibn Sa'd, *Al-Ṭabaqāt al-Kubrā*, vol. 7 (Cairo: Maktabat al-Khanjī, 2001), 135; Ibn Manthūr, *Tahdhīb Tārīkh Dimashq*, 5:292.

56 Al-Bukhārī, 20; Aḥmad, 3:317.

Indeed, the Messenger of Allah, may Allah bless him and grant him peace, said, "Whoever fears Allah then everything will fear Him, and the one who fears other than Allah, will fear everything."[57]

ʿĀ'isha, may Allah be pleased with her, reported, "I said, 'O Messenger of Allah, [does the verse] *Those who give whatever they give and whose hearts tremble* [al-Mu'minūn 23:60], refer to the person who steals and fornicates?' He, may Allah bless him and grant him peace, replied, 'No. Rather, [it refers] the one who fasts, gives charity, and prays, fearing that none of it will be accepted from him.'"[58] The Prophet, may Allah bless him and grant him peace, also said, "There is no believer who sheds tears from fearing Allah – even if they are [as little] as the size of a fly's head – realizing a lesson at the time they roll down [his cheeks], except that Allah makes him prohibited for the Hellfire [to consume him]."[59]

An Elucidation of the Prophets' Experiences of Fear

ʿĀ'isha, may Allah be pleased with her, narrates, "the Messenger of Allah, may Allah bless him and grant him peace, was such that when the weather would worsen and the winds would [start to] blow fiercely, his face would [visibly] change; he would stand up and pace around the house, going out and coming back in [again]. All of this was due to fear of Allah's punishment. Once, he recited verses from Surat al-Hāqqa and fainted."

Also, Allah the Exalted says, … *and Musa fell unconscious*, (al-Aʿrāf 7:143). When the Messenger of Allah, may Allah bless him and grant him peace, saw the [angelic] form of Jibrīl in the horizon, he lost consciousness. He, may Allah bless him and grant him peace, further said, "Jibrīl never came to me except that he would be trembling out of fear of [Allah,] the Compellor, The Magnificent." Additionally, it has been related that when what befell Iblis occurred, Jibrīl and Mīkāīl immediately began to weep. Allah, the Exalted, inspired them, [saying,]

---

57 Abū Muḥammad Zakī al-dīn al-Mundhirī, *Al-Targhīb Wa-l-Tarhīb Min al-Hadīth al-Sharif*, vol. 1 (Beirut: Dār Iḥyā' al-Turāth al-'Arabī, 1968), 26; ʿAlāuddīn al-Muttaqī al-Hindī, *Kanz Al-'Ummāl*, vol. 3 (Muassasat al-Risāla, 1981), 149; Ismāʿīl Ibn Muḥammad al-ʿAjlūnī, *Kashf Al-Khafā'*, vol. 2 (Cairo: Maktabat al-Qudsī, 1351), 249. Ḥāfiẓ al-ʿIrāqī grades this ḥadīth as severely weak (ʿIrāqī, *Al-Mughnī 'an Ḥaml al-Asfār*, 510).

58 Aḥmad, 6:159; Abū Nuʿaym al-Isfahānī, *Ḥilya al-Awliyā' wa Tabaqāt al-Aṣfiyā'*, vol. 10 (Cairo: Dār al-Ḥadīth, 2009), 278; Ibn Ḥajar al-ʿAsqalānī, *Fatḥ Al-Bāri bi-Sharḥ Ṣaḥīḥ al-Bukhārī*, vol. 11 (Egypt: al-Maktabat al-Salafiyya, 1380), 170; Jalāl al-Dīn al-Suyūṭī, *al-Durr al-Manthūr*, vol. 6 (Beirut: Dār Fikr, n.d.), 105.

59 Abū Muḥammad Zakī al-dīn al-Mundhirī, *al-Targhīb wa-l-Tarhīb min al-Hadīth al-Sharif*, vol. 4 (Beirut: Dār Iḥyā' al-Turāth al- 'Arabī, 1968), 231; al-Muttaqī al-Hindī, *Kanz al-'Ummāl*, 3:148.

"What has come over you, causing you to cry like this?" They replied, "O Lord! We are not secure from Your [Divine] designs!" Allah said, "You should be as such; never feel safe from My planning."

[About the Prophet, may Allah bless him and grant him peace,] Abū Dardā', [may Allah be pleased with him,] said, "The throbbing heart of Allah's closest, upon him be peace, on account of the fear of Allah, could be heard from the distance of a mile when he would stand to pray." Also, Mujāhid, may Allah be pleased with him, mentioned that Dāwūd, upon him be peace, cried for forty days in prostration; he did not raise his head until undergrowth sprouted [on the ground] through his tears. When his head was eventually covered [by foliage], it was called out, "O Dāwūd, are you hungry, that you should be fed? Or are you thirsty, that you should be given to drink? Or are you undressed, that you should be clothed? He then sighed heavily; the twigs ignited from the heat of his breath as Allah sent down His remission and forgiveness upon him. Dāwūd [upon him be peace] then said, 'My Lord, inscribe my mistakes onto my palm.' All his mistakes were then written onto his palm such that he would not extend his hand to eat or drink or for anything else except that he would see it, and it would consequently make him weep. Whenever he was handed a cup that was half full of water, when he would lift it [to drink], he would consider his mistakes; upon reaching his lips [the cup] would be overflowing due to his tears."

And it is also narrated about him, upon him be peace, that he never raised his head towards the sky until he passed away due to humility before Allah. Indeed, he used to privately entreat Allah, saying, "My Lord, whenever I remember my mistakes, the earth, in its vastness, constricts around me [as if I am dead]. But, when I remember Your Mercy, then [it is as if] my soul returns to me. Perfection is Yours! I have come to the physicians amongst your slaves to remedy my mistakes, and all of them direct me toward you, so wretched are those who despair of You Mercy."

Fuḍayl, may Allah have Mercy on Him, related, "It was narrated to me that Dāwūd, upon him be peace, remembered his mistake one day, so he jumped up abruptly with his hand upon his head until he reached the [nearby] mountains. Predatory animals gathered around him. He exclaimed, 'Go away! I do not want you! I only want those who profusely weep over their sins. No one should come to me unless they are crying. And who is free of sin? And what would one do with Dāwūd, the sinner, [anyways]?' He used to get rebuffed for weeping excessively, but he would say, 'Leave me to cry before the Day of Lament manifests; before the bones burn and the entrails are ignited; *before the stern, fierce, angels* (Al-Taḥrīm 66:6) are commanded, who *do not disobey Allah; they do as they are ordered* (Al-Taḥrīm 66:6).'"

ʿUmar ibn ʿAbdul Azīz mentioned that when Dāwūd [upon him be peace] was afflicted by [his] error, his voice faltered and he said, "O my Lord, my voice has become hoarse compared to the pure voices of those who are true [to You]."

It has additionally been narrated that after crying profusely to no avail, he, upon him be peace, felt inhibited and further saddened, saying, "O My Lord, will you not have Mercy on [account of] my crying?" Allah then inspired him, [saying], "O Dāwūd! You have forgotten your misdeed, yet you mention your crying?" He answered, "My Lord and Master, how could I forget my misdeed? When I would recite the Zabūr, the rivers would stop flowing; the winds would stop blowing; the birds would perch upon my head; and the wild animals would settle in my prayer niche (*miḥrāb*). But now, my Lord and Master, what is this estrangement that has [come] between me and You?" Allah, the Exalted revealed in response, "O Dāwūd, that was the succor of obedience, whereas this is alienation from transgression. O Dāwūd! Adam was a creature from amongst my creatures; I created him Myself; I blew My spirit into him; I had My angels bow down to him; I dressed him in the clothing of My benevolence; and I crowned him with the crown of My dignity; he felt lonely, so I married him to my servant, Ḥawāʾ, and I allowed him to dwell in My garden. However, when he disobeyed me, I expelled him from My Presence, naked and disgraced. O Dāwūd, listen to Me, and it is [only] the Truth that I speak: When you obeyed Us, we made [others] obey you; when you asked of Us, we gave you; and [even] when you disobeyed Us, We gave you respite. As such, if you come back to Us [now], [being] as you were before, We will [certainly] accept you."

Yaḥyā ibn Bukayr mentioned that it has been related that Dāwūd, when intending to go out, would remain in his place for seven days without eating or drinking anything; he would also abstain from approaching his wives. On the day prior, he would have his pulpit placed in front of all, and he would then order Sulaymān [upon him be peace] to call out with a [raised] voice that reached the [furthest] lands, along with their surrounding forests, mountains, and plains. The beasts would approach from the plains; the insects would swarm from the mountains; the birds would flock from their nests; the maidens would come out from their quarters; all would amass together on that day. Dāwūd, upon him be peace, would ascend his pulpit, with all the Children of Israel surrounding him; all types of creatures would likewise encircle him, with Sulaymān, upon him be peace, stationed by his head. He would then begin to praise his Lord whilst all would wail and cry. Upon mentioning Paradise, all the insects as well as a number of the wild animals and predatory beasts died. Thereafter, upon mentioning the horrors of the Day of Judgment whilst crying out himself, so many others also died. When Sulaymān saw the multitudes of those who had died, he exclaimed, "O my [respected] father! The entire audience has been torn to pieces [by] listening [to your words]! So many of the Children of Israel, the wild animals, and the insects have died!" Dāwūd then began to supplicate. Whilst he was doing so, a few of the monks from amongst the Children of Israel called out, "O Dāwūd! You have been hasty in seeking recompense from your Lord!" Dāwūd subsequently fell unconscious. When Sulaymān saw what had befallen him, he brought forth a pallet and hoisted him on it. He then summoned an announcer to call out, "Listen up! Whoever from amongst you has a relative or close friend alongside Dāwūd should [likewise] get a pallet and carry them upon it! Indeed, those who were with him were killed by the remembrance of Paradise and Hellfire!" Women then brought forth pallets, carrying their relatives, exclaiming, "O [dearest] one who has been killed by the remembrance of Paradise! O you who was killed by the fear of Allah, the Exalted!" Sometime afterwards, Dāwūd [upon him be peace] awoke. Placing his hand on his head, he entered his personal sanctuary [dedicated] for worship and closed the door. Therein, he prayed, "O Lord of Dāwūd! Are you angry with Dāwūd?" He continued to beseech [Allah] until Sulaymān, upon him be peace, came and sat by the door, seeking permission to enter. Thereafter, he entered, holding some barley bread. He said, "O my [dear] father, gain strength with this for what you are seeking." He ate from that bread as much as Allah, the Exalted, had willed. Thereafter, he went out to the Children of Israel to judge between them.

Yazīd al-Raqāshī stated that Dāwūd [upon him be peace] went out to the people one day to preach to them and warn them. He addressed forty thousand [people], and thirty thousand of them died, leaving behind only ten thousand. He had two maidservants that he took along with him so that when he was overwhelmed by fear to the extent that he would collapse and lose his senses, they would sit themselves upon his chest and legs out of fear that his limbs would detach [from his body].

Abū Bakr, may Allah be pleased with him, once addressed a bird, [saying], "Woe to me! If only I could be a bird like you and I was not made to be a [morally responsible] human." Abū Dharr, may Allah be pleased with him, once said, "I wish I was a supportive tree." ʿUthmān, may Allah be pleased with him, once said, "I would love it if it were such that when I die, I am not resurrected." ʿĀʾisha, may Allah be pleased with her, similarly expressed, "I wish I was a thing long forgotten." ʿUmar, may Allah be pleased with him, used to have two black lines [trailing] along his face from [his] tears. ʿUmar, may Allah be pleased with him, once said, "The one who fears Allah does not display his anger; the one who is conscious of Allah never does as he pleases. If it were not for the Day of Judgment, things would certainly not be as you see."

One day, upon completing the dawn prayer, Alī, may Allah be pleased with him, was visibly somber. Turning his hand over [in agitation], he said, "Indeed, I have seen the companions of the Messenger of Allah, may Allah bless him and grant him peace. Truly, to this day, I have never seen anything like them; they would awaken each morning pallid, disheveled, and dusty, as if trampled by goats; they had dedicated their nights to Allah, bowing, standing, and reciting the Book of Allah; they would spend equal time on their foreheads and on their feet [in prayer]. After reaching the morning and engaging in the remembrance of Allah, they would sway as trees do on a windy day. Their eyes would shed tears until their clothes were saturated with tears. I swear by Allah, [now] it seems as if I am in the midst of such heedless people!" He was never seen smiling after that until Ibn Muljim killed him.

ʿUmar, may Allah be pleased with him, would faint out of fear when he heard a verse from the Quran; people would visit him for days [until he recovered]. One day, he picked up a piece of dirt from the ground and said, "Woe is me, would that I could be this piece of dirt! I wish I was nothing – [not even] a memory! Woe is me, if only my mother did not give birth to me! Woe is me! I wish I could be long forgotten!"

ʿAlī, the son of Ḥusayn, may Allah have mercy on him, would often become pale when performing the ritual ablution (*wuḍūʾ*). His family would ask, "What is this that keeps happening to you when you perform *wuḍūʾ*?" He would reply, "Do you know in front of Whom I am intending to stand?"

It has been related that Fuḍayl, may Allah be pleased with him, was spotted on the Day of ʿArafa. Whilst everyone else was supplicating, he was weeping like a bereaved widow. Just before the sun had set, he clenched his own beard, looked up towards the sky. He said, "How ashamed am I before You, even when You have forgiven me?" Thereafter, he turned to join [the rest of] the people.

Ibn ʿAbbās, may Allah be pleased with him, was once asked regarding those who fear [Allah]. He thus replied, "Their hearts ache [tremendously] from the fear of Allah; they are constantly weeping; they often say, 'How can we rejoice when death is right behind us, and our graves are immediately in front of us; Judgment Day is our appointed time; our path [stretches] across the Hellfire; and [inevitably,] we [must] stand before our Lord.'"

When Hammād ibn ʿAbdi Rabbihi, used to sit, he did so restlessly on his feet. It was suggested to him, "If only you would relax [a bit]?" He answered, "That is how secure people sit. But I am not safe as I have disobeyed my Lord."

ʿUmar ibn ʿAbdul Azīz said, "Allah has made heedlessness a mercy within the hearts of His servants, so that they do not die out of the sheer fear of Allah, the Exalted."

It is narrated that fear of the Hellfire permeated the heart of a young boy from amongst the Ansār. When the Prophet, may Allah bless him and grant him peace, came, the boy hugged him and then immediately fell dead. The Prophet, may Allah bless him and grant him peace, said, "Prepare your companion [to be buried]; indeed, dread has destroyed him from within."

Understand [this well], and you will gain [so much]. Allah knows best what is correct, and to Him is our reference and ultimate return.

5 An Exposition on the Essential Nature of Anger. *Iḥyāʾ ʿUlūm al-Dīn* (*The Revival of Religious Sciences*) by Imam Abū Ḥāmid Muḥammad al-Ghazālī (d. 505 AH/1111 CE)

5.1 *Author's Biography*

See Author Biography under section 1 of Chapter 2.

5.2 *Text Overview and Significance*

In this translated chapter of the *Iḥyāʾ*, Imam al-Ghazālī provides an insightful overview of the nature and function of emotions, with a special focus on anger. He describes anger as an adaptive survival drive that is necessary for self-preservation and the protection of family. This is similar to evolutionary psychologists and emotion-focused theorists who posit that all emotions possess adaptive utility and survival properties. Using the specific case of anger, al-Ghazālī states that its adaptive need is to repel harm when a threatening situation is presented in the moment. Alternatively, anger aids the need to acquire justice for a past inequity that one has experienced. Imam al-Ghazālī further describes the physiological and cognitive states associated with anger. He highlights what is referred to as the "fight-flight response" in modern psychology, which can prompt action responses to approach and attack so as to ultimately subdue the threat. However, if perchance an individual deduces that they will not be able subdue the presenting threat, then the flight mechanism is activated, or a form of hopelessness sets in if they are unable to flee from harm. While the physiological correlates of anger he describes are more consistent with ancient medicine, they strikingly parallel many explanations of the physiology of anger in contemporary psychology. As for the cognitive correlates, he discusses the "all-or-nothing" and irrational reasoning tendencies that can sometimes set in. Also, while the adaptive need is to avoid harm or seek injustice, excessive anger leads to unproductive destructive tendencies. Once excessive anger sets in, al-Ghazālī states that one becomes irrational and any attempts to calm such an individual down will further add fuel to their fire of anger. Towards the end of the chapter, al-Ghazālī importantly points out how the intensity or frequency of the expression of emotions can vary from person to person based upon their biological predispositions, upbringing, socialization, and learning. He describes the need to keep one's emotional states regulated and balanced, never being unleashed in a manner that overpowers one's reason.

5.3 *Arabic Text*

بيان حقيقة الغضب

اعلم أن اللّٰه تعالى لما خلق الحيوان معرضاً للفساد والموتان بأسباب في داخل بدنه وأسباب خارجة عنه أنعم عليه بما يحميه عن الفساد ويدفع عنه الهلاك إلى أجل معلوم سماه في كتابه.

أما السبب الداخل: فهو أنه ركبه من الحرارة والرطوبة، وجعل بين الحرارة والرطوبة عداوة ومضادة؛ فلا تزال الحرارة تحلل الرطوبة وتجففها وتبخرها حتى تتفشى أجزاؤها بخاراً يتصاعد منها، فلو لم يتصل بالرطوبة مدد من الغذاء يجبر ما انحل وتبخر من أجزائها لفسد الحيوان، فخلق اللّٰه الغذاء الموافق لبدن الحيوان، وخلق في الحيوان شهوة تبعثه على تناول الغذاء؛ كالموكل به في جبر ما انكسر وسد ما انثلم؛ ليكون ذلك حافظا له من الهلاك بهذا السبب.

وأما الأسباب الخارجة التي يتعرض لها الإنسان: فكالسيف والسنان وسائر المهلكات التي يقصد بها، فافتقر إلى قوة وحمية تثور من باطنه فتدفع المهلكات عنه، فخلق اللّٰه الغضب من النار، وغرزه في الإنسان، وعجنه بطينته، فمهما صد عن غرض من أغراضه ومقصود من مقاصده اشتعلت نار الغضب، وثارت ثوراناً يغلي به دم القلب، وينتشر في العروق، ويرتفع إلى أعالي البدن كما ترتفع النار، وكما يرتفع الماء الذي يَغْلِي فِي الْقِدْرِ؛ فَلِذَلِكَ يَنْصَبُّ إِلَى الْوَجْهِ فَيَحْمَرُّ الْوَجْهُ وَالْعَيْنُ، وَالْبَشرَةُ لِصَفَائِهَا تَحْكِي لَوْنَ مَا وَرَاءَهَا مِنْ حُمْرَةِ الدَّمِ؛ كَمَا تَحْكِي الزجاجة لون ما فيها، وإنما ينبسط الدم إذا غضب على من دونه واستشعر القدرة عليه، فإن صدر الغضب على من فوقه، وكان معه يأس من الانتقام، تولد منه انقباض الدم من ظاهر الجلد إلى جوف القلب، وصار حزناً، ولذلك يصفر اللون، وإن كان الغضب على نظير يشك فيه تردد الدم بين انقباض وانبساط؛ فيحمر ويصفر ويضطرب.

وبالجملة: فقوة الْغَضَبِ مَحَلُّهَا الْقَلْبُ وَمَعْنَاهَا غَلَيَانُ دَمِ الْقَلْبِ بطلب الانتقام، وإنما تتوجه هذه القوة عند ثورانها إلى دفع المؤذيات قبل وقوعها وإلى التشفي والانتقام بعد وقوعها. والانتقامُ قوتُ هذه القوة وشهوتُها وفيه لذتها ولا تسكن إلا به.

ثُمَّ إِنَّ النَّاسَ فِي هَذِهِ الْقُوَّةِ عَلَى درجات ثلاث في أول الفطرة: من التفريط، والإفراط، والاعتدال.

أما التفريط فبفقد هَذِهِ الْقُوَّةِ أَوْ ضَعْفِهَا، وَذَلِكَ مَذْمُومٌ، وَهُوَ الَّذِي يُقَالُ فِيهِ ﴿إِنَّهُ لَا حَمِيَّةَ لَهُ﴾، ولذلك قال الشافعي رحمه الله: «من استغضب فلم يغضب فهو حمار».

فمن فقد قوة الغضب والحمية أصلاً فهو ناقص جداً، وَقَدْ وَصَفَ اللَّهُ سُبْحَانَهُ أَصْحَابَ النَّبِيِّ صَلَّى اللَّهُ عَلَيْهِ وَسَلَّمَ بِالشِّدَّةِ وَالْحَمِيَّةِ فَقَالَ: ﴿أَشِدَّاءُ على الكفار رحماء بينهم﴾، وَقَالَ لِنَبِيِّهِ صَلَّى اللَّهُ عَلَيْهِ وَسَلَّمَ: ﴿جَاهِدِ الكفار والمنافقين واغلظ عليهم﴾، وَإِنَّمَا الْغِلْظَةُ وَالشِّدَّةُ مِنْ آثَارِ قُوَّةِ الْحَمِيَّةِ، وَهُوَ الْغَضَبُ.

وَأَمَّا الْإِفْرَاطُ فَهُوَ أَنْ تَغْلِبَ هَذِهِ الصِّفَةُ حَتَّى تَخْرُجَ عَنْ سِيَاسَةِ الْعَقْلِ والدين وطاعته، ولا يبقى للمرء معها بصيرةٌ ونظرٌ وَلا فِكْرٌ وَلَا اخْتِيَارٌ، بَلْ يَصِيرُ فِي صُورَةِ المضطر.

وسبب غلبته: أمور غريزية، وأمور اعتيادية، فرب إنسان هو بالفطرة مستعد لسرعة الغضب، حتى كأن صورته في الفطرة صورة غضبان، ويعين على ذلك حرارة مزاج القلب؛ لأن الغضب من النار كما قال صلى الله عليه وسلم، وإنما برودة المزاج تطفئه وتكسر سورته.

وأما الأسباب الاعتيادية فهو أن يخالط قوماً يتبجحون بتشفي الغيظ وطاعة الغضب ويسمون ذلك شجاعة ورجولية، فيقول الواحد منهم: «أنا الذي لا أصبر على المكر والمحال، ولا أحتمل من أحد أمرا»، ومعناه: لا عقل لي ولا حلم، ثم يذكره في معرض الفخر لجهله، فمن سمعه رسخ في نفسه حسن الغضب، وحب التشبه بالقوم، فيقوى به الغضب.

ومهما اشتعلت نار الغضب وقوى اضطرامها أعمت صاحبها وأصمته عن كل موعظة، فإذا وُعِظَ لم يسمع، بل زاده ذلك غضباً، فإن استضاء بنور عقله وراجع نفسه لم يقدر؛ إذ ينطفئ نور العقل وينمحي في الحال بدخان الغضب؛ فإن معدن الفكر الدماغ، ويتصاعد عند شدة الغضب من غليان دم القلب دخان مظلم إلى الدماغ يستولي على معادن الفكر، وربما يتعدى إلى معادن الحس، فتظلم عينه حتى لا يرى بعينه، وتسود عليه الدنيا بأسرها، ويكون دماغه على مثال كهف اضطرمت فيه نار فاسود جوُّهُ، وحَمِيَ مستقره، وامتلأ بالدخان جوانبه، وكان فيه سراجٌ ضعيفٌ فانمحى أو انطفأ نوره، فلا تثبت فيه قدم، ولا يُسمَعُ فيه كلام، ولا تُرى فيه صورة، ولا يُقدر على إطفائه لا من داخل ولا من خارج، بل ينبغي أن يصبر إلى أن يحترق جميع ما يقبل الاحتراق، فكذلك يفعل الغضب بالقلب والدماغ.

وربما تقوى نار الغضب فتفنى الرطوبة التي بها حياة القلب فيموت صاحبه غيظاً، كما تقوى النار في الكهف فيتشقق وتنهد أعاليه على أسفاله، وذلك لإبطال النار ما في جوانبه من القوة الممسكة الجامعة لأجزائه، فهكذا حال القلب عند الغضب.

وبالحقيقة فالسفينة في ملتطم الأمواج عند اضطراب الرياح في لجة البحر أحسن حالاً وأرجى سلامة من النفس المضطربة غيظاً؛ إذ في السفينة من يحتال لتسكينها وتدبيرها وينظر لها ويسوسها، وأما القلب فهو صاحب السفينة وقد سقطت حيلته؛ إذ أعماه الغضب وأصمه.

وَمِنْ آثَارِ هَذَا الْغَضَبِ فِي الظَّاهِرِ: تَغَيُّرُ اللَّوْنِ، وَشِدَّةُ الرِّعْدَةِ فِي الْأَطْرَافِ، وَخُرُوجُ الْأَفْعَالِ عَنِ التَّرْتِيبِ وَالنِّظَامِ، وَاضْطِرَابُ الْحَرَكَةِ وَالْكَلَامِ، حَتَّى يَظْهَرَ الزَّبَدُ عَلَى الْأَشْدَاقِ، وَتَحْمَرَّ الْأَحْدَاقُ وَتَنْقَلِبَ الْمَنَاخِرُ، وَتَسْتَحِيلَ الْخِلْقَةُ، وَلَوْ رَأَى الْغَضْبَانُ فِي حال غَضَبِهِ قُبْحَ صُورَتِهِ لَسَكَنَ غَضَبُهُ حَيَاءً مِنْ قُبْحِ صُورَتِهِ وَاسْتِحَالَةِ خِلْقَتِهِ، وَقُبْحُ بَاطِنِهِ أَعْظَمُ مَنْ قُبْحِ ظَاهِرِهِ؛ فَإِنَّ الظَّاهِرَ عُنْوَانُ الْبَاطِنِ، وَإِنَّمَا قَبُحَتْ صُورَةُ الْبَاطِنِ أَوَّلًا ثُمَّ انْتَشَرَ قُبْحُهَا إِلَى الظَّاهِرِ ثَانِيًا، فَتَغَيُّرُ الظَّاهِرِ ثَمَرَةُ تغير الباطن، فقسِ الثمرة بالمثمرة فَهَذَا أَثَرُهُ فِي الْجَسَدِ.

وَأَمَّا أَثَرُهُ فِي اللِّسَانِ فَانْطِلَاقُهُ بِالشَّتْمِ وَالْفُحْشِ مِنَ الْكَلَامِ الَّذِي يَسْتَحِي مِنْهُ ذُو الْعَقْلِ، وَيَسْتَحِي مِنْهُ قَائِلُهُ عِنْدَ فُتُورِ الْغَضَبِ، وَذَلِكَ مَعَ تَخَبُّطِ النَّظْمِ واضطراب اللفظ.

أما أَثَرُهُ عَلَى الْأَعْضَاءِ فَالضَّرْبُ وَالتَّهَجُّمُ وَالتَّمْزِيقُ وَالْقَتْلُ والجرح عند التمكن من غير مبالاة، فإن هرب منه المغضوب عليه أو فاته بسببٍ وعجز عن التشفي رجع الغضب على صاحبه فيمزق ثَوْبَ نَفْسِهِ وَيَلْطُمُ نَفْسَهُ، وَقَدْ يَضْرِبُ بِيَدِهِ على الأرض، ويعدو عدو الواله السكران والمدهوش المتحير، وربما يسقط صريعاً لا يطيق العدو والنهوض بسبب شدة الغضب، ويعتريه مثل الغشية، وربما يضرب الجمادات والحيوانات، فيضرب القصعة مثلاً على الأرض، وقد يكسر المائدة إذا غضب عليها، ويتعاطى أفعال المجانين، فيشتم البهيمة والجمادات ويخاطبها ويقول: «إلى متى منك هذا يا كيت وكيت؟» كأنه يخاطب عاقلاً! حتى ربما رفسته دابة فيرفس الدابة ويقابلها بذلك.

وأما أثرة في القلب مع المغضوب عليه فَالْحِقْدُ، وَالْحَسَدُ، وَإِضْمَارُ السُّوءِ، وَالشَّمَاتَةُ بِالْمَسَاءَاتِ، وَالْحُزْنُ بِالسُّرُورِ، وَالْعَزْمُ عَلَى إِفْشَاءِ السِّرِّ وَهَتْكِ السِّتْرِ، وَالِاسْتِهْزَاءُ وَغَيْرُ ذَلِكَ مِنَ الْقَبَائِحِ.

فَهَذِهِ ثَمَرَةُ الْغَضَبِ الْمُفْرِطِ.

وَأَمَّا ثَمَرَةُ الْحَمِيَّةِ الضَّعِيفَةِ **فَقِلَّةُ الْأَنَفَةِ مِمَّا يُؤْنَفُ مِنْهُ** مِنَ التَّعَرُّضِ لِلْحُرَمِ والزوجة والأمة، واحتمال الذل من الأخساء، وصغر النفس والقماءة، وَهُوَ أَيْضًا مَذْمُومٌ إِذْ مِنْ ثَمَرَاتِهِ عَدَمُ الغيرة على الحُرَمِ وهو خنوثة، قَالَ صَلَّى اللَّهُ عَلَيْهِ وَسَلَّمَ: «إِنَّ سعدا لغيور، وأنا أغير من سعد، وإن اللّٰه أَغْيَرُ مِنِّي» ﴿رواه البخاري ومسلم﴾.

وَإِنَّمَا خُلِقَتِ الْغَيْرَةُ لِحِفْظِ الْأَنْسَابِ، وَلَوْ تَسَامَحَ النَّاسُ بِذَلِكَ لَاخْتَلَطَتِ الْأَنْسَابُ، وَلِذَلِكَ قِيلَ «كُلُّ أُمَّةٍ وُضِعَتِ الْغَيْرَةُ فِي رِجَالِهَا وُضِعَتِ الصِّيَانَةُ فِي نِسَائِهَا».

وَمِنْ ضَعْفِ الْغَضَبِ الْخَوَرُ، وَالسُّكُوتُ عِنْدَ مُشَاهَدَةِ الْمُنْكَرَاتِ، وَقَدْ قَالَ صلى الله عليه وسلم: «خير أمتي أحدَّاؤها» يعني: في الدين. وقال تَعَالَى: ﴿وَلَا تَأْخُذْكُمْ بِهِمَا رَأْفَةٌ فِي دِينِ اللَّهِ﴾.

بل من فقد الغضب عجز عن رياضة نفسه؛ إذ لا تتم الرياضة إلا بتسليط الغضب على الشهوة حتى يغضب على نفسه عند الميل إلى الشهوات الخسيسة.

فَفَقْدُ الْغَضَبِ مَذْمُومٌ، وَإِنَّمَا الْمَحْمُودُ غَضَبٌ يَنْتَظِرُ إِشَارَةَ الْعَقْلِ وَالدِّينِ فَيَنْبَعِثُ حَيْثُ تَجِبُ الْحَمِيَّةُ وينطفيء حَيْثُ يَحْسُنُ الْحِلْمُ، وَحِفْظُهُ عَلَى حَدِّ الِاعْتِدَالِ هُوَ الِاسْتِقَامَةُ الَّتِي كَلَّفَ اللَّهُ بِهَا عِبَادَهُ، وَهُوَ الْوَسَطُ الَّذِي وَصَفَهُ رَسُولُ اللَّهِ صَلَّى الله عليه وسلم حيث قال: «خير الأمور أوساطها»، فمن مال غضبه إلى الفتور حتى أحس من نفسه بضعف الغيرة وخسة النفس في احتمال الذل والضيم في غير محله فينبغي أن يعالج نفسه حتى يُقَوِّيَ غضبه، ومن مال غضبه إلى الإفراط حتى جره إلى التهور واقتحام الفواحش فينبغي أن يعالج نفسه ليَغُضَّ من سورة الغضب، ويقفَ على الوسط الحق بين الطرفين فهو الصراط المستقيم، وهو أرق من الشعرة وأحد من السيف، فإن عجز عنه فليطلب القرب منه، قال تعالى: ﴿ولن تستطيعوا أن تعدلوا بين النساء ولو حرصتم فلا تميلوا كل الميل فتذروها كالمعلقة﴾، فليس كل من عجز عن الإتيان بالخير كله ينبغي أن يأتي بالشر كله، ولكن بعض الشر أهون من بعض، وبعض الخير أرفع من بعض.

فهذه حقيقة الغضب ودرجاته نسأله الله حسن التوفيق لما يرضيه إنه على ما يشاء قدير.

5.4 *English Translation*

An Elucidation of the Reality of Anger

One should know that when Allah, the Exalted, created all creatures, he made them susceptible to harm and death on account of causes within and outside of their bodies. Furthermore, He bestowed upon them [inner propensities] to protect them from harm and safeguard them from their destruction until the appointed time [of death], that He specified in His [divine] Record.

As for the internal causes [of susceptibility for harm]: He created within created beings [both] heat and moisture and made a type of enmity and incongruity between them. Heat continuously loosens [the particles] of moisture, drying and evaporating it until its particles are transformed into steam that rises away from it. If there were no nutrients in food to replenish the particles that were dissolved and evaporated, the creature would fall ill. Therefore, Allah, the Exalted, created nourishment corresponding to the needs of [every] animal's body and created within each animal appetitive instincts that propel them to consume it, as if it were an agent [assigned] to fix what was broken, and rebuild what was destroyed, such that [it] would be saved from destruction on account of this instinct.

As for the external factors that a person is exposed to, they are like swords, spears, and other lethal armaments used to target him. Thus, he needs an inner faculty and zeal (*ḥamiyya*) that will erupt from the inside to repel these threats. Therefore, Allah created [the protective instinct of] anger from fire and ingrained it within human beings, embedding it within his [essentia] clay [composition]. As such, whenever he is hindered from actualizing an aspiration from amongst his different goals, or from fulfilling a purpose from amongst his various ambitions, the fire of anger is ignited within him; it surges, boiling the blood of the heart, spreading through the veins, and rising towards the upper areas of the body much like how fire rises, or the way boiling water rises in a pot.

Consequently, [the signs of] anger imbues the face, reddening both the face and eyes. Due to the skin's translucidity, it shows the redness of the blood beneath it, the way glass displays the color of what is contained within it. Blood expands when one becomes angry with someone whom he feels he has the power to subdue, [especially] if they are lesser than him [in strength or status]. However, if the anger is directed towards those who are greater than him and he has no hopes for [the possibility of] retribution, the blood retracts from the surface of the skin towards the inner core of the heart. [The anger] then transforms into sadness, and he becomes yellow [or pale]. Now, if his anger is directed towards [an adversary] who is his equal, then an oscillation of blood between expansion and constriction results, thus [resulting in him] becoming divided between turning red and yellow.

In sum, the locus of the faculty of anger is [within] the heart. It is defined as the boiling of the heart's blood in pursuit of retribution. This faculty, when aroused, directs focus towards the proactive repulsion of potential harm before it [actually] occurs, as well as the seeking of relief and retribution after harm is inflicted. Retribution is the nourishment and desire of this faculty – in it lies its satisfaction. In fact, it is not alleviated except by it.[60]

---

60 This is completely in convergence with emotion theory which posits that the underlying need for emotion is justice upon being wronged or mistreated. Without the need for justice being fulfilled, an individual may feel resentment and continuous anger inside. Al-Ghazālī normalizes this as a natural pre-wired instinct that is given to human beings as an adaptive faculty just as evolutionary psychologists also theorize.

People can be divided into three categories regarding [the intensity] of this faculty in their primordial nature: (i) deficient, (ii) excessive, and (iii) balanced.[61]

As for a lack [of anger]: the absence or weakness of this faculty is considered blameworthy. It is said about such a person that, "they have no passion". Thus, al-Shāfiʿī, may Allah have mercy on him, said "The one who is provoked and does not get angry is [like] a donkey."

Whoever totally lacks the drives of motivation and anger is extremely deficient. Allah, The Exalted, has described the companions of the Prophet, may Allah bless him and grant him peace, with vehemence and intensity, saying *Those with him are fierce with the disbelievers and compassionate with one another* (al-Fatḥ 48:29), and He said to His Prophet, may Allah bless him and grant him peace, *Struggle against the disbelievers and the hypocrites, and subdue them* (al-Tawba 9:73). Fierceness and subjugation are the effects of the faculty of vehemence, [at the root of] which is anger.

Excessive anger is when this attribute [i.e., anger] takes over, such that it strays from the command of reason and religious adherence. By this, a person is left with no insight, vision, conception, or volition; rather, it becomes as if one is being compelled.

The causes for the dominance of anger are predisposition and habituation.[62] To clarify, some people are inherently predisposed to become angry quickly, to the extent that it could be such that a person's resting face is the face of an angry person. What enables this is the heat in the inherent makeup of the heart because anger originates from fire, as the Prophet, may Allah bless him

61 Furthermore, the instinctual emotion of anger serves as a fundamental motivator for human beings, but it also possesses a potential for predatory aggression and destruction if not properly regulated. However, in its primitive adaptive form, it allows for self-preservation and the protection of offspring. In the context of humans as social beings, it also evokes a sense of righteousness and a desire for justice. The underregulation of this emotion is destructive anger and the over-regulation of it is cowardice (see Muḥammad Birgivī, *Al-Ṭarīqa al-Muḥammadiyya Wa-l-Sīra al-Aḥmadiyya* (Damascus: Dār al-Qalam, 2011), 254.). Thus, Islamic scholars acknowledge the survival instincts of the human being and that human emotions contain underlying adaptive needs, whilst likewise maintaining that predatory or hedonistic inclinations are destructive. The appropriate regulation of these emotions allows for its healthy expression.

62 In consideration of contemporary discourse and its context, it is remarkable that al-Ghazālī similarly provides a mutli-dimensional perspective on the underlying causes of anger, including both the possibility of it originating in one's temperament-nature as well as environmental learning and social modeling.

and grant him peace mentioned.[63] Indeed, only the coolness of the temperament extinguishes it and breaks its vehemence.

As for the means of habituation, such comes through socialization with people who boast about releasing their rage and obeying [the calls of] anger, considering it to be [indicative of] courage and manliness. Such people say, "I am such a person who cannot withstand plots or undesirable conditions, and I do not tolerate anything from anyone." This essentially translates to mean, "I have neither intelligence nor forbearance." He thus boastfully flaunts his ignorance. Accordingly, whosoever listens to such a person begins to internalize the [notion] that anger is commendable, and the love of imitating [such] people subsequently consolidate anger within them.

And whenever the fire of anger ignites and its blaze intensifies, it blinds the one who is enraged and deafens him to all words of reason. If someone offers him advice, not only does he not listen, but it amplifies his rage. Meanwhile, if he were to attempt to exercise his reason and check himself, he would fail to do so. This is because the rays of reason are snuffed out and extinguished by anger's smoke. For indeed, the source of cognition is the brain;[64] when anger surges, the blood boils, emitting steam that rises to the brain, which inundates the source of cognition.[65]

At times, it may even extend to the faculties of sensation, causing his eyes to black out to the extent that he is unable to see [anything], and the world

63 A multitude of complimentary prophetic traditions corroborate the fiery nature of anger. Consider the narration in which Abū Saʿīd al-Khudrī, may Allah be pleased with him, relates that the Prophet, may Allah bless him and grant him peace, said, "Verily anger is burning coal in the heart of the Son of Adam. Do you not see the redness of his eyes and the swelling of his jugular veins ..." (al-Tirmidhī, 2191). Also, ʿAṭiyyah al-Saʿdī, may Allah be pleased with him, narrates that the Prophet, may Allah bless him and grant him peace, stated, "Certainly anger is from Satan, and Satan was created from fire ..." (Abū Dāwūd, 4784).

64 Considering that al-Ghazālī was not a specialist in the field of medicine, by simply mentioning commonly known facts of medicine available to him, it can be deduced that Muslim physicians in al-Ghazālī's era were well-aware that cognitive processes are in fact associated with the brain.

65 Al-Ghazālī is describing the interrelated nature of emotion, cognition, and physiology in human beings. He adeptly underpins how intense emotional arousal can impair one's executive functioning. Although he utilizes the imagery and terminologies of ancient medicine to describe physiological expressions of anger, it is noteworthy to point out that he nonetheless acknowledges that excessive emotional activation, known today as the over-activation of the amygdala, can compromise executive functioning. Like many emotion theorists posit, al-Ghazālī seems to describe anger as an instinctual response in the body.

[around him] [seems to] blacken out entirely.[66] His brain becomes like a cave with a fire smoldering therein; its inside is dark, its floors are heated, and it is full of smoke. There is a faint lantern [visible] inside, the light of which has become extinguished and put out. In this cave, one cannot find their footing, nor can any speech be heard, and nothing is visibly perceptible. There is no way to extinguish the fire, neither from inside nor from the outside. The only option is to wait until all that is flammable burns up. This is [similar to] what anger does to the heart and brain. Sometimes, the fire of anger can become so fierce that the moisture containing the life of the heart dissipates; consequently, the person could die from anger. Such would be similar to the fire intensifying in the cave until it collapses, razing its ceiling to the ground. This is due to the fire's destruction of the cave's walls that functionally hold it up, keeping all of its parts structurally bound together. With anger, the state of heart can be just like that.

In reality, a ship struggling [to maneuver] through the virulent winds and waves of a violent sea storm is in a much better and hopeful state than that of a person overrun by anger. [At least] onboard the ship there is a captain who can look after, manage, and steer the ship. As for the heart, it is [as if] the captain of the ship has totally lost control; anger has blinded and deafened him.

Some of the apparent signs of anger include change of color; trembling of the limbs; acting in a disorderly or disorganized manner; dysregulated movement and speech to the extent that foam appears at the mouth, eyes become red, nostrils are widened, and one's face becomes contorted. If a person were able to see themselves enraged, their anger would quickly subside out of embarrassment from [observing] their unsightly appearance and absurd behavior – and the repulsiveness of one's inward state is even greater than the hideousness of one's outward appearance. Indeed, that which is outwardly visible is but a [slight] indication of one's inner condition. Accordingly, this vileness first permeates the inside, and then it spreads outwards thereafter; the changes that occur outside are only a result of the inner transformation. Consider the analogy of fruit produced by a fruit-bearing tree; the [manifestation of] anger is a mere side-effect of [what is occurring] inside the body.

As for the manifestation of anger on the tongue, it is the spewing of insults, obscenities, and detestable speech; such makes any reasonable person [who hears it] feel embarrassed; it makes the one who uttered such statements feel ashamed after their anger subsides. All of that occurs in tandem with a chaotic sense of order and muddled speech.

---

66 Here, al-Ghazālī highlights that anger can lead to psychosomatic complaints.

As for its influence on the body: hitting, attacking, tearing [clothes], and even killing and maiming without impunity [can occur] when [anger] fully takes over. If the person one is angry with runs away or escapes somehow, and one is unable to release their anger, then such a person [often] directs their rage towards their own self. Consequently, he may tear his clothing, hit himself, or slam the ground with his hands, running around like a drunken or perplexed and disoriented person. He may even succumb to a type of fit, immobilized due the intensity of his anger. He could even fall unconscious. He might lash out at inanimate objects and animals; for example, he might smash a bowl on the ground or even break a table if he were to direct his anger at it, behaving just as madmen do. He could curse and accost inanimate objects and animals, exclaiming, "How much longer will you continue like this!?" as if he were addressing a rational being. This would continue as such until perhaps he kicks an animal, and in return, the animal kicks him back.[67]

The following are [a few of] the ill-effects [of anger that manifest] in the heart in relation to the one with whom a person is angry: rancor; envy; suppressed negative sentiments; [the tendency] to rejoice at their adversities and lament over their triumphs; a firm resolve to divulge their secrets and uncover their faults; derision; and various other detestable things.

These are [only some of] the consequences of excessive anger.

On the other hand, the ill-effects of having an enfeebled [sense of] anger include a lack of honor with regards to the things for which one should have some sense of esteem, like how a person deals with that which is inviolable, including his wife or maidservant. Also, [spinelessly] tolerating humiliation from lowly people [is also included], as are [issues of] low self-esteem and self-respect. This state, [like excessive anger,] is similarly abhorred; from amongst its consequences is a complete lack of protective jealousy over things that are sacred; such is [unnaturally] effeminate. The Prophet, may Allah bless him and grant him peace, once said, "*Indeed Sa'd is a very jealous man. And I am more jealous than he is. And indeed, Allah is more jealous than I am.*"[68]

The feeling of [protective] jealousy was primarily created for the preservation of genealogy. If people were to become laxed with this, the lineages of people would get mixed up. It has thus been said, "for every nation in which protective jealousy has been instilled in men, their women will [likewise] have protection."

---

67 The signs of explosive anger mentioned here are similar to intermittent explosive anger found in the Diagnostic and Statistical Manual of Mental Disorders (DSM-5). Al-Ghazālī is drawing attention to the signs and indicators of this type of pathological anger.

68 Bukhārī (6846); Muslim (1499).

[Both] apathy and for one to remain silent upon encountering evil are also from an enfeebled [sense of] anger. The Prophet, may Allah bless him and grant him peace, said, "*The best of my ummah are those who are firm.*"[69] meaning, in their religion. Allah, Exalted is He, says "do *not let pity for them make you lenient in [upholding] the law of Allah*" (Nūr 24:2). In fact, those who have lost [the capacity to feel] anger are incapable of spiritual reform, as disciplining [the soul] cannot be fully accomplished unless anger is made to dominate over the appetitive drives (*shahwah*) such that a person can [effectively] direct their anger at their own self whenever they feel inclined towards vile passions.

To conclude, a lack of anger is also blameworthy. The type of anger that is praiseworthy is that which depends on the direction of reason and religion; it is [proportionately] unleashed in circumstances that require it, and [adequately] subdued when forbearance is most appropriate. This [approach to] anger preserves the balance, which is the steadfastness for which Allah has made his servants accountable; it is the middle path that the Messenger of Allah, may Allah bless him and grant him peace, described by saying, "*The best of affairs is that which is in the middle.*"[70]

Whosoever's anger is inclined towards apathy, such that he feels within himself weak [protective] jealousy and low self-respect by tolerating humiliation and injustice, it is necessary for him to remedy himself until he strengthens his faculty of anger. On the other hand, those whose anger inclines towards excessiveness such that it drives him to recklessness and the commission of immoral deeds, it is necessary for him to treat himself so as to reduce the intensity of his anger.[71] The person should stand in the correct middle point between the two extremes, which is the Straight Path that is thinner than a hair and sharper than a sword. If one is unable to do so, they should at least seek to be [as] close [as possible] to it. Allah the Exalted, states, *You will never be able to maintain [emotional] justice between your wives, no matter how keen you are. So do not totally incline towards one leaving the other hanging* (Al-Nisā' 4:129). Moreover, if someone cannot possibly do each and every good deed [with excellence], it does not mean that they should engage in every kind of evil [without restraint]. Indeed, some evil [actions] are less [in degree] than others; similarly, some good deeds are superior to others.

---

69 Al-Bayhaqī, *Shu'ab al-Imān*, 8301, 8302; al-Qaḍā'ī, *Musnad al-Shihāb*, 1276.

70 Al-Bayhaqī, *Shu'ab al-Imān*, 6601; al-Asbahānī, Abū Nu'aym, *M'arifa al-Ṣaḥābah*, 3171.

71 After listing the symptoms, indicators and unhealthy physiological and psychological consequences associated with excessive or deficient anger, al-Ghazālī concludes the discussion by urging the reader to engage in self-analysis. Accordingly, if one finds that such indicators exist, they are further advised to seek the requisite treatment to remedy this dysfunctional and dysregulated emotion.

Overall, this is the reality of anger and its [various] degrees. We ask Allah to enable us to do what is pleasing to Him, with excellence. Verily, He is entirely capable to do as He so wills.

6 The Heart's Delight. *Mufarriḥ al-Nafs* (*The Heart's Delight*) by Ibn Qādi Baalbek (d. 650 AH/1256 CE)

6.1 *Author's Biography*

Muẓaffar ibn ʿAbd al-Raḥmān ibn Ibrāhīm Abū Badr al-Dīn ibn Qāḍī Baalbek is more famously known as Ibn Qāḍī Baalbek. As his name suggests, his father, Majd al-Dīn, was an appointed judge in Baalbek (Lebanon) during the reign of ʿIzz al-Dīn Farrakshah. Upon his father's demise, Ibn Qāḍī relocated to Damascus where he began practicing as a physician. During his time in Damascus, he acquainted himself with medical and philosophical works, memorizing many of the famous texts prevalent at that time. He also became very close to his teacher, Muhadhab al-Dīn ʿAbd al-Raḥmān ibn ʿAli, who was the rector of a medical institution of learning. Muhadhab al-Dīn had a strong affinity towards Ibn Qāḍī due to his demonstrable intelligence. Ibn Qāḍī also studied advanced philosophy under Zayn al-Dīn al-Aʿma, who was a master in the field.

Alongside medicine, Ibn Qāḍī was also an accomplished *ḥāfiẓ* of the Holy Quran and he was well versed in the Islamic sciences. He was also well-known for his good character and generous contributions to expand the Islamic hospital (*bimāristān*) so as to serve more patients in need. Ibn Qāḍī passed away on Tuesday, the twenty-second of Ṣafar, in the year 650 AH when he was more than eighty years old. He was buried in his local cemetery, Bāb al-Ṣaghīr, in Damascus.

6.2 *Text Overview and Significance*

The book *Mufarriḥ al-Nafs* by Ibn Qāḍī Baalbek includes 10 sections. The first section addresses ontological remarks. The remaining 9 sections each addresses one type of elements that bring joy, happiness, and delight. There is one section on each of the physical senses (sight, smell, taste, sound, touch), one sections on medicines, one section on foods, one section on body movements, and a final section on the inner senses. This excerpt represents various sections of the books. In a unique style, this work discusses psychological states and emotions that arise through sensory stimulation. The author demonstrates the relationship between external stimulation and its subsequent effects; furthermore, he highlights the accompanying effects of such stimulation on inner emotional states. In this excerpt, the author discusses causes of happiness experienced through the sense of sight, through the sense of taste, through medicinal interventions, and through inner experiences. He supports the prominent belief that colors affect the mood of an individual and delves even deeper by comparing and contrasting the energy levels of people during the day versus their energy levels during the night. As for food intake, he mentions that consuming certain foods leads to varying emotional states, correlating certain tastes, like sweetness, for example, with a better sense of satisfaction and contentment.

6.3 *Arabic Text*

في اللذة المكتسبة للنفس من طريق حاسة البصر

اعلم أن المشهور عند الأطباء وعند أكثر الناس أن حاسة البصر محسوسها الألوان فقط، وليس كذلك، فإنها تحس بسبعة وعشرين جنسا من المدركات كل واحد يخالف الآخر بخلاف حاسة السمع، فإنها لا تحس إلا بالأصوات فقط.

فمدركات حاسة البصر:

الألوان والضوء والظلمة والأطراف والحجم والبعد والقرب والوضع والشكل والتفرق والاتصال والعدد والحركة والسكون والملامسة والخشونة والكثافة والشفيف والظل والحسن والقبيح والبشاشة والاختلاف والضحك والبكاء والرطوبة المعتبرة بالسيلان واليبس المعتبر بالتماسك.

وهذه الأمور قد حررتها العلوم الدقيقة الحكمية واطلعت عليها النفوس الفاضلة القدسية وهذه المدركات المعدودة بالحاسة البصر إليه ميل أكثر وفي إضافة ما تلتذ به النفس أعظم وأوفر كالألوان

وهي تنقسم إلى قسمين بسيط ومركب

فالبسيط عند بعضهم لونان: الأبيض والأسود وجميع الألوان المركبة منها على قدر اختلاف أجزائها.

وعند بعضهم أربعة: وهي الأبيض والأسود والأحمر والأصفر وما عدا هذه الألوان فمركب منها على قدر اختلاف أجزائها؟.

فالنفس تبتهج بما كان من الأجسام له اللون الأحمر والأخضر والأصفر والأبيض إما بسيط أو مركب بعضها من بعض فنظر هذه يوجب راحة النفس ولذة القلب وسرور العقل ونشاط ؟ الذهن وتوفر القوى وانبساط الأرواح وإنما قلنا ذلك لأنها ألوان مشرقة نيرة فالنفس لإشراقها ونورانيتها تميل إلى ما ناسبها فتحدث هذه الحالات المذكورة لأن النور محبوب ومعشوق.

وانظر الى فرحك وانبساطك وانشراحك وحركتك و تصرفك بالنهار، وفراغك وسكونك وتجمعك بالليل، وما سبب ؟ ذلك إلا النور تارة والظلمة أخرى.

واعلم أن النفس تسر وتلتذ وتبتهج بالنظر إلى المواضع الفسيحة لذة عظيمة، لأن الروح تلطف بنظرها إلى ذلك، فلا جرم أن المواضع المتنزهة كلما كانت أوسع كانت أنفع.

في اللذة الواردة على النفس من الواردات على البدن / من الأغذية

اعلم أن الأغذية المفرحة الواردة على البدن تنقسم على قسمين: مفردة ومركبة.

أما المفردة:

فالخبز: من الأغذية المفردة المفرحة الحسنة لا سيما إن كان من دقيق نقي مطيب بشيء من المصطكي والاشنة والأنيسون.

اللحم: من الأغذية الحسنة المفرحة المفردة النافعة السريعة الاستحالة إلى الدم، خصوصا ما كان من لحم ثني الغنم، أو من لحم الدجاج اللطيفة، أو من لحم الدراريج والفراريج والثيج بهذه الألوان، إما ملصوقة أو معرقة أو مطجنة أو مشوية قد طيبت بشيء من زعفران ودار صيني ومصطكي وماء ورد.

البيض: من الأغذية المفردة المفرحة المقوية للقلب على ما تقدم ذكره، وكان الأولى أن نذكره مع الأغذية المفردة المفرحة للنفس الحسنة البالغة النافعة في إحداث سرور القلب وقد أطنب في وصفه ومدحه عدة من الأطباء.

التفاح: قد تقدم ذكره، وهو من الأغذية المفرحة للنفس، خصوصا الحلو منه الشامي فإن النفس تبتهج به وترتاح بوروده لتوليد الدم الفاضل العَطِرِ الخالص.

الرمان: من الأغذية المفردة المفرحة للنفس لا سيما الحلو منه، وقد تقدم ذكره في الأدوية المفردة.

الحلاوات بأسرها مفرحة للنفس مزيدة في القوة منعشة للأرواح لتوليدها الدم الصالح خصوصا ما عمل منها بالسكر النقي وبشيء من أنواع الخبز مطيبة بشيء من المسك والزعفران وماء الورد والكافور.

الجلاب: مفرح للنفس، مقو للقوة، مجيد للهضم، وأطباء العرب يأمرون ملوكهم وكبراء بلدانهم أن يستعملوه على الأطعمة عوضا عن الماء، سيما ما كان بماء الورد، وهو رقيق القوام، مبرد بالفعل، فإنه يوجب سرور النفس، واحتواء المعدة على ما فيها من الطعام، فيجود الهضم. وتعديد أصناف الحلاوات مما يطول، فلا جرم ذكرناها إجمالا.

والله أعلم.

في اللذة المكتسبة للنفس من حركات البدن

اعلم أن حركات البدن مما يوجب لذة وسرورا من جهة أنها توجب تخلخلا للأعضاء، وتحليلا لفضلاتها، فتنبسط القوى والأرواح في البدن فتسر النفس لزوال العائق عن جواذبها.

ويسمى حركات البدن على الإطلاق الرياضية وينقسم إلى أقسام كثيرة:

فمنها ما يعم جملة البدن كحركة السفن والأراجيح والمهود فإن البدن يتحرك بالسواء في كل واحد منها.

ومنها ما يختص بعضو دون عضو كركوب الخيل فإنه يختص بحركة الرجلين والفخذين واللعب بالكرة الكبيرة والصوالجة على ما ذكر مما يحرك البدن أكثر من غيرها وما أشبه ذلك من الحركات المختصة بعضو دون عضو.

والتدليك في الحمام مما يحرك ظاهر البدن وينقي فضوله فإن كانت الفضول التي يراد من الرياضة تحليلها فهي هذه التي عند الجلد.

وكمال راحة الرياضة وتمام فعلها الذي يحصل به الانتفاع هو أن تربو الأعضاء وتحمر حمرة جيدة ليست بخارجة عن الاعتدال ولا تؤلمه فحينئذ تقوى القوى بها وترتاح النفس لورودها، ووجودها.

في اللذة المكتسبة للنفس من الحواس الباطنة

اعلم أن الحواس الباطنة لذتها وإدراكها يقترنان بفرح أشد وسرور أعظم وابتهاج أكثر مما يقترن به الحواس الظاهرة؛ وكيف لا يكون كذلك وهي تفضل عليها بإدراك المعاني.

وتنقسم اللذة منها على قدر النفوس فمنها:

النفوس الزكية العالمة الشريفة المتعلقة بملازمة الذكر اللطيف الجميل في الأمور الشريفة والاطلاع على الأحوال الدقيقة، واقتناص الأشياء الغامضة الخفية والمعاني الصعبة، كمن يبحث عن علوم الأفلاك وما حوت، وغيرها من العلوم الدقيقة وما جمعت، وحل المسائل المشكلة وما أوعت، فإن لمن علم شيئا من ذلك لذة عظيمة لا تنال إلا بالسكون في هذه الأحوال.

ولأصحاب العلوم العقلية مراتب في اللذات على قدر علومهم، كمن يقول الشعر فيقوى بفكرته الحسنة على تحصيل معان مبتكرة، فنفسه تشرف للقوة عليها وترتاح للوصول إليها، ويعرف ذلك من علمه وجربه.

واعلم أن النفس تلتذ وترتاح وتسر وتبتهج وتفرح ويزداد قواها قوة عند استعمال الأمور التي توجب قهر الأعادي وغلبتها لمناجزتها.

واعلم أن لذة الملوك والكبراء في ملازمة الصيد والقنص فإنها داخلة في هذا الباب، لأنهم يطلبون حيوانا يطلب النفور عنهم وعدم الانقياد إليهم، والنفس ترغب في ذلك وتهوى

التذلل والانقياد إليها، فكلما كان الصيد أبعد كانت اللذة محصولها أكثر، وسرور النفس بوقوعه أوفر.

واعلم أن الفكرة في عجائب أحوال الأفلاك، وما فيها من الكواكب، ومعرفة مقاديرها ومساحتها وشكلها وسيرها ووضعها، وأفعالها الظاهرة والخفية مما يوجب لذة عظيمة، لأن النفس تطلع على قدرة بارئها وموجدها ومبدعها جل ثناؤه وتقدست أسماؤه.

خاتمة الكتاب

فالذي يجب على الإنسان العالم الفاضل أن يحرص على اجتلاب ما يفرح نفسه.

- فإن اتفق أن يكون بحاسة فيكون بعض لذة، كمن يبصر المرائي الحسنة والصور المفرحة
- فإن اتفق أن يكون بحاستين كان أشرف من الذي يكون بحاسية واحدة، كمن يبصر المستنزهات ويسمع النغمات المطربات.
- فإن اتفق أن يكون بثلاث حواس كان أعظم، كمن يضيف إلى ذلك استنشاق الروائح الحسنة من البخورات والأنوار المذكورات.
- فإن اتفق أن يكون بأربع حواس كان أبهج للنفس، كمن يضيف إلى ذلك الاغتذاء بما كان من الأغذية حلوا، وشرب ما يلتذ به من الأشربة.
- فإن اتفق أن يكون بخمس حواس كان ألذ وأحسن، كمن يضيف إلى هذه القوة اللامسة ما كان أنعم من الملبوسات والمنكوحات.
- فإن اتفق أن يقترن بذلك لذة الحواس الباطنة فهو أكمل شيء ليحصل للنفس به الفرح والسرور وكحصول ما يختاره ويهواه من أي صنف كان من الموجودات، فذلك من أكمل المفرحات.

6.4 *English Translation*

Pleasure Acquired through the Sense of Sight

Recognize that the popular [understanding] amongst physicians and the majority of people is that the sense of sight only detects colors. This is not the case. In fact, the sense of sight encompasses twenty-seven [unique] types of perceptions, each distinct from the other; as opposed to the sense of hearing, which does not perceive anything other than sounds.

The elements perceived by the sense of sight include colors; light and darkness; dimensions and size; remoteness and closeness; position and shape; connectedness and separability; number; movement and stillness; smoothness and roughness; opacity, transparency, and translucence; beauty and ugliness; amiability and dissonance; laughter and weeping; moisture (indicated by fluidity), and stiffness (indicated by solidity).

All these matters have been clearly elucidated by precise knowledge and have been discerned by noteworthy, virtuous individuals. The sense of sight is even more attuned to this array of perceivable details than [it is regarding] colors. And, when combined with other things that typically satisfy the soul, [the effects] are even greater and more extensive.

Colors are of two types: basic and composite. Basic colors, according to some, are two: white and black; all [other] colors are composed of each, in various increments. However, according to others, [basic colors] are four: white, black, red, and yellow; thus, [all] other colors are composed of these in various proportions.[72]

Indeed, the soul delights in [regarding] red, green, yellow, or white objects in basic or composite form.[73] The sight of these colors soothes the soul, comforts the heart, eases the mind, invigorates the intellect, satisfies the senses, and relaxes the spirit. We believe this is the case because these are luminous, radiant colors that match [the nature of] the soul, which is inherently luminous and radiant. Accordingly, the soul is inclined towards them, resulting in the abovementioned states. [For the soul,] illumination is cherished and deeply desiderated.[74]

Examine your beatitude, cheerfulness, delight, energy, and activity during the daytime. Conversely, [consider] your [inclination towards] leisure, quiescence, and equanimity during the night. There is no other reason for this other than the [natural] alternation of light and darkness.[75]

It should also be known that the soul is immensely delighted, pleased, and uplifted by the sight of open spaces. This is because the spirit is appeased

72 The idea of primary colors evolved historically in different disciplines that study color and its perception, which yielded different primary color choices. Some of the disciplines that contributed to identifying primary colors include art history, philosophy, physics of light, and psychology of perception.

73 The author elaborated in a different section on the beauty of Allah's creation where these four colors are the main colors of delightful creations such lights, trees, fruits, gold, pearls, emerald, and ruby.

74 Studying the psychological impact of colors is an established discipline in the interior design industry. It is well-established that the use of certain colors and color combinations in an interior can result in a positive/negative impact or result in a wide range of emotional impacts.

75 In a subsequent paragraph, which was not included here for the sake of brevity, the author elaborates on the potentially aversive emotional impact of dark colors to the extent of producing negative biological influences (humoral imbalances). The author indicated that the impact of such dark colors is more pronounced when in clothing items. The latter is reminiscent of the Prophetic teaching "Wear white garments, for they are purer and better, and shroud your dead in them."

by such scenery. Undoubtedly, the wider the space, the more favorable it is for repose.

Pleasure Acquired through Food Intake[76]

Comforting food[77] that enters one's body is of two types: staple [food] and assorted [dishes].

Types of staples [food]:

Bread: A fine, simple, and fulfilling food, especially if it is baked with pure flour and flavored with mastic gum, asafoetida, or aniseed.

Meat: A wholesome, enjoyable, and nutritious staple food that assimilates quickly, contributing to the [production of] blood. Such is especially so with lamb meat, lean chicken meat, and meat from pigeons, sparrows, and quails.[78] Such is [best prepared] as a paste, braised, fried, or roasted; lightly seasoned with saffron, cinnamomum, mastic, and rosewater.

Eggs: A satisfying staple food that strengthens the heart. Although it was mentioned earlier, it is [arguably] more appropriate to mention it here alongside the [various] fine staple food items that are highly effective in promoting a sense of well-being in the heart. Accordingly, many medical practitioners have elaborated extensively on the qualities and benefits of eggs.

Apples: Such was [also] mentioned earlier. Apples are very invigorating – especially the sweet Syrian variety. They engender delight and comfort as they stimulate the production of healthful, wholesome, and pure blood.[79]

Pomegranate: A stimulating staple food, especially if it is sweet. It was mentioned previously amongst the simple [types of] medicine.

---

76 The concept of comfort food refers to foods that are thought to provide a feeling of well-being, improved mood, or emotional comfort. Comfort foods preferences emerge from a variety of sources including one's culture and childhood. While sweetness and high-caloric nature tends be common in comfort foods, this is not always the case, as evident in current literature on the topic but also as evident in this section of the book. For a review on the topic, see: Charles Spence, "Comfort Food: A Review," *International Journal of Gastronomy and Food Science* 9 (October 2017): 105–9.

77 The origins of the term comfort food trace back to the 1960s–1970s. However, the concept itself, as evident in this treatise, was explicitly tackled in this early Muslim treatise.

78 It is possible that the author is specifically referring to the attagen, francolin, heath-cock, or rail. The attagen, which in Latin means "a kind of bird", resembles the Arabic *ḥayquṭān*; it was a common bird of pre-modern Iraq, marked with distinct black and white spots.

79 The author alluded a few times in this section that one of the properties that contribute to comfort foods being so is the fact that they produce physiological and biological influences such as producing healthy blood. Contemporary research examined neurobiological impacts of comfort foods including the release of mood-enhancing opiates, serotonin, and the reduction of cortisol. However, research in this domain has not been conclusive.

Sweets, in general, are pleasurable to the soul; they provide an additional boost of energy and refresh the spirit as they stimulate the production of healthful blood. This is especially true for that which is made with pure sugar and some types of bread, [further] flavored with a little bit of musk, saffron, rose water, or camphor.

Julep: It improves one's mood, boosts energy, and promotes digestion. Accordingly, Arab physicians would direct their rulers and the elite of their lands to consume julep with their food instead of [using normal] water. [They] especially [encouraged the use of] julep with rose water. It is fine in its makeup, refreshing in its effect, and effectuates [a sense of] personal contentment. Moreover, it helps the stomach handle food better, thus improving digestion.

To enumerate all the various types of sweets would make matters too lengthy. Necessarily, we thus had to list them [here] in brief. Allah knows best.

Pleasure Acquired through Body Movements

[It] should be known that moving the body is another one of the things that foster [feelings of] pleasure and happiness.; such causes the limbs to loosen up, detoxifying them. This, in turn, satisfies the senses and spirit within the body, inducing a sense of well-being as obstacles are freed from where they would normally accumulate.[80]

- Movements of the body are generally called *sportive movements*, and they are categorized into many types:
- Movements that involve the whole body, such as the movement of ships, swings, and cradles. In each of these, the entire body moves synchronously.
- Movement that involves only specific parts of the body. For example, riding a horse specifically involves movement of the legs and thighs. Also, playing polo, as it is conventionally related, involves the movement of even more of the body as compared to anything else. There are likewise [many] other activities that similarly require [one to] move only specific parts of the body.

Massages in a *hammām* stimulate the outer parts of the body, ridding it of its waste products. In fact, these waste products under the skin are exactly what sports are meant to cleanse.[81]

Overall, the complete relaxing [effects] and adequate practice of sportive movements that would yield maximum benefit is [attained by] stretching the

80 In this sentence, the author succinctly summarizes the physical, physiological, and emotional benefits of physical activity. There is an increasing amount of evidence documenting the beneficial impacts of physical activity on mental health and its outcomes.

81 This is in line with the notion proposed by the father of Swedish massage, Hendrik Ling, that massage could bring about healing by improving the circulation of the blood and lymph. However, the exact biological underpinnings of the healing benefits of massage are understudied.

various body parts until they are moderately reddened in a way that does not elicit pain. It is only then that one's faculties would be strengthened, and a person would find [greater] satisfaction in their being.[82]

Pleasure Acquired through Inner Senses[83]

One must realize that perceptions and pleasures attained through the inner senses are associated with high spirits, greater happiness, and more immense joy than those attained through the external senses. And how could this not be so given that the inner perceptive capabilities are superior in detecting deeper meanings.

The pleasures derived from the aforementioned vary from person to person. For example:

Honorable and pure souls imbibed with knowledge continuously engage in careful reflections upon noble matters; explorations of the true nature of things; and capturing subtle, ambiguous, and complex realities. Examples of such are embodied by people who delve into astronomy and other forms of refined sciences with all that they entail, [exhibiting a keen interest in] solving intricate matters. Whoever acquires even a fraction of such knowledge experiences immense pleasure; a unique tranquility that cannot be obtained except in these [particular] conditions.

Indeed, scholars intellectually engaging with diverse forms of knowledge [accordingly] experience various levels of pleasure proportional to their knowledge. For example, a poet, equipped to capture creative meanings through his good ideas, feels exalted and fulfilled by doing just that. This can be affirmed by anyone who has practically observed and experienced it.

Realize that a person feels pleased, relieved, delighted, happy, elated, and their strength increases when engaging in matters that challenge them to defeat and overpower their enemies in a conflict scenario. Assuredly, the pleasure experienced by kings and rulers in hunting and shooting falls under this category. That is, they are hunting an animal which is fleeing and not surrendering to them, whilst they inwardly crave and covet that subjugation and submission. Thus, the farther the hunted animal, the more pleasure is derived; the soul is most thoroughly uplifted when [the prey] falls.

82 In later paragraphs in this section, the author elaborated on one form of physical movement and its connection to spiritual and emotional well-being, namely dance (in the way it is performed in some Sufi traditions).

83 This section delves into unique forms of activities and endeavors that bring forth supreme states of delight and tranquility through what the author named "inner senses". By inner senses-derived delight, the author refers to a range of intellectually-, spiritually-, and morally uplifting activities that inculcate connection with knowledge, science, wisdom, courage, and morality.

Furthermore, reflecting on the wonders of outer space and the celestial bodies therein, and knowing their numbers, sizes, shapes, movements, positions, and their apparent as well as subtler behaviors, all bring about immense pleasure to a person. [This is] because such reveals the might of one's Creator, Maker, and Originator – Exalted is His praise and Sacred are His names.[84]

Conclusion[85]

To conclude, it is incumbent upon every noble and conscious person to strive to acquire what uplifts their soul:

- If it happens to be through [only] one sense, such as seeing beautiful scenery and delightful images, then one acquires some pleasure.
- If it happens to be through two senses, then it is superior to that which is [experienced] through [merely] one sense; like the one beholding the scenery of captivating landscapes while listening to enchanting melodies.
- If it happens to be through three senses, then that is superior, such as breathing in pleasant aromas from various types of invigorating incense, in addition to the above.
- If it happens to be through four senses, then it is even more delightful, such as eating sweet foods and enjoying delicious drinks in addition to all the above.
- If it happens to be through five senses, then it is even more satisfying and pleasing, such as, in addition to the above, the tactile experience of soft clothing and soft-skinned spouses.
- If it happens that all of the above is [further] combined with pleasure acquired through the internal senses, then it is the most complete for experiencing overall satisfaction and contentment. Similarly, when a person gets what they want or selects from any of the aforementioned categories, that [also] elicits one of the more fulfilling [feelings] that palpably pleases [a person].

---

84 In later passages, the author further elaborates on delight obtained from reflecting on other natural phenomena such physical geography, climate, and weather. He also discusses supreme delight obtained through reflecting on and refining oneself.

85 It is helpful here to quote Elbaum (2016) who stated while reflecting on this work, "it is clear that *The Soul-Cheerer* was a unique medical text in its time. It takes a special intuition to try to create a single category out of disparate stimuli such as apples, Sufi dancing, poetry, and chebulic myrobalan, to posit that the soul-cheering effects of each are mediated by comparable physiological mechanisms – some 700 years before the discovery of dopamine reward pathways – and, finally, to resolve that what the world needs most is a textbook setting forth the secrets of synthesizing happiness." (Alan Elbaum, "The Pursuit of Happiness: T-S Ar.44.201," September 1, 2016.).

CHAPTER 5

Behavioral Themes

1 Character Traits: Definitions, Origins, Types, and How to Change Them. *Al-Ṭarīqa al-Muḥammadiyya wa-l-Sīra al-Aḥmadiyya* (*The Muhammadan Path*) by Imam Taqī al-Dīn Muḥammad al-Birgivī (d. 981 AH/1573 CE)

1.1 *Author's Biography*

Imam Taqī al-Dīn Muḥammad al-Birgivī was a sixteenth century prominent Muslim scholar who lived during the Ottoman period. He was born in the year 1522 CE in the Turkish city of what is now known as Balıkesir. His father, Pīr ʿAlī, was his first teacher; he was renowned for his good character and deep knowledge. Al-Birgivī was sent by his father to Istanbul to advance his knowledge of the Islamic sciences with the leading scholars of his time. There, he was initiated into the Bayramiyya Sufi order. As he progressed, al-Birgivī was offered the position of Judge of Estates in the Court of Edirne. However, he declined this position, preferring instead to fully dedicate his life to the worship of Allah. However, his spiritual master suggested that al-Birgivī serve as a teacher of the Islamic sciences, focusing on academic pursuits including the production of written works to benefit the Muslim nation. It was at this time that a famous scholar by the name of ʿAtāullah Efendī arranged for a religious institution to be built in Birgivī so that Imam al-Birgivī could teach as he was instructed. It was during this stage of his life that he became known as Imam al-Birgivī. During his time in Birgivī, he authored 27 books, becoming widely known for his scholarly works.

In his writings, he placed significant emphasis on the cultivation of character, ethics, and behavior. He openly criticized the ruling class for their shortcomings in these areas, stressing the importance of their embodiment of Islamic virtues as exemplars for the Umma. He was also extremely critical of the innovative excesses of Sufism that were in clear violation of traditional Islamic law. Al-Birgivī was a revivalist that advocated for the resurgence of Islamic orthodoxy through the return to the Prophetic Sunna. He lived in Birgivī until 1573 CE, where he died due to an outbreak of the plague.

1.2 *Text Overview and Significance*

The translated excerpts presented in this section are taken from Imam al-Birgivī's *Tariqa Muḥammadiyya*, which belongs to the genre of literature focused on Sufism and character development (Tadhīb al-Akhlāq). Albeit unique in its own right, this work bears resemblance to Imam al-Ghazālī's *Iḥyāʾ ʿUlūm al-Dīn*. While it is much more concise than the *Iḥyāʾ* of al-Ghazalī, it is very similar in its literary prose and reformative emphasis on spiritual and character development via a heavy reliance on canonical Islamic texts.

In the early sections of his work, Imam al-Birgivī emphasizes the importance of aligning spiritual practices with the principles of Islamic creed. He staunchly upholds Sunni orthodoxy and strongly criticizes heretical beliefs prevalent among certain Muslim groups, particularly the extreme and deviant Sufis. He opposes the excessive and monastic practices of these Sufi groups, viewing them as straying from the true essence of Islamic spirituality. It is likely for this reason that he titles his work *The Muhammadan Path*, highlighting the centrality of following Prophetic spirituality rather than adopting the practices of misguided Sufi leaders.

The first translated segment presented below focuses on Imam al-Birgivī's elucidation of the definition of character and good conduct. He delves into the fundamental human drives and how they give rise to cardinal virtues when balanced and vices when imbalanced. This particular section of his work is almost a verbatim quotation of some of the sections found in the fourteenth century writings of Imam al-ʿAdud al-Dīn al-Ījī, a scholastic theologian who wrote the famous treatise on character known popularly as *Akhlāq al-ʿAdudiyya* (al-Ījī & Taşköprüzade, 2018). Al-Ījī's work draws upon the Hellenistic and Islamic philosophical traditions, providing a theological undertone to the discussion of character. The text is a masterpiece, and its distinctiveness is in its concise, yet comprehensive synthesis of the large pre-existing literature pertaining to character development and virtue acquisition (Salem, 2022). Given its brevity, it was used as a reference work that was typically memorized by students in traditional Ottoman seminaries. It is likely for this reason that al-Birgivī, an Ottoman scholar, is so intimately familiar with al-Ījī's classification system; in the latter part of this translation, Imam al-Birgivī outlines and classifies key virtues according to al-Ījī's text, without quoting from him directly.

1.3 *Arabic Text*

الصِّنف الأَوَّل
في منكرات القلب وآفاته

اعلم أن إصلاحه أهم من كل شيء، إذ هو ملك مطاع نافذ الحكم، والأعضاء رعيّة وخدم له، ولذا قال ﷺ: «ألا وإنَّ في الجسد مضغة ...» الحديث.

وإصلاحه: تخليته عن الأوصاف، الذميمة، وتحليته بالأوصاف الحميدة، فلابد من قسمين:

القسم الأول

في تفسير الخلق، وبيان منشئه، وتقسيمه إلى المذموم والممدوح، وطريقة إزالة الأول وعلاجه إجمالاً، وتحصيل الثاني وإبقائه، وحفظ صحته وتقويته إجمالاً أيضاً

فنقول:

تفسير الخلق:

الخلق ملكة، تصدر عنها الأفعال النفسانية بسهولة من غير رؤية، ويمكن

تغييره لورود الشرع به، واتفاق العقلاء والتجربة، وتختلف الاستعدادات فيه بحسب الأمزجة.

منشؤه:

ومنشؤه قوى النفس، وهي ثلاث:

١ – **النطق**: وهو قوة الإدراك، فاعتداله : الحكمة؛ وهي ملكة للنفس تُدرك بها الصواب من الخطأ، وإفراطه الجربزة، وهي ملكة إدراك، تدعوإلى اطلاع ما لا يمكن معرفته كالمتشابهات وبحث القدر، أو يصدر بها أفعال يتضرر الغير بها، وتفريطه البلادة ، وهي ملكة يقصر بها صاحبها عن إدراك الخير والشر .

٢ – **والغضب**: وهو حركة للنفس دفعاً للمنافر، فاعتداله: الشجاعة؛ وهي ملكة بها يُقدم على أمور ينبغي أن يُقدم عليها، وإفراطه: التهوّر؛ وهو ملكة بها يُقدم على أمور لا ينبغي أن يُقدم عليها، وتفريطه: الجبن؛ وهو هيئة راسخة بها يُحجم عن مباشرة ما ينبغي.

٣ – **والشهوة**: وهي حركة للنفس طلباً للملايم، فاعتدالها: العفة؛ وهي ملكة بها يباشر المشتهيات على وفق الشرع والمروءة، وإفراطها: الشره والفجور؛ وهو ملكة بها يتناول المشتهيات مطلقاً حلالاً أو حراماً، وتفريطها: الخمود؛ وهو ملكة بها يقصر عن استيفاء ما ينبغي من المشتهيات.

والأوساط تحصل باستخدام الأوّل الأخيرين، والأطراف تحصل باستخدامهما إياه والأطراف مطلقاً والأوساط المشوب بها غرض فاسد: رذائل، فكل خلق مذموم ناشئ منها منفردة أو مجتمعاً بعضها أو كلّها.

طرق علاج الخلق المذموم:

وعلاجه الكلّي الإجمالي: معرفة حقائق الأمراض، وغوائلها، وأسبابها، وأضدادها وفوائدها وأسبابها، ثم معرفة وجود هذه الأمراض في نفسه بالتفتيش والتأمل، واختيار من يُنبهه على عيبه من أصدقاء الصدق، وتفحص قول أعدائه، فإنهم ينظرون إلى عيوبه ويذكرونه بها والنظر إلى الناس فإنهم مرآة(١)، وتذكرة لكل طالب مستبصر، ثم تمييز أسبابها، ثم إزالة الأسباب، وارتكاب الفضيلة المقابلة، والتكلّف في تحصيلها، إذ الأمراض تعالج بالأضداد، كما أن الصحة تحفظ بالأنداد

ثم التعنيف بالتعيير والتوبيخ في السرّ والعلانية، ثم الرذيلة المقابلة، فليحفظ حتى لا يتجاوز إلى الطرف الآخر، ثم الرياضات الشاقة؛ كالنذور والأيمان والعهود على التزام الأعمال الشاقة، حتى تذعن ما هو أسهل منها بالطيب والسهولة واستماع ما ورد في ذم سوء الخلق إجمالاً وتفصيلاً.

والثاني سيجيء في القسم الثاني إن شاء الله.

أدلة من السنة الشريفة على ذم سوء الخلق:

٨٨ – أما الأول : فمنه ما خرّج الأصفهاني: عن ميمون بن مهران رضي الله عنه قال: قال رسول الله ﷺ: «ما من ذنب أعظم عند الله من سوء الخلق؛ وذلك لأن صاحبه لا يخرج من ذنب إلا وقع في ذنب».

٨٩ – وخرّج الطبراني في «الأوسط»: عن عائشة رضي الله عنها ، قالت : قال رسول الله ﷺ: «الشؤم سوء الخلق».

٩٠ – وخرج الطبراني في «الأوسط»، وكذلك الأصفهاني: عن عائشة رضي الله عنها عن النبي ﷺ قال: «ما من شيء إلا له توبة؛ إلا صاحب سوء الخلق، فإنه لا يتوب من ذنب إلا عاد في شر منه».

٩١ – وخرّج الطبراني في «الكبير» و«الأوسط»، والبيهقي: عن ابن عباس رضي الله عنهما قال : قال رسول الله ﷺ: «الخُلق الحسن يذيب الخطايا كما يذيب الماء الجليد، والخلق السوء يفسد العمل كما يفسد الخلُّ العسل».

والأوساط الخالية عن الغرض الفاسد، فضائل فكل خلق محمود ناشئ منها منفردة أو مجتمعاً، بعضها، أو من مجموعها المسمّى بالعدالة، فمن حصل له بكسب أو طبع فليحفظه بملازمة أهله وعدم صحبة الأشرار، وإياه والاسترسال في الملاهي والمزاح والمراء، ولْيَرُضُ نفسه بوظائف علمية وعملية، وليذكر جلالته ودوامه وصفاءه، وحقارة الدنيا ونكدها، وباستماع ما ورد في حسن الخلق إجمالاً وتفصيلاً، والثاني سيجيء إن شاء الله تعالى.

الأدلة من الكتاب والسنة على مناقب حسن الخلق:

ومن الأول قوله تعالى: ﴿وَإِنَّكَ لَعَلَى خُلُقٍ عَظِيمٍ﴾ [القلم: ٤].

٩٢ – وقول النبي ﷺ فيما خرجه الطبراني في «الكبير»: عن أنس رضي الله عنه قال: قال رسول الله ﷺ: «إن العبد ليبلغ بُحسن خلقه عظيم درجات الآخرة، وشرف المنازل، وإنه لضعيف العبادة، وإنه ليبلغ بسوء خلقه أسفل درجة من جهنم».

٩٣ – وأخرج الإمام أحمد بن حنبل، والبيهقي والحاكم: عن أبي هريرة رضي الله عنه: أنه قال: قال رسول الله ﷺ: «بُعثت لأتمّم مكارم الأخلاق».

٩٤ – وأخرج الطبراني والبزّار: عن أنس رضي الله عنه: أن النبي ﷺ قال: «ذهب حسن الخلق بخيري الدنيا والآخرة».

٩٥ – وأخرج الطبراني في «الأوسط»: عن أبي هريرة رضي الله عنه قال: سمعت رسول الله ﷺ يقول: «ما حسّن الله خَلْقَ رجل وخُلقَه فتطعمه النار أبداً».

٩٦ – وأخرج البيهقي: عن أبي هريرة رضي الله عنه: أنه قال: قال رسول الله ﷺ: «يا أبا هريرة عليك بحسن الخلق»، قال: ما حسن الخلق يا رسول الله؟ قال: «تصل من قطعك، وتعفو عمن ظلمك، وتعطي من حرمك».

حقيقة التصوف:

فعليك أيها السالك بتخلية قلبك عن الرذائل وتحليته بالفضائل، فإن التصوّف عبارة عنهما، إذ قيل في تفسيره: هو الخروج من كل خلق دني، والدخول في خلق سنيّ.

فأمّا اتباع الهوى فهو السابع من آفات القلب:

[آيات قرآنية وأحاديث نبوية في التحذير من اتباع الهوى]:

قال الله تعالى: ﴿فَلَا تَتَّبِعُوا الْهَوَى أَن تَعْدِلُوا وَإِن تَلْوُا أَوْ تُعْرِضُوا فَإِنَّ اللَّهَ كَانَ بِمَا تَعْمَلُونَ خَبِيرًا﴾ [النساء: ١٣٥].

﴿وَلَا تَتَّبِعِ الْهَوَى فَيُضِلَّكَ عَن سَبِيلِ اللَّهِ﴾ [ص: ٢٦].

﴿وَأَمَّا مَنْ خَافَ مَقَامَ رَبِّهِ وَنَهَى النَّفْسَ عَنِ الْهَوَى ﴿٤٠﴾ فَإِنَّ الْجَنَّةَ هِيَ الْمَأْوَى﴾ [النازعات: ٤٠–٤١].

﴿أَرَيْتَ مَنِ اتَّخَذَ إِلَهَهُ هَوَىٰهُ﴾ [الفرقان: ٤٣].

﴿وَاتَّبَعَ هَوَىٰهُ فَمَثَلُهُ كَمَثَلِ الْكَلْبِ إِن تَحْمِلْ عَلَيْهِ يَلْهَثْ أَوْ تَتْرُكْهُ يَلْهَث﴾ [الأعراف: ١٧٦].

﴿وَاتَّبَعَ هَوَىٰهُ وَكَانَ أَمْرُهُ فُرُطًا﴾ [الكهف: ٢٨].

﴿بَلِ اتَّبَعَ الَّذِينَ ظَلَمُوا أَهْوَاءَهُم بِغَيْرِ عِلْمٍ﴾ [الروم: ٢٩].
﴿وَمَنْ أَضَلُّ مِمَّنِ اتَّبَعَ هَوَىٰهُ بِغَيْرِ هُدًى مِّنَ اللَّهِ﴾ [القصص: ٥٠].

١٠٣ – وأخرج البزّار: عن أنس رضي اللّٰه عنه، عن النبي ﷺ: أنه قال في آخر حديث طويل: «وأما المهلكات: فشُحٌّ مطاع، وهوى متبع، وإعجاب المرء بنفسه».

١٠٤ – وأخرج ابن أبي الدنيا: عن علي رضي اللّٰه عنه، عن النبي ﷺ: «إن أشدّ ما أخاف عليكم خصلتان: اتباع الهوى، وطول الأمل؛ فأما اتباع الهوى فإنّه يعدل بك عن الحق، وأما طول الأمل فإنّه يحبّب إليك الدنيا».

١٠٥ – وأخرج الترمذي: عن شدّاد بن أوس رضي اللّٰه عنه: أن رسول اللّٰه ﷺ قال: «الكيّس من دان نفسه وعمل لما بعد الموت، والعاجز من أَتْبَعَ نفسَه هواها وتمنّى على اللّٰه».

[معنى الهوى]:

فالهوى مصدر هويه يهواه من باب علم؛ أي: أحبّه واشتهاه، والنّفس بالطبع ميّالة إلى الشر أمارة بالسوء، فاتباع هواها يُردي ويُهلك لا محالة، أما في غير المباحات فظاهر، وأمّا فيها فبعد كونه صفة البهيمة، وركوناً إلى الدنيا الدنيئة، وشغلاً شاغلاً عن الطاعات وعن زاد الآخرة، مفضٍ إلى المحظور، وجارٌّ إلى الشرور، ومؤد إلى الفجور، وحِمًى للحرام، ومأوى للآلام والآثام، وصاحبه خسيس دنيء لئيم رذيل؛ بل هو لخنزير الشهوة خادم مطيع وعبد ذليل، وأنشدوا:

نونُ الهوانِ من الهوى مسروقةٌ فصريعُ كلِّ هوًى صريعُ هوانِ

ومقابله المجاهدة: وهي فطم النفس عن المألوفات، وحملها عن خلاف هواها في عموم الأوقات فهي بضاعة العبّاد ورأس مال الزهّاد ومدار صلاح النفوس وتذليلها، وملاك تقوية الأرواح وتصفيتها ووصولها.

فعليك أيها السالك بالتّشمُّر في منع النفس عن الهوى، وحملها على المجاهدة إن شئتَ من اللّٰه الهدى، قال اللّٰه تعالى:
﴿وَالَّذِينَ جَـٰهَدُوا فِينَا لَنَهْدِيَنَّهُمْ سُبُلَنَا﴾ [العنكبوت: ٦٩].
﴿وَمَن جَـٰهَدَ فَإِنَّمَا يُجَـٰهِدُ لِنَفْسِهِ إِنَّ اللَّهَ لَغَنِيٌّ عَنِ الْعَـٰلَمِينَ﴾ [العنكبوت: ٦].

– [تناول المباحات أحياناً لاسترداد النشاط في العبادة اتباع للشرع وليس الهوى]:

ثم اعلم أنَّ المذموم في اتباع الهوى في المباحات الإصرار عليه؛ إذ طبع البشر لا يتحمّل المخالفة الكلّية؛ ولأنه يؤدّي إلى الغلوّ والإفراط، وقد مرّ في فصل الاقتصاد أنّه منهيٌّ عنه؛ ولأنه يورث الملالة والسآمة المؤدّية إلى عدم المداومة المذموم جدّاً في العبادة.

١٠٦ – ولذا قال عليه الصلاة والسلام: «يا أيها الناس! خذوا من الأعمال ما تُطيقون فإن اللّٰه لا يَمَلُّ حتى تملُّوا وإن أحبَّ الأعمال إلى اللّٰه ما دام وإن قلّ» أخرجه البخاري ومسلم عن عائشة رضي اللّٰه عنها.

وفي رواية مسلم: «خذوا من العمل ما تطيقون فو اللّٰه لا يسأم اللّٰه حتى تسأموا».

١٠٧ – وعن علي رضي اللّٰه عنه: أنه قال: «روّحوا القلوب فإنها إذا أكرهت عَيَّت».

١٠٨ – وعن أبي الدرداء رضي اللّٰه عنه: أنه قال: «إنّي لأستجمّ نفسي باللّٰهو ليكون عوناً لي على الحق».

فحينئذ لا بدَّ أحياناً أن يتناول من المشتهيات المباحات استراحة من التعب، وتحرُّزاً عن السآمة، وتحريكاً للنشاط على العبادة؛ فلذا قال الإمام حجة الإسلام : لو سكن نشاطه وضعفت رغبته وعلم أن الترفه بالنوم أو الحديث أو المزاح في ساعة يردّ نشاطه؛ فذلك أفضل له من أداء الصلاة مع الملال». ففي الحقيقة هذا اتباع للشرع لا الهوى المحض.

[إجمال آفات القلب، أو ذكر بعض الأخلاق المذمومة]:

ولنذكر جملة الأخلاق السيئة المزبورة، والرَّذائل الردية المذكورة؛ ليسهل حفظها للطالب:

كفر، بدعة، رياء، كِبر، عُجب، حَسَد، بُخْل، إسراف، جهل، كُفران النعمة، سخط للقضاء، جَزَع، أمن، يأس، حب الظَّلَمة، بغض الصالحين، تعليق القلب بأسباب، حبُّ الجاه، خوف ذمّ، حبُّ المدحِ، اتباع الهوى، تقليد، طول الأمل، طمع، تذلّل، حقد، شَمَاتة، عَدَاوة، جُبْن، تهوّر، غدر، خِيَانة، خلف الوعد، سوء الظنّ، الطِّيرة، حبّ المال، حبّ الدّنيا، حرص، سَفه، بطالة، عَجَلة، تسويف عمل، فَظَاظة، وَقاحة، حُزن في أمر الدنيا، خوف فيه، غش، فتنة مداهنة، أُنس بمخلوق، خِفَّة، عناد، تمرّد، صلف، نفاق، جَرْبَزة، غَبَاوة، شره، خُمُود، إصرار.

ومن الأخلاق الحميدة غير ما ذكر ضمناً وتبعاً:

· **الاستقامة:** وهي الوفاء بالعهود كلِّها، وملازمة العدل، والتوسّط في كل الأمور، قال اللّٰه تعالى: ﴿فَاسْتَقِمْ كَمَا أُمِرْتَ﴾ [هود: ١١٢].

والأدبُ: وهو حفظ الحد بين الغلو والجفاء بمعرفة ضرر التعدي.

والفراسة: وهي خاطر ينشأ من قوة الإيمان يهجم على القلب فينفي ما يضاده.

٣٥٣ – أخرج القُشيري: عن أبي سعيد الخدري رضي اللّٰه عنه، قال: «اتقوا فراسة المؤمنِ فَإِنَّه ينظرُ بنور اللّٰه».

· **والتّفكر:** في نفسه: هل هي متصفة بمعصية فيتوب، أو متعرضة لها فيحترز، أو: لا، فيشكر اللّٰه على التوفيق.

وفي الطاعات: ليتدارك ما فات منها، ويحترز عن تركها، ويشكر على توفيق اللّٰه تعالى لما حصل منها.

وفي خَلْق اللّٰه تعالى وآياته في الأنفس والآفاق: حتى يزيد، وتعظم فيه معرفة عظمة اللّٰه تعالى وقدرته وعلمه، وحكمته فيحصل فيه محبَّة اللّٰه تعالى والشوق إليه، والأنس به، قال اللّٰه تعالى: ﴿وَيَتَفَكَّرُونَ فِي خَلْقِ السَّمَوَاتِ وَالْأَرْضِ﴾ [آل عمران: ١٩١].

والصدق: وهو في سبع:

١) في القول: ضدّ الكذب.

٢) وفي النيّة: الإخلاص.

٣–٤) وفي الوعد والعزم: قوتهما وخلوّهما من الضّعف والتردّد.

٥) وفي الوفاء: تحقيقه وإنجازه على وفق الوعد والعزم.

٦) وفي العمل: موافقته للباطن، وعدم دلالته على أمر لم يتصف به.

٧) وفي نحو الخوف: قوته وكثرته.

والصدِّيق من اتصف بهذه الأوصاف جميعاً.

والمرابطةُ: وهي ربط النفس على طاعة اللّٰه بخمس:

١) المشارطة على النّفس أولاً بترك المعاصي، وترتيب الوظائف والأوراد في كل يوم وليلةٍ.

٢) ثمَّ المراقبة بمراعاة القلب للرقيب باستدامة العِلم باطلاع الربّ، والنظر إليه في أثناء العمل وقبله ،وبعده هل يفي بالمشروط على وجهه أم يزيغ عنه؟.

٣) ثم المحاسبة بعد العمل هل أتم المشروط أم نقص؟.

٤–٥) ثمَّ المعاتبة والمعاقبة إن نقص؛ بنحو: الجوع، والعطش، والسهر، والنذر بالتصدّق ونحوه، حتى لا يرجع إليه ثانياً.

فمجموع ما ذكر من الأخلاق الحميدة تبعاً وأصالة ثمانية وسبعون:

إيمان، اعتقاد أهل السنة والجماعة، إخلاص، إحسان، تواضع، ذكر منَّة، نصيحة، تصوّف، غيرة، غِبْطة في عمل الآخرة، سخاء، إيثار، مروءة، فتوّة، حِكْمة، شُكْر، رضاء، صبر، خوف من اللّٰه تعالى، حُزن له، رجاء، بغضٌ في اللّٰه، حبٌّ في اللّٰه ، توكل، حب خمول، استواء ذم ومدح، مجاهدة تحقيق قصر أمل، ذكر ،موت تفويض تسليم، تملق في طلب العِلم، سلامة صدر عن حقد شجاعة حلم ،رفق، أناة، وفاء عهد، إنجاز وعد، حسن ظن، زهد، قناعة، رشد، سعي، إنابة، مبادرة في عمل الآخرة، رقة شفقة، حياء، صلابة في أمر دين أنس باللّٰه، شوق إليه، محبة اللّٰه، ،وقار، ذكاء، عفة، استقامة أدب ،فراسة ،تفكر ،صدق مرابطة مشارطة، مراقبة، محاسبة، معاتبة، معاقبة، كَظم غَيْظٍ، عفو، نيّة، إرادة طول حياة للعبادة، توبة، خشوع، يقين، عبودية، حرية، إرادة.

[أصول الفضائل]:

وللمتقدمين ومن سلك مسلكهم في ضبط الفضائل وحدودها طريقة لا بأس أن نذكرها، وإن وقع تكرار في بعض؛ لعدم خلوها عن الفائدة، وهي حصر أصولها وتفريع شعب كل منها عليه.

وقد علمْتَ أن أصولها أربعة: ثلاثة مفردة؛ وهي الحكمة والشجاعة والعفَّة، وواحدٌ مركَّب من مجموع هذه الثلاثة؛ وهو العدالة.

فشعب الحكمة: (ز):

أ - **صفاء الذهن:** استعداد النفس لاستخراج المطلوب بلا تشويش.

ب - **جودة الفهم:** صحة الانتقال من الملزوم إلى اللازم.

ج - **الذكاء:** سرعة اقتراح النتائج.

د - **حسن التصوّر:** البحث عن الأشياء بقدر ما هي عليه.

هـ - **سهولة التعلّم:** قوة النفس على درك المطلوب بلا زيادة سعي.

و - **الحفظ:** ضبط الصور المدركة.

ز - **الذكر:** استحضار المحفوظات.

وشعب الشجاعة: اثنتا عشرة:

أ - **كِبْرُ النفس:** استحقار اليسار والفقر والكِبَرِ والصّغر.

ب - **العفو:** ترك المجازاة بسهولة من النفس مع القدرة.

ج - **عِظَمُ الهمة:** عدم المبالاة بسعادة الدنيا وشقاوتها.

د - **الصبر:** قوة مقاومة الآلام والأهوال.

هـ - **النجدة:** عدم الجزع عند المخلوق.

و - **الحِلْمُ:** الطمأنينة عند سورة الغضب.

ز - **السُّكون:** التأني في الخصومات والحروب.

ح - **التّواضع:** استعظام ذوي الفضائل، ومَنْ دُوْنَه في المال والجاه.

ط - **الشهامة:** الحرص على ما يوجب الذكر الجميل من العظائم.

ي - **الاحتمال:** إتعاب النفس في الحسنات.

يا - **الحميّة:** المحافظة على الحُرَم والدِّين من التهمة.

يب - **الرّقة:** التأذّي عن أذى يلحق الغير.

وشعب العفّة اثنتا عشرة:

أ - **الحَيَاء:** انحصار النَّفس خوف ارتكاب القبائح.

ب - **الصبر:** حبسُ النَّفس عن متابعة الهوى.

ج - **الدِّعة:** السّكون عند هيجان الشهوة.

د – **النَّزاهة:** اكتسابُ المال من غير مَهَانة ولا ظلم، وإنفاقه في المصارف الحميدة.
هـ – **القَنَاعة:** الاقتصار على الكفاف.
و – **الوَقار:** التأني في التوجه نحو المطالب.
ز – **الرّفْق:** حُسْن الانقيادِ بما يؤدي إلى الجميل.
ح – **حُسْنُ السَّمت:** محبة ما يكمل النفس.
ط – **الوَرَع:** مُلازمة الأعمال الجليلة.
ي – **المروءة:** الرغبة الصادقة للنفس في الإفادة بقدر ما يمكن.
يا – **الانتظام:** تقدير الأمور وترتيبها بحسب المصالح.
يب – **السَّخاء:** إعطاء ما ينبغي لِمَنْ ينبغي، وهذا تحته ستة أنواع:
أ – **الكرم:** الإعطاء بالسهولة وطيب النفس.
ب – **الإيثار:** أن يكون مع الكف
ج – **النيل:** أن يكون مع السرور عن حاجته.
د – **المواساة:** أن يكون مع مشاركة الأصدقاء.
هـ – **السَّماحة:** بذل ما لا يجب تفضلاً.
و – **المسامحة:** ترك ما لا يجب تنزهاً.
وشُعَب العدالة: أربع عشرة:
أ – **الصداقة:** المحبّةُ الصَّادقة بحيثُ لا يشوبها غرض، ويؤثره على نفسه في الخيرات.
ب – **الألفة:** اتفاق الآراء في المعاونة على تدبير المعاش.
ج – **الوفاء:** ملازمة طريق المساواة، ومحافظة عهود الخلطاء.
د – **التَّودد:** طلب مودّة الأكفاء بما يوجب ذلك.
هـ – **المكافأة:** مقابلة الإحسان بمثله، أو زيادة عليه.
و – **حُسن الشركة:** رعاية العدل في المعاملات.
ز – **حسن القضاء:** ترك الندم والمن في المجازاة.
ح – **صلة الرحم:** مشاركة ذوي القرابة في الخيرات
ط – **الشَّفَقةُ:** صرف الهمّة إلى إزالة المكروه عن النّاس.
ي – **الإصلاح:** التوسّط بينَ النّاس في الخصومات بما يدفعها.
ك – **التوكُل:** تركُ السّعي فيما لا يسعه قدرة البشر.
ل – **التسليم:** الانقياد لأمر اللّه تعالى وترك الاعتراض فيما لا يلائم.
م – **الرّضاء:** طيبُ النّفسِ فيما يصيبه ويفوته مع عدم التغير.
ن – **العبادة:** تعظيم اللّه تعالى بما هو أهله وامتثال أوامره.
فمجموع الأصول والشُّعب خمسة وخمسون، وفيه زيادة ثلاثين فضيلة على ما ذكرنا.

فعليك أيُّها السّالك بالاحتراز عن جميع الخبائث المذكورة ودفعها، وحفظ أضدادها وباقي الفضائل، أو إزالتها ورفعها وتحصيل أضدادها وسائر الفضائل حتى يبقى أو تحصل لك تزكية النّفس، وتصفية الروح، وتخلية القلب وتَحْليته، فإن التصوّف والطريقة عبارة عن هذه الأمور، وخصوصاً سبعة من الرذائل؛ فإنَّها أمهات الخبائث، فعسى إن نجوت منها أن تنجو من غيرها أيضاً؛ وهن: الكُفْرُ، والبدعة، والرّياء والكبر، والحسد، والبُخْل، والإسراف.

1.4 *English Translation*

The First Category:
Sins and Sicknesses of the Heart

[One must] understand that its rectification is more imperative than all else. The heart [is like] a king who is obeyed [and whose] judgment is law; thus the [other] body parts are its subjects, [totally] servile to it. For this reason, the Prophet, may Allah bless him and grant him peace, said, "Indeed, in the body is a piece of flesh …"[1]

The heart's reformation [is achieved through] eliminating blameworthy traits and adorning it with praiseworthy ones. Two [distinct] discussions are thus needed:

The First Discussion:

[This discussion expounds] on the meaning of character, outlining its origins and categorizing it into that which is blameworthy and praiseworthy. [It] also generally [clarifies] the way one eradicates and remedies blameworthy traits. Likewise, how to attain, maintain, retain, and fortify praiseworthy traits, is generally [explained].

As such, we say:

---

1 On the authority of Nu'mān bin Bashīr, may Allah be pleased with him, [who] said, "I heard the Messenger of Allah, may Allah bless him and grant him peace, say, 'Verily, the permissible is distinct and the prohibited is distinct, but between both are doubtful matters concerning which many people are unaware. Accordingly, whoever carefully avoids that which is doubtful surely safeguards their religion and honor. However, the one who gets caught up in that which is doubtful [inevitably] falls for the forbidden, just as a shepherd pasturing [his flock] around a restricted territory all but grazes therein. Realize that every king has an inviolable domain – and Allah's inviolable domain is that which is unlawful. Indeed, within the body there is a piece of flesh, which, if it is healthy, then the entire body is [likewise] healthy. But, if it is compromised, then the rest of the body is [similarly] compromised. Verily, it is the heart.'" (Bukhārī 2051; Muslim 1599).

Meaning of Character:
Character is an acquired quality that readily produces automated actions without [much] deliberation. It is possible to [actively] modify it, as indicated by revealed scripture combined with the consensus of intellectual thinkers and [human] experience. The propensity for doing so differs according to [the variability of peoples'] temperaments.

Its Origin:
It originates [from] the faculties of the psyche; namely, [the following] three:[2]

1) **Rationality** (*nuṭq*):[3] Which is the faculty of reason. When balanced, [it manifests as] wisdom (*ḥikma*), which is the inherent capability of the psyche to distinguish right from wrong.

Opposedly, its intemperateness [fosters] obsession (*jarbaza*), which is when the capacity to ascertain prompts one to [closely] examine that which is [humanly] impossible to comprehend, like the elusive [verses of the Quran] (*mutashābihāt*),[4] or delving [too deeply] into [concepts like] predestination

---

2 This is consistent with Plato's, Aristotle's, and the Islamic philosophers' tripartite view of the core human drives.

3 According to Islamic scholars and philosophers, the distinctive difference between human beings and other living beings such as animals is the faculty of reason. Thus, human beings are known as living beings possessing the faculty of intellect (*ḥayawān nāṭiq*). Accordingly, humans share being in the genus of living creatures with other animals, however the distinctive difference (faṣl) between human beings and the various other categories of living beings is the possession of the faculty of reason and intellect. According to pure philosophical discourse, Islamic philosophers believe that a human being should not live like an animal as reason and intellect are the very properties that differentiate them from the animal kingdom. As such, humans should use their intellects for reasoning, acquisition of knowledge, reflection, and to tame and direct the appetitive and survival drives. The Quran describes humans who do not use their intellects, likening them to cattle: *Certainly, We have created for Hell many of the jinn and mankind; they have hearts with which they fail to understand; and they have eyes with which they fail to see; and they have ears with which they fail to hear. They are like cattle – rather, even more astray. Such are utterly heedless* (al-Aʿrāf: 7:179).

4 As per the seventh verse of Sura āl-ʿImrān, the vast majority of verses in the Quran are unequivocal in meaning (*muḥkamāt*), whereas a minority of verses are elusive (*mutashābihāt*). In other words, their meanings are not clearly interpretable, and may thus only be viewed and interpreted by filtering them through the clear-cut meanings of the bulk of the Quran with the underlying acknowledgement that Allah alone knows their true interpretation. The potential meanings of obscure verses are sometimes explored with speculative reflections by scholars but are essentially left uninterpreted as they are inherently deemed beyond human comprehension. Thus, Imam al-Birgivī points out that attempting to use the faculty of intellect as a tool to ascertain something that is not ascertainable by intellect alone is indicative of a spiritual problem; one needs to humble themselves before Allah, accepting their limitations in understanding everything.

(*qadr*). Because of such, [a person] could be incited [to] behave in ways that are detrimental to others.

Ignorance (*bilāda*) is [the term used to describe] when intellect is lacking. It is a chronic trait that inhibits a person from [appropriately] discerning between good and evil.

2) **Anger** (*ghaḍab*):[5] It is an inherent [protective] instinct [that serves] as a defense mechanism against threats. When balanced, it [manifests as] valor (*shujāʿa*), which is a trait that enables a person to confront the things that they should rightfully be taking on.

In excess, it [causes] rashness (*tahawwur*), which is a characteristic that causes one to [try to] take on that which they should not be dealing with [at all].

When this [instinct] is diminished, cowardice (*jubn*) [is engendered], which is a deep-rooted trait that hinders a person from facing what they rightfully ought to [be engaging with].

3) **Appetite** (*shahwa*): It is an inherent drive that incites one to seek comfort. Its balance [results in] temperance (*ʿiffa*), which is a quality through which one fulfills [their natural] desires in accordance with Islamic ethics (*sharīʿa*) and propriety. However, an unrestrained appetite [leads to] hedonism (*sharah*) and immorality (*fujūr*), due to which a person [endeavors] to satiate their desires by any means possible – be it permissible or forbidden. Moreover, an abated appetite [engenders] apathy (*khumūd*), which is an idiosyncrasy that causes a person to fall short when it comes to satisfying [even] the [most] vital of needs.

The first three virtues [wisdom, valor, and temperance] are attained by maintaining control over the last and second-last [of the aforementioned tendencies, namely, protective instincts and appetite]. Alternatively, the [six] vices [previously discussed][6] are established when both [protective instincts and appetite] are the ones that govern a person. Such vices, without exception, are depravities. It is likewise [the case] when virtues are tainted by a nefarious motive. Accordingly, every reprehensible characteristic that wholly or partially stems from such [is similarly blameworthy]; [it does not matter if] it is a solitary trait, or an array of [related] qualities.[7]

---

5 This may be understood more broadly as a 'survival' or 'self-protective' drive. The function of this drive serves to protect oneself from harm prior to or during its occurrence, and to seek justice after its occurrence. This is in accordance with what is mentioned by al-Ghazālī in the chapter entitled "The Elucidation of the Reality of Anger."

6 In order, they are obsession (*jarbaza*), ignorance (*bilāda*), rashness (*tahawwur*), cowardice (*jubn*), hedonism (*sharah*), and apathy (*khumūd*).

7 The moderation of the three major drives (i.e., appetite, anger, and rationality) leads to the acquisition of the three cardinal virtues (i.e. discipline, valor, and wisdom). The fourth

Approaches to Remedy Blameworthy Traits:
[The way to] a comprehensive treatment [is by] knowing the realities of these illnesses; their precursors; their causes; and their [corresponding] counter virtues with their advantages and causes. Thereafter, one must recognize the presence of such illnesses within oneself, through self-inspection, contemplation, and by [carefully] selecting a genuine friend to highlight one's flaws.[8] A person should also examine the words of their enemies as they [typically] look towards one's shortcomings and openly recount them. Also, by surveying other people, they are [like] a mirror and [serve as an] admonition for every perceptive person seeking [to discover their own defects].[9] Next, [one must] determine the causes of their vices, and then [proceed] to uproot them, whilst striving to enact and imbibe corresponding virtues.[10] This is because illnesses are [typically] treated with their [positive] opposites just as health is preserved through connaturally [healthful and balanced] things.[11]

Afterwards, [a person must] reprimand [their own self] with censure and blame internally as well as publicly, followed by [further treating oneself with] the negative opposite [extreme]. However, one must take care to not overdo it, [lest one becomes overly inclined] towards the opposite end [of the spectrum].[12]

---

cardinal virtue of justice is considered to be a byproduct of the effective moderation of the former three combined.

8 The first step mentioned for the treatment of the self is to first discover and learn what the virtues and vices are along with their associated subtypes, details, and underlying causes. Once an individual fully understands what health and sickness is, then they can attempt to analyze their own self, searching for the presence of these virtues or vices within.

9 It is not sufficient to undergo this process solely on one's own. Rather, it is necessary to seek feedback from multiple social networks, including via enemies, as they may most readily and unhesitantly highlight one's personal flaws.

10 For example, the corresponding virtue to the vice of arrogance is humility.

11 Using the analogy of ancient medicine, Imam al-Birgivī is establishing the central principle of moderation as it pertains to the health of the psyche and character development. Psychological health is indicated by the moderation and balance of all of one's elements and instinctive drives.

The treatment with the positive opposite is a commonly cited method by Islamic scholars that entails acting upon an incompatible and positive behavior in place of an unhealthy negative habit. For example, if one has excessive anger, then they shall exert effort to develop a behavioral plan of serving others, particularly those who are lesser than him in status.

12 The intervention being recommended here for those who are not responsive to the aforementioned positive opposite technique is to employ the 'negative opposite' or negative extreme behavior. To illustrate, if, for example, someone is struggling with personal arrogance then they should consciously act humbly, thus attempting to remedy their arrogance with the positive opposite. However, if this does not work in fully eradicating arrogance from within, then they should take it further, using the negative opposite

Next, [one should engage in] arduous [spiritual] exercises, [using] the likes of vows (*nudhūr*),[13] oaths (*aymān*),[14] and pledges (*ʿuhūd*) to [solemnly] commit to such practices.[15] [This must be upheld] until one aligns to easily and agreeably [perform] that which is comparatively less strenuous. [Only then will] listening to that which has been generally and comprehensively transmitted concerning the reprehensibility of bad character [prove to be most effective].

As for the second [more comprehensive discussion], it will be taken [up] in the second section, if Allah so wills.

The Condemnation of Bad Manners as Evidenced in the Noble Sunnah

As for the first [proof], al-Iṣfahānī relates on the authority of Maymūn bin Mahrān, may Allah be pleased with him, [who] reported that the Messenger of Allah, may Allah bless him and grant him peace, said, "With Allah, there is no

---

extreme. In this particular example, this means that they should exaggerate in their humility to the point of self-debasement, which is the opposite extreme of arrogance on the overall spectrum. This intervention is utilized for those resistant to the positive opposite behavior because it accounts for the rebound effect; by pressuring oneself to go to the other extreme, a person is able to find eventual balance. However, al-Birgivī cautions that an individual should exercise due care in using this approach, so that one does not inadvertently become habituated to the other undesirable extreme and thus suffer from yet another kind of imbalance.

13 A vow, in this context, may be of two types: 1) One may vow to perform a certain virtuous behavior or abstain from a vice, thereby converting this ordinarily voluntary act into an obligatory deed that they must fulfill, as Allah, the Exalted, states, *And let them fulfill their vows*, (al-Ḥajj 22:29). A person may vow to perform a separate act of worship such as fasting, prayer, or giving in charity if he is able to successfully enact the virtuous behavior or abstain from the vice, as a demonstration of gratitude for Allah's giving him the strength to succeed. If he were to violate the vow, then he would be required to pay an expiation (*kaffāra*) similar to that which is paid for violating an oath (*yamīn*), which entails feeding ten poor persons (two meals for each person), or clothing them (one garment per person), or giving them its equivalence in monetary value. Finally, if one is unable to do any of the three mentioned, then they must fast for three consecutive days (Ibn ʿĀbidīn, 1963).

14 An oath is similar to a vow, except that one takes an oath in the name of Allah, by saying, "*Wallāhi; billāhi; tallāhi*" or "I swear in the name of Allah" to perform a particular virtuous deed or abstain from a reprehensible action. Again, a violation of one's oath will require the same aforementioned expiation.

15 In this situation, an individual makes a promise or covenant with Allah that if he does not perform the virtuous action or if he were to act in a reprehensible way, he will consequently take upon a difficult task like spending the whole night in prayer, for example. This is to deter the lower ego from taking the easy path of comfort by either indulging in the seemingly pleasurable vice or avoiding the performance of the targeted virtuous deed. The rationale for the employment of this strategy is to reciprocally inhibit the undesirable action by providing a reasonable consequence of discomfort to come thereafter (Khādīmī, 2019, p. 163).

sin greater than bad character.[16] That is because the one who is guilty of it does not carry out a sin[ful act] except that he falls into yet another one."[17]

Al-Ṭabarānī relates in al-Awsaṭ that ʿAisha, may Allah be pleased with her, said that the Messenger of Allah, may Allah bless him and grant him peace, stated, "Pessimism is bad character."[18]

Al-Iṣfahānī, as well as al-Ṭabarānī in al-Awsaṭ, relate that ʿAisha, may Allah be pleased with her, reports that the Prophet, may Allah bless him and grant him peace, said, "There isn't a single deed except that repentance remediates it, other than [in the case of] someone with evil character. Verily, such a person does not repent from [any] sin except that he [easily] returns to that which is worse than it."[19]

In al-Kabīr and al-Awsaṭ, Al-Ṭabarānī as well as al-Bayhaqī relate on the authority of Ibn ʿAbbās, may Allah be pleased with him, who said, "The Messenger of Allah, may Allah bless him and grant him peace, said, 'Good character dissolves sin just as ice melts [to become] water. Likewise, evil character spoils deeds just as vinegar spoils honey.'"[20]

[All] balanced values devoid of nefarious motives are virtuous; thus, every individual, partial, or collective praiseworthy characteristic that stems from such is termed "justice" (*ʿadāla*). Whoever acquires such traits, naturally, or as a result of [exerting] effort, should maintain them by adhering to those who are [likewise] imbued with similar characteristics, whilst [simultaneously] avoiding bad company. Furthermore, a person must take care [to avoid] letting their guard down with regards to recreational activities, joking, and debating. Rather, one should become [sufficiently] inured so as to engage in knowledge-based pursuits and practices. One should [constantly] remember Allah's magnificence, everlastingness, and flawlessness, as well as the lowly and unsettling nature of this [ephemeral] world. Lastly, one should [mindfully] listen to that which has been generally and comprehensively related concerning good character.

---

16 This is because the foundations of bad character are embedded within the individual and if he has not extirpated the root of it, he will continue to show its symptoms or negative behavioral effects (Khādīmī, 2019, p. 164).

17 Al-Eṣbahānī, *al-Targhīb wa-l-Tarhīb*, 1197; al-Mundhirī, *al-Targhīb wa-l-Tarhīb*, 4045.

18 Al-Ṭabarānī, *al-Awsaṭ*, 4360; Aḥmad, 24591; al-Bayhaqi, *Shuʿab al-Imān*, 8022; al-Bukhārī, *al-Tārīkh al-Kabīr*, 2618.

19 Al-Ṭabarānī, *al-Ṣaghīr*, 553; al-Mundhirī, *al-Targhīb wa-l-Tarhīb*, 4044; al-Daylamī, *al-Firdaws*, 6155; al-Suyūṭī, *al-Jāmiʿ al-Ṣaghīr*, 2416.

20 al-Ṭabarānī, *al-Kabīr*, 1007 (19: 417); al-Bayhaqī, *Shuʿab al-Imān*, 8036; al-Mundhirī, *al-Targhīb wa-l-Tarhīb*, 4035.

As for the second [approach with more details], it will be addressed in the second section, if Allah so wills.

The Virtues of Good Character as Evidenced from The Book and The Sunna
Firstly, Allah, the Exalted, says, *Indeed, you are upon an exalted character* (al-Qalam 68:4).

Next, [is] the saying of the Prophet, may Allah bless him and grant him peace, as recorded by al-Ṭabarānī in al-Kabīr: Anas [bin Mālik], may Allah be pleased with him, reported, "the Messenger of Allah, may Allah bless him and grant him peace, said, 'Indeed, a servant could reach the [most] esteemed ranks and noblest of levels in the hereafter due to their good character, [even if] they are languid in their worship. One can likewise be demoted to the lowest levels of Hellfire due to their evil character.'"[21]

Imam Aḥmad bin Ḥanbal, al-Bayhaqī, and Al-Ḥākim relate that Abū Hurayra, may Allah be pleased with him, said, "The Messenger of Allah, may Allah bless him and grant him peace, stated, 'Indeed I was only sent to perfect good character.'"[22]

Al-Ṭabarānī and al-Bazzār relate on the authority of Anas, may Allah be pleased with him, that the Prophet of Allah, may Allah bless him and grant him peace, said, "Good character advances with the goodness of [both] this world and the hereafter."[23]

In al-Awsaṭ, al-Ṭabarānī transmits on the authority of Abū Hurayra, may Allah be pleased with him, who said, "I heard the Messenger of Allah, may Allah bless him and grant him peace, say, 'Allah never beautifies the [outward] form and [inward] characteristics of a person so as to thrust him [into] the fire.'"[24]

---

21 Al-Ṭabarānī, *al Kabīr*, 754 (1: 260); al-Daylamī, *al-Firdaws*, 713.

22 Aḥmad, 8939; al-Bayhaqi, al-Sunan al-Kubrā; al-Hākim, 2: 670: 4661.

23 Al-Ṭabarānī, *al-Awsaṭ*, 3141. 754; al-Daylamī, *al-Firdaws*, 3163.

Good character also provides individuals a more satisfactory life, overall. Bromley et al. (2006) found that adolescents at the average age of sixteen who possessed character strengths were at a decreased risk of developing psychiatric disorders, educational and occupational problems, interpersonal challenges, and criminal behaviors later in their early adulthood. Gilham et al. (2011) showed that character strengths predicted lower levels of depression and greater life satisfaction during adolescence. The possession of character strengths is correlated with life satisfaction and happiness at varying degrees (Park, Peterson, and Seligman, 2004; Peterson et. al., 2007).

24 Al-Ṭabarānī, *al-Awsaṭ*, 6780; al-Bayhaqī, *Shu'ab al-Imān*, 8037; al-Mundhirī, *al-Targhīb wa-l-Tarhīb*, 4020.

Good character also provides individuals a more satisfactory life, overall. Bromley et al. found that adolescents at the average age of sixteen who possessed character strengths were at a decreased risk of developing psychiatric disorders, educational and occupational

Al-Bayhaqī reported on the authority of Abū Hurayra, may Allah be pleased with him, who said that the Messenger of Allah, may Allah bless him and grant him peace, said, "O Abū Hurayra, it is [incumbent] upon you to have good manners." He replied, "What are good manners, O Messenger of Allah?" He explained, "To establish ties with those who sever [them], to forgive those who wrong you, and to give to those who withhold [from] you."[25]

The Reality of Spiritual Reformation (*Taṣawwuf*)

It is [imperative] that you, O seeker, clear your heart of all vices (*takhliya*) and adorn it with virtue (taḥliya); for indeed, the term *taṣawwuf* entails both of these [processes]. It has thus been said explanatorily: [*Taṣawwuf*] involves discarding every lowly characteristic and instilling sublime conduct.

Sicknesses of the Heart: Following One's Whims[26]

[The following] Quranic verses and prophetic traditions caution against following whimsical desires:

---

problems, interpersonal challenges, and criminal behaviors later in their early adulthood. (See Paul D. Bromley, Lynette D. Hodges, and David A. Brodie, "Physiological Range of Peak Cardiac Power Output in Healthy Adults," Clinical Physiology and Functional Imaging 26, no. 4 (July 2006): 240–46.) Gilham et al. (2011) showed that character strengths predicted lower levels of depression and greater life satisfaction during adolescence. (See Jane Gillham et al., "Character Strengths Predict Subjective Well-Being during Adolescence," The Journal of Positive Psychology 6, no. 1 (January 2011): 31–44.) The possession of character strengths is correlated with life satisfaction and happiness at varying degrees (see Nansook Park, Christopher Peterson, and Martin E.P. Seligman, "Strengths of Character and Well-Being," Journal of Social and Clinical Psychology 23, no. 5 (October 2004): 603–19; Christopher Peterson et al., "Strengths of Character, Orientations to Happiness, and Life Satisfaction," The Journal of Positive Psychology 2, no. 3 (July 2007): 149–56.).

25 Al-Bayhaqi, *Shu'ab al-Imān*, 8694.

Good character also provides individuals a more satisfactory life, overall. Bromley et al. (2006) found that adolescents at the average age of sixteen who possessed character strengths were at a decreased risk of developing psychiatric disorders, educational and occupational problems, interpersonal challenges, and criminal behaviors later in their early adulthood. Gilham et al. (2011) showed that character strengths predicted lower levels of depression and greater life satisfaction during adolescence. The possession of character strengths is correlated with life satisfaction and happiness at varying degrees (Park, Peterson, and Seligman, 2004; Peterson et al., 2007).

26 This section is taken from a different section of al-Birgivī's book. It lays down a detailed description of the Arabic term *hawā*, which is a commonly used term in Islamic character and Sufi literature. It refers to the unhealthy or excessive passions of the primitive self (*nafs al-ammāra*). The following of one's base passions leads an individual to the pursuit of hedonistic pleasures and a more materialistic lifestyle.

Allah the Exalted says, *So do not let your desires cause you to deviate. If you distort [testimony] or refuse [to give it], then Allah is fully aware of what you do* (al-Nisāʾ 4:135).

And do not follow desires lest it leads you astray from Allah's way (Ṣād 38:26).

As for the one who fears standing before his Lord and restrains himself from desire, then indeed, Paradise will be [their] abode (al-Nāziʿāt 79:40–41).

Have you seen the one who has taken his own desire as his god? (al-Furqān 25:43).

And he followed his desires. His example is thus like that of a dog; if you chase it, it pants with its tongue protruding, and if you leave it, it still pants with its tongue protruding (al-Aʿrāf 7:176).

Who has followed his desire and whose behavior has exceeded the limits (al-Kahf 18:28).

But the oppressors have followed their desires without knowledge (al-Rūm 30:29).

And who is more astray than the one who follows his desire without guidance from Allah? (al-Qaṣas 28:50).

Al-Bazzār relates on the authority of Anas, may Allah be pleased with him, that the Prophet, may Allah bless him and grant him peace, who, towards the end of a lengthy narration, said, "… as for the deadly sins, they are: greed that is assented to, lust that is pursued, and for a person to be infatuated with their own self."[27]

Ibn Abī Dunyā relates on the authority of ʿAlī, may Allah be pleased with him, that the Prophet, may Allah bless him and grant him peace, said, "Indeed, [there are] two qualities that I fear for you the most: following desires and wishful thinking. As for following desires, it causes you to swerve from the truth. As for wishful thinking, it makes the temporal world beloved to you."[28]

Al-Tirmidhī relates that Shaddād ibn Aws, may Allah be pleased with him, reports that the Messenger of Allah, may Allah bless him and grant him peace, said, "The prudent person is one who subdues their self[29] and strives for what comes after death, and the slacker is one who follows their desires with vain hope in Allah."[30]

---

27 Al-Bazzār, *Kashf al-Astār*, 80; al-Daylamī, *al-Firdaws*, 2475.

28 Ibn Abi Shayba, 34495; al-Bayhaqī, *Shuʿab al-Imān*, 10613.

29 The *nafs* is a term for that which contains both the aggressive and appetitive drives; it is not evil in and of itself, but necessary for survival. However, the term *hawā* does have a negative connotation as it carries the implication of the *nafs* following the base passions, meaning the excesses or perversions of the appetitive and aggressive drives. This consequently leads to a hedonistic lifestyle and the pursuit of worldly pleasures as opposed to seeking a higher, more meaningful life of seeking Allah's pleasure in submission to Him.

30 al-Tirmidhī, 2459.

The Meaning of Whimsical Carnal Passion (*hawā*)

[The term] *hawā* is a verbal noun of [the word] "to yearn" and "to covet" [that] follows the [same] morphological pattern [as the Arabic word] "to know." It means "to love" and "to crave" something. By nature, the [carnal] self is often inclined towards evil[31] and it emphatically pines for [that which is] wrong. As such, following its urges will inevitably lead to destruction. As for impermissible indulgences, then [such consequent ruin] is [quite] clear. But [even] regarding [the overindulgence in] permissible pleasures, beyond [the fact that] it is [how] animals [are] characterized, it [is indicative of] an [unhealthy] attachment to the temporal world. Such preoccupies a person from [performing] righteous deeds and [accumulating] provisions for the afterlife. Moreover, it drives [one] to that which is prohibited, leading to [all kinds of] evils; it steers towards transgression, fostering the forbidden; it is a hub for anguish and iniquities. The one who follows their desires is despicable, lowly, blameworthy, and [utterly] contemptible. Rather, they are actually [better likened to] an impulsive pig; servile, submissive, and disgracefully enslaved [to their whims].

Poetry:

> *[The letter] nūn [found] in "vileness" (hawān) is stolen from [the word] "passion" (hawā).*
> *Thus, to dominate every passion is to overcome vileness.*

Next, the opposite [of following desires] is striving (*mujāhada*), which entails weaning the [carnal] self from that which is desirous and compelling it to oppose its urges in most instances. Indeed, it is the commodity of the worshippers; the capital of the ascetics; the central axis for the subjugation and refinement of the self; and it is the framework for the soul's strengthening, purification, and achievement.

> O seeker, it is upon you to work diligently towards preventing your [inner] self from [unhealthy] passions; oblige it to strive if you wish to achieve guidance from Allah.
> Allah the Exalted says: *As for those who strive for Us, We will certainly guide them along Our ways* (al- ʿAnkabūt 29:69).

31 In its primitive, unrefined state, it will gradually gravitate towards vile hedonistic pursuits, especially if it is left untrained. But, if it is refined, then it will be of service just as the trained horse leads one to their desired destination despite the horse's original asocial nature that did not like human beings at the outset. Later, this animal comes to love their master and loves the journey with their master.

> *Whosoever strives, strives for their own benefit. Surely Allah is independent of all the worlds* (al-ʿAnkabūt 29:6).

Engaging in Permissible Things to Restore Vitality in Worship is in Accordance with Revealed Texts, and it is Not [The Same as Following One's] Whims: Next, [one should] know that what is blameworthy in following permissible desires is overindulgence. This is because human nature does not tolerate absolute abstinence.[32] It is also because it leads to immoderation and excessiveness, and this point has already been mentioned in a previous chapter indicating that it is forbidden. [Another reason is] because it cultivates weariness and dissatisfaction, which leads to a rather execrable [degree of] inconsistency in worship.

Accordingly, the Prophet, may Allah bless him and grant him peace, said, "O people! [Only] initiate the deeds that you can maintain, for Allah does not become weary, whereas you do. Verily, the most beloved of deeds to Allah are those which are continuous, even if they are few."[33] [This is] transmitted by Bukhārī and Muslim, on the authority of ʿA'isha, may Allah be pleased with her.[34]

Also, in a version [related] by Muslim: "[Only] initiate deeds that you can handle, for by Allah, Allah does not tire, but you do tire."[35]

[It is narrated] on the authority of ʿAlī, may Allah be pleased with him, who said, "Relax the hearts,[36] for if they are strained, they [will] falter."

[It is narrated] on the authority of Abū al-Dardā', may Allah be pleased with him, who stated, "Indeed, I [sometimes] try to relax my soul with entertainment so that it helps me [to be steadfast] upon the truth."[37]

---

32 This is a critical point. Islam does not encourage celibacy or monasticism; rather, it encourages the appropriate moderation of one's desires as opposed to the complete elimination of them.

33 What is desirable is to maintain consistency in performing good actions as opposed to engaging abundantly in some kind of worship followed by its abandonment. This lays down a very important behavioral principle of gradual and realistic change. It is important to draw emphasis on the notion that an individual must come to realistically evaluate their capabilities and then structure their character or behavioral development plan accordingly. Certainly, through steady progress, one can add greater increments of praiseworthy good deeds. However, in many cases, beyond the basic compulsory practices, one should not attempt to initiate actions that they will not be able to perform at all or will perform inconsistently.

34 Al-Bukhārī, 5862; Muslim, 782.

35 Muslim, 785.

36 Al-Suyūṭī, *al-Jāmiʿal-Saghīr*, 4484.

37 Ibid.

It is therefore necessary to occasionally indulge in permissible pleasures to relax after exerting [oneself], so as to avoid exhaustion and to induce vitality in worship. Imam Ḥujjat al-Islām [al-Ghazālī] thus stated, "If a worshiper's fervor were to dwindle and his aspiration [consequently] weakens, then [if he] knows that taking a break to sleep, talk, or joke will revitalize his diligence [in worship], such [would be] better for him than performing prayer with weariness."[38] And so, in actuality, this is in accordance with Islamic ethics (*sharīʿa*), and [it is] not outright [adherence to personal] desires.

An Overview of the Heart's Sicknesses and Reprehensible Characteristics:[39] We shall [now] list an assortment of blameworthy characteristics and pernicious vices so that it is easy for students to memorize them:

Sacrilege (*kufr*), innovation (*bidʿa*); ostentation (*riyāʾ*); arrogance (*kibr*); self-infatuation (*ʿujb*); envy (*ḥasad*); stinginess (*bukhl*); extravagance (*isrāf*); ignorance (*jahl*); ingratitude (*kufrān al-niʿma*); displeasure with [divine] decree (*sakhaṭ li-l-qaḍāʾ*); impatience (*jazaʿ*); [feeling] security [from divine justice] (*aman*); despondency (*yaʾs*); affinity for oppressors (*ḥubb al-ẓalama*); disdain for the righteous (*bughḍ al-ṣāliḥīn*); fixating the heart on [outward] means [instead of depending on Allah] (*taʿlīq al-qalb bi asbāb*); love for prestige (*ḥubb al-jāh*); fear of defamation (*khawf al-dhamm*); love of praise (*hubb al-madḥ*); following whims (*ittibāʿ al-hawā*); [blameworthy] imitation (*taqlīd*); vain hope (*ṭūl al-amal*); greed (*ṭamaʿ*); self-abasement (*tadhallul*); rancor (*ḥiqd*); finding pleasure in another person's pain (*shamāta*); enmity (*ʿadāwa*); cowardice (*jubn*); recklessness (*tahawwur*); treachery (*ghadr*); betrayal (*khiyāna*); violating contracts (*khalf al-waʿd*); ill-thought (*sūʾ al-ẓann*); superstition (*ṭiyara*); love of wealth (*ḥubb al-māl*); infatuation with the world (*ḥubb al-dunyā*); covetousness (*ḥirṣ*); vulgarity (*safah*); idleness (*baṭāla*); hastiness (*ʿajala*); procrastination (*taswīf*); harshness (*faẓāẓa*); insolence (*waqāḥa*); fear and grief over [temporal] worldly matters (*ḥuzn fī amr al-dunyā*); cheating (*ghish*); sedition (*fitna*); sycophancy (*mudāhana*); appeasing created beings [instead of the Creator] (*uns bi makhlūq*); flippancy (*khiffa*), recalcitrance (*ʿinād*), unruliness (*tamarrud*), superciliousness (*ṣalaf*), hypocrisy (*nifāq*), obsession (*jarbaza*), foolishness (*ghabāwa*), edacity (*sharah*), apathy (*khumūd*), and overindulgence (*iṣrār*).

38 Al-Ghazālī, *Iḥyāʾ ʿUlūm al-Dīn*, 4:375.

39 This segment is not a continuation of what precedes it; it is taken from a separate section of al-Birgivī's work.

Aside from what has [already] been mentioned, [here are] some of the praiseworthy characteristics that are contained within and complement [the other virtues]:

Integrity (*istiqāma*): It entails the fulfillment of all covenants, with adherence to justice and balance in all matters. Allah says, *So stay firm as you have been commanded* (Sura Hūd: 112).

Discipline (*adab*): It involves preserving the boundary between extremism and disregard by recognizing the harms of excessiveness.

Foresight (*firāsa*): It is [when] an inspiration stemming from strong faith descends upon the heart, dispelling what contravenes it.

Qushāyrī reports on the authority of Abū Saʿīd al-Khudrī, may Allah be pleased with him, who said, "Beware of the believer's intuition, for indeed he sees with the light of Allah."[40]

Self-reflection (*tafakkur*): [Which involves asking questions such as:] could this be deemed sinful? [If] so, one repents. Or [wondering:] am [I] prone to this? And [thus] exercising caution, whilst thanking Allah for [His gracious] enablement. [One should scrutinize] acts of obedience, [enabling one] to effortfully make up what acts of worship one has missed, and to be guarded against [ever] forsaking them. With that, one is grateful for Allah's assistance for whatever one was able to accomplish. Also, [beholding] Allah's creation and signs within oneself and in the horizons [is also needed]. Through this, one's awareness of Allah's greatness, power, knowledge, and wisdom is increased and amplified. This effectively establishes a love for Allah, a close bond, and [profound] yearning for Him. Allah the Exalted says: *And they ponder over the creation of the heavens and the earth* (Āl-ʿImrān 3:161).

Truthfulness (*ṣidq*): This manifests in seven [domains]:

1. Speech: [which is] the opposite of lying.
2. Intention: [which manifests as] sincerity.
3. Commitment.
4. Determination: [it is] both their firmness coupled with the absence of feebleness or hesitancy.
5. Integrity: [which means] to accomplish and fulfill something as promised and determined.
6. Action: [it entails the external] corresponding to the internal, without suggesting anything else extraneous to it.
7. Fear [of Allah]; [which includes] the strength of it and a [healthy] abundance of it.

40 Al-Qushayrī, *al-Risāla al-Qushayriyya*, 2:386; al-Tirmidhī, 3127; al-Ṭabarānī, *al-Awsaṭ*, 3254.

The [hyperbolic title] "truthful one" (*ṣiddīq*) is [afforded to] the one who possesses all the above-mentioned qualities.

Self-mastery: This [requires] committing oneself to the obedience of Allah in five [ways]:

1. Conditioning oneself to forsake sin first and foremost, whilst establishing a regular routine of spiritual practices and litanies for each day and night.
2. Closely observing and monitoring the heart to [ensure it is pure and presentable to] Allah, the Omniscient. [This is accomplished] by [inculcating] a continual awareness that the Lord oversees [all] – during, before, and after each [and every] action. [One should ask:] am I fulfilling what is required [exactly] as it should be done, or is something amiss?
3. Self-evaluation after [completing] each deed; have all requirements been completed [properly] or [is something] lacking?
4. Reprimanding
5. Or rebuking [oneself] for any deficiency. [This is done] with the likes of [self-induced] hunger and thirst, staying up at night, vowing to give charity, and similar acts that ensure one does not repeat the same [error] again.

The total of what was referenced [in this work] regarding good morals is seventy-eight:

Faithfulness (*īmān*); [adhering to] the Sunni creed (*iʿtiqād ahl al-sunna wa al-jamāʿa*); sincerity (*ikhlāṣ*); excellence (*iḥsān*); humbleness (*ṭawāḍuʿ*); acknowledging favors (*dhikr manna*); sincerely wishing well [for others] (*naṣīḥa*); spiritual reform (*taṣawwuf*); protective jealousy (*ghayra*); competitive desire for deeds [valued] in the Hereafter (*ghibṭa fī ʿamal al-ākhira*); munificence (*sakhāʾ*); altruism (*īthār*); civility (*murūʾa*); innocence (*futuwwa*); wisdom (*ḥikma*); gratitude (*shukr*); contentment (*riḍāʾ*); patience (*ṣabr*); fear of Allah (*khawf min Allah*); [enduring] grief for His sake (*ḥuzn lahū*); hope (*rajāʾ*); enmity for Allah's sake (*bughḍ fī Allāh*); love for Allah's sake (*ḥubb fī-llāh*); dependence [upon Him] (*tawakkul*); relishing placidity (*ḥubb khamūl*); indifference to praise and criticism (*istawāʾ dham wa madḥ*); striving (*mujāhada*); inquiry (*taḥqīq*); [having] realistic expectations (*qaṣr amal*); the remembrance of death (*dhikr mawt*); deference (*tafwīḍ*); acquiescence (*taslīm*); esteem for the seeking of [beneficial] knowledge (*tamalluq fī ṭalab al-ʿilm*); freedom from rancor in the heart (*salāmat al-ṣadr ʿan al-ḥiqd*); bravery (*shajāʿa*); forbearance (*ḥilm*); leniency (*rifq*); deliberation (*anāt*); upholding agreements (*wafāʾ bi-l-ʿahd*); fulfilling promises (*injāz al-waʿd*); thinking well [of others] (*ḥusn al-dhann*); asceticism (*zuhd*); satisfaction (*qanāʿa*); discretion (*rushd*); exerting effort [for good] (*saʿy*); penitence (*ināba*); [taking] initiative in acts related to the Hereafter (*mubādira fī ʿamal al-ākhira*); tenderness (*riqqa*); [genuine] concern (*shafaqa*); modesty (*ḥayāʾ*); firmness in [crucial] matters of religion (*ṣalāba fī amr dīn*); [seeking] comfort with Allah (*uns bi Allāh*); yearning for Allah (*shawq ilayhi*); loving Allah (*maḥabbat Allāh*); dignity (*waqār*); intelligence (*dhakāʾ*); temperance (*ʿiffa*); integrity (*istiqāma*); discipline (*adab*); foresight (*firāsa*); self-reflection (*tafakkur*); honesty (*ṣidq*); self-mastery (*murābaṭa*); accountability (*musharaṭa*); self-analysis (*murāqaba*); self-evaluation (*muḥāsaba*); [corrective] self-reproach (*muʿāqaba*) and reprimand (*muʿātaba*); suppressing anger (*kaẓm ghayẓ*); clemency (*ʿafw*); [good] intentions (*niyya*); desiring a long life for [the purpose of] worship (*irāda ṭūl ḥayā li-l-ʿibāda*); repentance (*tawba*); reverent humility (*khushūʿ*); certainty (*yaqīn*); servanthood [to Allah] (*ʿubūdiyya*); independence [of creation] (*ḥuriyya*); purpose (*irāda*).

The Roots[41] of Virtue:[42]

The advanced seekers and those who traverse their path have a [distinct] method for delineating virtuous [characteristics] and their parameters. There is no harm in listing them even if some repetition occurs. Such is not without benefit; namely, this [aids in] determining their roots and branching them out into each of their associated subcategories.

You have already come to know that there are four [main] roots of virtue; three of them are distinct [from one another]: wisdom (*ḥikma*), valor (*shajāʿa*), and temperance (*ʿiffa*). The [remaining] one – justice (*ʿadāla*) – is manifested as a combination of the three.

Subvirtues of Wisdom:

a. **Clarity of mind** (*ṣafāʾ al-dhihn*): [It is] the psyche's ability to distinguish matters without confusion.
b. **Sound comprehension** (*jawdat al-fahm*): [It is the ability] to deduce accurate conclusions from evidence.

---

41 Imam al-Birgivī has taken this section verbatim from Imam al-Ījī's al-Akhlāq al-ʿAdudiya. As mentioned earlier, given its widespread memorization and acceptance in Ottoman seminaries, it is being utilized as a primary reference here and is quoted exactly as it was presented in the original work.

42 Virtue ethics is a category of normative ethical theories that aims to explore and embody a life guided by moral character. It not only highlights the importance of moral virtues but also emphasizes the relationship between moral conduct and eudaimonia. Eudaimonia refers to the state attained by individuals who live a virtuous and fulfilling human life, an achievement that can be realized through the practice of virtues. In essence, by cultivating qualities such as honesty, justice, and generosity, individuals develop a moral character (Louis P. Pojman and James Fieser, *Ethics: Discovering Right and Wrong*, Eighth edition (Boston, MA: Cengage Learning, 2017), 146–69).

c. **Fluid intelligence** (*dhakāʾ*): [It constitutes] expeditiousness in deriving conclusions.
d. **Sound conceptualization** (ḥusn al-taṣawwur): [It entails] examining things to their [proper] extent.
e. **Ease of learning** (*suhūlat al-taʿallum*): [It is] the psyche's faculty to grasp ideas without excessive effort.
f. **Memory** (*ḥifẓ*): [It involves] the retention of images captured [by the mind].
g. **Recollection** (*dhikr*): [The ability] to [actively] recall that which is committed to memory.

Subvirtues of Valor:
a. **Vast-heartedness** (*kibr al-nafs*): [To] disdain opulence, dependance, arrogance, and inferiority.
b. **Clemency** (*ʿafuw*): Easily forsaking retribution despite having the capability [to exact it].
c. **Perseverance** (*ʿiẓam al-himma*): Unrelenting in the face of life's pleasures and pains.
d. **Patience** (*ṣabr*): The faculty to withstand various types of agony and pain.
e. **Courage** (*najda*): A lack of anxiety in relation to the creation.
f. **Forbearance** (*ḥilm*): Composure [at times] when anger is incited.
g. **Serenity** (*sukūn*): Deliberation in the face of arguments and conflicts.
h. **Humility** (*tawāḍuʿ*): Duly honoring those with virtue, as well as those with comparably less wealth and prestige.
i. **Resolve** (*shahāma*): A determination to perform extraordinary tasks that are commemorated as admirable [actions].
j. **Endurance** (*iḥtimāl*): Travailing oneself in [performing] good deeds.
k. **Protectiveness** (*ḥamiyya*): [A sense of] defensiveness against attacks on sacred matters and religion.
l. **Compassion** (*riqqa*): To empathize with another person's pain.

Subvirtues of Temperance:
a. **Modesty** (*ḥayāʾ*): Restraining oneself for fear of committing indecencies.
b. **Self-regulation** (*ṣabr*): Inhibiting oneself from pursuing whims.
c. **Self-restraint** (*diʿa*): [Maintaining] composure when appetites are roused.
d. **Probity** (*nazāha*): Appropriating wealth without disgrace or injustice and [likewise] spending it in commendable ways.
e. **Contentment** (*qanāʿa*): [Acquiescently] limiting [oneself] to that which suffices.

f. **Dignity** (*waqār*): Deliberation when proceeding toward [one's] objectives.
g. **Agreeableness** (*rifq*): Excellent tractability that [effectively] promotes courtesy.
h. **Civility** (*ḥusn al-samt*): Love for personal accomplishment.
i. **Piety** (*waraʿ*): Adhering to [the performance of] reverential deeds.
j. **Goodwill** (*murūʾa*): A genuine inner desire for others to benefit as much as possible.
k. **Orderliness** (*intiẓām*): Prioritizing and organizing all of one's affairs based on superior goals.
l. **Generosity** (*sakhāʾ*): To give what is appropriate to those for whom it is appropriate; there are six variations of this subvirtue:
    a. **Bountifulness** (*karam*): Giving openheartedly, with ease.
    b. **Altruism** (*īthār*): [To give] whilst forgoing one's own needs.
    c. **Acceptance** (*nayl*): To be cheerfully [accepting].
    d. **Openhandedness** (*muāsāt*): To mutually share with friends.
    e. **Munificence** (*samāḥa*): To spend extra when it is not required.
    f. **Leniency** (*musāmaḥa*): Voluntarily forgoing what one does not need.

Subvirtues of Justice:

a. **Sincere friendship** (*ṣadāqa*): [It is] genuine amity that is untainted by ulterior motives, and to give preference over oneself in matters of goodness.
b. **Compatibility** (*ulfa*): [It involves] the harmonizing of viewpoints to cooperate in managing the demands of life.
c. **Loyalty** (*wafāʾ*): [It entails] adhering to the path of equity and upholding all agreements with one's cohorts.
d. **Affection** (*tawaddud*): To seek the affection of one's peers through [behaviors] that engender this.
e. **Reciprocity** (*mukāfaʾa*): To complement goodness with its like or what is better than it.
f. **Excellence in partnership** (*ḥusn al-sharika*): To uphold balance in one's interactions.
g. **Excellence in recompense** (*ḥusn al-qaḍā*): To compensate others without [causing them] remorse or [reminding them of one's] favors.
h. **Familial connection** (*ṣilat al-raḥm*): To direct acts of goodness towards one's relatives.
i. **Harm reduction** (*shafaqa*): To direct [one's] energy towards the removal of that which is disliked by others.

j. **Reconciliation** (*iṣlāḥ*): [It involves acting as] an intermediary between people in discrepancies to bring about a settlement.
k. **Reliance on Allah** (*tawakkul*): [It necessitates] abandoning efforts [to attempt] that which is not humanly possible.
l. **Surrender** (*taslīm*): To submit to Allah's commands and refraining from objecting to that which one deems unsuitable.
m. **Satisfaction** (*riḍā*): To maintain a calmness of spirit towards afflictions and losses, without [wishing] to change [the outcome].
n. **Servitude** (*ʿibāda*): To show reverence to Allah as is [rightfully] due to Him, and to adhere to His commands.

In conclusion, the roots of virtue and their subcategories total fifty-five; there are thirty additional virtues beyond what we have already mentioned.

It is [incumbent] upon you, O seeker, to take due precaution against, and resist, all the aforementioned evil traits whilst [carefully] safeguarding their [corresponding] opposites alongside the remaining [other] virtues. [Focus on] extirpating and removing them whilst simultaneously acquiring their counter virtues as well as all the other virtuous traits until they become [deeply] imbibed, or [until] the purification of the self, soul, and heart is attained. Indeed, spirituality (*taṣawwuf*) and its path (*ṭarīqa*) are terms that encompass these matters.

Especially [regarding] the seven vices, they are the roots of all evils. Hopefully, if you are saved from those you shall be saved from others as well. They are Sacrilege (*kufr*), innovation (*bidʿa*), ostentation (*riyāʾ*), arrogance (*kibr*), envy (*hasad*), stinginess (*bukhl*), and wastefulness (*isrāf*).

2 Chapter on *Waswasa*. *Mirqāt al-Mafātīḥ* by Mulla ʿAlī al-Qarī (d. 1014 AH/1620 CE)

2.1 *Author's Biography*

Imam Nūr al-Dīn Abū al-Hasan ʿAlī ibn Sulṭān Muḥammad al-Qārī al-Ḥarawī, more famously known as Mulla ʿAlī al-Qārī, was an accomplished Islamic scholar. Despite his depth of knowledge in various fields, it was his expertise in reciting the Quran that earned him the title "al-Qārī." Born in Herat, Afghanistan, he began his pursuit of knowledge under the guidance of local scholars before embarking on a journey to Makkah in search of further sacred learning.

Al-Qārī possessed exceptional calligraphy skills and annually crafted handwritten copies of the Quran for sale. The proceeds from these endeavors sustained him and his scholarly pursuits throughout the year. Amongst Hanafi scholars, he was recognized as an authority in the sciences of Hadīth, jurisprudence, and spirituality.

Included amongst his esteemed works are his commentaries on *Miskhāt al-Maṣābīḥ*, Qādī 'Iyyād's *al-Shifa'*, and the *Shamā'il* compiled by Imam al-Tirmidhī. Imam al-Qārī passed away in the year 1014 AH and was laid to rest within the sacred precincts of Makkah. His legacy endures as an exemplar of scholarship and spirituality; many of his works are still widely studied and taught throughout the Islamic world until today.

2.2 *Text Overview and Significance*

Mulla ʿAlī al-Qarī's *Mirqāt al-Mafātīḥ* stands as one of the most renowned Arabic commentaries on the famous compilation *Mishkāt al-Maṣābīḥ*, by the distinguished Hanafi traditionalist, Muḥammad Khatīb al-Tabrīzī. *Mishkat al-Maṣabīḥ* is a compilation of Prophetic statements encompassing various subjects, with an aim to provide readers with a comprehensive understanding of the Islamic tradition through the words of the Prophet Muhammad, may Allah bless him and grant him peace.

The translated segment below presents a collection of Prophetic narrations that address the concept of *waswasa*, which refers to intrusive thoughts and inclinations instigated by the devil. In his commentary, Mulla ʿAlī Qārī, offers a systematic classification of the thoughts that human beings may experience. He distinguishes between ruminative thoughts related to actions such as prayer and fasting, and mental obsessions like blasphemy. Furthermore, he delves into the question of whether individuals are held accountable for their thoughts in Islam, exploring diverse scholarly perspectives on the matter.

In summary, al-Qārī concludes that accountability primarily pertains to voluntary actions, thereby indicating that non-volitional thoughts do not bear the weight of accountability in Islam. This scholarly discussion analyzing the nature of thoughts, their impact on behavior, and other related considerations illustrate the depth and precision of Islamic scholarly discourse. Such a classification of thoughts and its legal implications can offer valuable insights for clinical treatment, particularly in addressing anxiety disorders and religious obsessive compulsive disorders (OCD) associated with excessive scrupulosity.

2.3 *Arabic Text*

بَاب الْوَسْوَسَة
الْفَصْلُ الْأَوَّلُ

63 – عَنْ أَبِي هُرَيْرَةَ رَضِيَ اللَّهُ عَنْهُ قَالَ: قَالَ رَسُولُ اللَّهِ – صَلَّى اللَّهُ عَلَيْهِ وَسَلَّمَ – : "«إِنَّ اللَّهَ (تعالى) تَجَاوَزَ عَنْ أُمَّتِي مَا وَسْوَسَتْ بِهِ صُدُورُهَا، مَا لَمْ تَعْمَلْ بِهِ، أَوْ تَتَكَلَّمْ»" مُتَّفَقٌ عَلَيْهِ.

بَابٌ فِي الْوَسْوَسَةِ

الْخَوَاطِرُ إِنْ كَانَتْ تَدْعُو إِلَى الرَّذَائِلِ فَهِيَ وَسْوَسَةٌ، وَإِنْ كَانَتْ إِلَى الْفَضَائِلِ فَهِيَ إِلْهَامٌ، وَالْأَصَحُّ أَنَّهُ لَيْسَ بِحُجَّةٍ مِنْ غَيْرِ الْمَعْصُومِ؛ لِأَنَّهُ لَا ثِقَةَ بِخَوَاطِرِهِ.

(الْفَصْلُ الْأَوَّلُ)

63 – (عَنْ أَبِي هُرَيْرَةَ رَضِيَ اللَّهُ عَنْهُ قَالَ: قَالَ رَسُولُ اللَّهِ – صَلَّى اللَّهُ عَلَيْهِ وَسَلَّمَ – : (إِنَّ اللَّهَ تَجَاوَزَ) أَيْ: عَفَا (عَنْ أُمَّتِي) أَيْ: أُمَّةِ الْإِجَابَةِ، وَفِي رِوَايَةٍ: "تَجَاوَزَ لِي عَنْ أُمَّتِي"، أَيْ: لَمْ يُؤَاخِذْهُمْ بِذَلِكَ لِأَجْلِي فَلَهُ الْمِنَّةُ الْعُظْمَى الَّتِي لَا مُنْتَهَى لَهَا عَلَيْنَا (مَا وَسْوَسَتْ بِهِ صُدُورُهَا) : بِالرَّفْعِ فَاعِلًا أَيْ: مَا خَطَرَ فِي قُلُوبِهِمْ مِنَ الْخَوَاطِرِ الرَّدِيئَةِ، فَهُوَ مِنْ مَجَازِ الْمُجَاوَرَةِ، وَيَجُوزُ نَصْبُهُ مَفْعُولًا بِهِ. قِيلَ: فِيهِ نَظَرٌ؛ لِأَنَّ الْوَسْوَسَةَ لَازِمٌ، لَنِعْمَ وَجْهُ النَّصْبِ الظَّرْفِيَّةُ إِنْ سَاعَدَتْهُ الرِّوَايَةُ، وَرُوِيَ مَا حَدَّثَتْ بِهِ أَنْفُسُهَا بِالرَّفْعِ، وَالنَّصْبُ بَدَلُهُ (مَا لَمْ تَعْمَلْ بِهِ) أَيْ: مَا دَامَ لَمْ يَتَعَلَّقْ بِهِ الْعَمَلُ إِنْ كَانَ فِعْلِيًّا (أَوْ تَكَلَّمَ) : بِهِ أَيْ: مَا لَمْ تَتَكَلَّمْ بِهِ إِنْ كَانَ قَوْلِيًّا كَذَا فِي الْأَزْهَارِ، قَالَ صَاحِبُ الرَّوْضَةِ فِي شَرْحِ صَحِيحِ الْبُخَارِيِّ: الْمَذْهَبُ الصَّحِيحُ الْمُخْتَارُ الَّذِي عَلَيْهِ الْجُمْهُورُ أَنَّ أَفْعَالَ الْقُلُوبِ إِذَا اسْتَقَرَّتْ يُؤَاخَذُ بِهَا، فَقَوْلُهُ – صَلَّى اللَّهُ عَلَيْهِ وَسَلَّمَ –: «إِنَّ اللَّهَ تَجَاوَزَ عَنْ أُمَّتِي مَا وَسْوَسَتْ بِهِ صُدُورُهَا» مَحْمُولٌ عَلَى مَا إِذَا لَمْ تَسْتَقِرَّ، وَذَلِكَ مَعْفُوٌّ بِلَا شَكٍّ؛ لِأَنَّهُ لَا يُمْكِنُ الِانْفِكَاكُ عَنْهُ بِخِلَافِ الِاسْتِقْرَارِ، ثُمَّ نَقَلَ صَاحِبُ الْأَزْهَارِ عَنِ الْإِحْيَاءِ مَا حَاصِلُهُ: أَنَّ لِأَعْمَالِ الْقَلْبِ أَرْبَعَ مَرَاتِبَ. الْأَوَّلُ: الْخَاطِرُ كَمَا لَوْ خَطَرَ لَهُ صُورَةُ امْرَأَةٍ مَثَلًا خَلْفَ ظَهْرِهِ فِي الطَّرِيقِ لَوِ الْتَفَتَ إِلَيْهَا يَرَاهَا. وَالثَّانِي: هَيَجَانُ الرَّغْبَةِ إِلَى الِالْتِفَاتِ إِلَيْهَا، وَنُسَمِّيهِ مَيْلُ الطَّبْعِ، وَالْأَوَّلُ حَدِيثُ النَّفْسِ، وَالثَّالِثُ: حُكْمُ الْقَلْبِ بِأَنْ يَفْعَلَ أَيْ: يَنْظُرُ إِلَيْهَا فَإِنَّ الطَّبْعَ إِذَا مَالَ لَمْ تَنْدَفِعِ الْهِمَّةُ وَالنِّيَّةُ، مَا لَمْ تَنْدَفِعَ الصَّوَارِفُ، وَهِيَ الْحَيَاءُ، وَالْخَوْفُ مِنَ اللَّهِ تَعَالَى، أَوْ مِنْ عِبَادِهِ، وَنُسَمِّيهِ اعْتِقَادًا. وَالرَّابِعُ: تَصْمِيمُ الْعَزْمِ عَلَى الِالْتِفَاتِ، وَجَزْمِ النِّيَّةِ فِيهِ، وَنُسَمِّيهِ عَزْمًا بِالْقَلْبِ، أَمَّا الْخَاطِرُ فَلَا يُؤَاخَذُ بِهِ، وَكَذَا الْمَيْلُ، وَهَيَجَانُ الرَّغْبَةِ؛ لِأَنَّهُمَا لَا يَدْخُلَانِ تَحْتَ الِاخْتِيَارِ، وَهُمَا الْمُرَادَانِ بِقَوْلِهِ – عَلَيْهِ الصَّلَاةُ وَالسَّلَامُ –: (إِنَّ اللَّهَ تَجَاوَزَ عَنْ أُمَّتِي) الْحَدِيثَ. وَأَمَّا الثَّالِثُ، وَهُوَ الِاعْتِقَادُ: فَهُوَ مُرَدَّدٌ بَيْنَ أَنْ يَكُونَ اخْتِيَارًا لَا يُنْكِرُهُ، وَاضْطِرَارًا يُنْكِرُهُ، فَالِاخْتِيَارِيُّ يُؤَاخَذُ،

وَالِاضْطِرَارِيُّ لَا يُؤَاخَذُ، وَأَمَّا الرَّابِعُ وَهُوَ الْعَزْمُ، وَالْهَمُّ بِالْفِعْلِ، فَإِنَّهُ يُؤَاخَذُ بِهِ، وَعَلَيْهِ تَنْزِلُ الْآيَاتُ الَّتِي دَلَّتْ عَلَى مُؤَاخَذَةِ أَعْمَالِ الْقُلُوبِ إِلَّا أَنَّهُ إِنْ تَرَكَ خَوْفًا مِنَ اللَّهِ تَعَالَى كُتِبَتْ لَهُ حَسَنَةٌ؛ لِأَنَّ هَمَّهُ سَيِّئَةٌ، وَامْتِنَاعَهُ عَنْهَا مُجَاهَدَةٌ مَعَ نَفْسِهِ فَتَكُونُ حَسَنَةً تَزِيدُ عَلَيْهَا، وَإِنْ تَرَكَهَا لِعَائِقٍ، أَوْ فَاتَهَا ذَلِكَ لِعَدَمِ الْحُصُولِ كُتِبَتْ عَلَيْهِ سَيِّئَةٌ لِلْعَزْمِ، وَالْهِمَّةِ الْجَازِمَةِ، وَالدَّلِيلُ الْقَاطِعُ عَلَى ذَلِكَ قَوْلُ رَسُولِ اللَّهِ – صَلَّى اللَّهُ عَلَيْهِ وَسَلَّمَ – فِي الْحَدِيثِ الصَّحِيحِ الْمُتَّفَقِ عَلَى صِحَّتِهِ: (إِذَا الْتَقَى الْمُسْلِمَانِ بِسَيْفَيْهِمَا فَالْقَاتِلُ، وَالْمَقْتُولُ فِي النَّارِ) قِيلَ: يَا رَسُولَ اللَّهِ فَمَا بَالُ الْمَقْتُولِ؟ قَالَ: (إِنَّهُ كَانَ حَرِيصًا عَلَى قَتْلِ صَاحِبِهِ). وَهَذَا صَرِيحٌ فِي أَنَّهُ صَارَ إِلَى النَّارِ، وَوَقَعَ فِيهَا بِمُجَرَّدِ الْعَزْمِ، وَالنِّيَّةِ، وَإِنْ مَاتَ وَلَمْ يَعْمَلْ وَقُتِلَ مَظْلُومًا، وَكَيْفَ لَا يُؤَاخَذُ بِأَعْمَالِ الْقَلْبِ الْجَازِمَةِ، وَالْكِبْرُ، وَالْعُجْبُ، وَالنِّفَاقُ، وَالْحَسَدُ، وَغَيْرُهَا مِنَ الْأَوْصَافِ الذَّمِيمَةِ يُؤَاخَذُ بِهَا. وَقَالَ رَسُولُ اللَّهِ – صَلَّى اللَّهُ عَلَيْهِ وَسَلَّمَ –: (الْإِثْمُ مَا حَاكَ فِي الصَّدْرِ). وَقَالَ: (الْبِرُّ مَا اطْمَئِنَّ إِلَيْهِ الْقَلْبُ، وَاطْمَأَنَّتْ إِلَيْهِ النَّفْسُ، وَالْإِثْمُ مَا حَاكَ فِي نَفْسِكَ، وَتَرَدَّدَ فِي صَدْرِكَ، وَإِنْ أَفْتَاكَ النَّاسُ) اهـ.

أَقُولُ: الِاسْتِدْلَالُ بِالْحَدِيثِ الْأَخِيرِ فِيهِ نَظَرٌ؛ لِأَنَّهُ جَعَلَ الْإِثْمَ عَيْنَ مَا تَرَدَّدَ فِي الصَّدْرِ، وَتَقَدَّمَ أَنَّ مَا لَمْ يَسْتَقِرَّ لَا يَكُونُ إِثْمًا، فَمَعْنَى الْحَدِيثِ أَنَّ مَا تَرَدَّدَ فِي الصَّدْرِ أَنَّهُ إِثْمٌ أَوْ غَيْرُ إِثْمٍ فَفِعْلُهُ إِثْمٌ احْتِيَاطًا، كَمَا إِذَا تَعَارَضَ دَلِيلُ التَّحْرِيمِ، وَالتَّحْلِيلِ فِي شَيْءٍ فَيَحْرُمُ. قِيلَ: الْحَدِيثُ يَدُلُّ عَلَى أَنَّ التَّجَاوُزَ الْمَذْكُورَ خَاصِّيَّةُ هَذِهِ الْأُمَّةِ، وَعَلَى التَّوْجِيهِ الَّذِي نَقَلَهُ صَاحِبُ الْأَزْهَارِ مِنَ الرَّوْضَةِ وَالْإِحْيَاءِ يَلْزَمُ أَنَّهُ يَكُونُ عَامًّا لِجَمِيعِ الْأُمَمِ؛ لِأَنَّ مَا لَا يَدْخُلُ تَحْتَ الِاخْتِيَارِ لَا يُؤَاخَذُ بِهِ شَخْصٌ مِنَ الْأَشْخَاصِ لِقَوْلِهِ تَعَالَى: ﴿لَا يُكَلِّفُ اللَّهُ نَفْسًا إِلَّا وُسْعَهَا﴾ [البقرة: 286] فَالصَّوَابُ مَا قَالَهُ الطِّيبِيُّ مِنْ أَنَّ الْوَسْوَسَةَ ضَرُورِيَّةٌ، وَاخْتِيَارِيَّةٌ، فَالضَّرُورِيَّةُ: مَا يَجْرِي فِي الصُّدُورِ مِنَ الْخَوَاطِرِ ابْتِدَاءً، وَلَا يَقْدِرُ الْإِنْسَانُ عَلَى دَفْعِهِ، فَهُوَ مَعْفُوٌّ عَنْ جَمِيعِ الْأُمَمِ، وَالِاخْتِيَارِيَّةُ: هِيَ الَّتِي تَجْرِي فِي الْقَلْبِ، وَتَسْتَمِرُّ، وَهُوَ يَقْصِدُ، وَيَعْمَلُ بِهِ، وَيَتَلَذَّذُ مِنْهُ كَمَا يَجْرِي فِي قَلْبِهِ حُبُّ امْرَأَةٍ، وَيَدُومُ عَلَيْهِ، وَيَقْصِدُ الْوُصُولَ إِلَيْهَا، وَمَا أَشْبَهَ ذَلِكَ مِنَ الْمَعَاصِي، فَهَذَا النَّوْعُ عَفَا اللَّهُ عَنْ هَذِهِ الْأُمَّةِ خَاصَّةً تَعْظِيمًا، وَتَكْرِيمًا لِنَبِيِّنَا – عَلَيْهِ الصَّلَاةُ وَالسَّلَامُ –، وَأُمَّتِهِ، وَإِلَيْهِ يَنْظُرُ قَوْلُهُ تَعَالَى: ﴿رَبَّنَا وَلَا تَحْمِلْ عَلَيْنَا إِصْرًا كَمَا حَمَلْتَهُ عَلَى الَّذِينَ مِنْ قَبْلِنَا﴾ [البقرة: 286] وَأَمَّا الْعَقَائِدُ الْفَاسِدَةُ، وَمَسَاوِئُ الْأَخْلَاقِ، وَمَا يَنْضَمُّ إِلَى ذَلِكَ فَإِنَّهَا بِمَعْزِلٍ عَنِ الدُّخُولِ فِي جُمْلَةِ مَا وَسْوَسَتْ بِهِ الصُّدُورُ اهـ.

وَهُوَ كَلَامٌ حَسَنٌ. وَلِهَذَا قَيَّدَهُ النَّبِيُّ – صَلَّى اللَّهُ عَلَيْهِ وَسَلَّمَ – بِقَوْلِهِ: (مَا لَمْ تَعْمَلْ، أَوْ تَتَكَلَّمْ) إِشَارَةٌ إِلَى أَنَّ وَسُوسَةَ الْأَعْمَالِ وَالْأَقْوَالِ مَعْفُوَّةٌ قَبْلَ ارْتِكَابِهَا، وَأَمَّا الْوَسْوَسَةُ الَّتِي لَا تَعَلُّقَ لَهَا بِالْعَمَلِ وَالْكَلَامِ مِنَ الْأَخْلَاقِ وَالْعَقَائِدِ فَهِيَ ذُنُوبٌ بِالِاسْتِقْرَارِ. وَذَكَرَ الْإِمَامُ النَّوَوِيُّ أَنَّ مَذْهَبَ الْقَاضِي أَبِي بَكْرِ بْنَ الطَّيِّبِ أَنَّ مَنْ عَزَمَ عَلَى الْمَعْصِيَةِ وَوَطَّنَ نَفْسَهُ عَلَيْهَا أَثِمَ فِي اعْتِقَادِهِ وَعَزْمِهِ، وَيُحْمَلُ مَا وَقَعَ فِي أَمْثَالِ قَوْلِهِ – عَلَيْهِ الصَّلَاةُ وَالسَّلَامُ –: (إِذَا هَمَّ

عَبْدِي بِسَيِّئَةٍ فَلَا تَكْتُبُوا عَلَيْهِ فَإِنْ عَمِلَهَا فَاكْتُبُوهَا سَيِّئَةً) الْحَدِيثَ فِيمَنْ لَمْ يُوَطِّنْ نَفْسَهُ عَلَى الْمَعْصِيَةِ، وَإِنَّمَا مَرَّ ذَلِكَ بِفِكْرٍ مِنْ غَيْرِ اسْتِقْرَارٍ، وَيُسَمَّى هَذَا هَمًّا، وَيُفَرِّقُ بَيْنَ الْهَمِّ وَالْعَزْمِ، وَهَذَا مَذْهَبُ الْقَاضِي أَبِي بَكْرٍ، وَخَالَفَهُ كَثِيرٌ مِنَ الْفُقَهَاءِ وَالْمُحَدِّثِينَ وَأَخَذُوا بِظَاهِرِ الْحَدِيثِ. وَقَالَ الْقَاضِي عِيَاضٌ: عَامَّةُ السَّلَفِ وَأَهْلُ الْعِلْمِ مِنَ الْفُقَهَاءِ وَالْمُحَدِّثِينَ عَلَى مَا ذَهَبَ إِلَيْهِ الْقَاضِي أَبُو بَكْرٍ لِلْأَحَادِيثِ الدَّالَّةِ عَلَى الْمُؤَاخَذَةِ بِأَعْمَالِ الْقُلُوبِ، لَكِنَّهُمْ قَالُوا: إِنَّ هَذَا الْعَزْمَ يُكْتَبُ سَيِّئَةً، وَلَيْسَتِ السَّيِّئَةُ الَّتِي هَمَّ بِهَا لِكَوْنِهَا لَمْ يَعْمَلْهَا، وَقَطَعَ عَنْهَا قَاطِعٌ غَيْرُ خَوْفِ اللَّهِ تَعَالَى وَالْإِنَابَةِ، لَكِنَّ الْإِصْرَارَ وَالْعَزْمَ مَعْصِيَةٌ، فَصَارَ تَرْكُهُ لِخَوْفِ اللَّهِ تَعَالَى وَمُجَاهَدَتِهِ نَفْسَهُ الْأَمَّارَةِ حَسَنَةً، فَأَمَّا الْهَمُّ الَّذِي لَا يُكْتَبُ فَهِيَ الْخَوَاطِرُ الَّتِي لَا يُوَطِّنُ النَّفْسَ عَلَيْهَا، وَلَا يَصْحَبُهَا عَقْدٌ وَلَا نِيَّةٌ وَعَزْمٌ، وَذَكَرَ بَعْضُ الْمُتَكَلِّمِينَ خِلَافًا فِيمَا إِذَا تَرَكَهَا لِغَيْرِ خَوْفِ اللَّهِ تَعَالَى بَلْ لِخَوْفِ النَّاسِ هَلْ تُكْتَبُ حَسَنَةً؟ قَالَ: لَا، لِأَنَّهُ إِنَّمَا حَمَلَهُ عَلَى تَرْكِهَا الْحَيَاءُ، وَهَذَا الْخِلَافُ ضَعِيفٌ لَا وَجْهَ لَهُ. هَذَا آخِرُ كَلَامِ الْقَاضِي، وَهُوَ ظَاهِرٌ حَسَنٌ لَا مَزِيدَ عَلَيْهِ، وَقَدْ تَظَاهَرَتْ نُصُوصُ الشَّرْعِ بِالْمُؤَاخَذَةِ بِعَزْمِ الْقَلْبِ الْمُسْتَقِرِّ، مِنْ ذَلِكَ قَوْلُهُ تَعَالَى: ﴿إِنَّ الَّذِينَ يُحِبُّونَ أَنْ تَشِيعَ الْفَاحِشَةُ فِي الَّذِينَ آمَنُوا لَهُمْ عَذَابٌ أَلِيمٌ﴾ [النور: 19] وَقَوْلُهُ: ﴿اجْتَنِبُوا كَثِيرًا مِنَ الظَّنِّ إِنَّ بَعْضَ الظَّنِّ إِثْمٌ﴾ [الحجرات: 12] وَالْآيَاتُ فِي هَذَا كَثِيرَةٌ. وَقَدْ تَظَاهَرَتْ نُصُوصُ الشَّرْعِ وَإِجْمَاعُ الْعُلَمَاءِ عَلَى تَحْرِيمِ الْحَسَدِ، وَاحْتِقَارِ الْمُسْلِمِينَ، وَإِرَادَةُ الْمَكْرُوهِ بِهِمْ، وَغَيْرِ ذَلِكَ مِنْ أَعْمَالِ الْقُلُوبِ وَعَزْمِهَا، وَقَدْ تَقَدَّمَ الْفَرْقُ بَيْنَ مَا لَهُ تَعَلُّقٌ بِالْعَمَلِ وَبَيْنَ مَا لَيْسَ لَهُ تَعَلُّقٌ بِهِ، وَاللَّهُ تَعَالَى أَعْلَمُ. وَقِيلَ: يُؤَاخَذُ بِالْهَمِّ بِالْمَعْصِيَةِ فِي حَرَمِ مَكَّةَ دُونَ غَيْرِهَا، وَهُوَ رِوَايَةٌ عَنْ أَحْمَدَ، وَبِهِ قَالَ ابْنُ مَسْعُودٍ لِقَوْلِهِ تَعَالَى: ﴿وَمَنْ يُرِدْ فِيهِ بِإِلْحَادٍ بِظُلْمٍ﴾ [الحج: 25] الْآيَةَ. وَيُرَدُّ بِأَنَّ الْإِرَادَةَ هِيَ الْقَصْدُ، وَهُوَ الْعَزْمُ الَّذِي هُوَ أَخَصُّ مِنَ الْهَمِّ. (مُتَّفَقٌ عَلَيْهِ) فِي الْجَامِعِ الصَّغِيرِ: رَوَاهُ الْجَمَاعَةُ عَنْ أَبِي هُرَيْرَةَ بِلَفْظِ: (إِنَّ اللَّهَ تَجَاوَزَ لِأُمَّتِي عَمَّا حَدَّثَتْ بِهِ أَنْفُسَهَا مَا لَمْ تَتَكَلَّمْ، أَوْ تَعْمَلْ بِهِ) .

64 – وَعَنْهُ قَالَ: «جَاءَ نَاسٌ مِنْ أَصْحَابِ رَسُولِ اللَّهِ – صَلَّى اللَّهُ عَلَيْهِ وَسَلَّمَ – إِلَى النَّبِيِّ – صَلَّى اللَّهُ عَلَيْهِ وَسَلَّمَ –، فَسَأَلُوهُ: إِنَّا نَجِدُ فِي أَنْفُسِنَا مَا يَتَعَاظَمُ أَحَدُنَا أَنْ يَتَكَلَّمَ بِهِ! قَالَ: "أَوَقَدْ وَجَدْتُمُوهُ؟" قَالُوا: نَعَمْ: قَالَ: (ذَاكَ صَرِيحُ الْإِيمَانِ)». رَوَاهُ مُسْلِمٌ.

---

64 – (وَعَنْهُ) أَيْ: عَنْ أَبِي هُرَيْرَةَ رَضِيَ اللَّهُ عَنْهُ (قَالَ: جَاءَ نَاسٌ) أَيْ: جَمَاعَةٌ («مِنْ أَصْحَابِ رَسُولِ اللَّهِ – صَلَّى اللَّهُ عَلَيْهِ وَسَلَّمَ – إِلَى النَّبِيِّ – عَلَيْهِ الصَّلَاةُ وَالسَّلَامُ – فَسَأَلُوهُ: إِنَّا نَجِدُ») : وَاقِعٌ مَوْقِعَ الْحَالِ أَيْ: سَأَلُوهُ مُخْبِرِينَ إِنَّا نَجِدُ، أَوْ قَائِلِينَ عَلَى احْتِمَالِ فَتْحِ الْهَمْزَةِ، وَالْكَسْرِ، وَقِيلَ: عَلَى الْفَتْحِ مَفْعُولٌ ثَانٍ لِسَأَلُوهُ، ثُمَّ الْكَسْرُ أَوْجَهُ حَتَّى يَكُونَ بَيَانًا لِلْمَسْئُولِ عَنْهُ، وَهُوَ مُجْمَلٌ يُفَسِّرُهُ الْحَدِيثَانِ الْآتِيَانِ (فِي أَنْفُسِنَا مَا يَتَعَاظَمُ أَحَدُنَا أَنْ يَتَكَلَّمَ بِهِ) أَيْ: نَجِدُ فِي قُلُوبِنَا أَشْيَاءَ قَبِيحَةً نَحْوَ: مَنْ خَلَقَ اللَّهَ؟ وَكَيْفَ هُوَ؟ وَمِنْ أَيِّ شَيْءٍ؟ وَمَا أَشْبَهَ ذَلِكَ مِمَّا يَتَعَاظَمُ النُّطْقُ بِهِ لِعِلْمِنَا أَنَّهُ قَبِيحٌ لَا يَلِيقُ شَيْءٌ مِنْهَا أَنْ نَعْتَقِدَهُ، وَنَعْلَمَ أَنَّهُ

قَدِيمٌ، خَالِقُ الْأَشْيَاءَ، غَيْرُ مَخْلُوقٍ، فَمَا حُكْمُ جَرَيَانِ ذَلِكَ فِي خَوَاطِرِنَا؟ وَتَعَاظَمَ: تَفَاعَلَ بِمَعْنَى الْمُبَالَغَةِ؛ لِأَنَّ زِيَادَةَ الْمَبْنَى لِزِيَادَةِ الْمَعْنَى، فَإِنَّ الْفِعْلَ الْوَاحِدَ إِذَا جَرَى بَيْنَ اثْنَيْنِ يَكُونُ مُزَاوَلَتُهُ أَشَقَّ مِنْ مُزَاوَلَتِهِ وَحْدَهُ، وَلِذَا قِيلَ: الْمُفَاعَلَةُ إِذَا لَمْ تَكُنْ لِلْمُغَالَبَةِ فَهِيَ لِلْمُبَالَغَةِ، أَيْ: نَسْتَعْظِمُ غَايَةَ الِاسْتِعْظَامِ، وَقَوْلُهُ: أَحَدُنَا؛ رُوِيَ بِرَفْعِ الدَّالِ، وَمَعْنَاهُ يَجِدُ أَحَدُنَا التَّكَلُّمَ بِهِ عَظِيمًا لِقُبْحِهِ، وَيَجُوزُ النَّصْبُ عَلَى نَزْعِ الْخَافِضِ أَيْ: يَعْظُمُ وَيَشُقُّ التَّكَلُّمُ بِهِ عَلَى أَحَدِنَا (قَالَ: (أَوَقَدْ وَجَدْتُمُوهُ؟) الْهَمْزَةُ لِلِاسْتِفْهَامِ التَّقْرِيرِيِّ، وَالْوَاوُ الْمَقْرُونَةُ بِهَا لِلْعَطْفِ عَلَى مُقَدَّرٍ أَيْ: حَصَلَ ذَلِكَ وَقَدْ وَجَدْتُمُوهُ؟، وَالضَّمِيرُ لِمَا يَتَعَاظَمُ أَيْ: ذَلِكَ الْخَاطِرُ فِي أَنْفُسِكُمْ تَقْرِيرًا وَتَأْكِيدًا، فَالْوِجْدَانُ بِمَعْنَى الْمُصَادَفَةِ، أَوِ الْمَعْنَى أَحَصَلَ ذَلِكَ الْخَاطِرُ الْقَبِيحُ وَعَلِمْتُمْ أَنَّ ذَلِكَ مَذْمُومٌ غَيْرُ مَرْضِيٍّ؟ فَالْوِجْدَانُ بِمَعْنَى الْعِلْمِ. (قَالُوا: نَعَمْ. قَالَ: ذَاكَ): إِشَارَةٌ إِلَى مَصْدَرِ وَجَدَ، أَيْ: وِجْدَانُكُمْ قُبْحَ ذَلِكَ الْخَاطِرِ، أَوْ مَصْدَرُ يَتَعَاظَمُ، أَيْ: عِلْمُكُمْ بِفَسَادِ تِلْكَ الْوَسَاوِسِ، وَامْتِنَاعُ نُفُوسِكُمْ وَتَجَافِيهَا عَنِ التَّفَوُّهِ بِهَا (صَرِيحُ الْإِيمَانِ) أَيْ: خَالِصُهُ يَعْنِي أَنَّهُ أَمَارَتُهُ الدَّالَّةُ صَرِيحًا عَلَى رُسُوخِهِ فِي قُلُوبِكُمْ، وَخُلُوصِهَا مِنَ التَّشْبِيهِ وَالتَّعْطِيلِ؛ لِأَنَّ الْكَافِرَ يُصِرُّ عَلَى مَا فِي قَلْبِهِ مِنْ تَشْبِيهِ اللَّهِ سُبْحَانَهُ بِالْمَخْلُوقَاتِ، وَيَعْتَقِدُهُ حَسَنًا. وَمَنِ اسْتَقْبَحَهَا وَتَعَاظَمَهَا لِعِلْمِهِ بِقُبْحِهَا وَأَنَّهَا لَا تَلِيقُ بِهِ تَعَالَى كَانَ مُؤْمِنًا حَقًّا، وَمُوقِنًا صِدْقًا فَلَا تُزَعْزِعُهُ شُبْهَةٌ وَإِنْ قَوِيَتْ، وَلَا تَحُلُّ عُقَدَ قَلْبِهِ رِيبَةٌ وَإِنْ مُوِّهَتْ، وَلِأَنَّ مَنْ كَانَ إِيمَانُهُ مَشُوبًا يَقْبَلُ الْوَسْوَسَةَ وَلَا يَرُدُّهَا. وَقِيلَ: الْمَعْنَى أَنَّ الْوَسْوَسَةَ أَمَارَةُ الْإِيمَانِ؛ لِأَنَّ اللِّصَّ لَا يَدْخُلُ الْبَيْتَ الْخَالِيَ، وَلِذَا رُوِيَ عَنْ عَلِيٍّ رَضِيَ اللَّهُ عَنْهُ وَكَرَّمَ اللَّهُ وَجْهَهُ أَنَّ الصَّلَاةَ الَّتِي لَا وَسْوَسَةَ فِيهَا إِنَّمَا هِيَ صَلَاةُ الْيَهُودِ، وَالنَّصَارَى. (رَوَاهُ مُسْلِمٌ).

65 – وَعَنْهُ قَالَ: قَالَ رَسُولُ اللَّهِ – صَلَّى اللَّهُ عَلَيْهِ وَسَلَّمَ –: «يَأْتِي الشَّيْطَانُ أَحَدَكُمْ، فَيَقُولُ: مَنْ خَلَقَ كَذَا؟ مَنْ خَلَقَ كَذَا؟ حَتَّى يَقُولَ: مَنْ خَلَقَ رَبَّكَ؟ فَإِذَا بَلَغَهُ، فَلْيَسْتَعِذْ بِاللَّهِ وَلْيَنْتَهِ». مُتَّفَقٌ عَلَيْهِ.

---

65 – (وَعَنْهُ) أَيْ: عَنْ أَبِي هُرَيْرَةَ رَضِيَ اللَّهُ عَنْهُ (قَالَ: قَالَ رَسُولُ اللَّهِ – صَلَّى اللَّهُ عَلَيْهِ وَسَلَّمَ –: يَأْتِي الشَّيْطَانُ) أَيْ: يُوَسْوِسُ إِبْلِيسُ، أَوْ أَحَدُ أَعْوَانِهِ مِنْ شَيَاطِينِ الْإِنْسِ وَالْجِنِّ عَلَى طَرِيقِ التَّلْبِيسِ (أَحَدَكُمْ فَيَقُولُ: مَنْ خَلَقَ كَذَا؟) : يَعْنِي السَّمَاءَ مَثَلًا (مَنْ خَلَقَ كَذَا؟) : يَعْنِي الْأَرْضَ، وَغَرَضُهُ أَنْ يُوقِعَهُ فِي الْغَلَطِ، وَالْكُفْرِ، وَيُكْثِرُ السُّؤَالَ عَلَى هَذَا الْمِنْوَالِ (حَتَّى يَقُولَ: مَنْ خَلَقَ رَبَّكَ؟) وَهُوَ قَدِيمٌ خَالِقُ كُلِّ شَيْءٍ (فَإِذَا بَلَغَهُ) ضَمِيرُ الْفَاعِلِ لِأَحَدِكُمْ، وَضَمِيرُ الْمَفْعُولِ رَاجِعٌ إِلَى مَصْدَرِ يَقُولُ أَيْ: إِذَا بَلَغَ أَحَدُكُمْ هَذَا الْقَوْلَ يَعْنِي مَنْ خَلَقَ رَبَّكَ، أَوِ التَّقْدِيرُ بَلَغَ الشَّيْطَانُ هَذَا الْقَوْلَ (فَلْيَسْتَعِذْ بِاللَّهِ) طَرْدًا لِلشَّيْطَانِ إِشَارَةً إِلَى قَوْلِهِ تَعَالَى: ﴿إِلَّا عِبَادَكَ مِنْهُمُ الْمُخْلَصِينَ﴾ [الحجر: 40] وَإِيمَاءً إِلَى قَوْلِهِ – عَلَيْهِ الصَّلَاةُ وَالسَّلَامُ –: (لَا حَوْلَ وَلَا قُوَّةَ إِلَّا بِاللَّهِ) فَإِنَّ الْعَبْدَ بِحَوْلِهِ، وَقُوَّتِهِ لَيْسَ لَهُ قُوَّةُ الْمُغَالَبَةِ مَعَ الشَّيْطَانِ، وَمُجَادَلَتِهِ، فَيَجِبُ عَلَيْهِ أَنْ يَلْتَجِئَ إِلَى مَوْلَاهُ، وَيَعْتَصِمَ بِاللَّهِ مِنَ الشَّيْطَانِ الَّذِي

أَوْقَعَهُ فِي هَذَا الْخَاطِرِ الَّذِي لَا أَقْبَحَ مِنْهُ، فَيَقُولُ بِلِسَانِهِ: أَعُوذُ بِاللَّهِ مِنَ الشَّيْطَانِ الرَّجِيمِ، وَيَلُوذُ بِجَنَانِهِ إِلَى جَنَابِهِ أَنْ يَدْفَعَ عَنْهُ شَرَّهُ وَكَيْدَهُ، فَإِنَّهُ مَعَ اللُّطْفِ الْإِلَهِيِّ لَا أَضْعَفَ مِنْهُ، وَلَا أَذَلَّ، فَإِنَّهُ مُشَبَّهٌ بِالْكَلْبِ الْوَاقِفِ عَلَى الْبَابِ، وَلِذَا قَالَ تَعَالَى: ﴿إِنَّ كَيْدَ الشَّيْطَانِ كَانَ ضَعِيفًا﴾ [النساء: 76] أَيْ: بِالنِّسْبَةِ إِلَى الْقُوَّةِ الْإِلَهِيَّةِ فَلَا يُنَافِي قَوْلَهُ تَعَالَى حِكَايَةً: ﴿إِنَّ كَيْدَكُنَّ عَظِيمٌ﴾ [يوسف: 28] (وَلْيَنْتَهِ) بِسُكُونِ اللَّامِ، وَتُكْسَرُ، أَيْ: لِيَتْرُكِ التَّفَكُّرَ فِي هَذَا الْخَاطِرِ، وَلْيَشْتَغِلْ بِأَمْرٍ آخَرَ؛ لِئَلَّا يَسْتَحْوِذَ عَلَيْهِ الشَّيْطَانُ، فَإِنَّهُ إِنَّمَا أَوْقَعَهُ فِيهِ رَجَاءَ أَنْ يَقِفَ مَعَهُ، وَيَتَمَكَّنَ فِي نَفْسِهِ فَيَحْصُلَ لَهَا شَكٌّ وَرَيْبٌ فِي تَنْزِيهِهِ تَعَالَى عَنْ سِمَاتِ الْحُدُوثِ وَإِنْ دَقَّتْ وَخَفِيَتْ، فَمَنْ تَنَبَّهَ وَكَفَّ عَنِ الِاسْتِرْسَالِ مَعَ ذَلِكَ الْخَاطِرِ، وَأَشْغَلَ نَفْسَهُ حَتَّى انْصَرَفَتْ عَنْهُ فَقَدْ خَلَصَ، وَمَنْ لَا فَقَدِ ارْتَبَكَ فَيُخْشَى عَلَيْهِ مَزَلَّةُ الْقَدَمِ فِي قَعْرِ جَهَنَّمَ، وَإِنَّمَا أُمِرَ بِذَيْنِكَ دُونَ الِاحْتِجَاجِ وَالتَّأَمُّلِ لِأَمْرَيْنِ: أَحَدُهُمَا: أَنَّ الْعِلْمَ بِاسْتِغْنَاءِ اللَّهِ تَعَالَى عَنِ الْمُؤَثِّرِ وَالْمُوجِدِ ضَرُورِيٌّ لَا يَقْبَلُ احْتِجَاجًا، وَإِنَّمَا ذَلِكَ شَيْءٌ يُلْقِيهِ الشَّيْطَانُ إِمَّا لِيُحِجَّكَ إِنْ جَادَلْتَهُ؛ لِأَنَّهُ مُسَلَّطٌ عَلَى الْقُلُوبِ بِإِلْقَاءِ الْوَسَاوِسِ عَلَيْهَا لِيَخْتَبِرَ إِيمَانَهَا، وَوَسَاوِسُهُ غَيْرُ مُتَنَاهِيَةٍ فَمَتَى عَارَضْتَهُ بِمَسْلَكٍ وَجَدَ مَسْلَكًا آخَرَ إِلَى مَا يُرِيدُهُ مِنَ الْمُغَالَطَةِ وَالتَّشْكِيكِ، وَإِمَّا لِيُضَيِّعَ وَقْتَكَ وَيُكَدِّرَ عَيْشَكَ إِنِ اسْتَرْسَلْتَ مَعَهُ، وَإِنْ حَجَجْتَهُ فَلَا أَخْلَصَ لَكَ مِنَ الْإِعْرَاضِ عَنْهُ جُمْلَةً، وَالِالْتِجَاءِ إِلَى اللَّهِ تَعَالَى بِالِاسْتِعَاذَةِ مِنْهُ كَمَا قَالَ عَزَّ مِنْ قَائِلٍ ﴿وَإِمَّا يَنْزَغَنَّكَ مِنَ الشَّيْطَانِ نَزْغٌ فَاسْتَعِذْ بِاللَّهِ﴾ [الأعراف: ٢٠٠] ثَانِيهِمَا: أَنَّ الْغَالِبَ فِي مَوَارِدِ هَذِهِ الْخَوَاطِرِ أَنَّهُ إِنَّمَا يَنْشَأُ مِنْ رُكُودِ النَّفْسِ، وَعَدَمِ اشْتِغَالِهَا بِالْمُهِمَّاتِ الْمَطْلُوبَةِ مِنْهَا، فَهَذَا لَا يَزِيدُهُ فِكْرُهُ فِي ذَلِكَ إِلَّا الزَّيْغَ عَنِ الْحَقِّ، فَلَا عِلَاجَ لَهُ إِلَّا الِالْتِجَاءَ بِحَوْلِ اللَّهِ وَقُوَّتِهِ، وَالِاعْتِصَامَ بِكِتَابِ اللَّهِ وَسُنَّةِ رَسُولِهِ. قَالَ الْخَطَّابِيُّ: لَوْ أَذِنَ رَسُولُ اللَّهِ – صَلَّى اللَّهُ عَلَيْهِ وَسَلَّمَ – فِي مُحَاجَّتِهِ لَكَانَ الْجَوَابُ سَهْلًا عَلَى كُلِّ مُوَحِّدٍ أَيْ: بِإِثْبَاتِ الْبَرَاهِينِ الْقَاطِعَةِ عَلَى أَنْ لَا خَالِقَ لَهُ تَعَالَى بِإِبْطَالِ التَّسَلْسُلِ وَنَحْوِهِ كَاسْتِحْضَارِ أَنَّ جَمِيعَ الْمَخْلُوقَاتِ دَاخِلَةٌ تَحْتَ اسْمِ الْخَلْقِ، فَلَوْ جَازَ أَنْ يُقَالَ: "مَنْ خَلَقَ الْخَالِقَ" لَأَدَّى إِلَى مَا لَا يَتَنَاهَى، وَهُوَ بَاطِلٌ قَطْعًا، وَفِيهِ إِشْعَارٌ بِمَذَمَّةِ عِلْمِ الْكَلَامِ، وَدَلَالَةٌ عَلَى حُرْمَةِ الْمِرَاءِ وَالْمُجَادَلَةِ فِيمَا يَتَعَلَّقُ بِذَاتِ اللَّهِ وَصِفَاتِهِ، وَإِيمَاءٌ إِلَى صِحَّةِ إِيمَانِ الْمُقَلِّدِ. (مُتَّفَقٌ عَلَيْهِ)

2.4 *English Translation*

The Chapter on *Waswasa* (Intrusive Thoughts)

63 – (1) **On the authority of Abū Hurayra, may Allah be pleased with him, the Messenger of Allah, may Allah bless him and grant him peace, said, "Indeed, Allah overlooks for my nation what their hearts whisper to them as long as they do not act upon it or speak of it." Agreed Upon.**[43]

43 Al-Bukhārī, 2528; Muslim, 127; Abū Dawūd, 2209; Al-Nasā'ī, 3434; Al-Tirmidhī, 1183; Ibn Mājah, 2040.

[With regards to] passing thoughts (*khawāṭir*), whenever they call towards reprehensible deeds, they are [termed] *waswasa*, whereas if they [motivate one] towards [performing] virtuous actions, they are [called] *ilhām*. The soundest opinion [about the authority and significance of *ilhām*] is that it is not authoritative evidence when originating in other than divinely protected persons,[44] as [most] fleeting thoughts are [otherwise] unreliable.[45]

Section 1

63 – **On the authority of Abū Hurayra, may Allah be pleased with him, the Messenger of Allah, may Allah bless him and grant him peace, said, "Indeed Allah overlooks ..."** meaning, "He has forgiven."

"For my nation (*umma*) ..." i.e., the nation that answers the [divine] call (*ummat al-ijāba*). In another narration, **"He has pardoned my nation for me,"** meaning, He will not hold them accountable, for my sake. His favor upon us is the [absolute] greatest; it is limitless.

"What their hearts whisper to them," [Grammatically, the word for "hearts" is] the subject [of the sentence, which gives the] meaning "what occurs within their hearts of vile thoughts." This is a metaphorical expression [associated with] proximity.[46] [It can] also validly be [in] the accusative case as the object. It is said [that] this is debatable, as [the word] *waswasa* is intransitive [and therefore has no object]. Indeed, the most plausible approach [in considering it to be] accusative [would be] as an adverb [indicating time or place], if it was supported in the narration. [An additional report] has been transmitted

---

44 Meaning, prophets, who are divinely protected from being inspired by Shayṭān and committing sin.

45 To clarify, *ilhām*, or divine inspiration, only holds authoritative weight when it originates from the infallible prophets. In this context, in the case of non-prophets, "authoritative" implies that this form of knowledge does not impose an obligation on others to believe unless such is accompanied by objective means of verification.

For instance, if one claims to have received inspiration regarding certain "truths" about human psychology, the validity of such claims can only be established through empirical evidence. Otherwise, they would be regarded as personal opinions or beliefs without broader validity. However, when it comes to prophets, their dreams and inspirations are a form of revelation, carrying religious obligations for all to believe and uphold. The distinction lies in the nature of the source – divinely inspired knowledge from prophets is recognized as binding due to its origin, while inspirations from non-prophets require additional verification for broader acceptance, as such could be from Shayṭān.

46 In other words, it is not the heart that produces such thoughts, although it may seem to be the case because it is in proximity to that which does. Accordingly, the heart is expressed as the doer of the action, or the subject of the sentence. Thus, it is stated, "what their hearts whisper to them" instead of "what is whispered into their hearts."

[with the wording], "what their [inner] selves say to them," with [the word for "selves" in] the nominative case; and the genitive case [as] its substitute.

"As long as they do not act upon it ..." meaning, as long as it does not pertain to any misdeed [like] if it is [a vile thought] related to an action.

"Or speak of it," meaning, as long as one does not speak of it, if it is [a negative thought] associated with speech. [This is] as it was [explained] in *al-Azhār*.[47] The author of *al-Rawḍa* states in [his] commentary of *Ṣaḥīḥ al-Bukhārī*:

> The sound and preferred opinion held by the majority [of scholars] is that the workings of the heart will [in fact] be taken into account if they are entertained. As for the statement of the Messenger of Allah, may Allah bless him and grant him peace, "Indeed Allah overlooks for my nation that which their hearts whisper to them ..." [It is] understood [to mean] so long as such [thoughts] do not linger [in the heart]. Those [thoughts which merely occur briefly] are undoubtedly forgiven, as [completely] freeing oneself from them is impossible, which is not the case for [thoughts that become] deeply ingrained.[48]

Thereafter, the author of *al-Azhār* cites [al-Ghazālī's] *Iḥyā'*, the summary of which [is the following]:

The workings of the heart are of four types:

First: An [automatic] thought (*khāṭir*);[49] like if the image of a woman were to come to mind, [who,] for example, is behind someone on the street, [so] if they were to turn around, they would [actually] see her.

Second: An impulse (*hayajān al-raghba*) to look at her. We call this natural predilection (*mayl al-ṭabʿ*),[50] whereas the first is [termed] the insinuation of the soul (*ḥadīth al-nafs*).

---

47 *Al-Azhār* likely refers to Yūsuf al-Ardabīlī's (d. 779 AH) still unpublished *al-Azhār Sharḥ al-Maṣābīḥ*, a commentary on al-Baghawī's *Maṣābīḥ al-Sunna*.

48 Sirāj al-dīn Ibn al-Mulaqqīn, *Al-Tawḍīḥ Li-Sharḥ Jāmiʿ al-Ṣaḥīḥ*, vol. 2 (Dimashq: Dār al-Nawādir, 2008), 275. There is a distinction being made between fleeting negative thoughts that are involuntary and inescapably occur in everyone, versus the acceptance, deliberation, and commitment to such thoughts which is volitional and within one's control.

49 According to Imam al-Ghazālī, automatic thoughts (*khawāṭir*) may or may not be reflective of one's beliefs as they typically occur non-volitionally; sometimes as satanic whispers or mere inner fleeting thoughts that occur without deliberation.

50 Imam al-Ghazālī's thought-action process theory is being cited here by Mulla ʿAlī al-Qārī. Al-Ghazālī is demonstrating a clear connection between thoughts that occur automatically and their accompanying emotional and physiological reactions. This is a clear

Third: The heart's decision to act (*ḥukm al-qalb*); meaning, one would look at her. Indeed, when [a person's] instinct inclines [towards something], they do not [typically] resist [such] an impulse or resolve, unless [it is] suppressed by [certain] virtues that deter [one from acting]. This includes modesty, fear of Allah Most High, or [even fear of] His servants. We call this conviction (*iʿtiqād*).[51]

Fourth: A firm resolution to turn [towards her] with a willful intention [to act]. We name this [the] determination of the heart (*ʿazm bi-l-qalb*).

As for a [mere] passing thought (*khāṭir*), one will not be held accountable for it. It is the same for [one's natural] inclinations (*mayl al-ṭabʿ*) and impulses (*hayajān al-raghba*) as both of them are [similarly] non-volitional, thus they are both what is meant by the prophetic narration, "Indeed, Allah overlooks for my nation …"[52]

Regarding the third [category], which is conviction (*iʿtiqād*), it varies; it could be entirely volitional, or ineluctable [and] against one's will. As such, one is [morally] responsible for that which is by choice, whereas that which is non-volitional is overlooked.[53]

As for the fourth [stage in] which [a person has] a [willful] determination and incentive to act (*ʿazm bi-l-qalb*), one is certainly held accountable for that. Verses have accordingly been revealed that establish [personal] accountability for the workings of the heart, unless [one] forsakes [such intentions] fearing Allah Most High, [in which case] it is recorded as a good deed. This is because such an intent is a sin; stifling it [entails] a struggle with one's inner self which merits a reward [that] supersedes it. Furthermore, if one abandons it because

---

display of the mind-body relationship that precedes cognitive behavioral therapy by nearly a millennium.

51 In the context of erratic thoughts of blasphemy, such a distinction becomes critically important. Only at the stage where an individual makes a decision or commitment to the initially automatic or fleeting thought does it become a mental action or belief. The former two stages, i.e., *khawāṭir* and the excitatory physiological and emotional responses (*mayl al-ṭabaʿ*) that accompany non-volitional thoughts may simply be considered mental processes while the remaining stages are considered mental actions.

52 On account of such automatic thoughts being non-volitional and mere mental processes, they are not taken into account from a religious standpoint.

53 The central point of affirming religious responsibility versus negating it goes back to the degree of one's control and volition over their thoughts. While it is conceivable for a person to control some automatic thoughts, it would be considered undue hardship to try to control all thoughts. Thus, given the hardship in doing so, all fleeting thoughts are not within one's realm of responsibility. Even in the third stage outlined in the text, volition is the central consideration for responsibility. That is, if one non-volitionally, mindlessly, or instinctively inclines toward a vile thought without having performed the associated action, this too is not within the purview of moral responsibility.

of some [incidental] obstacle or it [simply] does not take place, it is [nonetheless] recorded as a sin due to [one's] willful determination and resolve [to carry it out].[54] The definitive proof for this is the statement of the Messenger of Allah, may Allah bless him and grant him peace, in an authentic tradition for which the veracity is agreed upon: "'If two Muslims [were to] fight each other with their swords [drawn], then the one who killed and the one who was killed [will both be] in the Fire.' [A companion] asked, 'O Messenger of Allah, what [was] the fault of the one who was killed?' He responded, 'he was vehemently intent upon killing his companion.'"[55] This explicitly [states] that he will end up in the Fire solely because of a firm resolution and intention despite having died without killing; rather, he was wrongfully killed. Then again, how could one not be taken to account for the resolute workings of the heart when arrogance, self-infatuation, hypocrisy, envy, and other blameworthy [inward] traits will [necessarily] be judged? Indeed, the Messenger of Allah, may Allah bless him and grant him peace, said, "Sin is what agitates the heart."[56] He also stated, "Righteousness is that which brings comfort to the heart and tranquility to the soul. Sin is what perturbs your soul, and wavers within your heart, even if people [try to] legitimize it."[57]

In my opinion, using the latter narration as proof [for this] is debatable because it [seems to] construe sin itself to be what wavers in the heart. However, it was mentioned previously that a [fleeting thought] is not a sin so long as it is not accompanied by a firm resolve. Accordingly, the [above-mentioned] narration means that whatever causes discomfort in the heart could [potentially] be a sin, although it may not [actually] be [a sin].[58] Practically, it [should be treated as] a sin, out of precaution. [This is] just like when there are contradicting proofs regarding the prohibition and permissibility of something; such [a thing] is [considered] unlawful.

---

54 In the case of a full commitment, the establishment of an intention, and behaviors directed toward the commitment of the inspired misdeed, all of these would be considered mental actions and thus punishable. However, if regret and fear of Allah interrupts the completion of this action, then the previously established mental action is likewise removed, and one is absolved of accountability regarding it. This is a divine grace for the believer. However, if one is unable to fulfill the action for some other reason, i.e., some worldly barrier that rendered him incapable of actualizing his intentions, he will still be held accountable for this behavior despite not having performed it, on account of the mental action and commitment.

55 Al-Bukhārī, 31; Muslim 1752.

56 Muslim, 2553; al-Tirmidhī 2389.

57 Aḥmad, 18001.

58 Considering the ḥadīth that specifies, "so long as he does not act upon it or speak of it."

[Next,] it is said that the [main] narration [of this chapter] indicates that the [divine] pardoning mentioned [therein] is a special dispensation for this nation (*umma*). This is in accordance with what the author of *al-Azhār* quoted from *al-Rawḍa*, whereas [al-Ghazālī's] *Iḥyā'* contends that it is general, [extending] to all nations.[59] [This is] because [absolutely] no one is accountable for that which is non-volitional, as per Allah's [broad] statement: *Allah does not confer responsibility* [*upon*] *anyone unless* [*it is within*] *their capability*, (al-Baqara 2:286). The correct [understanding] is what al-Ṭībī stated, in that thoughts are [either] non-volitional or volitional. Accordingly, the non-volitional type [includes] the fleeting thoughts that initially cross the mind which a person cannot avoid. Such is overlooked for all of humanity. Conversely, volitional thoughts are those that overrun the heart and abide; a person forms intentions and acts according to them. One [often] derives pleasure from it, like [when] infatuation for a woman foments in a man's heart; he continually fixates on it [until] he resolves to get together with her. Such is similarly the case with other sins. Now, this [particular] type [of thought is what] Allah has uniquely forgiven for this nation (*umma*), as an honor and favor for our Prophet and his people, may Allah bless him and grant him peace.[60] Regarding this, [one should] consider Allah's statement: *Our Lord! Do not place a burden upon us like the one you placed on those before us* ... (al-Baqara 2:286). As for corrupt beliefs, abhorrent characteristics, and anything else thereto related, such are beyond the purview of what is generally meant by "what their hearts whisper ..."[61]

It is a well-founded viewpoint. [Presumably,] it was on this basis [that] the Prophet, upon him blessings and peace, stipulated, "as long as they do not

59 The first view presented indicates that other nations were in fact held morally responsible for fleeting inner thoughts. The second view, which is that of al-Ghazalī and others, holds that no nation is responsible for such transient non-volitional inner thoughts.

60 Despite all that has been mentioned previously regarding the fact that volitional thoughts would be considered punishable, based upon this view, even such vile volitional thoughts are overlooked due to the special mercy accorded to the Prophet, may Allah bless him and grant him peace, and his followers. Thus, mental processes regarding the performance of a vile action, even if volitional, are considered to be forgiven according to this interpretation.

61 The aforementioned exclusion only applies to those thoughts that have an action potential, like entertaining the thought of eating impermissible food, for example. However, vile thoughts that do not have any actionable behavioral outputs such as the willful acceptance of blasphemous beliefs or blameworthy inner character vices like jealousy, negative views of others, pride, etc. do not fall within the aforementioned exclusion of accountability. Rather, these thoughts are regarded as mental actions for which one is held accountable.

act [upon it] or speak [of it]." [which is] an indication that [mere] urges to act or speak are remitted until they are [actually] carried out. [On the other hand,] regarding intrusive thoughts that have no bearing on deeds or speech, like [those] pertaining to [negative] characteristics and beliefs, then they are [regarded as] as sins when they are rooted [in the heart].[62]

Imam al-Nawawī mentioned that the opinion of al-Qaḍī Abū Bakr bin al-Ṭayyib is that whosoever intends to commit sin and prepares oneself accordingly has incurred sin through their resolve and intention. What comes in the likes of the prophetic narration, "[Allah says to the angels] 'When my servant is tempted to sin, do not record it against him; but if he does end up committing it, then record it as one misdeed …'" applies to someone who does not inwardly prepare to [actually] sin. Rather, one circumvents this as a [mere] idea without [letting it] take hold. This is called temptation (*hamm*); there is a [crucial] difference between temptation and the willful determination [to act] (*ʿazm*).[63] [In summary,] this is the interpretation of al-Qaḍī Abū Bakr. Whilst a multitude of jurists and traditionalists disagree with him and prefer the apparent [meaning] of the text,[64] al-Qaḍī ʿIyāḍ asserts [that] the majority of the pious predecessors as well as the expert jurists and traditionalists are upon that which al-Qaḍī Abū Bakr has concluded due to the [various] narrations that [clearly] prove the accountability for the [inner] workings of the heart. However, they say [that] this resolve is in fact recorded as a sin, although [it is] not the [same] sin that one was tempted to commit, as that deed was not [actually] perpetrated. [Assuming] it was prevented by something other

62 In other words, vile thoughts like envy or blasphemy that are non-action based are only sinful when they become settled and embedded in the heart; one would not be held accountable for their mere occurrence.

63 The concept of thought-action fusion in Acceptance and Commitment Therapy (ACT) also discusses the problems with equating thoughts with actions since this can be a source of distress for patients with obsessive compulsive disorder (OCD) or other anxiety disorders. ACT thought fusion falsely entails that: (a) the belief that thinking about a negative event makes it more likely to happen or (b) the belief that having a negative thought is morally equal to carrying out the very same action (see Roz Shafran, Dana S. Thordarson, and S. Rachman, "Thought-Action Fusion in Obsessive Compulsive Disorder," Journal of Anxiety Disorders 10, no. 5 (September 1996): 379–91.). While this concept is useful, it is important to consider the greater specifications provided by Islamic scholarship as outlined above; most notably, differentiating between volitional versus non-volitional thoughts. And, in the case of even volitional thoughts, pinpointing whether they are mental processes that are actionable or if they are mental actions that do not contain external action potentials. Such a distinction and education can be very important in the treatment of Muslim patients with anxiety or OCD.

64 As is consistent with what Ṭībī mentioned earlier that even deliberations regarding actionable thoughts as long he does not actually act upon them are considered overlooked.

than the fear of Allah and repentance, then the persistence and resolve [to act] are [what are counted as] sin. On the other hand, forsaking it due to fear of Allah and the quelling of one's evil-inciting self is a good deed. So, as for the [kind of] temptation that is not recorded, then it is [when it occurs as] passing thoughts that do not marshal the soul [to act] upon them, and do not coincide with any conviction, intention, or resolute decision. Some of the theologians (*mutakallimīn*) mention a different view, in that if one forsakes sin for other than the fear of Allah – [like] for the sake of people instead – would that be recorded as a good deed? They say no because it was only shyness that motivated them to abandon the sin. But this opposing view is weak and has no merit.[65] This is the last of what al-Qaḍī [ʿIyāḍ] has mentioned, and it is clear and well-stated; nothing more [can really be said] to add to it.

Indeed, the sacred legal texts clearly support the [idea of personal] accountability for [whoever] firmly intends [sin] in their heart. From amongst such [texts]: *Verily, those who crave that indecency propagates amongst the believers will suffer a painful punishment,* (al-Nūr 24:19). Also: *Avoid most suspicion [as] some suspicion is sinful …* (al-Ḥujurāt 49:12); and the verses in this [regard are] numerous. Additionally, the sacred legal texts and scholarly consensus affirm the impermissibility of envy, debasing Muslims, as well as desiring adversity for them, alongside other sins of the heart, [which includes] the firm resolve to [commit] such [sins].[66] The difference between that which corresponds to [taking] action and that which does not was [already] discussed previously, and Allah the Exalted knows best.[67]

---

65 The author seems to consider the abandonment of evil actions on account of modesty (*ḥayāʾ*) as sufficient for the acquisition of reward since modesty is amongst the most important character virtues of a believer. Accordingly, he considers the contrary view as mentioned by some of the theologians as weak. Being concerned with the perceptions of others does not necessarily negate sincerity in performing deeds for the sake of Allah. This is on account of the fact that violations of Islamic norms in Muslim communities are considered reprehensible; not because they violate social norms per se, but ultimately, because they are displeasing to Allah.

66 This further corroborates that any commitment towards particular thoughts become mental actions or beliefs. Thus, having jealousy, holding grudges or resentments, and other similar deeds are all considered inner vices if they have settled within an individual, thereby becoming volitional mental actions as opposed to involuntary transient ideas or feelings.

67 Meaning, as mentioned previously, if the thought is related to an actionable sin, then whether it is sinful or not is debated in the case where one does not properly enact it. However, in the case of non-actionable thoughts such as thoughts of envy, arrogance, or blasphemy, then all are considered sins for which one will be held accountable if they become commitments, taking root in the heart.

It is also said [that a person] will be held accountable for the [mere] temptation (*hamm*) to sin exclusively within the sacred precincts of Makkah. This is a transmitted opinion [attributed] to [Imam] Ahmad [bin Ḥanbal]; Ibn Masʿūd [may Allah be pleased with him] also held this view given the verse, *And whosoever intends to deviate by doing wrong in it* ... (al-Hajj, 22:25). This is countered by [understanding] that [the word] "to want" (*irāda*) means "to seek" (*qaṣd*), which is the willful determination [to act] (*ʿazm*) that is more specific than temptation (*hamm*).

"Agreed upon." [As defined] in [Imam al-Suyūṭī's] *al-Jāmiʿ al-Ṣaghīr*: that [which is] narrated by the group[68] on the authority of Abū Hurayra [may Allah be pleased with him], with the wording, "Indeed, Allah overlooks for my nation whatever their souls insinuate to them, as long as they do not speak or act in accordance with it."[69]

64 – (2) **Also on his authority, he says, "People from amongst the Companions of the Messenger of Allah, Allah bless him and grant him peace, came to the Prophet, Allah bless him and grant him peace, and said to him puzzledly, 'Verily, we find within ourselves that which is too appalling for any of us to speak of.' He said, 'Do you really find it as such?' They answered, 'yes'. He said, 'That is clear faith.'" Narrated by Muslim.**

64 – **"Also on his authority,"** meaning, on the authority of Abū Hurayra, may Allah be pleased with him.

"He says, people ..." "... came," meaning, a group [of people].

"From amongst the Companions of the Messenger of Allah, Allah bless him and grant him peace, came to the Prophet ..." upon him blessings and peace, **"and said puzzledly, 'Verily, we find ...'"** [This] stands in the place of a circumstantial adverb, meaning, they actually asked him [as a way of] informing [him, saying,] "we find ..." Alternatively, they could have said it employing the accusative or genitive case. It is said [to be] accusative as an additional direct object, [thus,] "to ask him ..."

Next, the genitive case is a sounder view, rendering it that which underscores what is being asked about. Hence, it is ambivalent; the following two narrations [in the chapter serve to] clarify it.

---

68 This group is in reference to the narrators of the six authenticated canonical works of hadith (*al-siḥāḥ al-sitta*).

69 al-Suyūṭī, *al-Jāmiʿal-Ṣaghīr*, 1704.

While there is the view that even fleeting thoughts are punishable if they occur whilst one is present within the sacred boundaries of Makkah, the author reiterates that there is a distinction between a temptation (*hamm*) and a volitional mental commitment (*ʿazm*). He does not seem to favor the idea that there could be an exception to the rule as all fleeting thoughts are non-volitional and are thus overlooked.

"'Within ourselves that which is too appalling for any of us to speak of,'" meaning, "We find within our hearts [such] horrid things, like: Who created Allah? How is He? From what? And other thoughts like that[70] which are too appalling to speak of given our [inherent] knowledge that such is heretical [and therefore] completely inappropriate to [seriously] internalize. Plus, we know that He is pre-existent [without origin]; the creator of absolutely everything; uncreated." Accordingly, what is the verdict of such thoughts running through our minds?

"Too appalling ..." [on the morphological pattern] that signifies hyperbole, considering [the linguistic axiom]: the more additional [non-root letters employed to] form [a word], the more meaning [it conveys]. Hence, when one verb is enacted [mutually] by two [subjects], its function is [necessarily] more forceful than when it is enacted alone [by a single subject]. Based on this, it is said [that] this [particular morphological pattern] is hyperbolic [even] when it is not used hyperbolically. [So, this word in the narration] means, "we regard [this to be] of utmost concern."

As for the saying **"any of us,"** it has been related in the nominative case, which means, "anyone amongst us [would] deem speaking of it [to be] tremendous due to its vileness." Likewise, it [could be] validly interpreted [as being] accusative via the omission of the [implied] preposition, [thus] meaning, "it is tremendous, and mentioning it [would] be difficult for any one of us."

"He said, 'Do you really find it as such?'" The interrogative particle is employed [rhetorically] as a statement. The [following] particle affixed to it is a connecting [particle] preceded by an implicit [sentence], inferred to be "that [does] happen ... and you have really found it to be so." As for the pronoun, [it] represents that which is appalling, meaning, "the fleeting thoughts within your minds." [It is used] to ascertain and emphasize. Furthermore, [the verb] "to find" means "to take place." Or, it means, "did that inappropriate thought [actually] occur whilst you knew it to be ignoble and objectionable?" In that case, "to find" means "to know" [here].

"They answered, 'yes'. He said, 'That ...'" The demonstrative pronoun [goes back] to the verbal noun "to find" [which produces the] meaning, "your finding of depravity [in] that passing thought." Alternatively, [it could refer back to] the verbal noun "to be appalled", [which gives the] meaning, "your recognition of the corruption of those intrusive thoughts, your conscientious objections [against them], as well as your refraining from [even] speaking of them."

---

70 Meaning, other involuntary thoughts of a blasphemous nature.

"Clear faith" meaning, pure faith, in that, "such is a sign clearly indicating it is firmly rooted in your hearts; untainted by anthropomorphism and the denial [of Allah's attributes]." Indeed, a disbeliever affirms that which [comes] into his heart concerning [beliefs like] comparing Allah the Magnanimous, with created beings, and accepting that as a good thing. Whereas the one who deems it [to be] abhorrent and is appalled by such [thoughts] because he recognizes their contemptuousness and that they are unbefitting of Allah the Exalted, [such a person] is a true, resolute, and sincere believer. [There is] no misconception [that can] shake him, no matter how compelling, and no doubt [that can] sway his heart, no matter how convoluted. This is because one whose faith is tarnished will [readily] entertain intrusive thoughts and will not repel them. Moreover, it is [also] said that intrusive thoughts [themselves] are a sign of faith, as a robber [would] never break into a barren home. In this sense, it was related on the authority of ʿAlī, may Allah be pleased with him and ennoble his countenance, that the only prayer in which there are absolutely no intrusive thoughts is that of the Jews and Christians.[71]

65 – (3) **Also on his authority, he reported the Messenger of Allah, may Allah bless him and grant him peace, said, "Shayṭān will come to one of you and say, 'Who created this? Who created that?' Until he says, 'who created your Lord?' When it reaches that point, one should seek refuge in Allah and desist." Agreed Upon.**[72]

65 – (3) **"Also on his authority,"** meaning, on the authority of Abū Hurayra, may Allah be pleased with him.

"He reported the Messenger of Allah, may Allah bless him and grant him peace, said, "Shayṭān will come ..." meaning, Iblīs will whisper; or one of his assistants from amongst the devils of humankind or the *jinn* [will insinuate] by way of deceit.

71 This is a complete reframing of the initial concern that the Companions presented to the Prophet, may Allah bless him and grant him peace, wherein he informed them that this phenomenon is in fact an indicator of manifest faith – not its absence. Thus, the naturally occurring, negative, fleeting types of thoughts are things that necessarily occur in all human beings. The feeling of discomfort with such thoughts is also an additional indicator of their faith, given that they find these thoughts to be reprehensible and therefore reject them; this provides further distinction between belief and fleeting thoughts or mental processes. The author reiterates this notion with yet another cognitive reframe, by mentioning that a thief does not steal from an empty house just as Shayṭān is not concerned with whispering vile thoughts into the hearts of people who are already misguided. Rather, he is concerned with beguiling those with stronger faith.

72 Al-Bukharī, 3276; Muslim, 389.

"To one of you and say, 'who created this?" Thus, for example, [who created] the sky?

"'Who created that?'" meaning, the earth [for example]. His purpose being to beguile one into error and [eventual] disbelief, prompting many questions in this [particular] manner.

"Until he says: 'who created your Lord?' ..." whereas He is pre-eternal [without origin], the Creator of everything.

"When it reaches that point," The [hidden] pronoun [after "reaches"] refers to the subject "one of you," whereas the [connecting] pronoun [attached to the verb] is the direct object, which refers to the verbal noun of "he will say," rendering the meaning, "when this saying, 'who created your Lord?' reaches you." Alternatively, it could be interpreted, "[when] Shayṭān [eventually] reaches this saying."[73]

"One should seek refuge in Allah ..." so as to thwart Shayṭān, pointing to the Quranic verse, ... *except your chosen servants amongst them* (al-Ḥijr 15:40), and alluding to the Prophet's saying, may Allah bless him and grant him peace, "There is no capability or power except by Allah."[74] Indeed, a servant, with all of his [apparent] ability and strength does not have the capacity to fight or argue with Shayṭān.[75] Hence, he must [completely] rely on his Master, seeking protection with Allah from Shayṭān, who has flung him into this incomparably grotesque thought-pattern. As such, he verbally says, "I seek refuge in Allah from the accursed Shayṭān," pleading for His protection so as to ward off

73 The prophetic narration is clearly demonstrating how initial negative thoughts, when entertained, progressively worsen until they prompt one to question the existence of God altogether. Engaging with ruminative negative thoughts tends to magnify them, not eradicate them. These are common challenges of those who struggle with obsessive compulsive disorder (OCD). Rumination is a core feature of OCD that is defined as the tendency to spend excessive time over-focusing on, worrying about, and analyzing a thought and its accompanying discomforting feelings (see Susan Nolen-Hoeksema, Blair E. Wisco, and Sonja Lyubomirsky, "Rethinking Rumination," *Perspectives on Psychological Science* 3, no. 5 (September 2008): 400–424.).

74 Al-Tirmidhī, 3426; Abū Dāwūd 5095.

75 Yusuf & Haddad, outline the RIDA model of dealing with negative ruminative thought problems. RIDA, which stands for Recognition, Identification, Denial-Decoupling, and Alternative formulation is a cognitive technique used in Traditional Islamically Integrated Psychotherapy (TIIP). In such a circumstance, one would *recognize* the negative emotions of fear that is brought on by the worrisome thoughts; *identify* what the thought is; *deny* the thought, ascribing it to Shayṭān and not to themselves; and then provide an *alternate formulation* for the thought, such as "the presence of such a thought is an indication of the strength of my faith and Shayṭān does not come to the heart of an unfaithful person." (See: Yusuf and Elhaddad, "The Use of the Intellect ('aql) as a Cognitive Restructuring Tool in an Islamic Psychotherapy.")

Shayṭān's evil and manipulative tactics. By divine design, there is [thankfully] no one weaker or more debased than Shayṭān; he is much like a [snarling] dog standing by the door. Accordingly, Allah the Exalted says, *Indeed, the treachery of Shayṭān is ever so feeble.* (al-Nisā 4:76). To clarify, [this is] in relation to divine power, thus it does not negate Allah's statement quoting [the Egyptian governor in Sura Yūsuf], *Verily, your treachery is great.* (Yūsuf 12:28).[76]

"And desist." [Here, the jussive case allows] for the absence of a vowel as well as vowelization, conveying the following meaning: "One should cease dwelling upon these intrusive thoughts, and subsequently focus on something else so that Shayṭān does not take control." Afterall, he only imposes such [thoughts] in [people's] minds out of hope that they will pay attention to him so he can manipulate their minds, fostering even the most minute and subtle of doubts and suspicions regarding Allah's [absolute] transcendency above all attributes of creation. Verily, a person who exercises caution, refrains from entertaining those [types of] ideas, and [effectively] preoccupies their mind until such thoughts pass, becomes truly liberated. Conversely, whoever does not [do so] is certainly confounded, and it is consequently feared that they will slip up [and fall] into a pit of Hellfire.

Overall, [when dealing with intrusive thoughts] one is only instructed to do those two things [as mentioned in the narration], without careful scrutiny or expostulation. This is due to two considerations:

Firstly, knowledge that Allah is [totally] independent from all influences and causes is necessarily known and cannot be disputed. It is just something that Shayṭān projects to get you to raise objections [hoping] you will contend with him, as he was conferred sway over the hearts through insinuating whispers in order to test peoples' faith. And his whispers are [seemingly] endless; whenever you traverse a path to oppose him, he finds another way until [he achieves] what he desires, [in terms of] inculcating delusion and skepticism. Alternatively, [his whispers are meant] to waste your time and muddle your life, [especially] if you were to lower your guard with him. If you were to refute him, then that is not nearly as liberating as shunning him completely whilst relying on Allah the Exalted and seeking protection from him, as valuably affirmed by Allah [Himself]: *If you are tempted by Shayṭān, then seek refuge with Allah …* (al-ʿArāf 7:200).

---

76 Through the assignment of these negative thoughts to Shayṭān, one is able to externalize these thoughts and distance them from one's own beliefs. Externalization of negative thoughts to other than oneself is a modern technique in Acceptance and Commitment Therapy (ACT) (see Shafran, Thordarson, and Rachman, "Thought-Action Fusion in Obsessive Compulsive Disorder.").

Secondly, the predominant source of these intrusive thoughts springs from none other than inner stagnation, [when] the mind is not engaged with what it should [rightfully] be focused on. One does not gain anything by obsessing over such [trivial ideas] other than gradual divergence from the truth. So, there really is no remedy for such [a person] other than seeking refuge in the light and power of Allah, with a firm adherence to the Book of Allah as well as the way (*sunna*) of His Prophet [may Allah bless him and grant him peace]. Al-Khaṭṭābī says: "[Hypothetically,] if the Messenger of Allah, may Allah bless him and grant him peace, had permitted [people] to contend with Shayṭān, it would be rather easy for any monotheist to react by [broadly] affirming the categorical proofs [establishing] that Allah the Exalted is non-originated, thereby offsetting the progressive sequence [of devious questions].[77] Similarly, [one can] keep in mind that all created beings are integrated under the category of that which is created [by the Creator]. Consequently, if it were [rationally] acceptable to ask who created the Creator, that would lead to a never-ending cycle [of the same],[78] which is utterly fallacious; it portrays the depravity of scholastic theology (*ʿilm al-kalām*); it also [serves as] an evidence for the prohibition of [superfluous] debating and arguing over that which relates to Allah's essence and attributes; it likewise alludes to the vitality of faith for those who adhere to and trust [well-established scholarship].

77 Many of these concepts are deeply ingrained across civilizations; consider the proverbs, 'the devil is in the details' and 'an idle mind is the devil's workshop.'

78 A mental tactic to break the vicious cycle is to remind oneself and think, "I am going to engage in circular reasoning that has no end." Thus, becoming cognizant of what one is doing and how it is not beneficial can help defuse the engagement of the process, and aid in avoiding the tiresome process of chasing a never-ending line of questioning. Another strategy offered by al-Qārī here is to remind oneself of a definitive conclusive statement or principle that helps one avoid the details, by simply being reminded that by definition, the creation is that which has a creator. So, if one were to ask the question of 'who created the creator' then they would have to ask, 'who created the creator's creator', leading to infinite regress; and infinite regress is an impossible logical fallacy.

CHAPTER 6

Themes on General Well-Being

1 Man's Discovery of His Own Vices. *Al-Ṭibb al-Ruhānī* (*Psycho-Spiritual Medicine*) by Abū Bakr Muḥammad ibn Zakariyā al-Rāzī (d. 251 AH/925 CE)

1.1 *Author's Biography*

Abu Bakr al-Rāzī is one of the most eminent Muslim physicians of the classical period. He acquired much of his medical education under the tutelage of the famous polymath Imam Muḥammad ibn Jarīr al-Ṭabarī. He lived during the rule of the Abbasid caliph al-Muktafi, who appointed him as the director of one of the first hospitals in the Islamic world, situated in Baghdad. Al-Rāzī authored numerous medical treatises, embracing a holistic approach that embraced both the physical and psychological aspects of health and treatment. Notably, al-Rāzī recognized and valued the significance of what we presently refer to as the therapeutic alliance between the practitioner and patient. He emphasized that "the physician, even if he has his doubts [in the treatability of the patient], must always make the patient believe he will recover, for the state of the body is linked to the state of the mind."

Al-Rāzī's pioneering work extends beyond medicine. He holds recognition as the first person to describe and document classically conditioned responses, predating Pavlov's research by a thousand years. Although many of al-Rāzī's works have unfortunately been lost over time, *al-Tibb al-Rūḥānī* serves as a testament to the profound richness of his thinking, which centered on rectifying the psyche from a spiritual, moral, and psychological perspective.

1.2 *Text Overview and Significance*

In this translated excerpt from *al-Tibb al-Rūḥānī*, Imam al-Rāzī delves into the importance of nurturing one's mental and spiritual well-being, highlighting the need for guidance from an accomplished mentor, or what he refers to as a "supervisor." He argues the impossibility for an individual to be fully aware of all of one's personal flaws as each person has a self-serving bias that blinds them or makes them defensive when it comes to being cognizant of their own shortcomings. To address this, al-Rāzī suggests that a person should take the advice of a wise person or supervisor who can assist in identifying areas for personal improvement and growth. Additionally, he emphasizes the value of paying attention to the opinions of one's neighbors, associates, and fellow believers, as their perspectives – both positive and negative – can provide insight into one's character. Al-Rāzī further contends that one's enemies can serve as a valuable source of recognizing personal faults, as their motives may lead them to expose his flaws and weaknesses.

This section principally underscores the importance of mentorship or supervision for self-improvement and development. Despite the widespread stigma amongst contemporary Muslim populations when it comes to treating mental health, al-Rāzī's treatise illustrates the indigenous and deeply ingrained notion of seeking support and help; such was and is very much an inherently Islamic practice.

Finally, it is worth noting that al-Rāzī draws extensively from the Greek philosophers throughout his work. He references Galen's writings and acknowledges that the chapter at hand serves as a condensed summary of the most crucial points from Galen's work on the same subject matter.

1.3 *Arabic Text*

الفصل الرابع
في تعرف الرجل عيوب نفسه

من أجل أن كل واحد منا لا يمكنه منع الهوى؛ محبة منه لنفسه، واستصوابا واستحسانا لأفعاله، وأن ينظر بعين العقل الخالصة المحضة إلى خلائقه و سيرته لا يكاد يستبين ما فيه من المعايب والضرائب الذميمة، و متى لم يستبن ذلك فيعرفه لم يقلع عنه؛ إذ ليس يشعر به؛ فضلا عن أن يستقبحه، ويعمل في الإقلاع عنه.

فينبغي أن يسند الرجل أمره في هذا إلى رجل عاقل، كثير اللزوم له والكون معه، ويسأله و يضرع إليه ويؤكد عليه أن يخبره بكل ما يعرفه فيه من المعايب، ويعلمه أن ذلك أحب الأشياء إليه وأوقعها عنده، وأن المنة عليه منه تعظم في ذلك والشكر يكثر، ويسأله ألا يستحييه في ذلك ولا يجامله، ويعلمه أنه متى تساهل وضجع في شيء منه فقد أساء إليه وغشه واستوجب منه اللائمة عليه.

فإذا أخذ الرجل المشرف يخبره ويعلمه ما فيه، وما ظهر وبان له منه، لم يظهر له اغتماما ولا استخزاء، بل أظهر له سرورا بما يستمع، وتشوقا إلى ما لم يستمع منه. فإن رآه في حال ما قد كتمه شيئا؛ استحياء منه، أو قصر في العبارة عن تقبيح ذلك، أو حسنها لامه على ذلك، وأظهر له اغتماما به، وأعلمه أنه لا يحب ذلك منه، ولا يريد إلا التصريح وإعلامه ما يراه على وجهه.

فإن وجده في حال أخرى قد زاد وأسرف في تقبيح شيء رآه منه وتهجينه لم يغضبه ذلك، بل حمده عليه وأظهر له بشرا وسرورا بما رآه منه.

وينبغي أن يجدد سؤال هذا المشرف عليه حالا بعد حال؛ فإن الأخلاق والضرائب الرديئة قد تحدث بعد أن لم تكن.

وينبغي أن يستخبر ويتحسس ما يقول فيه جيرانه ومعاملوه و إخوانه، وبماذا يمدحونه وبماذا يعيبونه؛ فإن الرجل إذا سلك في هذا المعنى هذا المسلك لم يكد يخفى عليه شيء من عيوبه وإن قل وخفي.

فإن اتفق له ووقع عدو ومنازع محب لإظهار مساوئه ومَعَايِبِه، لم يستدرك من قبله معرفة عيوبه، بل اضطر وألجئ إلى الإقلاع عنها، إن كان ممن لنفسه عند نفسه مقدار، وممن يحب أن يكون خيرا فاضلا.

وقد كتب في هذا المعنى جالينوس كتابا جعل رسمه: "في أن الأخيار ينتفعون بأعدائهم"، فذكر فيه منافع صارت إليه؛ من أجل عدو كان له. وكتب أيضا "في تعرف الرجل عيوب نفسه"، مقالة قد ذكرنا نحن جوامعها وجملتها هنا.

و فيما ذكرنا من هذا الباب، كفاية وبلاغ، ومن استعمله لم يزل كالقدح مقوما مثقَّفًا.

1.4 *English Translation*

Regarding Man's Discovery of His Own Vices

Indeed, each and every one of us is [inherently] unable to [completely] suppress [our] base desires (*hawā*). This is due to [man's innate] infatuation with his own self, and [his tendency] to consider his own actions [to be] correct and upright. He [cannot] evaluate his own character and lifestyle with an unbiased, purely rational perspective; [as such] he can barely detect his own vices and blameworthy habits. Since such [tendencies] cannot be detected, he does not acknowledge them, or get rid of them. After all, he does not [even] perceive them, let alone deem them inappropriate and [thus] work to uproot them.[1]

1 This highlights an inherent Islamic civilizational value in which all individuals are required to undergo some degree of mentorship or supervision for the personal refinement of character. While the philosophers may favor wise counsel, spiritual practitioners (Sufis) often advocate for qualified spiritual masters to supervise them. In contemporary societies marked by growing individualism, the conscious and deliberate focus on character development is steadily waning. Esteemed treatises that discuss character development, like al-Rāzī's, assert that becoming a good human being necessitates not only facing personal struggles and employing strategic approaches, but also having proper supervision.

Positive psychology seems to be among the few areas of psychology concerned with character development (see Christopher Peterson and Martin E.P. Seligman, *Character Strengths and Virtues: A Handbook and Classification* (Washington, DC: New York: American Psychological Association; Oxford University Press, 2004)). Notably, Peterson and Seligman

In consideration [of the above], one should rely, in this regard, on another [particularly] astute person. One [should] often accompany him, ask him, be humble towards him, and be sure to inform him of whatever deficiencies one recognizes to be within their own self. [Indeed,] they should let it be known to him that this is the most beloved and most significant of things, and that this favor of his is tremendous, and oft appreciated.[2] They should ask him not to be timid in this and to avoid flattery. They should inform him that if they are lax or sluggish in anything related to this, then they will have wronged and misled him, and [will thus be] deserving of rebuke [by him].

Now, when this person [acting as a] supervisor starts apprising one and disclosing what has become apparent and manifest to him regarding whatever is in one, [it is crucial to] avoid displaying any [sense of] dejection or disgrace. On the contrary, one should be delighted with whatever one hears from him, and eagerly anticipate what one has not yet heard. If one believes [that the overseer] has concealed something out of timidness, or has held back in his expression of reprimand, or [has even] presented it in a favorable light, one should [politely] censure him and express his discontent with that. One should then let him know that one does not like this of him but [rather] prefers nothing other than forthrightness in stating what he evidently observes.

[On the other hand,] if [the person] finds that [one's supervisor] has, in another situation, exaggerated and overstated his censure and condemnation of what he has observed, it should not upset them. Instead, one [should] thank him and rejoice, expressing delight due to what he has observed from him.[3]

It is crucial to renew one's request for this overseer['s help] every now and then, as bad habits and characteristics can [always] come into being where they did not exist [before].

Moreover, a person should [regularly] consult and make enquiries from his neighbors, colleagues, and [fellow] brothers regarding one's own self: what [exactly] do they find praiseworthy in him and in what do they [likewise] find fault. If a person adopts this approach in these matters, hardly any of his vices will [likely] remain hidden to him, no matter how small or obscure.[4]

---

discuss character and virtue literature within the Islamic intellectual heritage (Peterson & Seligman, 2004).

2 Such an individual as described by al-Rāzī would be willing to undergo significant critique on account of the degree of importance they assign to their personal development.

3 Such is the attitude of an individual who is willing to err on the side of caution on account of his emphasis and desire to espouse lofty character.

4 Self-awareness and understanding one's strengths and weaknesses are important components of psychological well-being. Getting input from other people can yield insightful information that advances self-awareness.

Indeed, if before one is able to redress the recognition of their faults, they come across an antagonist or adversary who is keen on exposing one's vices and weaknesses, then they will be compelled and forced to remove them. [This is, of course,] if they are a person of self-respect who desires to be good and virtuous.

Galen has written a treatise on this matter entitled, *That the Best Men Profit from their Enemies*, in which he mentions the benefits he gained from an enemy of his. He also wrote *On a Man's Discovery of His Own Vices*, [which is] an article that we have given a summary of, mentioning its main points.[5]

What we have explained in this chapter is quite sufficient, and whosoever makes use of this would resemble a [sharp] arrow on route [to reach its target].[6]

2 The Means of Recognizing One's Own Flaws. *Iḥyāʾ ʿUlūm al-Dīn* (*The Revival of Religious Sciences*) by Imam Abū Ḥāmid Muḥammad al-Ghazālī (d. 505 AH/1111 CE)

2.1 *Author's Biography*

See Author Biography under section 1 of Chapter 2.

Mainstream psychological frameworks recognize the necessity of seeking external perspectives for self-improvement and self-awareness, even though the unique cultural and religious setting may be different. It is consistent with the notion that relationships with others and constructive criticism are important components of human development. Some therapeutic approaches, such as cognitive behavioral therapy (CBT) or interpersonal therapy for example, involve exploring interpersonal dynamics and seeking feedback from others to gain insights into one's behavior and thought patterns.

A similar concept of "outsider witness" is also found in narrative theory that aims to achieve better self-awareness and consistency of one's behavior with their professed identity by helping patients receive recognition from the broader community (see Maggie Carey and S. Russell, *Re-Authoring: Some Answers to Commonly Asked Questions* (2003: Dulwich Centre, n.d.).; Margaret M. Leahy, Mary O'Dwyer, and Fiona Ryan, "Witnessing Stories: Definitional Ceremonies in Narrative Therapy with Adults Who Stutter," *Journal of Fluency Disorders* 37, no. 4 (December 2012): 234–41.).

5 This is a clear demonstration of Islamic philosopher-physicians not shying away from the usage of the ancient Greek and Hellenistic works in their writings. Islamic scholars inherited the philosophic and medical tradition from the ancient Greeks, adopting and adapting it to their civilizational values.

6 While al-Rāzī is not shy to cite Galen in his writing here and throughout his book, his disclaimer demonstrates that while he accepted Greek ideas, he was not uncritical of them. Here, al-Rāzī summarizes only that much of what he finds useful from Galen and integrates it into his work amidst his own unique approach to human psychology.

2.2 *Text Overview and Significance*

In this translated segment of the renowned *Iḥyā*, Imam al-Ghazālī highlights the four ways through which a person may become cognizant of their own vices and deficiencies. This particular chapter is strikingly similar to al-Rāzī's writings in *al-Ṭibb al-Ruhānī*. It is clear that al-Ghazālī drew these ideas as well as others from the available works of the philosophers and physicians of his time. While he was a fierce critic of their theology, he was not shy to acknowledge any good they had to offer, especially regarding elements of human nature, health, or pathology that did not contravene Islamic beliefs, practices, or principles. In fact, al-Ghazālī's work stands out as it uniquely and eloquently filters philosophical discourse through Islamic scripture; such knowledge was taken by al-Ghazālī to be both supportive and complementary of Islamic principles derived from Islamic holy texts.

In this translated excerpt, the first two modes of gaining self-awareness that are mentioned by al-Ghazālī are relational modalities. The first method is through the relationship between the seeker and a qualified spiritual master (shaykh) who is well-experienced, scholarly, and capable of discerning the negative traits within an individual. Although finding such a person can be challenging, when such an individual is identified, one should inform him of their shortcomings so that the spiritual master can guide them in their treatment. Overall, the most significant difference between this work and other philosophical works revolving around character development is the inclusion of the qualified spiritual master as the central means for gaining self-awareness and rectification. The second relational modality mentioned is to draw from a religious colleague or peer who possesses both experience and uprightness. In modern psychological discourse, perhaps such a role could be fulfilled by the mental health practitioner. The third approach to gaining awareness of one's flaws is by attending to the criticism of one's enemies. This is because a friend may be hesitant to disclose faults whereas an enemy will not withhold their criticisms in the same way. While one should take such statements with a grain of salt, it is duly important to examine whether or not there is some truth to them. The last modality mentioned is to socially mingle with people and consider the possibility of others' apparent flaws existing within one's own self.

2.3 *Arabic Text*

بَيَانُ الطَّرِيقِ الَّذِي يَعْرِفُ بِهِ الْإِنْسَانُ عُيُوبَ نَفْسِهِ

اعْلَمْ: أَنَّ اللَّهَ عَزَّ وَجَلَّ إِذَا أَرَادَ بِعَبْدٍ خَيْرًا بَصَّرَهُ بِعُيُوبِ نَفْسِهِ، فَمَنْ كَانَتْ بَصِيرَتُهُ نَافِذَةً لَمْ تَخْفَ عَلَيْهِ عُيُوبُهُ، فَإِذَا عَرَفَ الْعُيُوبَ أَمْكَنَهُ الْعِلَاجُ، وَلَكِنَّ أَكْثَرَ الْخَلْقِ جَاهِلُونَ بِعُيُوبِ أَنْفُسِهِمْ، يَرَى أَحَدُهُمُ الْقَذَى فِي عَيْنِ أَخِيهِ وَلَا يَرَى الْجِذْعَ فِي عَيْنِ نَفْسِهِ.

فَمَنْ أَرَادَ أَنْ يَعْرِفَ عُيُوبَ نفسه فله أربعة طرق:

الْأَوَّلُ: أَنْ يَجْلِسَ بَيْنَ يَدَيْ شَيْخٍ بَصِيرٍ بعيوب النفس، مطلع على خفايا الآفات، ويحكِّمَهُ في نفسه، ويتبعَ إشارتَهُ في مجاهدته، وهذا شأن المريد مع شيخه، والتلميذ مع أستاذه، فيعرِّفُهُ أستاذُهُ وشيخُهُ عيوبَ نفسِهِ، ويعرِّفُهُ طريقَ علاجِه، وهذا قد عَزَّ في الزمان وجودُهُ.

الثَّانِي: أَنْ يَطْلُبَ صَدِيقًا صَدُوقًا بَصِيرًا مُتَدَيِّنًا، فينصبَهُ رقيباً على نفسه ليلاحظ أَحْوَالَهُ وَأَفْعَالَهُ، فَمَا كَرِهَهُ مِنْ أَخْلَاقِهِ وَأَفْعَالِهِ، وعيوبه الباطنة والظاهرة ينبهه عليه.

فهكذا كانَ يفعل الأكياس والأكابر مِنْ أَئِمَّةِ الدِّينِ، كانَ عمر رَضِيَ اللَّهُ عَنْهُ يَقُولُ: (رَحِمَ اللَّهُ امْرَأً أَهْدَى إِلَيَّ عيوبي). وكان يسأل سلمانَ عن عيوبه لما قدم عليه، وقال له: ما الذي بلغكَ عني مما تكرهُهُ؟ فاستعفى، فألح عليه، فقال: بلغني أنك جمعت بين إدامين على مائدة، وأن لك حُلَّتَيْنِ، حلَّةً بالنهار وحلَّةً بالليل، قال: وهل بلغك غير هذا؟ قال: لا، قال: أما هذان فقد كفيتهُما. وَكَانَ يَسْأَلُ حذيفة وَيَقُولُ لَهُ: أَنْتَ صَاحِبُ سِرِّ رَسُولِ اللَّهِ صَلَّى اللَّهُ عَلَيْهِ وَسَلَّمَ فِي الْمُنَافِقِينَ، فَهَلْ تَرى عَلَيَّ شَيْئًا مِنْ آثَارِ النِّفَاقِ؟

فَهُوَ عَلَى جَلَالَةِ قَدْرِهِ وَعُلُوِّ مَنْصِبِهِ هَكَذَا كَانَتْ تُهْمَتُهُ لِنَفْسِهِ رَضِيَ اللَّهُ عَنْهُ، فَكُلُّ مَنْ كَانَ أَوْفَرَ عَقْلًا وَأَعْلَى مَنْصِبًا كَانَ أَقَلَّ إِعْجَابًا، وَأَعْظَمَ اتِّهَامًا لِنَفْسِهِ.

إلا أن هذا أيضاً قد عَزَّ، فقلَّ في الأصدقاء من يترك المداهنة، فيخبرُ بالعيبِ، أو يتركُ الحسدَ، فلا يزيدُ على قدر الواجب، فلا تخلو في أصدقائِكَ عن حسود، أو صاحب غرضٍ يرى ما ليس بعيب عيباً، أو عن مداهن يخفي عنك بعض عيوبك.

ولهذا كان داود الطائي قد اعتزل الناس، فقيل له: لم لا تخالط الناس؟ فقال: وماذا أصنع بأقوام يخفون عني عيوبي؟!

فقد كانت شهوةُ ذوي الدين أن يتنبهوا لعيوبهم بتنبيه غيرهم، وَقَدْ آلَ الْأَمْرُ فِي أَمْثَالِنَا إِلَى أَنَّ أَبْغَضَ الْخَلْقِ إِلَيْنَا مَنْ يَنْصَحُنَا وَيُعَرِّفُنَا عُيُوبَنَا، وَيَكَادُ هَذَا أَنْ يَكُونَ مُفْصِحًا عَنْ ضَعْفِ الْإِيمَانِ؛ فَإِنَّ الْأَخْلَاقَ السَّيِّئَةَ حَيَّاتٌ وَعَقَارِبُ لَدَّاغَةٌ، فَلَوْ نَبَّهَنَا مُنَبِّهٌ عَلَى أَنَّ تَحْتَ ثَوْبِنَا عَقْرَبًا لَتَقَلَّدْنَا مِنْهُ مِنَّةً، وَفَرِحْنَا بِهِ وَاشْتَغَلْنَا بإزالة العقرب وإبعادها وقتلها، وإنما نكايتها على البدن، ويدوم أَلَمُهَا يَوْمًا فَمَا دُونَهُ، وَنِكَايَةُ الْأَخْلَاقِ الرَّدِيئَةِ عَلَى صَمِيمِ الْقَلْبِ، وَيُخْشَى أَنْ تَدُومَ بعد الموت أبداً، أو آلافاً من السنين، ثُمَّ لَا نَفْرَحُ بِمَنْ يُنَبِّهُنَا عَلَيْهَا، وَلَا نَشْتَغِلُ بِإِزَالَتِهَا، بَلْ نَشْتَغِلُ بِمُقَابَلَةِ النَّاصِحِ بِمِثْلِ مَقَالَتِهِ، فَنَقُولُ لَهُ: (وَأَنْتَ أَيْضًا تَصْنَعُ كَيْتَ وَكَيْتَ)، وَتَشْغَلُنَا الْعَدَاوَةُ مَعَهُ عَنِ الِانْتِفَاعِ بِنُصْحِهِ، وَيُشْبِهُ أَنْ يَكُونَ ذَلِكَ مِنْ قَسَاوَةِ الْقَلْبِ الَّتِي أَثْمَرَتْهَا كَثْرَةُ الذُّنُوبِ، وَأَصْلُ ذلك ضعف الإيمان، فنسأل الله عز وجل أَنْ يُعَرِّفَنَا رُشْدَنَا، وَيُبَصِّرَنَا بِعُيُوبِنَا، وَيَشْغَلَنَا بِمُدَاوَاتِهَا، وَيُوَفِّقَنَا لِلْقِيَامِ بِشُكْرِ مَنْ يُطْلِعُنَا عَلَى مَسَاوِئِنَا بِمَنِّهِ وَفَضْلِهِ.

الطَّرِيقُ الثَّالِثُ: أَنْ يَسْتَفِيدَ مَعْرِفَةَ عُيُوبِ نَفْسِهِ مِنْ أَلْسِنَةِ أَعْدَائِهِ، فَإِنَّ عَيْنَ السُّخْطِ تُبْدِي الْمَسَاوِئَ، وَلَعَلَّ انْتِفَاعَ الْإِنْسَانِ بِعَدُوٍّ مشاحن يذَكِّرُهُ عُيُوبَهُ أَكْثَرُ مِنِ انْتِفَاعِهِ بِصَدِيقٍ مُدَاهِنٍ يُثْنِي عَلَيْهِ وَيَمْدَحُهُ، وَيُخْفِي عَنْهُ عُيُوبَهُ، إِلَّا أَنَّ الطَّبْعَ مَجْبُولٌ عَلَى تَكْذِيبِ الْعَدُوِّ، وَحَمْلِ مَا يَقُولُهُ عَلَى الْحَسَدِ، وَلَكِنَّ الْبَصِيرَ لَا يَخْلُو عَنِ الِانْتِفَاعِ بِقَوْلِ أَعْدَائِهِ؛ فَإِنَّ مَسَاوِئَهُ لَا بُدَّ وَأَنْ تَنْتَشِرَ عَلَى أَلْسِنَتِهِمْ.

الطَّرِيقُ الرَّابِعُ: أَنْ يُخَالِطَ النَّاسَ، فَكُلُّ مَا رَآهُ مَذْمُومًا فِيمَا بَيْنَ الْخَلْقِ فَلْيُطَالِبْ نَفْسَهُ بِهِ وَيَنْسُبْهَا إِلَيْهِ؛ فَإِنَّ الْمُؤْمِنَ مِرْآةُ الْمُؤْمِنِ، فَيَرَى مِنْ عُيُوبِ غَيْرِهِ عُيُوبَ نَفْسِهِ، وَيَعْلَمُ أَنَّ الطِّبَاعَ مُتَقَارِبَةٌ فِي اتِّبَاعِ الْهَوَى، فَمَا يَتَّصِفُ بِهِ واحد من الأقران لا ينفك القرن الآخر عَنْ أَصْلِهِ، أَوْ عَنْ أَعْظَمَ مِنْهُ، أَوْ عن شيء منه، فليتفقد نفسه ويطهرها من كُلِّ مَا يَذُمُّهُ مِنْ غَيْرِهِ، وَنَاهِيكَ بِهَذَا تَأْدِيبًا، فَلَوْ تَرَكَ النَّاسُ كُلُّهُمْ مَا يَكْرَهُونَهُ من غيرهم لاستغنوا عن المؤدب.

قيل لعيسى عليه السلام: من أَدَّبَكَ؟ قال: ما أدبني أحد، رأيت جهل الجاهل شينا فاجتنبته.

وهذا كله حِيَلُ من فقد شيخاً عارفاً زكياً، بصيراً بعيوب النفس، مشفقاً ناصحاً في الدين، فارغاً من تهذيب نفسه، مشتغلاً بتهذيب عباد الله تعالى، ناصحاً لهم، فمن وجد ذلك فقد وجد الطبيب، فليلازمه، فهو الذي يخلصه من مرضه، وينجيه من الهلاك الذي هو بصدده.

2.4 *English Translation*

The Means of Recognizing One's Own Flaws

[One should] realize that if Allah wants goodness for a servant [of His], He makes him cognizant of his own flaws. If he is [sufficiently] discerning, none of his flaws would remain undetected. By recognizing [one's own] faults, reform thus becomes possible. However, most people are oblivious to their own shortcomings; noticing the [tiniest] defect in others, whilst failing to detect the most blatant [of vices] within their own self.

There are four ways in which a person may recognize their own flaws:[7]

7 It is noteworthy that Imam al-Ghazālī's four methods completely converge with Abū Bakr al-Razī's suggestions of how to discover one's vices. This demonstrates Imam al-Ghazālī's willingness to draw directly from existent philosophical and medical works in his synthesis. The difference between the two styles of writing is evident in al-Ghazālī's reliance on scriptural sources to justify and discuss such issues of character development. This chapter

First: One [should] consult a shaykh[8] who has [deep] insight into inner deficiencies, [and is thus] well-aware of subtle [spiritual] illnesses. They [should] depute him as an authority over one's self, and [thereafter] adhere to his directives for their [eventual] rectification. This is [the nature of] the relationship between a disciple (*murīd*)[9] and his shaykh, or a student with his teacher; [both] the teacher and shaykh alert [the seeker concerning] his flaws and [likewise] enlighten him [as to] the method of treatment. However, this [approach] has become uncommon over time.

Second: [A person] may seek [assistance from] a sincere, insightful, and religious friend,[10] appointing him to [carefully] observe and take note of one's demeanor and deeds. He [may] subsequently draw their attention towards whatever he dispraises of their manners, actions, and flaws – apparent or hidden. This is precisely what the prominent, astute, religious scholars [of the past] used to do. ʿUmar, may Allah be pleased with him, used to say, "May Allah have mercy on whoever guides me to [recognize] my shortcomings."[11] When Salmān [may Allah be pleased with him] would come to him, ʿUmar used to ask him about his own flaws, saying, "What has reached you concerning me that you dislike?" Salmān would try to avoid [the question], but ʿUmar insisted.

---

is a clear display of adopting and adapting Greek and philosophical works into a uniquely Islamic and theological literary discourse.

8 This is a reference to a shaykh of Sufism; a qualified spiritual master who undertakes various Islamic disciplines and practices to develop character and spirituality. This is a living practice-based tradition of Islam that continues until today. A shaykh is one who has received spiritual training from their teachers and has been formally authorized to initiate disciples in the spiritual path (*ṭarīqa*). Such a system of authorization originates from an unbroken chain that reaches back to the Master of all spiritual masters, the Prophet Muhammad, may Allah bless him and grant him peace.

9 A disciple is the one who is formally initiated into a spiritual path by making a solemn pledge of allegiance (*bayʿa*) to an accomplished spiritual master. Thereafter, one is expected to faithfully strive upon the spiritual path, working upon themselves and fully adhering to the spiritual counsel of the shaykh, to the best of their ability.

10 Imam al-Ghazālī outlines a second relational modality for character development that is unlike the typical one prescribed by the theologians. This relational modality seems to indicate a more authoritative relationship rather than an authoritarian one. The contemporary Muslim psychologist could potentially largely fulfill this role. However, it is important to note that al-Ghazālī outlines the important prerequisite quality of such an individual, i.e., of being Islamically upright or righteous. One of the most common definitions of uprightness, or *ʿadāla*, as outlined in Islamic law, is to abstain from all major sins and to refrain from persisting upon committing minor sins, with personal righteousness being preponderant, overall. (al-Sayyid al-Sharīf al-Jurjānī, *Kitāb al-Taʿrīfāt* (Lebanon: Maktabat Lubnān, 1985), 147.)

11 (Al-Ismāʿīlī and al-Dhahabī, *Manāqib ʿUmar*).

He thus answered, "I have heard that you [reportedly] conjoined two [different] dishes on a [single] spread, and that you have two outfits; one for the daytime and the other for night."[12] 'Umar [then] asked, "Have you heard [anything else] other than this?" Salman replied, "No." 'Umar said, "As for those two [concerns], I have taken care of them." He would [likewise] implore Ḥudhayfa [may Allah be pleased with him] saying, "Concerning the hypocrites, you are the [appointed] confidant of the Prophet, may Allah bless him and grant him peace. So, do you see any of the characteristics of hypocrisy in me?" This is how he would scrutinize himself despite his eminence and high status, may Allah be pleased with him. Hence, the greater a person's intelligence and rank, the more critical they [should] be regarding their own self and [thus] further away [from] self-infatuation.[13]

However, this is also rare, as few friends [can] resist adulation so as to [accurately] disclose [one's] flaws. Conversely, [few can] avoid envy, due to which they do not say more than what is required [of them]. As such, amongst your friends there will inevitably be someone with envy or an ulterior motive, contriving that which is not even a deficiency to be a vice. Or [there will be others] who [excessively] flatter, concealing some of your flaws from you.

For this reason, Dāwūd al-Ṭā'ī isolated himself from others. He was consequently asked, "Why do you not associate with people?" He responded, "What am I to do with people who hide my flaws from me?"

Indeed, the [ardent] desire of the faithful was to have their flaws pointed out to them by others. But this has degenerated [significantly] amongst people like us [nowadays]; [amongst] all of creation, the most despised to us are those

12 While this may not be seen as reprehensible according to the general norms of most people, the companions of the Prophet, may Allah bless him and grant him peace, held a very stringent standard of asceticism and vigilance in abstaining from the dangers of the love of wealth. Given the weight of responsibility they had over the community in serving as role models, they were particularly meticulous in ensuring that they did not demonstrate even the slightest inclination towards luxury or worldly comforts, even if they were technically permissible. As a famous Arabic proverb states, "The good deeds of the righteous are considered to be misdeeds for those closest to Allah."

13 Taking account of oneself on a daily basis can elicit the emergence of positive characteristics from within a person and engender holistic health and balance (see Hooman Keshavarzi et al., eds., Applying Islamic Principles to Clinical Mental Health Care: Introducing Traditional Islamically Integrated Psychotherapy, 1st ed. (Routledge, 2020), 263.). Individuals are encouraged to reflect upon their behaviors, analyze their actions as well as their thoughts, and struggle against their lower ego's negative inclinations (Keshavarzi et al., 257–59.).

who advise us and make us aware of our deficiencies.[14] This is a clear indication of weak faith.

Verily, bad morals are [like] vicious snakes and scorpions. So, if someone were to warn us that there is a scorpion [hidden] in our clothes, we would readily believe them and [immediately] take action to remove, kill, and get rid of it, well-pleased and grateful for the warning. The sting of a scorpion only affects the body, its pain lasting for a day or even less. However, immorality injures the innermost [part] of the heart,[15] [its harm] potentially extends beyond death, lasting for thousands of years or [even] eternity. Yet, we are displeased with whoever alerts us concerning it, and we do not take action to extirpate it. Instead, we exonerate [ourselves] by confronting the one advising us and retorting, "well, you also do such and such …".[16] Enmity [thus] preoccupies us from deriving benefit through their advice. This appears to come from hard-heartedness caused by an abundance of sins, the root of which is [essentially] weakness of faith.

We ask Allah the Exalted, through his generosity and favor, to help us come to our senses, enabling us to recognize our deficiencies and strive to rectify them; and to guide us to be grateful towards those who reveal our flaws to us.

Third: To gain insight [into] one's flaws via the claims of one's enemies. Indeed, the contemptuous eye finds all faults. Hence, it is likely that a person would benefit more from an impudent enemy who recounts one's flaws as opposed to a polite friend who praises one and obscures one's faults. But [our] natural disposition is inclined to discredit [our] enemies and interpret whatever they say [to be rooted] in envy. Nonetheless, an astute person still derives

---

14 It is interesting how al-Ghazālī is pointing out the moral decline of his time, at a period when there was still a lot of literature being produced on virtue, ethics, character, and spirituality. With an increasingly materialistic society and the spread of western individualism globally, the consequent excess of emphasis, acceptance, tolerance, and sensitivity has created a social environment that is not conducive to social rectification or negative feedback. Resiliency is on the decline among the newer generations, particularly with the increased sensitivity and need for unchecked self-expression seen in generations Y and Z (American Psychological Association, Stress in America Survey, 2022).

15 Abu Hurayra, may Allah be pleased with him, reported, "the Messenger of Allah, peace and blessings be upon him, said, 'Verily, when the servant commits a sin, a black mark appears upon his heart. If he abandons the sin, seeks forgiveness, and repents, then his heart will be polished. If he returns to the sin, the blackness will increase until it [eventually] overcomes his heart. This is the covering that Allah has mentioned: *No, rather a covering is over their hearts from what they have earned.* (Al-Muṭaffifīn, 83:14)" (Al-Tirmidhī, 3334).

16 *Tu quoque* or "you too" fallacy, is a statement that intends to discredit an individual's claim by attacking their own behaviors and actions as being inconsistent with their claim. It is an appeal to hypocrisy.

benefit from the sayings of his enemies, as [the reality of] his shortcomings will undoubtedly come out of their mouths.

Fourth: To mingle with [other] people. Whenever a person sees something reprehensible in others, he should check himself regarding it, and [furthermore] ascribe it to himself, as a believer is [like] a mirror to [other] believer[s]. He thus sees his own flaws through the faults of others and knows that natural tendencies are [relatively] similar to one another when it comes to following [one's] desires. As such, whatever characteristics are apparent in an individual are bound to exist in another person amongst peers; essentially, for the most-part, or [at least] in some sense. So, one should scrutinize their own self, and cleanse it of everything one deems blameworthy in others. This alone would be sufficient for rectification;[17] [hypothetically,] if absolutely everyone were to forsake what they disapprove of in others, there would be no need for a reformer.

'Īsā, upon him be peace, was [once] asked, "Who taught you good comportment?" He replied, "No one taught me; I saw the sullying ignorance of the ignorant, and subsequently kept away from it."

All of these are [possible] alternatives for those who are bereft of a discerning and righteous shaykh; [one who is] insightful regarding spiritual weaknesses; compassionate; admonitory in religion; accomplished [in terms] of his own self-rectification; genuinely devoted to the reformation of Allah's servants. Whosoever finds such [a person] has found [their spiritual] doctor, and should thus cling [firmly] to him, as he is the one who can [help] rid a person of their ailments and save them from impending destruction.

3 The Need for the Management of the Psyche. *Maṣāliḥ al-Abdān wa-l-Anfus* (*Sustenance of the Body and the Psyche*) by Abū Zayd al-Balkhī (d. 322 AH/934 CE)

3.1 *Author's Biography*

Abū Zayd Aḥmad ibn Sahl al-Balkhī was born in modern day Afghanistan in a city called Balkh. He was recognized as a polymath and spent significant

17 Imam al-Ghazālī is drawing this from classical Greek and Islamic philosophical works, emphasizing its utility in this particular approach to character change. He outlines this methodology as among the most powerful tools for gaining personal insight and transforming the self. By seeing one's behaviors in others, one is able to externally observe the degree of repugnance in one's own behavior, which can engender a feeling of adaptive shame and disgust. This effectively deters one from behaving in a similar way again in the future.

time in Baghdad to further his education. His life was dedicated to the fields of psychology, science, literature, geography, Islamic theology, and theoretical medicine. He was a student of the renowned physician al-Kindī. He laid a great deal of importance to spirituality viewing religion as the greatest of all philosophies, understanding that in order to be a good philosopher one needed to be grounded in spirituality and be a sincere worshiper of Allah. The discovery of his treatise on physical and mental health entitled *Maṣālih al-Abdān wa al-Anfus* has led to an immense interest in the works of the classical Islamic scholars regarding human psychology. It is noteworthy that in his work, al-Balkhī's classification and symptomatology of obsessive disorders parallels the fifth edition of the modern Diagnostic and Statistical Manual of Obsessive-Compulsive Disorders (OCD). al-Balkhī was well versed in the Islamic sciences as well, so his writings encourage patients to seek treatment for illnesses by reminding them of the prophetic tradition that Allah has created a cure for every illness.

3.2 *Text Overview and Significance*

The original treatise *Maṣālih al-Abdān wa al-Anfus* by al-Balkhī is composed of two larger sections. The first section is devoted to physical health, while the second section of his book deals with psychological health. The psychology-focused section of his book can be further subdivided into two parts. The first part, spanning from chapters one to four contains several general public guidelines related to mental health. For the purposes of this compilation, only these first four chapters have been translated. In these chapters, he outlines general ways to preserve psychological health, utilizing mostly a cognitive psychological approach. He attempts to provide important education about human psychology and the stressors of the world in order to engender resilience in his readers. The second part, spanning from chapters five through seven was not included in this compilation; these are more interventionally oriented, providing practical guidelines and assessments of particular emotional states and disorders.

Overall, al-Balkhī concludes that psychological disorders arise out of emotional dysregulation; thus, he views emotions as the central indicators of health or pathology. Accordingly, in his view, the ultimate goal of health is to acquire regulated and balanced emotions, mostly through a healthy cognitive orientation to life preventatively, and to restore or cognitively restructure one's thinking in order to reverse psychopathology. Al-Balkhī emphasizes the importance of mental health and ascertains that human beings are bound to experience both physical and mental health disorders. Thus, it is imperative to give equal and sometimes even more importance to the maintenance of one's psyche.

He demonstrates how much the psyche is interconnected with physical health and how the absence of caring for one's mental health can also contribute to the onset of physical ailments.

Furthermore, it is also noteworthy that while al-Balkhī is a trained theologian in his own right, his literary style is similar to the other philosophers and physicians, making few explicit scriptural references. While he does write like a philosopher physician in that regard, he also clearly states that he has simplified the language employed in his book. To explain further, by omitting exhaustive theological discourse and complex philosophical debates pertaining to the soul or psyche, he sought to make his book practical and accessible to the average reader.

3.3 *Arabic Text*

الباب الأول
في الإخبار عن مبلغ الحاجة إلى تدبير مصالح الأنفس

قد أتينا في المقالة الأولى من هذا الكتاب على ما تلزم الحاجة إلى معرفته واستعماله في تدبير مصالح الأبدان، وحفظ الصحة عليها إذا كانت موجودة، وإعادتِها إليها إذا فُقِدَت بعارضٍ يعرضُ لها من العلل والأسقام بالقول المجمل الذي يعرفُ معه الناظرُ فيه ما يجب أن يجريَ عليه تدبيرُ بدنه في معنى الأغذية والأدوية لاستدامة السلامة، واستبقاء الصحة.

ونحن نقصدُ في هذه المقالة للإخبار بوجه تدبير مصالح الأنفس، وحفظِ قواها على سبيل الصلاح والاعتدال، وجهةِ التدبيرِ في نفي الأعراض النفسانية التي تعرض لها. ونبدأ فنقول:

إن الإنسان لما كان مركباً من بدن ونفس، صارَ يوجدُ له من قِبَلِ كلٍّ منهما صلاحٌ وفسادٌ، وصحةٌ ومرضٌ وسقمٌ، وأعراض تعرضُ له في صحتها، فتفسدُها عليه، وينسبُ إليه خصوصا.

فالأعراض التي تعرِضُ للبدن فتفسد صحته هي مثلُ: الحمى، والصداع، وسائر الأوجاع التي تعرض له في كل من أعضائه، والأعراض النفسانية هي مثل: الغضب، والغم، والخوف، والجزع، وما أشبهها.

وهذه الأعراض النفسانية هي ألزم للإنسان، وأكثرُ اعتراءً له من الأعراض البدنية؛ وذلك أن الأعراض البدنية قد يَسْلَمُ الواحد بعد الواحد منها حتى لا يكاد يعرضُ له في أكثر أيام عمرِهِ منها أو من عامَّتِها شيءٌ. فأما الأعراض النفسانية فإن الإنسان مدفوع في أكثر أوقاته إلى ما يتأذى به منها؛ إذ ليس يخلو في كافة أحواله من استشعار غم أو غضب أو حزن، وما أشبهها من الأعراض النفسانية، إلا أنه ليس قدرُ ما يصلُ منها إلى كل واحد من الناس

قدراً واحداً، فإنهم مختلفون فيما يحصل إليهم من هذه الأعراض، وذلك أن كلاً منهم إنما يأخذ منها بحسب مزاجه، وأصل تركيبه في القوة والضعف، فمنهم من يُلفَى سريعَ الغضب، ومنهم من يُلفَى بطيءَ الغضب، وكذلك منهم من يشتد خوفه وجزعُه من الشيء الهائل، ومنهم من يكون متجلداً رابط الجأش.

وكذلك توجدُ أحكامُ النساءِ والصبيانِ وأصحاب الطبائع الضعيفة مخالفةً لأحكام الرجال الأقوياء الطبائع في قدرِ ما يخلصُ منها إلى كل منهم؛ إلا أنه لا بد أن يأخذ كلٌّ بحظه منه، قل ذلك فيه أو كثر منه، واشتد عليه أو ضعف.

ومن أجل ذلك لا يستغني أحد من الناس عن تقديم العناية بمصالح الأنفس، والاجتهاد فيما ينفي عنه ما يعتريه منها، فيؤدِّيهُ إلى القلقِ، وتنغُّصِ العيش. وتكون تلك الأعراض نظيرة الأمراض الجسمانية التي تعرض له فتؤلمُه وتسقمُهُ، وتؤديه إلى الحالة المكروهة.

على أن الكلام في هذا الباب أمر لم تجرِ عادة الأطباء بذكره وإيقاعه في الكتب التي كانوا يؤلفونها في الطب ومصالح الأبدان ومعالجات العلل العارضة لها؛ وذلك لأن القول ليس هو من جنس صناعتهم، ولأن معالجات الأمراض النفسانية ليست من جنس ما يتعاطونه من الفصد وسقي الأدوية وما أشبههما من وجوه المعالجات، غير أنهم وإن لم يفعلوا ذلك، ولم تجر العادة به منهم، فإن إضافة تدبير مصالح الأنفس إلى تدبير مصالح الأبدان أمر صواب، بل هو مما تمس الحاجة إليه، ويعظم الانتفاع؛ لاشتباك أسباب الأبدان بأسباب الأنفس؛ فإن الإنسان إنما قِوَامُهُ بنفسِه وبدنِه، وليس يُتوهم له بقاءٌ إلا باجتماعهما، لتظهرَ منه الأفعال الإنسانية، فهما يشتركان في الأحداث النائبة، والآلام العارضة، وكما أن البدن إذا سقمَ وألِمَ وعرضَتْ له الأعراض المؤذية، مَنَعَ ذلك قوى النفسِ من الفهمِ والمعرفةِ وغيرها أن تفعلَ أفعالها على وجهها، ويتفرَّغَ معها الإنسان للقيام بما يقلقها ويؤذيها كان في ذلك ما يشغل الإنسان عن الاستمتاع باللذات البدنية، وأخذ شيء منها على سبيله، وَوَجَدَ عيشه مكدرةً، وحياتَهُ متنغِّصَةً عليه، بل ربما أداه تحاملُ الآلام النفسانية عليه إلى الأمراض البدنية!

وإذا كان ذلك كذلك فبكل إنسان حاجةٌ – وخصوصا بمن تغلبُ عليه الأعراض النفسانية المؤذية – إلى أن يعلم كيف جهة التدبير في مقابلتها بما ينفيها أو يقلل منها، وإذا وجد ذلك مجموعاً له، مضافاً إلى ذكر مصالح الأبدان في كتاب، أو أمكنه أن يعرف ما يلزمُه الحاجة إليه من ذلك؛ فيداوي نفسَه به مما يعتريه من تلك الآلام، واستغنى عن تطلُّبِ تلك الأشياء في المواضع التي توجد متفرقة فيها من كتب الحكماء وأهل الموعظة والتبصير، ثم لعله لا يقدرُ على أن يجد ما يحتاج إليه من ذلك مستجمَعًا له في كتاب واحد يكون رجوعه فيه إليه، فقد عُلِمَ أن مطلبَ ذلك يعسرُ، ولا يتسهَّلُ السبيلُ نحو تسهيلها إلى تدبير مصالح الأبدان وحفظ الصحة عليها وإعادتها إليها، فإن كتب الأطباء في ذلك كثيرة، ولهم أقاويل مشروحة – وإن لم يكن مذهبهم تسهيلها فيها المذهبَ الذي

نحوناه في الإيجاز والاختصار والتخريج له على جهة الوصية والتذكرة –، فأما هذا النوع الذي هو تدبير مصالح الأنفس، فلا نعلم أحداً قال فيه قولاً مشروحاً وافياً بقدر الحاجة، فنحن نتكلم فيه بما تبلغه المعرفة، وبالله التوفيق.

3.4 *English Translation*

Articulation of the Immense Need for Fostering the Sustenance of the Psyche

In the first section of this book,[18] we expounded upon that which needs to be known and applied in managing the interests of the body, by maintaining its well-being when healthy and restoring it back to health whenever compromised by symptoms of disorder and disease. [This was discussed] in a comprehensive manner, effectively informing the reader how they must take care of their body in terms of consuming suitable foods and medicine in order to sustain [physical] well-being and retain health.

In this section, we endeavor to elucidate the methods of sustaining the psyche, as well as [how] to safeguard its faculties on the path towards well-being and equilibrium.[19] We furthermore explore avenues to mitigate [various] psychological symptoms that afflict it.

We begin by saying that since human beings are composed of a body and psyche, both components [inevitably] experience [various degrees of] well-being and disorder, health, and sickness, as well as particular ailments and symptoms that adversely affect one's [overall] well-being.

The symptoms that adversely affect bodily health are the likes of fever, headaches, and all other types of [physical] pain that afflict each of the body's various organs. Conversely, psychological symptoms include anger, grief, fear, panic, and other similar conditions.[20] [Generally,] these psychological conditions are more abiding and recurrent than physical symptoms. To elucidate, it

18 In the initial portion of Al-Balkhī's work, he focuses on the development, sustenance, and treatment of physical ailments. This section marks the start of the second part of his book, dedicated to the nourishment of the psyche.

19 This is in reference to the theory of homeostasis regarding the health of both the body and the psyche which was prevalent in Greek medicine and adopted by Islamic philosophers and physicians. Al-Balkhī is expanding the analogy of homeostasis of physical fluids in the body to the psyche. While this theory may be relatively marginalized in contemporary medicine, the notion of adaptive versus maladaptive, emotional regulation, and equilibrium continue to hold significance in modern psychology. In fact, Keshavarzi, Khan, Ali & Awaad have defined psychological health as an equilibrium across all components of the psyche. (See: Keshavarzi et al., *Applying Islamic Principles to Clinical Mental Health Care.*)

20 Al-Balkhī's classification of psychological disorders seems to be primarily rooted in emotional disturbances. In his view, the presence of debilitating emotional states seem to indicate the presence of psychological pathology.

is conceivable that a person may almost never suffer from any physical symptoms throughout most or all of their lifetime. As for psychological symptoms, human beings are susceptible to suffering from them most of the time, in some way [or another]. It is inconceivable that a person could ever be [completely] free from experiencing feelings of sorrow, anger, grief, or similar psychological states.[21] However, not every person bears the same symptom in the same way; people differ in their responses to these symptoms, as each person is affected according to the strength or weakness of their innate temperament and make-up.[22] Some people are quick-tempered whereas others are slow-to-react. Likewise, some may become extremely upset and panic-stricken in the face of atrocity, whilst others [easily] maintain their composure, [predominantly] undisturbed.

Thus, one can contradistinguish between the [expected] responses of women, children, and those with a weak disposition compared to those with a disposition that is naturally stronger.[23] Each individual's [experience]

21 Despite being written over a millennium ago, it is remarkable how al-Balkhī underscores the mind-body connection and the pervasiveness of psychological turmoil. It is worth noting that the first four chapters of al-Balkhī's treatise on psychological health are mostly preventative in nature, while the last few chapters are dedicated to treatment of an existing psychological disorder. Al-Balkhī is outlining the necessity of psychological hygiene and pre-emptive approaches to engendering resilience to psychological suffering before environmental challenges are presented.

22 Al-Balkhī importantly outlines the relationship between temperament and psychological states. Each individual's biological temperament and inherent tendencies substantially influence their capacity to control and regulate their emotions. Those who are neurotic in their disposition may have a more difficult time with feelings of anxiety and experience higher degrees of psychological symptoms, particularly in comparison to those with an easy temperament (see Thomas A. Widiger, *The Oxford Handbook of the Five Factor Model* (Oxford University Press, 2017).

Al-Balkhī's perspective represented the prevailing stance amongst Islamic philosophers, physicians, and spiritual practitioners and it was well established despite the debate of nature versus nurture; such has only recently been resolved within the field of psychology.

23 While modern psychological discourse may contend with the gender similarities (Janet Shibley Hyde, "The Gender Similarities Hypothesis.," American Psychologist 60, no. 6 (September 2005): 581–92.) versus gender differences debate, empirical evidence supports the existence of gender differences in psychology, with distinct emotional states typically exhibiting greater prominence in each respective gender (Giolla & Kajonous (2018)). For example, neuroticism seems to be higher in women whilst aggression is typically higher in males (Hyde). While Hyde espouses the gender similarities hypothesis, her meta-analysis of 128 studies on gender differences across psychological variables found that more than 20% effect sizes were large, while most of the remainder demonstrated at least small to moderate effect sizes (below a mean difference of d = 0.35). Although it is true that males and females exhibit more similarities than differences, her findings appear to clearly indicate significant psychological differences between the genders.

will inevitably be based on the nature of their disposition, be it diminutive, abundant, intense, or moderate.

For these reasons, no one can do without giving precedence to the sustenance of the psyche and actively striving to ward off what [adversely] affects it. [Negligence in this regard can easily] lead to disquietude and dysfunction. Such [psychological] symptoms are comparable to physical illnesses that beset the body, causing a person pain, inducing sickness, and bringing about an agonizing situation [overall].[24]

Nonetheless, [conventional] physicians scarcely discuss this topic, and it is [generally] not included in their written works that deal with medicine, the sustenance of the body, and the treatment of its various illnesses. This is [likely] because it is a subject that goes well beyond their professional interests; the treatment of psychological disorders is vastly different from bloodletting, prescribing medications, and other similar treatments that they typically administer. Even though they largely ignore psychology in their normative [medical] practices,[25] it is most [appropriate and] correct to combine the careful management of both the mind and body, with due consideration for what sustains each of them, [respectively]. In fact, it is a much needed [approach] that [could only] yield tremendous benefit, as functional matters of the psyche and the body are [deeply] interrelated. Indeed, each [and every] human being is made up of both an [inner] psyche and an [outer] body; it is unfathomable for a person to exist without the simultaneous integration of both [essential] components. This [vital combination] is what one needs to behave as [and be] human, since it is both [the mind and body] that concomitantly react to unfavorable circumstances and experience pain. Hence, when the body experiences sickness, pain, or other unsettling symptoms, the psyche's capacity to discern and understand is hindered or functionally weakened, as are various other mental faculties. [Naturally,] a person suffering from such agitation fixates on their troubles, which effectively diminishes the [body's] ability to properly experience most forms of physical satisfaction. This can distort one's outlook and experience of life itself. More still, it could even be such that psychological afflictions carry over and induce physical ailments too.[26] Considering all of the above, it is imperative for everyone, especially those

24 Al-Balkhī once again lays special emphasis on psychological care and psychological development in order to generate resilience to future disorder.

25 Even during al-Balkhī's time, it appears that physicians tended to undervalue psychological health, thus motivating al-Balkhī to write this treatise, describing and emphasizing the potential consequences of its negligence.

26 Al-Balkhī demonstrates the interconnection between the mind and body. He describes how physical ailments can be the result of psychosomatic experiences or that stressful conditions can adversely affect the body.

[frequently] struggling with psychological issues, to understand the modalities of [personal] management in countering these ailments with that which repels them or minimizes them.

Accordingly, if one can find such [key information] compiled in a book that also includes what is needed to take care of the body, then such a person would be able to treat their own self without having to scour for such things through the scattered writings of traditional healers, religious orators, [and others].

Then again, one might not be able to find all of those things incorporated together in one singular resource.[27] In fact, procuring such [a reference] would [likely] be quite challenging and not as easy as finding works that are solely dedicated to physical remedies for the restoration and preservation of bodily health. Although [conventional] physicians have [produced] numerous books detailing medical matters [pertaining to the sustenance of the body], it seems that their overall approach makes this [knowledge] inaccessible [to the average layperson], whereas our uniquely condensed, concise style, crafted in the form of simple reminders and advice, [proves to] be much easier. Indeed, we do not know of anyone else who has effectively discussed and sufficiently explained the sustenance of the psyche in this way.[28] On this matter, we speak [solely] to the extent of our knowledge, and Allah alone grants success.

4 Preservation of the Health of the Psyche. *Maṣāliḥ al-Abdān wa al-Anfus* (*Sustenance of the Body and the Psyche*) by Abū Zayd al-Balkhī (d. 322 AH/934 CE)

4.1 *Author's Biography*

Abū Zayd Aḥmad ibn Sahl al-Balkhī was born in modern day Afghanistan in a city called Balkh. He was recognized as a polymath and spent significant time in Baghdad to further his education. His life was dedicated to the fields of psychology, science, literature, geography, Islamic theology, and

27 Al-Balkhī is illustrating the scarcity of written works solely devoted to this topic during his time.

28 One of the unique features of this particular work is al-Balkhī's intention to write it in vernacular Arabic, ensuring its accessibility as a self-help guide for the general population. While discussions of psychology found in the books of the physicians of that era tended to be overly technical or philosophical, al-Balkhī endeavored to simplify his approach in order to provide maximal benefit to the average reader. It is worth noting that in this work, al-Balkhī does not really delve into theories of change, philosophical discussions revolving around the nature or location of the psyche or soul, or other complex matters. He seems to be focused more on practical wisdoms and strategies for the masses.

theoretical medicine. He was a student of the renowned physician al-Kindī. He laid a great deal of importance to spirituality viewing religion as the greatest of all philosophies, understanding that in order to be a good philosopher one needed to be grounded in spirituality and be a sincere worshiper of Allah. The discovery of his treatise on physical and mental health entitled *Maṣāliḥ al-Abdān wa al-Anfus* has led to an immense interest in the works of the classical Islamic scholars regarding human psychology. It is noteworthy that in his work, al-Balkhī's classification and symptomatology of obsessive disorders parallels the latest edition of the modern Diagnostic and Statistical Manual of Obsessive-Compulsive Disorders (OCD). al-Balkhī was well versed in the Islamic sciences as well, so his writings encourage patients to seek treatment for illnesses by reminding them of the prophetic tradition that Allah has created a cure for every illness.

4.2 *Text Overview and Significance*

After likening the health of the psyche to one's physical health, al-Balkhī states that when the psyche is calmed and regulated it achieves health. However, in order to achieve this state one must be free of and protect themselves from psychological disorders. Additionally, he says any emotional states such as intense anger, fear, or anxiety should be regulated in order for the psyche to experience holistic psychological well-being.

In a practical sense, al-Balkhī warns that one should avoid external triggers that contribute to provoking the psyche with intense feelings of anger, panic, grief, or fear. Moreover, one should avoid ruminative thoughts leading to further self-doubt and confusion. In order to deal with such threats, whilst in a state of psychological health (i.e. prior to becoming distressed), one should proactively internalize a core belief that the world is filled with challenges and cannot completely satiate all their desires. Through this, one can achieve the resilience to withstand threats and challenges when they arise. Further more it leads a person to be content with divine decree, the effect of which is such that one would naturally experience less intense negative reactions to smaller adversities and grievances that are a normal part of human life.

4.3 *Arabic Text*

الباب الثاني

في تدبير حفظ صحة الأنفس عليها

إن لنفس الإنسان صحة وسقماً، كما إن لبدنه صحة وسقماً؛ فصحة نفسه أن تكون قواها ساكنة، ولا يهيج به شيء من الأعراض النفسانية، ولا يغلبَ عليه، كالغضب، أُو الفزع،

أو الجزع، وما نحن ذاكروه منها عند تعديدنا إياها، فيكون سكون النفس منها صحتها وسلامتها. كما أن صحة البدن وسلامته يكونان بأن توجد الأخلاط التي فيها من الدم والمرتين والبلغم ساكنةً، ولا يهيج شيء منها، فيغلبَ على غيره .

فكما أنه يجب أن يبدأ في باب مصلحة البدن بحفظ صحته عليه، ثم يتبع ذلك بإعادة صحته إليه إذا فقدت، كذلك يجب في مصلحة النفس أنه يبدأ بحفظ صحتها عليها إذا وُجِدَت، وإذا كانت صحتها إنما هي في سكون قواها كما وصفنا، فينبغي لمن أراد حفظ الصحة أن يجتهد في استدامة سكون قوى نفسه، وأن لا يهيجَ به منها هائج.

وكما أن البدن إنما يُحفظُ صحتَه عليه بوجهين: أحدهما: أن يصان عن الآفات الخارجة كالحر و البرد والنكبات المؤلمة. والآخر: أن يُصانَ عن الآفات الداخلة، وهو أن لا يترك شيئاً من أخلاطه الأربعة يهيج به، فيغلبُ سواه، وذلك بتعديل الغذاء، وأخذ النافع، واجتناب الضار منه، وبما يتبع ذلك من المعاني التي ذكرناها في المقالة الأولى في باب حفظ صحة البدن، كذلك النفس إنما تُحفظُ صحتُها عليها من وجهين:

أحدهما: أن تصان عن الأعراض الخارجة التي هي ورودُ ما يَرِدُ عليها من الأشياء التي يسمعها الإنسان أو يبصرها، فتقلقُه وتضجرُه، وتحرِّكُ منه قوةَ غضبٍ أو فزعٍ أو غمٍّ أو خوفٍ وما أشبه ذلك.

والآخر: أن تصانَ عن الأعراضِ الداخلةِ التي هي التفكيرُ فيما يؤديه إلى شيءٍ مما وصفنا من هذه الأعراض، فيُشْغَلُ قلبُهُ وينقسمُ ضميرُه .

وليس يتهيأ له ذلك إلا لمعنيين:

أحدهما: أن يُشعِرَ قلبَه وقتَ سلامةِ نفسهِ وسكونِ قواها ما أُسِّسَتْ وجُبِلَتْ عليه أحوال الدنيا من أن أحداً لا يصل فيها إلى تحصيل إرادته، ونيلِ شهواته على سبيل ما يتمناه و يهواه، من غير أن يشوب كلا من ذلك شائبةُ تنغُّصٍ وتكدُّرٍ، أو يعرِضَ له فيه عارضُ أذى أو مكروهٍ. ويعلمَ أن هذا هو ما استمر عليه الطباع، وجرت به العادة، فلا يطلب من دنياه ما ليس في أصل بُنْيَتِها، ويدعُ – لمعرفته لذلك – الاستقصاء في وجوه معاملاته ومعاشراته لمن هو فوقه أو مثله أو دونه، ويتغافلُ عن كثير من الأمور التي تَرِدُ عليه بخلاف مرادِهِ و محبته ما وسعَهُ ذلك، وجاز أن يغضيَ عنه، ولا يعوِّدَ نفسَهُ أن يضجَرَ لكل صغير من الأمور التي يسمعها أو يبصرها، ويَسيرٍ من الحوادث التي تقعُ بكراهتِه، فإنه إذا عوِّدَ احتمالَ الصغير ومقارَّةَ النفسِ عليه صار ذلك عادةً له في احتمال ماهو أجلُّ شأناً، وأعظم خطباً من المهمات التي تبدهُهُ، والمكارهِ التي تردُ عليه.

ويكون حاله في ذلك حالَ من يمرِّنُ نفسهُ على احتمال الأذى اليسيرِ من الحر والبرد وآلام النكبات، و تركِ إظهارِ الجزعِ لكل منها، حتى تستمر طباعه على ذلك، ويصير احتمال اليسير منها سبباً لاحتمال ما هو أكثر و أعظم منه إذا ابتلي به أو دفع إليه؛ فإن هذه هي السبيل في رياضة الأبدان، وهي السبيل في رياضة الأنفس.

والمعنى الآخر: أن يعرف بنيةَ نفسِه، ومبلغَ ما عندها من الاحتمال للأمور الملمَّةِ الواردة عليه، فإن لكل إنسان مقدارا من قوة القلب أو ضعفه، وسعة الصدر أو ضيقه؛ فمن الأنفس ما يوجد فيه محتمَلٌ للخطوب العظيمة، حتى لا يقدحَه شيءٌ منها، ولا يُضعِفَ متنَه، ومتَّسَعٌ لأشغال كثيرة مهمة حتى يتفرغ لكل منها ويقابله بما يخفف عنها من الحيل، ومنها ما يوجد فيه من الانخزال لكل ما يفجؤه من الهموم، حتى تدهشَه وتحيِّرَه وتجعله وشيك انحلال القوة من كل ما يلم به من النوائب، حتى تكربَه وتضيق عليه مذاهب التصرف والاحتيال، وحتى تؤديه إلى حالةٍ تُعقِبُه علةً في البدن مضرةً به.

فإذا عرف الإنسان طبيعته ومنتهى قوتها ومبلغ استقلالها بالأمور، بني على حسب ذلك تدبيره في مطالبه ومقاصده، مَلِكاً كان أو سُوقةً؛ فإن وجد نفسه مستقلة بعظائم الأمور، مقويةً بجلائل الخطوب، تعرض لذلك، وإن أحس منها برقِّةِ بنيةٍ أو ضعفِ تركيبٍ في أغراضه ومقاصده، تجنب وجوه المخاطرات وأنواع التغريرات، وما يتعاطاه ذوو الأنفس القوية، والصدور الواسعة، والطبائع المستحصفة، وجعل غرضه فيهما غرض من يكون تحصيل سلامة النفس ودعتها وراحة القلب وطمأنينته – مع فوت كثير من الآمال والرغائب – أحب إليه، وآثر عنده من نيل أوفر الحظوظ منها مع ركوب المخاطرة، وحمل النفس على التغرير والتعرض لما إن دُفِعَ في عقباه إلى خلاف ما يحبه، ضاق به صدرُه، وقلقَتْ له نفسُه، (و) لم يأمن إيصاله بضرر عظيم يناله في نفسه وبدنه.

فإنه متى لزم هذا المذهب في البابين اللذين وصفناهما طابت عيشته، ودامت راحته، وحَصَّل الحظ الأوفر من سلامة نفسه، وحفظَ عليها صحتها، واستكمل بذلك السعادة الدنيوية؛ لأن كمال هذه السعادة إنما هي في صحة البدن و النفس وراحتهما، واندفاع الآفات والمكاره عنهما مدة الحياة في هذه الدنيا. ومتى خالف هذه الطريقة في مطالبه ومقاصده تنغصت عليه حياتُه، وتكدرت عيشته، واجتلب إلى نفسه الأمراض النفسانية التي تُضجِرُه وتقلقُه، كما يجتلب الأمراض البدنية إليه من لا يصون نفسه من الآفات الخارجة، ويتناول من أغذية المطاعم والمشارب وغيرهما مِن حاجة الأبدان أكثر مما تتحمله قوته، وتستقل به طبيعته.

4.4 *English Translation*

Preservation of the Health of the Psyche

The human psyche can be healthy or unhealthy, much like the human body. The psyche's well-being is [characterized by] the quietude of its [various] faculties. [A healthy mind] is not overwhelmed by any substantial psychological symptoms, including anger, anxiety, depression, or other conditions that we have already enumerated previously.[29] And so, it is this inner composure that is [indicative] of psychological health and wellness. Similarly, the health and well-being of the body is based on the [balance and welfare] of its humors, wherein the blood, phlegm, and both [the yellow and black] types of bile are harmoniously placid; none of them prevails over the others.

[Previously,] the chapter pertaining to the sustenance of the body necessarily commenced [with valuable information] for maintaining bodily health, followed by [a discussion of] its restoration [and treatment] when unwell. A similar approach is likewise befitting for the sustenance of the psyche.

Thus, if the psyche's well-being is [rooted] in the quietude of its faculties as we have described, then whosoever endeavors to preserve its health must strive to maintain that composure and protect it from anything [and everything] that may disrupt [it].[30]

The body's health can be safeguarded in two principal ways: the first is to shield it from unhealthy external conditions, like excessive heat, cold, and physical trauma. Next, is to protect it from an adverse internal imbalance of the four humors; at no point should any of them be aroused [to the extent] that one of them dominates over the others. This is [accomplished] by carefully managing one's diet; consuming what is wholesome [and effective] whilst avoiding that which causes harm. To that end, we have already provided details in the first part [of this book], in the chapter [about] preserving the health of the body.

The same [applies] to the health of the psyche; it is [also] sustained in two ways, the first of which entails protecting [it] from [harmful] external influences, like disturbing sights and sounds. These [influences] can upset a person, triggering rage, panic, depression, fear, or other similar responses.[31] The second approach [necessitates] safeguarding [the psyche] from internal disturbances incited by [negative] thinking.[32] This induces some of the adverse states that we have already described, [often] causing one to be distraught due to [excessive] mental preoccupation.

No individual can be [effectively] equipped to deal with such except [by adopting] a two-pronged approach: firstly, at a time of [relative] mental calm,

29 Sickness is indicated by one's being overwhelmed with emotions; such that normative rational faculties are no longer governing one's behavior.

30 Al-Balkhī is pointing to the necessity of exercising and training the psyche preventively during times of calm when there is an absence of psychological disarray.

31 This is in reference to environmental triggers that may cause one to become overwhelmed or excessively emotionally aroused.

32 Like modern cognitive behavioral therapy (CBT), al-Balkhī elucidates that the roots of many emotional disturbances can be traced back to one's ways of thinking and thoughts.

one should internalize [the fact that] this ephemeral world, by design, was not inherently created for anyone to get what they want or to satisfy their urges as they please. Indeed, everything, in that regard, is [inescapably] tainted and sullied by some [sort of] pain, disappointment, or distressing drawback.

[Ultimately,] one will internalize this as a reality in nature that always has been, and always will be.[33] Thereafter, he would not expect anything unrealistic out of life. [Drawing] from this [newfound] awareness, he will cease to overanalyze his various dealings and interactions [with others], regardless of whether they are superior, inferior, or equal to him [in status]. He will largely ignore much of what comes his way that goes against his personal will and preference, to the best of his ability. It is [even] possible that he may disregard it [altogether]. He will [gradually] recondition himself [to avoid] overreacting

---

33 Generally, modern psychological literature, to the exclusion of existential psychologists, views human beings as psychologically healthy by default; health and happiness are seen as the natural homeostatic states of human existence. From this perspective, psychological suffering is typically viewed as abnormal; diseases or syndromes driven by unusual pathological processes of the mind. Until recently, psychological well-being was seen as the absence of psychological disease (Tracey Peter, Lance W. Roberts, and Jennifer Dengate, "Flourishing in Life: An Empirical Test of the Dual Continua Model of Mental Health and Mental Illness among Canadian University Students," *International Journal of Mental Health Promotion* 13, no. 1 (January 2011): 13–22.). Here, al-Balkhī embraces the idea that psychological suffering is the normal state of affairs in life. This is due to the fact that this world is neither a place of total happiness nor a place where one acquires all of their wants and wishes.

Imam al-Birgivī further suggests that hopelessness and unhappiness are the causes of excessive attachment to this world. When a person is overly attached and has a longing for worldly life, he is devastated if any pleasure he craves is denied to him (Muḥammad Birgivī, *Al-Ṭarīqa al-Muḥammadiyya Wa-l-Sīra al Aḥmadiyya* (Damascus: Dār al-Qalam, 2011).). Imam al-Birgivī's observations about excessive attachment to the world align with the psychological concept of the illusion of control, as both involve a person's perceptions and beliefs about their ability to influence and control certain aspects of their life for the sake of happiness. The illusion of control (see Ellen J. Langer, "The Illusion of Control.," *Journal of Personality and Social Psychology* 32, no. 2 (August 1975): 311–28.) is the tendency for people to overestimate their ability to control events and may be tied to psychological maladjustment (see Jack Block and C. Randall Colvin, "Positive Illusions and Well-Being Revisited: Separating Fiction from Fact.," *Psychological Bulletin* 116, no. 1 (July 1994): 28–28; Colvin & Block, 1994; Iain Chalmers and Robert Matthews, "What Are the Implications of Optimism Bias in Clinical Research?," *The Lancet* 367, no. 9509 (February 2006): 449–50.; Daniel Kahneman, *Thinking, Fast and Slow*, 1st pbk. ed (New York: Farrar, Straus and Giroux, 2013).). Accurate perceptions of self and the world are essential for mental health (see Marie Jahoda, "The Meaning of Psychological Health," *Social Casework* 34, no. 8 (October 1953): 349–54.; Abraham H. Maslow, "Self-Actualizing People: A Study of Psychological Health," *Personality, Symposium 1* (1950): 11–34.).

to every insignificant sight, sound, and other trivial matters that he [previously] considered to be irritating.

Indeed, once he habituates himself to tolerate these minor frustrations, he will naturally develop [a better] ability to handle that which is much more significant and comparatively more difficult. He would then be quite similar to someone who [actively] develops pain tolerance or acclimatizes their body to heat or cold; they persevere without outwardly showing their discomfort until it becomes [second] nature. In [this way,] enduring minor aches [and pains] becomes an [important] means for withstanding that which is quantitatively and qualitatively greater, should there be [a need to be] exposed to it. This is typically how the body is trained, and it is [likewise] the way in which the psyche is conditioned [as well].[34]

Next, the second approach [entails] being cognizant of a person's own make-up and what their maximum limit is that their mind can handle. Every individual has a unique capacity in terms of mental strength and weakness, as well as scope. Indeed, some people can withstand tremendous hardship without thinking much of it or being triggered in any [significant] way. They can endure a multitude of onerous stressors [at once], adeptly attending to each

---

34 Third-wave cognitive-behavioral methods such as acceptance and commitment therapy (ACT) (Steven C. Hayes, "Acceptance and Commitment Therapy, Relational Frame Theory, and the Third Wave of Behavioral and Cognitive Therapies," *Behavior Therapy* 35, no. 4 (2004): 639–65.; Harold W. Kohl et al., "The Pandemic of Physical Inactivity: Global Action for Public Health," *The Lancet* 380, no. 9838 (July 2012): 294–305) and dialectical behavior therapy (DBT) (Matthew McKay, Jeffrey C. Wood, and Jeffrey Brantley, *The Dialectical Behavior Therapy Skills Workbook: Practical DBT Exercises for Learning Mindfulness, Interpersonal Effectiveness, Emotion Regulation, and Distress Tolerance* (New Harbinger Publications, 2019) adopt an acceptance-based approach, which encourages coming into contact with every internal and external experience directly, fully, and without the need to change, rid or alter one's thoughts or feelings towards them. Techniques employed can include observing and identifying fearful emotions, labeling unpleasant emotions, giving form to the emotions, and reflecting upon the experience that helps one psychologically distance themselves from the negative internal associations.

Contemporary psychologists also incorporate the principle of gradual exposure to anxiety-provoking stimuli as a means to desensitize and gain mastery over them. Behavioral methods employed by modern psychologists involve a variety of exposure techniques such as directly confronting the feared stimulus (in-vivo); imagined exposure when the former is not feasible; and interoceptive exposure, which involves stimulating the physiological sensations of fear in response to the stimuli. Behaviorists also utilize flooding as an alternative to gradual exposure, whereby individuals confront the entirety of the feared stimuli, like having someone suffering from a cat phobia sit in a room full of cats. Here, it appears that al-Balkhī favors a gradual approach; similar to behavioral gradual exposure theories, he advises that a person becomes acquainted with their tolerance limits in order to construct an exposure regimen accordingly.

and every one until they are minimalized. Contrarily, there are some who are totally overrun when faced with stress. [Their minds] become muddled to the point where they are [almost entirely] incapacitated by whatever is stressing them [out]. This can eventually deteriorate into a debilitating state of depression so severe that it could even cause adverse physical illness within the body.

And so, if an individual were to understand their own innate disposition, its limitations, and its maximal tolerance of [various] matters, one can correspondingly construct a [personal] development plan to [properly] manage [all of] their affairs and [achieve] their aims – regardless of whether one is a [mighty] monarch or a [lowly] layperson.[35]

If a person finds [that they have] the [intrinsic] psychological fortitude to tolerate adversity, [they can] proceed to confront it [accordingly]. Alternatively, if someone feels they have a softer disposition or weaker temperament, such [a person] can purposefully avoid certain types of challenges and harms that are [more appropriately] taken on by those who are stronger and better-equipped by nature. By doing so, one caters to both, fostering psychological well-being, inner comfort, and tranquility. Even though many personal hopes and dreams must be relinquished, this approach is [nonetheless] more preferable than attempting to confront overly precarious circumstances and what one simply cannot withstand. Indeed, forcing the psyche to grapple with difficult matters it cannot readily contend with invariably causes a sense of perplexity and strain, risking immense psychological and physiological harm.

Whenever anyone adheres to this methodology [as outlined] in the previous two chapters we have described, [such a person] will [surely] experience wholesomeness in their life, with a [relatively] lasting feeling of contentment. [They would] have attained the greatest fortune of having a healthy, well-preserved psyche, and thus achieved worldly fulfillment. This is because total well-being can only be [garnered] through the health and comfort of both the body and the psyche [together], whereby all afflictions and disturbances are kept in check throughout life.

If anyone were to wilfully disregard this approach, their life would become overwhelming and complicated. They would [inadvertently] induce various psychological illnesses within their own mind, that would [further] aggravate and frustrate them, much like how bodily illnesses are brought on: a person fails to avoid unhealthy external conditions by eating and drinking excessively

---

35 One definition for self-awareness is having a clear perception of one's personality, including strengths, weaknesses, thoughts, beliefs, motivations, and emotions (see Kirsten Jack and Eula Miller, "Exploring Self-Awareness in Mental Health Practice," Mental Health Practice 12, no. 3 (November 13, 2008): 31–35.).

and overindulging in other bodily needs beyond what one can naturally handle [and thus becomes unwell].

5 When One Loses It: Methods of Restoring Mental Health. *Maṣāliḥ al-Abdān wa al-Anfus* (*Sustenance of the Body and the Psyche*) by Imam Abū Zayd al-Balkhī (d. 322 AH/934 CE)

5.1 *Author's Biography*

Abū Zayd Aḥmad ibn Sahl al-Balkhī was born in modern day Afghanistan in a city called Balkh. He was recognized as a polymath and spent significant time in Baghdad to further his education. His life was dedicated to the fields of psychology, science, literature, geography, Islamic theology, and theoretical medicine. He was a student of the renowned physician al-Kindī. He laid a great deal of importance to spirituality viewing religion as the greatest of all philosophies, understanding that in order to be a good philosopher one needed to be grounded in spirituality and be a sincere worshiper of Allah. The discovery of his treatise on physical and mental health entitled *Maṣāliḥ al-Abdān wa al-Anfus* has led to an immense interest in the works of the classical Islamic scholars regarding human psychology. It is noteworthy that in his work, al-Balkhī's classification and symptomatology of obsessive disorders parallels the fifth edition of the modern Diagnostic and Statistical Manual of Obsessive-Compulsive Disorders (OCD). al-Balkhī was well versed in the Islamic sciences as well, so his writings encourage patients to seek treatment for illnesses by reminding them of the prophetic tradition that Allah has created a cure for every illness.

5.2 *Text Overview and Significance*

In this section, Imam al-Balkhī reiterates that all human beings are prone to experiencing psychological issues just as they are prone to experiencing physical pain. In fact he asserts that psychological issues are more prevalent than physical problems given that it is conceivable for a person to be free of major medical problems throughout most of their life should they live a generally healthy lifestyle, on the other hand emotional ups and downs are common place throughout life and at times these can reach a clinical threshold rendering the individual psychologically ill. The emotional variability he discusses include anger, resentment, sadness, and grief. Thereafter, al-Balkhī proceeds to explore the interventional strategies and treatment approaches. He draws the analogy for treating the psyche with treating the body by pointing out that for every physical illness or pain there is a corresponding dietary supplement or medication for its healing. Similarly, he states that for every psychological issue, there is an accompanying psychospiritual intervention to alleviate it of suffering. He further emphasizes that such treatments should be deferred to a specialist, even if the sufferer is himself a specialist. There are two reasons he provides: firstly, most individuals are naturally inclined to accept the advice of others instead of relying on their own thoughts which they may doubt. Next, when a person suffers from psychological issues, their emotional states may cloud their judgement and cannot rid themselves of distress whilst experiencing it intensely. He gives the example of a physician who is inundated by physical illness as a demonstration of how he is unable to treat himself and is in need of another doctor to treat him.

5.3 *Arabic Text*

الباب الثالث

في تدبير إعادة صحة النفس – إذا فقدت – إليها

إن الذي ذكرناه من حفظ سلامة النفس عليها أمر ليس يتهيأ في كل الأوقات والأحوال؛ إذ كان غير ممكن في طبيعة الإنسان أن يحفظ قوى نفسه على سبيل السكون والهدوء حتى لا يهيج به هائج من أعراض الغضب والفزع والجزع، وما أشبهها من الأعراض النفسانية. وهي من دنياه في دار هموم وأحزان ومحل نوائب و نكبات.

ولا يزال يرد فيها عليه من حوادث الأمور، ونوازل الخطوب مايقع بخلاف محبته وضد إرادته. كما أنه غير ممكن في معنى بدنه أن يخلو من الأعراض البدنية حتى لا يعتريه منها شيء في أعضائه يؤذيه ويؤلمه. فإن سلم مما يكبر منها في كثير من الأوقات لم يسلم مما يصغر، بل الأمر في الأعراض النفسانية تعاقبها على الإنسان في عامة أوقاته أقوى منه في الأعراض البدنية. فإن الإنسان ربما بقي مدة من الزمان لا يعرض له فيها وجع من الأوجاع البدنية تصيبه في بعض أعراضه، ولا يكاد يمضي به يوم لا يرد عليه فيه ما تحرك منه قوة غضب أو زجر أو حزن أو غم؛ وذلك للطف جوهر النفس، وسرعة تغيرها، وكثرة استحالتها.

فمن أجل ما وصفناه يلزم الإنسان الحاجة في مصالح نفسه إلى تعهد قواها لئلا يهيج به منها شيء، وإذا هاج منها شيء بادر بتسكينه، ورده إلى أفضل أحواله. وكما أن معالجة البدن إذا عرض له عارض كألم أو سقم إنما يكون بشيء جسماني يجانسه من أصناف الأغذية والأدوية يستصلح به ذلك الفساد وينفي ذلك الأذى، كذلك معالجة النفس إذا عرض لها عارض هيجان من إحدى قواها إنما يكون بشيء روحاني يجانسها.

وكما أن العلاج البدني إما أن يكون بشيء من داخل كالاحتماء و الامتناع مما لا يجب تناوله، ومد اليد إليه. وإما أن يكون بشيء خارج مثل ما وصفناه من الأغذية

والأدوية. وكذلك معالجة النفس مما يعرض لها إما أن يكون: شيء من داخل وهو فكرة يثيرها الإنسان من نفسه؛ فيقمع بها ذلك العارض، ويسكن ذلك الهائج. وإما أن يكون بشيء خارج؛ وهو كلام يعظه به غيره فينجع فيه ويعمل في تسكين الهائج، وإصلاح الفاسد من قوى نفسه. فالإنسان المعني بصلاح نفسه جدير بأن لا يخليها من تعهدها بهذين الوجهين لكيلا يتسلط عليه من الأعراض النفسانية الردية ما ينغص به عليه عيشه. وربما أداه عند إفراطه عليه إلى بعض العلل البدنية عند اندفاعه إلى شيء منها من خارج كالأغذية والأشربة. وأما مكلفة الطبيب القائم بمداواته يوجد في أكثر الأحوال أنفع له وأرد عليه من المعونة التي تخلص إليه من داخل بضبط بدنه واحتمائه.

كذلك الحكم في الأعراض النفسانية من أن المعونة التي تلحقه من خارج بالعظة والتذكير يوجد أنجع وأعمل فيه، وأرد بالنفع والفائدة عليه لمعنيين: أحدهما أن الإنسان يقبل من غيره أكثر مما يقبل من نفسه؛ وذلك أن رأيه في كل الأحوال مغلوب بهواه وأحدهما ممتزج بالآخر. والثاني أن الإنسان في وقت اهتياج عارض من الأعراض النفسانية به مشغول بما يقاسيه من ذلك العارض، مقهور على عزمه ورأيه، مفتقر إلى من يلي عليه تدبير أمره، وإصلاح فساده. وحاله في ذلك شبيهة بحال الطبيب الذي يعتل علة جسدانية فيشتغل بها عن التطبيب لنفسه، ويفتقر إلى طبيب آخر يقوم بمداواته ومعالجته.

ومن أجل ما وصفناه كانت العادة جرت من الملوك الحزمة بأن تكون لحضرتهم حكماء يداوون منهم الأعراض النفسانية إذا هاجت نحو الغضب والفزع، والضجر بالوصايا والمواعظ؛ فيقبلونها منهم وينتفعون بسماعها، والعمل بها. وكانوا يرتبطونهم لذلك كما يرتبطون أطباءً حذاقاً يراؤون منهم الأعراض البدنية إذا أصابهم شيء منها علماً منهم بأنه لا غنى بهم عن اقتناء الصنفين معاً. وأن الحاجة إلى أحد الصنفين في وقت الحاجة إلى أن يكون لكل منهما غذاء ودواء في نوعه ومن جوهره.

على أن المعونة التي تلحق الإنسان من خارج في نفي الأعراض النفسانية، وإن كانت أرد وأنفع فإنه ليس يستغني مع ذلك عن معونة تلحقه من داخل بوصايا فكرية تتهيأ أن يقمع بها الأعراض النفسانية إذا هاجت؛ فيجمعها في نفسها في وقت صحتها، وسكون قواها، ويستودعها قوة الحفظ منها ليخطرها بباله، ويعظ بها نفسه إذا لم يحضره واعظ مذكر من خارج، كما يفعله المحتاط في الأعراض البدنية لنفسه بأن يتطلب أدوية تصلح للأمراض البدنية فيجمعها، ويستودعها خزائنه لكي إن عرض له عارض من الأمراض والأوجاع في وقت لا يحضره فيه طبيب يعالجه، تناولها لينتفع بها وينزع أذى العارض عن نفسه.

ولذلك يجب أن نجمع في هذه المقالة من الكتاب الوصايا التي قد يجب أن تستعمل في معالجة الأمراض النفسانية التي نسميها، ونحصيها في الباب الذي يتلو هذا الباب في موضعها وقت الحاجة إليها فينتفع بها إن شاء الله تعالى.

5.4 *English Translation*

When One Loses It: Methods of Restoring Mental Health

Verily, that which we stated [previously] regarding the preservation of the psyche's well-being is not something that can be sustained at all times and in every given circumstance. Human nature rules out [the] possibility of perpetuating a serene and tranquil [internal] state that is totally free of disturbances like anger, fear, anxiousness, and other similar psychological symptoms. [Afterall,] stress, sadness, calamities, and misfortune are [all inherently] central to the [nature of] this temporal world.[36]

[Indeed,] each [person] will inevitably face unfavorable circumstances and situations that oppose their personal will and desires. On that note, it is likewise impossible to be totally free from [experiencing some sort of] physical symptoms that cause pain and discomfort in one's body. Even if one were to almost never experience any major physical complications, minor complications are [inescapably] bound to occur [at least once in a while]. With that, the likelihood of [having to cope with] various psychological problems are even more pronounced than anything [exclusively] related to the body. Assuredly, a person may live for quite some time without suffering from any kind of bodily aches or pains. However, hardly a day goes by in which something [or another] occurs to arouse feelings of anger, frustration, sadness, or grief.[37] In essence, this is due to the psyche's inherent sensitivity, volatility, and ever-changing nature.

On account of what we have detailed [above], it is crucial for each [and every] human being to purposefully monitor and take care of their psychological needs so as to avoid being distempered. If [anyone finds that] their psyche is in disarray, they [should] do their best to soothe it and restore it to its optimal condition.[38]

Also, when the body is afflicted with [physical] pain or sickness, such symptoms are counterbalanced with treatments like [selected] types of dietary supplements and medications that are correspondingly physical [in nature]. Treating the psyche is similar; whenever a [psychological] symptom upsets

36 Yet again, al-Balkhī is attempting to inculcate the acceptance of suffering and challenges of worldly life in the mind of the reader.

37 Here, al-Balkhī is highlighting the prevalence of emotional dysregulation.

38 Existential therapy advocates that responsibility assumption is an essential first step in the therapeutic process (Irvin D. Yalom, *Existential Psychotherapy*, 235–36.). Existential psychotherapists encourage patients to take responsibility – that is, to apprehend how they contribute to their distress – to facilitate therapeutic change (Irvin D. Yalom, *Staring at the Sun: Overcoming the Terror of Death*, 139.).

any of the mind's faculties, a psychological remedy that [appropriately] corresponds to it is needed.

Furthermore, physical treatments of the body include internal [remedies], like refraining from that which the body does not need. External remedies could also [be used], which we have [already] discussed regarding dietary regimens and medications. Likewise, [both] external and internal [types of] remedies [are applied when] treating the psyche. [To explain] further, a person suffering from [psychological] problems [can alleviate their discomfort] internally, [by] using their own mind to keep symptoms in check and pacify [the psyche's] overarousal.[39] [Moreover, an example of] an external influence [that effectuates psychological healing is] when another person offers [personalized,] heart-felt advice that enacts a healthful change [of state], calming and curing the psyche's faculties.[40] All in all, whosoever purports to have any sense of care for their own mental well-being should not willfully ignore these two approaches. Otherwise, one risks being [imminently] overcome by degenerative psychological issues that adversely impact one's [quality of] life and could even cause certain illnesses within the body if one impetuously self-medicates and overindulges with dietary supplements and other external remedies. For the most-part, an expert doctor commissioned to treat someone is generally more adept and effective than merely monitoring and safeguarding one's own body internally. Again, the same is [true] for the treatment of psychological symptoms; external interventions like [personal] advice and admonition prove to be more practically effective and beneficial [than mere self-monitoring]. [There are] two reasons for this: firstly, human beings [tend to] more readily accept what others assert over their own personal thoughts.[41] This is because human desires constantly pervade rational thought; both are [perplexingly] inseparable from one another. Secondly, in the midst of struggling with a psychological problem, a person is [deeply] preoccupied with whatever it is they are going through; overwhelmed and enfeebled, one must rely on external help for [decisive] treatment to improve one's condition.[42] In that state, such an

39 Two cognitive modalities of addressing emotional disturbances within the psyche are being addressed here by al-Balkhī. The first of which is to cognitively reframe, restructure, or counter one's thoughts so as to alter one's negative emotions.

40 Today, this is one of the key purposes and functions of counseling and psychotherapy.

41 This can be especially true for anxiety disorders or trauma where patients struggle with a significant lack of reassurance and experience unhealthy levels of self-doubt and self-critique.

42 In a calm state of mind, individuals may be able to think more reasonably and in a way that is psychologically healthier. However, when an individual is emotionally triggered and experiencing high degrees of emotional arousal, it can prove increasingly difficult to

individual is much like a physician who falls [so severely] ill that he can no longer treat himself; he needs another doctor to diagnose and treat him.

It is for [precisely] this reason that the judicious kings [of the past] would customarily appoint wise advisors to counsel them, encourage them, and [actively] treat [many of] their psychological problems, like anger, anxiety, and weariness.[43] They would listen to their advice, accept it, and [avidly] adhere to it. [Indeed,] they would consult them in the same way that they would refer to expert physicians when afflicted with physical illnesses. This [was] because they understood that they could not possibly do without [due] consideration for both [the mind and body], in tandem. Necessarily, when either [the mind or body] requires [treatment], each of them is [accordingly remedied] with dietary and medicinal [interventions], in [correspondence] with their [respective] essence and type.

[Now,] with regards [to the earlier statement] that psychological symptoms are best remedied via external [means of] treatment, it does not obviate the need for the inward [type of] aid [driven] by [introspection and] self-talk, [especially] when subduing psychological symptoms as they flare up. At times when the faculties of the psyche are relaxed and well, a person may store such constructive thoughts in his memory, recalling them [at will] to [effectively] admonish himself, [especially] if there is no one else present [to help].[44] This is the same as someone who is careful regarding physical hazards; they procure

---

maintain rational thinking and behavior. During such instances, individuals have lower degrees of self-awareness or insight. Therefore, seeking the assistance of a professional who can help activate those feelings through graduated exposures accompanied by self-soothing and redirection can be helpful for psychological treatment and well-being.

43 Al-Balkhī is normalizing seeking assistance and treatment for one's psychological issues. He highlights how this has always been a common practice of the rich and powerful elite. However, he also emphasizes that this practice should not be solely limited to the elite.

44 It appears that al-Balkhī is utilizing a cognitive approach to address emotional disarray. He is highlighting the importance of storing protective thoughts and beliefs that may prove useful during distressing life circumstances. This practice can be found in Dialectical Behavioral Therapy (DBT). In an exercise called "Emergency Coping Plan for Dealing with Situations" (see Matthew McKay, Jeffrey C. Wood, and Jeffrey Brantley, *The Dialectical Behavior Therapy Skills Workbook: Practical DBT Exercises for Learning Mindfulness, Interpersonal Effectiveness, Emotion Regulation & Distress Tolerance* (Oakland, CA: New Harbinger Publ, 2007), 61.) DBT therapists encourage clients to prepare for distressing situations and create new coping thoughts that they can use in the future if and when they find themselves in similar types of situations (see McKay, Wood, and Brantley, 57–60.).

[I.e., "This too shall pass," "I can be anxious and still deal with the situation," "This is an opportunity for me to learn how to cope with my fears," (see McKay, Wood, and Brantley, 47–48.); "There is a purpose to my life, even though I might not always see it," (see McKay, Wood, and Brantley, 56.).]

and store [various] medications just in case there is a need, when symptoms or pains crop up and a physician is unavailable. If they happen to experience any sort of sickness or pain, they can [easily] access the appropriate remedies [they require] to find relief on their own.

So, at this juncture, we will proceed to outline all the advice that may be practically necessary to treat psychological disorders, which we shall detail in the following chapter. [By doing so,] anyone can benefit as per their [individual] need, by the will of Allah, the Exalted.

6 Explaining and Enumerating Psychological Symptoms. *Maṣāliḥ al-Abdān wa-l-Anfus* (*Sustenance of the Body and the Psyche*) by Imam Abū Zayd al-Balkhī (d. 322 AH/934 CE)

6.1 *Author's Biography*

Abū Zayd Aḥmad ibn Sahl al-Balkhī was born in modern day Afghanistan in a city called Balkh. He was recognized as a polymath and spent significant time in Baghdad to further his education. His life was dedicated to the fields of psychology, science, literature, geography, Islamic theology, and theoretical medicine. He was a student of the renowned physician al-Kindī. He laid a great deal of importance to spirituality viewing religion as the greatest of all philosophies, understanding that in order to be a good philosopher one needed to be grounded in spirituality and be a sincere worshiper of Allah. The discovery of his treatise on physical and mental health entitled *Maṣāliḥ al-Abdān wa al-Anfus* has led to an immense interest in the works of the classical Islamic scholars regarding human psychology. It is noteworthy that in his work, al-Balkhī's classification and symptomatology of obsessive disorders parallels the fifth edition of the modern Diagnostic and Statistical Manual of Obsessive-Compulsive Disorders (OCD). Al-Balkhī was well versed in the Islamic sciences as well, so his writings encourage patients to seek treatment for illnesses by reminding them of the prophetic tradition that Allah has created a cure for every illness.

6.2 *Text Overview and Significance*

In this chapter, al-Balkhī discusses the accompanying physical responses that can arise from acute emotional disturbances, such as panic or depression. As an example, he explains that intense anger can result in disorientation, tremors, and a pale complexion. However, he posits that the underlying cause of anger is rooted in grief. Regardless of the specific negative trait, al-Balkhī asserts that grief is the fundamental cause of all adverse physical responses, while happiness serves as the foundation for all that brings about an overall state of serenity. Furthermore, al-Balkhī emphasizes that those who prioritize physical health must necessarily strive to alleviate distress in order to preserve and safeguard themselves. Given his belief that grief is the primary cause of all mental illness, he similarly suggests that individuals concerned with the well-being of their psyche should work towards freeing their consciousness of anxiety, and subsequently cultivating a state of serenity within it.

6.3 *Arabic Text*

الباب الرابع

في ذكر الأعراض النفسانية وتعديدها

إنا إذ وصفنا جهة التدبير في معالجة الأعراض النفسانية، فمن الواجب بعد ذلك أن نصف ما هي ونعدَّها كما تفعلُها الأطباء من ابتدائهم في كتبهم تعديد الأمراض البدنية وماهيتها، ثم العودَ بعد ذلك في وصفِ ما يعالج به كل منها، فنقول:

إن الأشياء التي تنسب إلى النفس كثيرة، منها قوًى فاضلةٌ كالعقلِ والفهمِ والحفظِ، والأخرى مسترذَلةٌ هي أضداد لها، ومنها أخلاق محمودة كالعفة والسخاء والكرم، والأخرى مذمومة مضادة لها، ومنها أشياء عارضة تقع وترتفع سريعًا كالغضب والفزع وما أشبههما.

والمقصود منا فيما نصفه مما يضاف إلى الأنفس إنما هو الشيء الأخير – نعني الأعراض التي تحدث وتزول – لأنها هي التي تتصل أسبابها بأسباب البدن فتقلقُه وتغيِّرُه، أو تؤثر فيه آثارًا كثيرًا ما ترجع بالضرر عليه. فقد عُلِم أن لكل واحد من هذه الأعراض النفسانية تأثيرًا في البدن تغيِّرُه تغييرًا ظاهرًا قويا، وذلك مثلُ ما يفعله الغضب الشديد في الأحيانِ من الاختلاط والارتعاش للبدن، واصفرار اللون، وشبيه بذلك ما يفعله الفزع والخوف، حتى يسخن البدن عن ذلك أو يبرد، ويحدث فيه أحداث موحشة المناظر.

فما وُجِد من أعراض النفس على هذه السبيل فواجب على المعنيّ بصلاح بدنه أن يدبر في دفعه عن نفسه، وتسكين هائجه تدبيرًا يكفيه مؤنته، ويقيه غائلته، فنقول:

إن الذي يرأسُ هذه الأعراض المؤذية، وهو لها كالأصل إنما هو الغم، وهو مقدمة لجميعها، وموجود مع كل منها، كالغضبان، فإنه يغتمُّ من الأمر، ثم يغضب بسببه، وكذلك الجزِعُ والخائفُ.

وضد الغمِّ السرورُ، فإنه أصل لكل ما يوجد له الإنسان مرتاحا ومهتزا له؛ فالغم من أعراض النفس موضوعٌ بإزاء كل مكروه يخلص إلى الإنسان، والسرور موضوع بإزاء كل محبوب يناله، فالغم أقوى أسباب مرض النفس، والسرور أقوى أسباب صحتها، ولذلك يجب على المعني بمصالح نفسه أن يجتهد في نفي الغم عنها، واجتلاب السرور إليها،

كما يجب على المعني بمصلحة بدنه أن يجتهد في نفي الأسقام عنه، واجتذاب الصحة إليه.

ونقول بعد ذلك: إن من أعراض قوى النفس التي تتولد من الغم الغضب، وهو عرض يبلغ في تهييج الإنسان وإقلاقه وإثارة الدم في جسده وتغيير لونه وتحريك بدنه بالحركات المضطربة الموحشة ما لا يبلغه غيره من أعراض النفس، حتى يخرجه إلى مثل صورة المجنون؛ فربما يسخن الجسد – في حال الاستشاطة له – تسخينا يُعقِب الحمَّى والحرارة المستبطنةَ للقلبِ المستوليةَ عليه.

ثم من قوى أعراض النفس الفزعُ، وهو عَرَضٌ يعتري الإنسان من شيء، ومخافتِه إياه، فالخوف مقدمة للفزع، والفزعُ إفراطُه؛ وإذا قويَ ربما وقعَ على الإنسان منه القلق، حتى يصفر لونه لغؤورِ الدم من ظاهر جسده إلى باطنه، وترتعشَ أطرافُه من يديه ورجليه حتى لا يتماسك، وتتعطل عن أفعالها، ويُدهِشَ الإنسانَ و يحيِّرَه، حتى يعجز عن وجه الاختيار للتخلص من الشيء الذي يحتفُّه ويفزعُه، فربما عرضت له في مثل تلك الحالة علةٌ بدنيةٌ قويةٌ لتموُّجِ أخلاطِ بدنه واضطرابها، وزوال كل شيء منها عن سبيل الاعتدال.

وإنما يعتري الإنسان هذا العرض الذي هو الفزع – ومقدمتُه الخوفُ – من شيء يفكر فيه، ويروعُه تخيُّلُه في نفسه، أو من شيء ينظر إليه، فيَهُولُهُ منظرُهُ، أو من شيء يسمعه، كصوتٍ شديدٍ يتأدَّى إلى سمعِه، فلا يحتملُه لشدته وجهارته، فينجِبُ قلبَه، أو خبرٍ يردُ عليه يكونُ تحته أمرٌ مكروهٌ ومخيفٌ، فيرتاعُ لذلك، وتتغير منه نفسه، حتى يتأدَّى إلى الحالةِ التي وصفناها، وما يشبهها.

ومن قوى أعراض النفس الجزعُ، وهو عرض يعتري الإنسان من فقد محبوب من أهل أو مال أو شيء يحل موقعَه منه، فيكون عزيزًا عليه، محببا إليه، فتألم نفسه لفقده، ويعتريه لذلك حزن، ثم يشتد ذلك الحزن حتى يصير جزعا. فحال الجزع مع الحزن كحال الفزع مع الخوف، وذلك أن الجزع إنما هو شدة الحزن، كما أن الفزع إنما هو شدة الخوف.

والجزع عرض يؤثر في الإنسان آثارًا موحشة من الإقلاق، وإعدام الصبر، حتى يُتخيَّلَ الذي يغلِبُ عليه هذا العَرَضُ – في عين الناظر إليه – بأوحش هيئة، ويُقدِمَ على أفعال تحاكي الجنون من مثلِ لطم الوجه، ونتف الشعر، والصراخ، وتمزيق الثياب، وأمور ليس لها نظائر دالة على ارتفاع حكم العقل والحياء عن صاحبها. وكثيرا ما يؤدي ذلك متعاطيه إلى علل بدنية تهتاج به، وتثور في تلك الحال حتي يصعب عليه تلافيها، ويشتد عليه معالجتها.

ومن قوى أعراض النفس الوسواس الذي يعتلج في صدر الإنسان، ويثير منه الخواطر الرديئة، وينغص عليه عيشه، ولا يكاد يتهيأ (*يهنأ) معها بلذة من لذات بدنه، حتى تَناوَلُها على وجهها. وهذا العرض هو الذي يُدعى حديث النفس، و هو من قوى أعراضها.

فهذه المعاني التي ذكرناها هي الأعراض النفسانية التي قلنا إنها تتصل بمضار الأبدان، وتؤدي في بعض الأوقات إلى عللها. وهي نظيرة الأوجاع التي تهيج بالإنسان في أعضاء بدنه، فتؤلمه وتقلقه، وتمنعه من تناول الأغذية والمرافق الجسدانية، والاستمتاع بشيء منها.

فكما تلزم الحاجة في المصالح البدنية إلى مداراة تلك الأوجاع بما يقمعها من الأدوية، ويبرؤها من الأسقية كذلك تلزم الحاجة في هذه الأعراض النفسانية التي هي أوجاعها إلى مقابلتها من العلاجات التي بينا ما حدُّها وجهتها في الباب المتقدم ما يشفيها، ويخلِّصُ من مكروهها. ونحن ذاكرون ما يجب أن يقابَلَ به كل منها فيما يتلو من القول إن شاء اللّه تعالى.

6.4 *English Translation*

Explaining and Enumerating Psychological Symptoms

As we have already discussed the [main] ways to treat psychological problems, it is now necessary to describe what they are and enumerate them in the same manner that physicians do in the beginnings of their works. They [typically] categorize the physical diseases [first], [explaining details pertaining to] their nature. They then proceed to explain possible treatments for each of them.

We thus [begin by] stating that there are many features attributed to the psyche.[45] Some of them are virtuous, such as the faculties of intellect, comprehension, and memory.[46] Their opposites, by contrast, are [regarded as] reprehensible. Additionally, certain praiseworthy traits [are also attributed to the psyche] like self-control, munificence and nobility.[47] Their opposites are [similarly regarded as] vices, as are transitory emotions that [characteristically] arise and subside quickly such as anger, panic, and the like.[48]

---

45 Here, al-Balkhī is providing a clarification of his usage of the Arabic term *nafs* which has been translated as "psyche" throughout the text. In order to avoid confusion, al-Balkhī is outlining some of the potential contextual usages of the term, as *nafs* can have multiple meanings depending on the usage and context of the author.

46 *Nafs* can be used in the context of cognitive neuroscience or in the medical treatises in their discussions of cognitive faculties of the brain such as memory, executive functioning, etc.

47 Another usage of *nafs* and its accompanying discussions is within the context of character development, virtues, and vices.

48 Finally, al-Balkhī identifies his intended usage of *nafs*, situating his writing within a psychological context and in reference to psychological health or pathology, i.e., emotional disturbances, as he clarifies in the following paragraph.

Our sole purpose in outlining that which is affiliated with the psyche is the last [aforementioned] point: specifically, the symptoms that appear and disappear. This is because their causes are related to the causes of the body; they unsettle and alter it, or affect it tremendously in many ways, resulting in harm. It has [already] been well-established that each of these psychological symptoms has an effect on the body, provoking a considerably noticeable reaction. For example, severe anger can sometimes cause confusion, trembling of the body, and discoloration. In much the same way, panic and fear [can] increase or decrease the temperature of the body and contort one's [physical] appearance, making it unsightly.

Based on this, it is incumbent upon the one who cares about the health of their body to [actively] strive to eradicate all existent symptoms that afflict the psyche; one [must] adequately sedate triggers and [carefully] prevent that which causes them distress.

As such, we propose that the chief cause of all adverse symptoms is none other than grief. Indeed, it is the root [cause] and starting point of all other symptoms, and it [continues to] coexist with each of them. Hence, an angry person is [first] afflicted with grief over [a particular] issue, and then they become infuriated because of it.[49] Panic and fear are likewise similar.

Conversely, the opposite of grief is delight, which is the root [cause] of human solace and contentment. And so, grief is the [core] psychological symptom that accompanies every upheaval that a person [may] face, whereas delight coincides with everything desirable that one can encounter.[50] Furthermore, grief is the leading cause of mental illness, whilst delight is the main basis for mental well-being. Consequently, a person with due concern for the sustenance of their own psyche must strive to extricate all grief from [within] it and [likewise] imbue it with delight. [This should be done] in the same manner

49 Contemporary studies similarly find a relationship between anger and grief. While this is not always the case, there are certainly instances when underlying frustrations can be the source of anger (see Lucia M. Walsh et al., "The Relationship Between Anger and Anxiety Symptoms in Youth with Anxiety Disorders," *Journal of Child and Adolescent Counseling* 4, no. 2 (May 4, 2018): 117–33.).

50 Cognitive models of anxiety describe it as the tendency to overestimate the perceived likelihood of harm; to overestimate the perceived negative outcomes of expected harm; or to underestimate the perceived ability to cope (see Aaron T. Beck, Gary Emery, and Ruth L. Greenberg, *Anxiety Disorders and Phobias: A Cognitive Perspective* (Cambridge, MA: Basic Books, 2005); Michel J. Dugas et al., "Worry and Problem Solving: Evidence of a Specific Relationship," *Cognitive Therapy and Research* 19, no. 1 (February 1995): 109–20; David A. Clark and Aaron T. Beck, *Cognitive Therapy of Anxiety Disorders: Science and Practice* (New York: Guilford Press, 2011); Mark Papworth et al., *Low Intensity Cognitive Behaviour Therapy: A Practitioner's Guide* (Los Angeles: SAGE, 2013).).

that someone concerned about their bodily health must endeavor to ward off all types of [physical] sicknesses and foster [physical] health.

Having said this, [one] of several symptoms engendered by inner grief that afflicts the faculties of the psyche is: anger. Indeed, anger is one of the most intensive symptoms that can aggravate a person. To a degree that exceeds all other psychological symptoms, it increases blood pressure in the body, causes discoloration, and [may even] trigger involuntary convulsions to such an extent that one might seem psychotic.[51] When it surges, [anger] can engulf the heart completely, causing it to boil from within; this can sometimes overheat the body, resulting in a fever.

Moreover, another symptom of the psyche's faculties is panic. It is a symptom that besets a person when they encounter something frightful. Hence, fear precedes panic, as panic is [a type of] excessively heightened fear. When intensified, it may incite anxiety within a person, [potentially] leading to pallidness because of blood rushing inwardly, [away] from the extremities of the body. [Consequently,] one's hands and feet could [start] trembling uncontrollably, [temporarily] hindering their normative function. Additionally, one may become so distraught, unfocused, and indecisive that they can not eradicate whatever is evoking their [sense of] fear and panic. In such a state, the onset of severe physical illness is also quite possible given the disturbance of balance and complete disarray of the body's humors.

A person only really experiences the onset of panic and fear by imagining or thinking about something that frightens them. Similarly, one may look at something [unsightly] which, in turn, horrifies them. Or one may hear something; either an overwhelming sound that is unbearable due to its startling intensity and loudness; or some unpleasant, dreadful news. As a result, such a person feels fear. Their psyche is [thus] affected by it like the extent to which we have described.

Next, another [similar] symptom of the psyche's faculties is depression.[52] It is a symptom that afflicts a person when they face the loss of a loved one,

---

51 This is very similar to Imam al-Ghazālī's discussion of anger. Similarly, both anxiety and worry are responses to threat.

52 The original Arabic term (*al-jazaʿ*) seems to have no equivalent in English that adequately conveys its meaning. While it does denote extreme sorrow, worry, and overwhelm, a person afflicted with such a condition functionally lacks the requisite forbearance to endure and overcome their condition. It is this inability to be patient that is associated with the term more so than the severity of sadness, although all such meanings are nonetheless included (see Malik Badri, *Abū Zayd Al-Balkhī's Sustenance of the Soul* (Herndon: Virginia: The International Institute of Islamic Thought, 2013), 38). Interestingly, the same trilateral roots of the word, if slightly rearranged, form the word that denotes inability (*al-ʿajz*).

property, or anything else deemed personally significant and is therefore endeared. One suffers psychologically due to such a loss, and the consequent grief [gradually] deepens until it devolves into [a form of] depression.[53] The correlation between depression and grief is comparable to that of panic and fear; essentially, depression is acute sadness in the same way that panic is heightened fear.[54] Moreover, depression is a phenomenon that evokes rather dismal reactions [from] within a human being. [This] includes discomposure as well as a [distinct] lack of forbearance. Conceivably, one who is overcome by this symptom may appear to an onlooker as being totally uncivilized; mimicking actions [characteristic] of insanity like slapping [one's own] face, pulling out hair, shouting, tearing [one's] clothes, and many other [bizarre] things that have no parallel yet are completely indicative of a person who has lost both their mind and [sense of] propriety. Often, people who do those things eventually develop bodily ailments which further aggravate their condition, thereby making it hard to prevent it [from worsening] and more difficult to remedy. More rigorous treatment is then required.

Yet another symptom of the psyche's faculties is intrusive thoughts (*waswasa*). It intrudes upon the human mind, stirring up negative thoughts. Life becomes straitened [by it]; one can hardly enjoy any single bodily delight unless it is done in a particular way [as per the obsession]. This symptom is referred to as the [inner] speech of the psyche, and it is [one] of the most pervading of its symptoms.[55]

---

53 In his essay, Mourning and Melancholia, Freud argues that mourning occurs when a person is grieving the loss of a loved object, which is a healthy and a natural part of the grieving process. (see Freud Sigmund, *Mourning and Melancholia* (Merck, Sharpe & Dohme, 1972)). On the other hand, melancholia (depression) occurs when the person grieves for a loss that one is unable to fully comprehend or identify, and this form of sadness he considers as pathological.

54 This is an important distinction that al-Balkhī makes between grief and depression. While grief can be adaptive and necessary to process the loss of a loved one, prolonged grief is associated with features of hopelessness and can turn into dysfunctional depression (see Paul A. Boelen, Jan Van Den Bout, and Jos De Keijser, "Traumatic Grief as a Disorder Distinct From Bereavement-Related Depression and Anxiety: A Replication Study With Bereaved Mental Health Care Patients," *American Journal of Psychiatry* 160, no. 7 (July 2003): 1339–41.; Paul A. Boelen and Jan Van Den Bout, "Complicated Grief, Depression, and Anxiety as Distinct Postloss Syndromes: A Confirmatory Factor Analysis Study," *American Journal of Psychiatry* 162, no. 11 (November 2005): 2175–77.).

55 In the latter half of this section of his book, al-Balkhī goes on to describe obsessive compulsive disorders in detail. Awaad & Ali (2015) have conducted an analysis of al-Balkhī's classification of obsessive-compulsive disorder (OCD) and have found a full convergence between the diagnostic categories listed by al-Balkhī and the Diagnostic and Statistical Manual of Mental Disorders (DSM) for OCD.

To conclude, the concepts that we have discussed are precisely those psychological symptoms that, as we have stated, interlink [directly] with that which can harm the body, and may even lead to [various] bodily illnesses at times. They are [all] comparable to the bodily aches and pains that cause a person distress and discomfort, preventing them from eating food and enjoying any of the other [functional] amenities of the body. Consequently, just as the sustenance of the body necessitates treating such pains with medications and supplements for [subsequent] relief and cure, there is likewise a similar need to treat these psychological symptoms – which are sufferings of the psyche – with their corresponding remedies which we have clarified in the previous chapter. [This includes] their [general] scope, approach, what cures them, and eradicates their ill-effects. And we will elucidate what is required to deal with each of them [specifically] in what is to follow, if Allah so wills.

Bibliography

Abramson, Lyn Y., Gerald I. Metalsky, and Lauren B. Alloy. “Hopelessness Depression: A Theory-Based Subtype of Depression.” *Psychological Review* 96, no. 2 (April 1989): 358–72.

ʿAjlūnī, Ismāʿīl Ibn Muḥammad. *Kashf al-Khafāʾ*. Vol. 2. Cairo: Maktabat al-Qudsī, 1351.

Aldao, Amelia, Susan Nolen-Hoeksema, and Susanne Schweizer. “Emotion-Regulation Strategies across Psychopathology: A Meta-Analytic Review.” *Clinical Psychology Review* 30, no. 2 (March 1, 2010): 217–37.

Ālūsī, Shihāb al-dīn al-. *Rūḥ al-Maʿānī*. Vol. 12. Beirut: Dār al-Kutub al-ʿIlmiyya, 1415.

Asbahānī, Abū Nuʿaym al-. *Ḥilya Al-Awliyāʾ Wa Tabaqāt al-Aṣfiyāʾ*. Vol. 1. Cairo: Dār al-Ḥadīth, 2009.

ʿAsqalānī, Ibn Ḥajar. *Fatḥ al-Bāri bi-Sharḥ Ṣaḥīḥ al-Bukhārī*. Vol. 11. Egypt: al-Maktabat al-Salafiyya, 1380.

Baʿalbak, Ibn Qādī. *Mufarriḥ al-Nafs*. Lebanon: Dār al-Kutub al-ʿIlmiyya, 1971.

Badri, Malik. *Abū Zayd Al-Balkhī's Sustenance of the Soul*. Herndon: Virginia: The International Institute of Islamic Thought, 2013.

Bājūrī, Ibrāhīm ibn Muḥammad. *Tuḥfat Al-Murīd ʿalā Jawhara al-Tawḥīd*. Cairo: Dār al-Salām, 2002.

Balkhī, Abū Zayd. *Maṣālih al-Abdān wa-l-Anfus*. Lebanon: Dār Iḥyāʾ al-Turāth al-ʿArabī, 1994.

Bandura, A. *Social learning theory*. Englewood Cliffs, NJ: Prentice Hall, 1977.

Bayhaqī, Abū Bakr Aḥmad ibn ʿAlī al-. *Kitāb Shuʿab al-Īmān*. Beirut: Maktaba Dār al-Rushd, 2003.

Bayhaqī, Abū Bakr Aḥmad ibn ʿAlī. *al-Sunan al-Kubrā*. Beirut: Dār al-Kutub al-ʿIlmiyya, 2003.

Bayhaqī, Abū Bakr Aḥmad ibn ʿAlı al-. *Al-Zuhd al-Kabīr*. Beirut: Dār al-Jinān Muʾassasa al-Kutub al-Thaqāfiyya, 1987.

Beck, Aaron T., Gary Emery, and Ruth L. Greenberg. *Anxiety Disorders and Phobias: A Cognitive Perspective*. Cambridge, MA: Basic Books, 2005.

Birgivī, Muḥammad. *al-Ṭarīqa al-Muḥammadiyya wa-l-Sīra al-Aḥmadiyya*. Damascus: Dār al-Qalam, 2011.

Block, Jack, and C. Randall Colvin. “Positive Illusions and Well-Being Revisited: Separating Fiction from Fact.” *Psychological Bulletin* 116, no. 1 (July 1994): 28–28.

Boelen, Paul A., and Jan Van Den Bout. “Complicated Grief, Depression, and Anxiety as Distinct Postloss Syndromes: A Confirmatory Factor Analysis Study.” *American Journal of Psychiatry* 162, no. 11 (November 2005): 2175–77.

Boelen, Paul A., Jan Van Den Bout, and Jos De Keijser. "Traumatic Grief as a Disorder Distinct from Bereavement-Related Depression and Anxiety: A Replication Study with Bereaved Mental Health Care Patients." *American Journal of Psychiatry* 160, no. 7 (July 2003): 1339–41.

Bromley, Paul D., Lynette D. Hodges, and David A. Brodie. "Physiological Range of Peak Cardiac Power Output in Healthy Adults." *Clinical Physiology and Functional Imaging* 26, no. 4 (July 2006): 240–46.

Bukhārī, Muḥammad. *Ṣaḥīḥ al-Bukhārī*. Damascus: Dār Ibn Kathīr, 2002.

Bukhārī, Muḥammad. *al-Tārīkh al-Kabīr*. Riyadh: al-Nāshir al-Mutamayyiz li-l-Ṭabʿa wa-l-nashr wa-l-tawzīʿ, 2019.

Bukhārī, Muḥammad al-. *The Interpretation of Dreams*. Courier Dover Publications, 2015.

Buss, David M. *Evolutionary Psychology: The New Science of the Mind*. Psychology Press, 2015.

Carey, Maggie, and S. Russell. *Re-Authoring: Some Answers to Commonly Asked Questions*. 2003: Dulwich Centre, n.d.

Chalmers, Iain, and Robert Matthews. "What Are the Implications of Optimism Bias in Clinical Research?" *The Lancet* 367, no. 9509 (February 2006): 449–50.

Clark, David A., and Aaron T. Beck. *Cognitive Therapy of Anxiety Disorders: Science and Practice*. New York: Guilford Press, 2011.

Daylamī, Abū Shujāʿ. *al-Firdaws bi-Maʾthūr al-Kitāb*. Beirut: Dār al-Kutub al-ʿIlmiyya, 1986.

Dugas, Michel J., Hélène Letarte, Josée Rhéaume, Mark H. Freeston, and Robert Ladouceur. "Worry and Problem Solving: Evidence of a Specific Relationship." *Cognitive Therapy and Research* 19, no. 1 (February 1995): 109–20.

Elbaum, Alan. "The Pursuit of Happiness: T-S Ar.44.201," September 1, 2016.

Esbahānī, Abū Nuʿaym. *Maʿrifat al-Ṣaḥāba*. Riyadh: Dār al-Waṭan li-l-nashr, 1998.

Esbahānī, Abū Nuʿaym. *al-Targhīb wa-l-Tarhīb*. Vol. 2. Cairo: Dār al-Hadīth, 1993.

al-Farhārawī al-Multānī, ʿAbd al-ʿAzīz ibn Aḥmad. *Nibrās: Sharḥ Sharḥ al-ʿAqāʾid al-Nasafiyya*. Istanbul: Maktaba Yāsīn, 2012.

Freud, Sigmund. *Civilization and Its Discontents*. In *Princeton University Press eBooks*, 523–29, 2018.

Gardner, H. *Frames of mind: The theory of multiple intelligences*. New York: Basic Books, 1983.

Ghazālī, Abū Ḥāmid. *Mukhtaṣar Iḥyāʾ ʿUlūm al-Dīn*. Beirut: Muassasat al-Kutub al-Thaqāfiyya, 1990.

Ghazālī, Abū Ḥāmid. *Iḥyāʾ ʿUlūm al-Dīn [The Revival of the Religious Sciences]*. Jeddah Saudi Arabia: Dār al-Minhāj, 2011.

Gillham, Jane, Zoe Adams-Deutsch, Jaclyn Werner, Karen Reivich, Virginia Coulter-Heindl, Mark Linkins, Breanna Winder, et al. "Character Strengths Predict

Subjective Well-Being during Adolescence." *The Journal of Positive Psychology* 6, no. 1 (January 2011): 31–44.
Goldstein, E. Bruce. *Cognitive Psychology: Connecting Mind, Research, and Everyday Experience*. 4th ed. Cengage Learning, 2017.
Groff, Peter S. "Al-Kindi and Nietzsche on the Stoic Art of Banishing Sorrow." *The Journal of Nietzsche Studies* 28, no. 1 (January 1, 2004): 139–73.
Ḥākim, Muḥammad. *al-Mustadrak ʿala al-Ṣaḥiḥayn*. Beirut: Dār al-Kutub al-ʿIlmiyya, 1990.
Haydar, ʿAlī. *Durar al-Ḥukkām Sharḥ Majallat al-Aḥkām*. Riyadh: Dār Ālam al-Kutub, 2003.
Hayes, Steven C. "Acceptance and Commitment Therapy, Relational Frame Theory, and the Third Wave of Behavioral and Cognitive Therapies." *Behavior Therapy* 35, no. 4 (2004): 639–65.
Hayes, Steven C., PhD. *A Liberated Mind: How to Pivot Toward What Matters*. National Geographic Books, 2020.
Hindī, ʿAlā'uddīn al-Muttaqī. *Kanz al-ʿUmmāl*. Vol. 3. Muassasat al-Risāla, 1981.
Hyde, Janet Shibley. "The Gender Similarities Hypothesis." *American Psychologist* 60, no. 6 (September 2005): 581–92.
Ibn ʿAbd al-Barr, Abū ʿUmar. *al-Istidhkār*. Vol. 2. Beirut: Dār al-Kutub al-ʿIlmiyya, 2000.
Ibn Abī ʿĀṣim, Abū Bakr. *al-Sunna*. Vol. 1. Beirut: al-Maktaba al-Islāmiyya, 1400.
Ibn Abī al-Dunyā, ʿAbd Allāh. *al-Hamm aa-l-Ḥazan*. Cairo: Dār al-Salām, 1991.
Ibn Abī Shayba, Abū Bakr Muḥammad Ibn Ibrāhīm. *al-Muṣannaf*. Vol. 17. Riyadh: Dār Kunūz Ishbiliyya li-l-nashr wa-l-tawzīʿ, 2015.
Ibn ʿAsākir, Thiqat al-Dīn. *Muʿjam al-Shuyūkh*. Vol. 2. Dimashq: Dār al-Bashāir, 2000.
Ibn Ḥanbal, Aḥmad. *Faḍāil al-Ṣaḥāba*. Vol. 1. Beirut: Muassasat al-Risāla, 1983.
Ibn Ḥanbal, Aḥmad. *Musnad Aḥmad*. Muassasat al-Risāla, 2001.
Ibn Ḥanbal, Aḥmad. *Musnad al-Imām Aḥmad Ibn Ḥanbal*. Lebanon: Mu'assasat al-Risāla, 1995.
Ibn Māja, Abū ʿAbdillah. *Sunan Ibn Māja*. Halab: Dār Iḥyā al-Kutub al-ʿArabiyya, nd.
Ibn Mubārak, Abū ʿAbd al-Raḥmān. *Al-Zuhd Wa-l-Raqā'iq*. Amman: Dār al-Fārūq, 2022.
Ibn al-Mulaqqīn, Sirāj al-dīn. *al-Tawḍīḥ li-Sharḥ Jāmiʿ al-Ṣaḥīḥ*. Vol. 2. Dimashq: Dār al-Nawādir, 2008.
Ibn Saʿd, Muḥammad. *al-Ṭabaqāt al-Kubrā*. Vol. 3. Cairo: Maktabat al-Khanjī, 2001.
Ibn Saʿd, Muḥammad. *al-Ṭabaqāt al-Kubrā*. Vol. 7. Cairo: Maktabat al-Khanjī, 2001.
Ibn Sīnā, Abū ʿAlī. *Al-Qānūn Fī al-Ṭibb*. Lebanon: Dār al-Kutub al-ʿIlmiyya, 1999.
Ibn Sīna, al-Ḥussayn. *Al-Qānūn fī al-Ṭibb*. Lebanon: Dār al-Kutub al-ʿIlmiyyah, 1999.
Ibn Sīrīn, Muḥammad. *Muntakhab al-Kalām fī Tafsīr al-Aḥlām*. Ḥalab: Sharikat Maktaba wa Maṭbaʿat Muṣṭafā al-Bāb al-Ḥalabī, 1940.
ʿIrāqī, Abū al-Faḍl. *Al-Mughnī ʿan Ḥaml al-Asfār*. Lubnān: Dār Ibn Ḥazm, 2005.

Isfahānī, Abū Nuʿaym al-. *Ḥilyat al-Awliyāʾ wa Tabaqāt al-Aṣfiyāʾ*. Vol. 10. Cairo: Dār al-Ḥadīth, 2009.

Jack, Kirsten, and Eula Miller. "Exploring Self-Awareness in Mental Health Practice." *Mental Health Practice* 12, no. 3 (November 13, 2008): 31–35.

Jahoda, Marie. "The Meaning of Psychological Health." *Social Casework* 34, no. 8 (October 1953): 349–54.

Jawziyya, Muḥammed Ibn Qayyim. *Madārij al-Sālikīn Bayna Manāzil Iyyāka Naʿbudu aa-Iyyāka Nastaʿīn*. Saudi Arabia: Dār al-Ṣamīʿī, 2011.

al-Jawziyya, Muḥammed Ibn Qayyim. *al-Ṭibb al-Rūḥānī*. Beirut: Maktabat al-Thaqāfa al-Dīniyya, 1986.

Joseph, Wolpe. *Psychotherapy by Reciprocal Inhibition*. California: Stanford University Press, 1958.

Jurjānī, al-Sayyid al-Sharīf. *Kitāb al-Taʿrīfāt*. Lebanon: Maktabat Lubnān, 1985.

Kahneman, Daniel. *Thinking, Fast and Slow*. 1st pbk. ed. New York: Farrar, Straus, and Giroux, 2013.

Kalābadhī, Abū Bakr. *Al-Taʿarruf Li-Madhhab Ahl al-Taṣawwuf*. Beirut: Dār al-Kutub al-ʿIlmiyya, nd.

Keshavarzi, Hooman, and Bilal Ali. "Forensic Psychology in Islamic Jurisprudence." In *Oxford Encyclopedia of Islamic Bioethics*, 2016.

Keshavarzi, Hooman, Fahad Khan, Bilal Ali, and Rania Awaad, eds. *Applying Islamic Principles to Clinical Mental Health Care: Introducing Traditional Islamically Integrated Psychotherapy*. 1st ed. Routledge, 2020.

Kharāʾiṭī, Abū Bakr Muḥammad ibn Jaʿfar. *Iʿtilāl al-Qulūb Fī Akhbār al-ʿushshāq Wa al-Muḥibbīn*. Vol. 1. Makkah: Maktabat Bilāl Muṣṭafā al-Bāz, 2000.

Kohl, Harold W., Cora Lynn Craig, Estelle Victoria Lambert, Shigeru Inoue, Jasem Ramadan Alkandari, Grit Leetongin, and Sonja Kahlmeier. "The Pandemic of Physical Inactivity: Global Action for Public Health." *The Lancet* 380, no. 9838 (July 2012): 294–305.

Langer, Ellen J. "The Illusion of Control." *Journal of Personality and Social Psychology* 32, no. 2 (August 1975): 311–28.

Laqqānī, Ibrāhīm al-. *Hidāya Al-Murīd Lī Jawhar al-Tawḥīd*. Beirut: Dār al-Kutub al-ʿIlmiyya, 2012.

Laqqānī, Ibrāhīm al-. *Umdat Al-Murīd Li-Jawharat al-Tawḥīd*. Beirut: Dār al-Nūr, 2016.

Leahy, Margaret M., Mary O'Dwyer, and Fiona Ryan. "Witnessing Stories: Definitional Ceremonies in Narrative Therapy with Adults Who Stutter." *Journal of Fluency Disorders* 37, no. 4 (December 2012): 234–41.

Leahy, Robert L. *Cognitive Therapy Techniques, Second Edition: A Practitioner's Guide*. Guilford Publications, 2017.

Linehan, Marsha. *Skills Training Manual for Treating Borderline Personality Disorder*. Diagnosis and Treatment of Mental Disorders. New York: Guilford Press, 1993.

Makkī, Abū Ṭālib al-. *Qūt Al-Qulūb Fī Mu'āmala al-Maḥbūb*. Vol. 1. Beirut: Dār al-Kutub al-ʿIlmiyya, 2005.

Marwazī, ʿAbd al-Karīm al-Samʿānī al-. *Al-Muntakhab Min Muʿjam Shuyūkh al-Samʿānī*. Riyadh: Dār ʿĀlam al-Kutub, 1996.

Marwazī, ʿAbd al-Karīm al-Samʿānī al-. *Al-Taḥbīr Fī al-Muʿjam al-Kabīr*. Vol. 2. Baghdād: Riāsāt Dīwān al-Awqāf, 1975.

Maslow, Abraham H. "A Theory of Human Motivation." *Psychological Review* 50, no. 4 (1943): 370–96.

Maslow, Abraham H. "Self-Actualizing People: A Study of Psychological Health." *Personality, Symposium* 1 (1950): 11–34.

McKay, Matthew, Jeffrey C. Wood, and Jeffrey Brantley. *The Dialectical Behavior Therapy Skills Workbook: Practical DBT Exercises for Learning Mindfulness, Interpersonal Effectiveness, Emotion Regulation & Distress Tolerance*. Oakland, CA: New Harbinger Publications, 2007.

McKay, Matthew, Jeffrey C. Wood, and Jeffrey Brantley. *The Dialectical Behavior Therapy Skills Workbook: Practical DBT Exercises for Learning Mindfulness, Interpersonal Effectiveness, Emotion Regulation, and Distress Tolerance*. New Harbinger Publications, 2019.

Morgan, Jane. "On Becoming a Person (1961) Carl Rogers' Celebrated Classic in Memoriam." *Journal of Psychological Issues in Organizational Culture* 2, no. 3 (October 1, 2011): 95–105.

Multānī, ʿAbd al-ʿAzīz ibn Aḥmad al-Farhārawī al-. *Nibrās: Sharḥ Sharḥ al-ʿAqāʾid al-Nasafiyya*. Istanbul: Maktabat Yāsīn, 2012.

Mundhirī, Abū Muḥammad Zakī al-dīn. *al-Targhīb wa-l-Tarhīb min al-Hadīth al-Sharif*. Vol. 1. Beirut: Dār Iḥyāʾ al-Turāth al-ʿArabī, 1968.

Mundhirī, Abū Muḥammad Zakī al-dīn. *al-Targhīb wa-l-Tarhīb min al-Hadīth al-Sharif*. Vol. 4. Beirut: Dār Iḥyāʾ al-Turāth al-ʿArabī, 1968.

Muslim, Ebū al-Ḥusayn. *Jāmiʿ al-Ṣaḥīḥ*. Turkiye: Dār al-Ṭibāʿa al-Āmira, 1334.

Nabulsī, ʿAbd al-Ghanī. *Taʿṭīr al-Anām fī Taʿbīr al-Manām*. Cairo: Maṭbaʿat al-Azhariyya, 1306.

Najem, K., & Margolin, E. (2023). Diplopia. StatPearls (2023 Feb.).

al-Nasafī, Abū Muʿīn Maymūn. *Tabsira al-Adilla fī Usūl al-Dīn*. Cairo: Maktaba al-Azhariyya li al-Turāth, 2011.

Nasāī. *Sunan al-Nasāʾī*. Cairo: Maktabat al-Tijāriyya al-Kubrā, 1930.

Nolen-Hoeksema, Susan, Blair E. Wisco, and Sonja Lyubomirsky. "Rethinking Rumination." *Perspectives on Psychological Science* 3, no. 5 (September 2008): 400–424.

Papworth, Mark, Theresa Marrinan, Brad Martin, Dominique Keegan, and Anna Chaddock. *Low Intensity Cognitive Behaviour Therapy: A Practitioner's Guide*. Los Angeles: SAGE, 2013.

Park, Nansook, Christopher Peterson, and Martin E. P. Seligman. "Strengths of Character and Well-Being." *Journal of Social and Clinical Psychology* 23, no. 5 (October 2004): 603–19.

Peter, Tracey, Lance W. Roberts, and Jennifer Dengate. "Flourishing in Life: An Empirical Test of the Dual Continua Model of Mental Health and Mental Illness among Canadian University Students." *International Journal of Mental Health Promotion* 13, no. 1 (January 2011): 13–22.

Peterson, Christopher, and Martin E. P. Seligman. *Character Strengths and Virtues: A Handbook and Classification.* Washington, DC: New York: American Psychological Association; Oxford University Press, 2004.

Peterson, Christopher, Willibald Ruch, Ursula Beermann, Nansook Park, and Martin E. P. Seligman. "Strengths of Character, Orientations to Happiness, and Life Satisfaction." *The Journal of Positive Psychology* 2, no. 3 (July 2007): 149–56.

Pinker, Steven. "The Blank Slate: The Modern Denial of Human Nature." *Choice Reviews Online* 40, no. 07 (March 1, 2003): 40–4305.

Pojman, Louis P., and James Fieser. *Ethics: Discovering Right and Wrong.* Eighth edition. Boston, MA: Cengage Learning, 2017.

Qārī, ʿAlī. *Mirqāt al-Mafātīḥ.* Vol. 3. Lebanon: Dār al-Kutub al-ʿIlmiyya, 2001.

Qārī, ʿAlī. *Mirqāt al-Mafātīḥ.* Vol. 5. Lebanon: Dār al-Kutub al-ʿIlmiyya, 2001.

Qārī, ʿAlī. *Mirqāt al-Mafātīḥ.* Vol. 7. Lebanon: Dār al-Kutub al-ʿIlmiyya, 2001.

Qārī, ʿAlī. *Mirqāt al-Mafātīḥ.* Vol. 9. Lebanon: Dār al-Kutub al-ʿIlmiyya, 2001.

Qushayrī, ʿAbd al-Karīm. *al-Risāla al-Qushayriyya.* Cairo: Dār al-Maʿārif, nd.

Rathee, M., & Jain, P. (2023). "Ageusia." *StatsPearls (2023 Jan.).*

Rāzī, Abū Bakr. *al-Ṭibb al-Ruḥānī.* Cairo: Maktaba al-Nahḍa al-Miṣriya, 1978.

Rogers, Carl R. *On Becoming a Person: A Therapist's View of Psychotherapy.* Boston: Houghton Mifflin, 1961.

al-Sābūnī, Nūr al-Dīn. *al-Bidāya min al-Kifāya fī Uṣūl al-Dīn.* Cairo: Dār al-Māʿrif, 1969.

al-Sābūnī, Nūr al-Dīn. *al-Kifāya fi-l-Hidaya.* Beirut: Dār Ibn Ḥazam, 2014.

Sanʿānī, Muḥammad b. Ismāʿīl. *al-Tanwīr Sharḥ al-Jāmiʿ al-Ṣaghīr.* Vol. 3. Riyadh: Maktabat Dār al-Salām, 2011.

Shafran, Roz, Dana S. Thordarson, and S. Rachman. "Thought-Action Fusion in Obsessive Compulsive Disorder." *Journal of Anxiety Disorders* 10, no. 5 (September 1996): 379–91.

Sigmund, Freud. *Mourning and Melancholia.* Merck, Sharpe & Dohme, 1972.

Sijistānī, Abū Dāwūd. *Sunan Abī Dāwūd.* Lebanon: Dār al-Risāla al-ʿĀlamiyya, 2009.

Silberstein, Laura R., Dennis Tirch, Robert L. Leahy, and Lata McGinn. "Mindfulness, Psychological Flexibility and Emotional Schemas." *International Journal of Cognitive Therapy* 5, no. 4 (December 2012): 406–19.

al-Sirhindī, Aḥmad, Al-Mirānī, Muḥammad Ashraf, & Senturk, Recep. *al-Mukhtārāt Min Maktūbāt al-Imām al-Rabbāni al-Sirhindī*. Amman: Dār al-Nūr al-Mubīn, 2016.

Skinner, Burrhus Frederic. *Beyond Freedom and Dignity*. Hackett Publishing Company Incorporated, 2002.

Snow, Nancy E. *Virtue as Social Intelligence: An Empirically Grounded Theory*. New York: Routledge, 2010.

Spence, Charles. "Comfort Food: A Review." *International Journal of Gastronomy and Food Science* 9 (October 2017): 105–9.

Sternberg, R. J. *Beyond IQ: A Triarchic Theory of Intelligence*. Cambridge University Press, 1985.

Suhrawardī, Shihab al-Din. *ʿAwārif al-Maʿārif*. Makkah: al-Maktabat al-Makkiyya, 2001.

Sulamī, Abū ʿAbd al-Raḥmān al-. *Ḥaqāiq Al-Tafsīr*. Vol. 1. Beirut: Dār al-Kutub al-ʿIlmiyya, 2001.

Suyūṭī, Jalāl al-Dīn. *al-Durr al-Manthūr*. Vol. 6. Beirut: Dār Fikr, n.d.

Suyūṭī, Jalāl al-Dīn al-. *al-Jāmiʿ al-Kabīr*. Cairo: al-Azhar al-Sharīf, 2005.

Suyūṭī, Jalāl al-Dīn. *al-Jāmiʿ al-Ṣaghīr*. Lebanon: Dār al-Kutub al-ʿIlmiyya, 2004.

Ṭabarānī, Abū al-Qāsim Sulaymān ibn Aḥmad. *al-Muʿjam al-Awsaṭ*. Cairo: Dār al-Ḥaramayn, 1995.

Ṭabarānī, Abū al-Qāsim Sulaymān ibn Aḥmad. *Al-Muʿjam al-Kabīr*. Cairo: Maktabat Ibn Taymiyya, 1994.

Ṭabarānī, Abū al-Qāsim Sulaymān ibn Aḥmad. *Muʿjam al-Ṣaghīr*. Madina: al-Maktabat al-Salafiyya, 1968.

Taftāzanī, Saʿd al-Dīn Masʿūd ibn ʿUmar al-. *Sharḥ Al-ʿAqāʾid al-Nasafiyya*. Karachi: Maktabat al-Bushrā, 2000.

Teasdale, John D., Zindel Segal, and J. Mark G. Williams. "How Does Cognitive Therapy Prevent Depressive Relapse and Why Should Attentional Control (Mindfulness) Training Help?" *Behaviour Research and Therapy* 33, no. 1 (January 1995): 25–39.

Thaʿlabī, Abū Isḥāq. *Al-Kashf Wa-l-Bayān ʿan Tafsīr al-Qurʾān*. Vol. 29. Jidda: Dār al-Tafsīr, 2015.

Tirmidhī, Abū ʿĪsā. *al-Jāmiʿ al-Kabīr*. Beirut: Dār al-Gharb al-Islāmī, 1996.

Tirmidhī, al-Ḥakīm al-. *Nawādir Al-Uṣūl Fī Aḥādīth al-Rasūl*. Vol. 3. Beirut: Dār al-Jīl, nd.

Walsh, Lucia M., Courtney Benjamin Wolk, Emily M. Becker-Haimes, Amanda Jensen-Doss, and Rinad S. Beidas. "The Relationship Between Anger and Anxiety Symptoms in Youth with Anxiety Disorders." *Journal of Child and Adolescent Counseling* 4, no. 2 (May 4, 2018): 117–33.

Walter, Mischel and Yuichi Shoda. "A Cognitive-Affective System Theory of Personality: Reconceptualizing Situations, Dispositions, Dynamics, and Invariance in Personality Structure." *Psychological Review* 102, no. 2 (1995): 246–68.

Watson, John Broadus. *Behaviorism*. London: Kegan paul, Trench, Trubner & Co., Ltd., 1930.

Weng, Helen Y., Andrew S. Fox, Alexander J. Shackman, Diane E. Stodola, Jessica Z. K. Caldwell, Matthew C. Olson, Gregory M. Rogers, and Richard J. Davidson. "Compassion Training Alters Altruism and Neural Responses to Suffering" 24, no. 7 (2013): 1171–80.

Westen, Drew, and Pavel S. Blagov. "A Clinical-Empirical Model of Emotion Regulation: From Defense and Motivated Reasoning to Emotional Constraint Satisfaction." In *Handbook of Emotion Regulation*, 373–92. The Guilford Press, 2007.

Widiger, Thomas A. *The Oxford Handbook of the Five Factor Model*. Oxford University Press, 2017.

Yalom, Irvin D. *Existential Psychotherapy*. New York: Basic Books, 1980.

Yalom, Irvin D. *Staring at the Sun: Overcoming the Terror of Death*. 1. ed., PB printing. San Francisco, CA: Jossey-Bass, 2009.

Yusuf, A., and H. Elhaddad. "The Use of the Intellect ('aql) as a Cognitive Restructuring Tool in an Islamic Psychotherapy." In *Applying Islamic Principles to Clinical Mental Health Care: Introducing Traditional Islamically Integrated Psychotherapy*, 1st ed., 209–35. Routledge, 2020.

Zabīdī, al-Sharīf Muḥammad al-. *Itḥāf Al-Sādah al-Muttaqīn Bi Sharḥ Iḥyā' 'Ulūm al-Dīn*. Vol. 1. Lebanon: Dār Iḥyā' al-Turāth al-'Arabī, 1994.

Ziriklī, Khayr al-Dīn al-. *Kitāb Al-A'lām*. Vol. 1. Beirut: Dār al-'Ilm al-Malāyīn, 2002.

Index

ʿAbdullah Ibn ʿUmar 99*n*2
Abū Bakr al-Ṣiddīq 92, 92*n*5
Abū Jahl ibn Hishām 98
Acceptance and Commitment Therapy (ACT) 77, 80*n*1, 212*n*2, 218*n*, 244*n*
Ādam 47, 51, 131
Ahl al-sunna wa al-jamaʿa 21, 196
Ali Haydar Efendi 3, 65, 66
accountability (*muhāsabah*) 70*n*2, 197, 201, 209–213
acquired knowledge (*iktisābī*) 9
acquired (*kasbī*) (*c.f. crystallized intelligence*) 36
adaptive shame 231*n*
aggressive drives 81*n*1, 84
ahliyya (mental competence) 3, 70*n*2
ʿālam al-ʾamr (divine world) 26*n*2, 53*n*
Angel (*malak*) 77, 82, 83, 84, 85, 95, 96, 97
analogy 15, 30, 144*n*2, 160, 186*n*5, 235*n*2, 246
anger (*ghaḍab*) 39*n*2, 62*n*, 63–65, 150, 152–163, 185–186, 197–198, 235–236, 239, 241, 246, 249, 251–252, 255–257
animalistic soul 46, 47*n*1, 49
animal or life soul (*rūḥ ḥayawānī*) 41, 46
anxiety 102, 106, 107, 109*n*1–2, 110*n*, 143*n*4, 236*n*2, 239, 241, 244*n*, 250*n*3, 251, 253, 256*n*2, 257, 257*n*1
Applying Islamic Principles to Clinical Mental Health Care: Introducing Traditional Islamically Integrated Psychotherapy 70*n*1, 84*n*1, 229*n*2, 235*n*2
apathy (*khumūd*) 162, 185*n*2, 194
appetitive drives 77, 80, 81, 81*n*1, 84, 84*n*2, 85
ʿaql (intellect) 21, 22, 25, 31, 32, 33, 34, 36, 37*n*3, 38*n*2, 39*n*, 40*n*2, 46*n*, 48*n*3, 49, 53*n*, 70
ʿaraḍ (accident) 31, 37
al-Ashʿarī 6, 29, 33, 145
attachment 106, 107, 108, 108*n*, 111, 116*n*1, 117*n*1, 118*n*1, 130*n*1, 132*n*
automatic thought (*khāṭir*) 208–209
Ayyūb (prophet) 94

Baghdad 21, 40, 102, 124, 220, 232, 238, 246, 252
badīhī (self-evident truths) 11–18*n*
al-Bājūrī, Ibrāhīm ibn Muḥammad 3, 33, 36, 38*n*5–6, 46*n*1, 48*n*3
al-Balkhī 231, 235*n*1–2–3, 236*n*1–2, 237*n*1–2–3, 238, 238*n*1–2, 242*n*2–4, 243*n*, 244*n*, 246, 249*n*1–2, 250*n*1, 251*n*1–2, 252, 253, 255*n*1–4, 258*n*2–3
al-Bayhaqī, Abū Bakr Aḥmad ibn ʿAlī 29*n*1, 31*n*2, 145*n*2, 162*n*1, 188*n*5, 189*n*3, 190, 191*n*2
behavioral interventions 3, 16
behaviorist 11*n*5, 12*n*2, 30*n*1 63*n*1, 244*n*1
al-Bidāya fī Uṣūl al-Dīn 6, 9*n*1
biological temperamental predispositions 60
blank slate 11*n*5, 30*n*1, 63*n*2
blameworthy 50–52, 117*n*1, 121*n*, 130*n*3, 158, 162, 183, 185–186*n*5, 192–194, 210–211*n*3, 222, 231

Cognitive Behavioral Therapy (CBT) 77, 80*n*1, 106*n*3, 109*n*1, 110*n*, 224*n*1, 242*n*4
categories of dreams 86, 94, 94*n*2, 95, 95*n*
cerebral cortex 57*n*3, 58*n*1, 60*n*1
certainty (*yaqīn*) 19, 197
character development 60, 62*n*, 102, 174, 186*n*5, 222*n*, 225, 227, 228*n*1, 228*n*3, 255*n*3
character strengths 189–190*n*3–5, 222*n*
character traits (*akhlaq*) 4, 52, 60, 61, 62, 65, 80, 173
children in dreams 96, 101
cognitive faculty (s) 15, 40, 54, 57, 58, 59, 75, 255*n*2
cognitive-affective personality system (CAPS) 81*n*4
cognitive impairments 18
cognitive psychology 56*n*1, 58*n*2
cognitive reframing 106*n*2, 144*n*2
cognitive theories 111
contentment (*riḍā*) 110, 123*n*1, 164, 170, 172
conviction (*iʿtiqād*) 19, 52, 142, 209, 213
comprehension (quwwa mudrika) 18
context in dream interpretation 87, 93*n*1, 98, 98*n*, 101, 101*n*4
cultural influence on dreams 98, 98*n*
cowardice (*jubn*) 65, 158*n*1, 185*n*2, 194

critiques of Śramaṇa and Brahmins 11*n*6–12*n*3

Danyāl (prophet) 96
Diagnostic and Statistical Manual of Mental Disorders (DSM) 143*n*4, 161*n*, 232, 239, 246, 252, 258*n*3
Dialectical Behavior Therapy (DBT) 108*n*, 244*n*, 251*n*2
dār al-ghurūr (realm of delusion) 49
dār al-khulūd (realm of permanence) 49
deceased person in dreams 101
delayed and immediate gratification 81*n*4, 84, 84*n*3
delusion (*ghurūr*) 141, 142
depression 102, 106*n*1, 143*n*4, 241, 242, 245, 252, 257, 258, 258*n*1–2
desires (*shahawāt*) 31, 47*n*2, 48*n*2, 50–51, 54, 84–85, 93*n*2, 102, 108*n*, 111, 142, 185, 190–194, 218, 222, 224, 231, 239, 249, 250
despair (*qunūṭ*) 135, 144, 148
detachment 108*n*, 111
determination (*himma*) 49, 195, 198, 209–210, 212, 214
devil (shayṭān) 29, 31, 80, 82, 83, 84, 84*n*1, 85, 85*n*, 93, 94, 94*n*1, 95, 96, 116, 123, 201, 216, 219*n*1
dimāgh (brain) 39, 49*n*3
disciple (*murīd*) 14, 33*n*, 41, 65, 135, 228
discursive theology (*ʿilm al-kalām*) 6, 9*n*1, 34
divine command (*ʿālam al-amr*) 46, 47, 124
divine deprivation (*ighwā wa khidhlān*) 82
divine enablement (*tawfīq*) 82
divinely endowed (*ʿāṭāʾī*) (c.f. spiritual intelligence) 34, 37
divine manifestation (*tajallī*) 122
divinity (*ilāhiyyāt*) 6
dream interpretation (*taʿbīr al-manām*) 85, 86, 87, 92*n*3–5, 93*n*, 94, 94*n*2, 95*n*, 96, 98, 98*n*, 99, 99*n*2, 100, 100*n*2, 101, 101*n*4
dream interpreter 87, 97, 99, 99*n*2, 100, 101, 101*n*4
dunyā (material world) 49, 141
al-Dunyā 111, 117*n*1, 124, 125, 130*n*3

Egypt 12, 31, 33, 147, 218
empirical knowledge 41
ennobled (*sharafī*) intellect 37
eternal (*qadīm*) knowledge 9*n*1
executive functioning 159*n*3
existentialists 108*n*
existential therapy 249*n*3
exposure 110*n*, 244*n*

fear (*khawf*) 110*n*, 116, 121, 122, 129*n*, 134, 135, 141, 143, 143*n*4, 144, 144*n*1–2, 145, 146, 147, 148, 150, 151, 235, 239, 242, 244*n*, 249, 251*n*2, 256, 257, 258
fiṭra (innate disposition) 15, 84*n*2
five senses 77, 80, 172
forensic psychology 66, 67, 70*n*1
forgiveness (*ʿafw*) 230*n*2
Freud, Sigmund 30*n*1, 86, 87, 258*n*1

Galen 26*n*1, 221, 224, 224*n*2
ghaflah (heedlessness) 151
al-Ghazālī, Abū Ḥāmid 2, 3, 4, 20*n*, 21, 22, 26*n*2, 27*n*, 30*n*, 31*n*, 32*n*, 37*n*3, 38*n*1, 39*n*2, 40*n*2, 46*n*1, 60, 61, 62*n*, 63*n*1, 64*n*2, 77, 80*n*1–2, 81*n*3, 82*n*1, 84*n*2, 102, 134, 135, 142*n*1, 143*n*4, 144*n*1–3, 152, 153, 157*n*, 158*n*2, 159*n*2–3, 160*n*, 161*n*1, 162*n*3
gnosis 27, 53, 122
good character 50, 60–61, 119, 163, 173, 188–189*n*3–4, 190*n*2
Greek
and Hellenistic works 224*n*1
and Islamic philosophical works 231*n*
and philosophical works 227*n*
ideas 224*n*2; medicine 235*n*2
grief (*huzn*) 102, 105, 106*n*1, 107, 108, 110, 111, 116, 116*n*1, 117, 117*n*1–3, 118, 118*n*1–3, 119, 119*n*1, 120, 120*n*1, 121, 121*n*, 123, 124, 125, 129, 129*n*, 130*n*1–3, 131, 132, 133, 134, 235, 239, 246, 249, 252, 253, 256, 256*n*1, 257, 258, 258*n*2

habituation 62–63*n*, 84*n*2, 110*n*, 158–159
hadith 32*n*1, 37*n*2, 40, 48*n*1, 49*n*3, 51*n*1, 62*n*1, 63*n*1, 93*n*1, 105, 124, 128*n*1, 145, 214*n*1
hāfiẓa (capacity to retain) 59, 60
happiness (*surūr*) 129*n*, 130*n*2, 132, 142*n*1, 163, 164, 170, 171, 172*n*2
al-Ḥarawī 111, 119*n*2, 120, 120*n*2, 121, 124
hawā (whimsical carnal passion) 49, 190–192, 194, 222
Hawwāʾ (Eve) 47

heart 77, 80, 80*n*1–2, 81, 82, 83, 84, 85, 85*n*, 94, 97
heart (*qalb*) 20*n*2, 21, 22, 25, 26, 27, 28, 29, 31, 32, 34, 37*n*3, 46*n*1, 47*n*2, 49*n*3, 52, 53, 62, 82*n*1
hedonism (*sharah*) 41, 49, 158, 185*n*2, 190–192
Ḥilyat al-Awliyā᾽ wa Tabaqāt al-Aṣfiyā᾽ 32*n*1, 48*n*1
holistic approaches to knowledge 7, 9*n*2, 64*n*1, 83*n*4
homeostasis 235*n*2
hope 105–121–134–135–141–142–143–144–144*n*2–145–146; in Allah (*rajā᾽*), 106*n*1–145–191
hopelessness 106*n*1, 143, 152
human drives 22, 29, 38*n*6, 84*n*2, 174, 184*n*1
human inclinations 77, 84, 84*n*2, 85*n*
humoral medicine 26*n*1, 144*n*1
humoral theory 81, 93, 93*n*2, 95
hypocrite 47, 117*n*1, 158, 229

ʿibādāt (acts of worship) 22
Ibrāhīm (prophet) 95
ignorance (*bilāda*) 26, 51, 76, 159, 185*n*2, 194, 231
Iḥyā᾽ ʿUlūm al-Dīn (The Revival of the Religious Sciences) 21, 22, 29, 32, 37, 60, 62, 77, 134, 152, 174, 194, 224
ijāza (transmission-certification) 50, 66
ilhām 77, 82, 85, 207*n*2
illusion of control 243*n*
imagination (*mutakhayyala*) 57, 58, 59
Imam ʿAbd al-Ghanı al-Nabulsī 85, 86, 93*n*2, 94*n*2, 95*n*, 98*n*, 99*n*1, 100*n*1
Imam al-Haramayn 21
Imam Ḥasan al-Baṣrī 83
Imam Muḥammad ibn Jarīr al-Ṭabarī 220
Imam Nūr al-Dīn al-Ṣābūnī 6–9
Imam Taqī al-Dīn al-Birgivī 158*n*1, 173–197, 243*n*
inferential (*istidlalī*) knowledge 11, 58–60
inferential faculty (*wahm*) 59, 60
innate (*gharīzī*) (c.f. fluid intelligence) 36
insane person (*majnūn*) 70, 71, 72, 73, 74, 75
insanity (*Junūn*) 65, 71, 72, 73*n*2, 74*n*1, 75
intelligence of the ascetics (*ʿaql al-zuhhād*) (c.f. inspired intelligence) 37
intermittent insanity (*majnūn ghayr muṭbaq*) 71, 73*n*2, 74*n*1
Interpersonal Therapy 223*n*3
intuitive knowledge (*ẓarūrī*) 9–10, 38
irāda (willful intent) 70*n*2, 120, 120*n*3, 197, 214
al-Isfahānī, Abū Nuʿaym 32*n*1, 48*n*1, 147*n*2
Islamic Law (*sharīʿa*) 17*n*2, 19*n*1, 76, 185, 194
Islamic spirituality (*tasawwuf*) 22, 41, 174
istikhāra 122, 122*n*2, 123, 122*n*3
Itḥāf al-Sāda al-Muttaqīn bi-Sharḥ Iḥyā᾽ ʿUlūm al-Dīn 29*n*1, 32*n*1

Jaʿfar al-Ṣādiq 97
al-Jawzī 102, 106
jealousy (*ḥasad*) 52, 161, 162
al-Juwaynī, Abu al-Maʿālī Abd al-Mālik 21, 31*n*1, 38
justice (*ʿadāla*) 7, 66, 152, 157*n*, 158*n*1, 162, 185*n*1, 188, 194, 195, 197*n*2, 198, 199, 225, 228*n*3, 228*n*4

khabar mutawātir (massively transmitted reports) 10, 118
Kharā᾽iṭī, Abū Bakr Muḥammad ibn Jaʿfar 29*n*1
al-Kindī 108*n*

al-Laqānī, Ibrāhīm 33, 34
Laṭīfa Rabbāniyya Rūḥāniyya (divine, spiritual substance) 26, 46
legal insanity 66, 70*n*1
legal opinion (*fatwā*) 66, 72
legal theory (*uṣūl al-fiqh*) 72, 74

madrasa (Islamic seminaries) 21, 66
al-Makkī, Abū Ṭālib 33*n*2, 83*n*2
malakūtī (metaphysical realm) 26*n*2
Maṣālih al-Abdān wa al-Anfus (Sustenance of Body and Soul) 231, 232, 238, 239, 246, 252
Māturīdī theology 6–11*n*5, 17*n*2
Mulla ʿAlī al-Qārī 62*n*, 129*n*, 200–201, 208*n*4
meaningless dreams 93*n*1, 94
metaphysical soul (*rūh samāwī ʿulwi*) 41
modesty (*ḥayā᾽*) 197, 198, 209, 213*n*1
motivation 77, 81, 81*n*3
muʿāmalāt (Social Aspects of Life) 22
mudhakkira (capacity to recall) 59, 60

Muhammad (prophet) 83, 84, 92, 92*n*2–5, 93*n*1, 94, 94*n*1, 95, 96, 98, 99*n*2
muhlikāt (destructive actions) 22
al-Muʿjam al-Kabīr 31*n*2, 50*n*5
munjiyāt (Actions that lead to ultimate Salvation) 22

al-Nafs al-ammāra bi-l-sūʾ (the self that commands to evil) 19, 20, 31, 48, 52, 190*n*3
al-Nafs al-lawāmma (the blaming self) 28
al-Nafs al-muṭmainna (the tranquil self) 29
Naqshbandī 14, 33
narrative theory 224*n*1
nature vs nurture 2, 22
nawawī 22, 212
naẓarī 19, 38
neocortex 58*n*1
nifāq (hypocrisy) 47, 194, 210, 229, 230*n*3
nightmares 94, 94*n*2
non-remittant insanity (*junūn muṭbiq*) 72, 73, 74, 74*n*1

obsession (*jarbaza*) 184, 185*n*2, 194, 201, 258
obsessive compulsive disorder (OCD) 70*n*1, 77, 83*n*4, 201, 212*n*2, 217*n*1, 218*n*, 232, 239, 246, 252, 258*n*3
origins of dreams 93*n*2, 94*n*2
ordinary dreams 94*n*2, 97*n*1
Ottoman 65, 66, 71*n*4, 85, 86, 173, 174, 197*n*1

panic 235, 236, 239, 242, 252, 255, 256, 257, 258
passing thoughts (*khawāṭir*) 32, 80*n*1, 81, 81*n*2–3, 85*n*, 207, 208*n*3, 209*n*2
patience (*sabr*) 51, 109, 118*n*2, 119*n*1, 194, 196, 198
perception 10–15, 40*n*2, 41, 46, 53, 56–60, 75, 80, 98, 167, 168*n*1, 171, 243*n*
perceptual recall faculty (*khayāl*) 57, 58, 59
Peterson and Seligman 189*n*3, 221*n*, 223*n*1
positive psychology 190*n*1, 222*n*
positivist 30*n*1
primitive drive 30*n*1
prophetic dreams 93
prophetic spirituality 174
prophethood (*nubuwwāt*) 7, 11*n*2, 15, 18, 101
psychosomatic experiences 160*n*, 237*n*3
purity (*wuḍūʾ*) and righteous dreams 99

al-Qayyim 110, 111, 117*n*1, 119*n*1, 122*n*3, 125, 130*n*3
Qurʾan 10*n*1, 32, 40*n*1
Qūt al-Qulūb fī Muʿāmalat al-Maḥbūb 33*n*2, 83*n*2
qabḍ (feeling of constrain) 116*n*1

radical acceptance 108*n*
rashness (*tahawwur*) 51, 185*n*2
rationality (*nuṭq*) 184, 185*n*3
rational soul (*nafs nātiqa*) 40*n*2
al-Razi, Fakhr al-Dīn 6, 33, 38*n*5, 72*n*2
rectification 225, 228, 230*n*1, 231
rectify 220, 230. *See also* rectification
reflection 110, 111, 135, 171
regret (*taʾassuf*) 119, 122*n*3
remorse 105, 109
repentance (*tawbah*) 49, 188, 197, 213
repression 30*n*2
resilience 108*n*, 109*n*1, 232, 236*n*1, 237*n*1, 239
reviver (*mujaddid*) 14, 17
RIDA 217*n*3
righteous dreams (*ruʾyā sāliḥa*) 92, 94, 95, 99
Rogers, Carl 30*n*1, 63*n*1

saʿāda (felicity) 49
sadness 105, 105*n*1–3, 106, 106*n*1, 107, 108, 117*n*1–3, 119, 121, 125, 130*n*1–2–3, 131, 132, 132*n*, 133, 157
sane person (*ʿāqil*) 75
satanic distressing dreams 94
secret (*sirr*) 53
seeker 110, 111, 116, 120, 120*n*3, 122, 122*n*1–3, 123, 141, 225, 228. *See also* disciple
self
  awareness 223*n*3–225–245*n*-250*n*4
  control 84, 84n3
  discipline (*mujāhada*) 63, 102
  improvement 223*n*3
  infatuation 229
  monitoring 250
  rectification 231
  respect 224

scholastic theology (*ʿilm al-kalām*) 27*n*2, 33–34, 38*n*1, 174, 219
Shāfī 33, 38*n*1–4, 39
shahwa (appetitive drive) 29, 51, 61, 162, 185
shajāʿa (courage) 65, 196, 197
shaqāwa (misfortune) 49
Shaykh (spiritual guide) 38*n*4, 50, 61, 65, 225, 228*n*1, 231
Skinner, Burrhus Frederic 30*n*1
social learning theory 63*n*1
sorcery-induced dreams 95
sources of knowledge 6–14
sorrow (*huzn*) 102, 105, 105*n*3, 106, 106*n*1, 107, 110, 118, 118*n*1, 124, 130, 131, 133
speaking animals in dreams 101
spiritual exercises (*riyāḍa al-nafs*) 50, 60, 62, 63, 187, 247
spiritual illnesses 15, 18–19, 106*n*2, 228
spiritual path (*ṭarīqa*) 228*n*1
spiritual practitioners (*Sufis*) 222*n*, 236*n*2
al-Suhrawardī 39*n*2, 40, 41, 46*n*1, 49*n*1, 53*n*1, 116
Sunna 32, 92*n*3, 173, 187, 189, 219
Sunni 17*n*2, 21, 33, 174, 196
supervision 221, 222*n*
supervisor 220, 223
supplication (*duʿa*) 99, 122, 132
survival instincts 58*n*2, 77, 158*n*1
survival of the fittest 30*n*1
Stoic philosophy 108*n*
symbolism in dreams 87, 92, 95*n*, 96, 98, 98*n*, 101, 101*n*4

tafsīr 46*n*1
al-Taftāzanī, Saʿd al-Dīn Masʿūd ibn ʿUmar 27*n*1, 39*n*1
takhliya and *taḥliya* 190
Taʿṭīr al-Anām fī Taʿbīr al-Manām 85
taʾwīl 10*n*1, 46*n*1
tazkiya (purification) 19–20, 64, 192, 200
temperance (*ʿiffa*) 185, 197–198
temporal knowledge (*ḥādith*) 9
theologians (*mutakallimīn*) 17*n*2, 33*n*1, 34, 38*n*6, 39*n*1–2, 213*n*1, 228*n*4
therapeutic alliance 220
thought-action theory 77, 81*n*3
al-Tibb al-Rūḥānī 102, 220, 225
tranquility (*iṭmiʾnān*) 20, 29*n*2, 52, 95, 171*n*2, 210
trauma-induced dreams 95
tripartite classification of dreams 94
true dreams (*ruʾyā sādiqa*) 92*n*2, 93*n*1, 94*n*2, 95, 95*n*, 97, 97*n*1, 99, 99*n*1, 100*n*1
true reports 9–12
Tuḥfat al-Murīd ʿalā Jawahart al-Tawḥīd 33, 36
al-Tustarī, Salh 33*n*1

Umm al-Faḍl 98

valor (*shujāʿa*) 185*n*3, 197, 198
vices and virtues 53, 102, 129*n*, 143, 173, 174, 185–186, 189–190, 194–200, 209, 211*n*3, 213*n*1–2, 220, 221, 222, 223, 225, 227, 227*n*, 229, 255, 255*n*3

waswasa (intrusive thoughts) 77, 80, 81*n*3, 82, 200–201, 206–207, 212, 215–219, 258
well-being 220, 223*n*3, 235, 239, 241, 242, 243*n*, 245, 249, 250*n*4, 253, 256
wisdom (*ḥikma*) 96, 105, 108*n*, 171*n*2, 184–185*n*3, 195–197, 238*n*2
wishful thinking (*tamannī*) 142, 191
worry (*hamm*) 110*n*, 116, 117, 119, 124, 129*n*, 130, 130*n*1, 131, 133, 146
wujūd (entity) 31

Yūsuf (prophet) 86, 93, 96, 100, 100*n*1

al-Zabīdī, al-Sharīf Muḥammad 29, 32
zuhd (asceticism) 37, 196
al-Zuhd al-Kabīr 29*n*1, 32*n*1

www.ingramcontent.com/pod-product-compliance
Lightning Source LLC
Chambersburg PA
CBHW071457110726
47908CB00003B/637
* 9 7 8 9 0 0 4 7 2 5 2 1 8 *